THINKING
INSIDE
THE BOX

THINKING
INSIDE
THE BOX

a reader in interior design
for the 21st century

Middlesex
University
PRESS

First published in 2007 by Middlesex University Press

Copyright © Middlesex University Press

Authors retain copyright of individual chapters

ISBN 978 1 904750 22 2

A CIP catalogue record for this book is available from The British Library

Cover design by Helen Taylor
Typesetting by Carnegie Book Production
Printed in the UK by Cambridge Printing

Middlesex University Press
North London Business Park
Oakleigh Road South
London N11 1QS

Tel: +44 (0)20 8411 4162: +44 (0)20 8411 4161
Fax: +44 (0)20 8411 4167

www.mupress.co.uk

CONTENTS

WHAT IS INTERIOR DESIGN?

WHY DO WE DO INTERIOR DESIGN?

HISTORIES OF INTERIOR DESIGN

HOW DO WE TEACH INTERIOR DESIGN?

Leonie BELL

The Lighthouse, Scotland's Centre
for Architecture, Design and the City

FOREWORD

The Lighthouse is 'Scotland's Centre for Architecture, Design and the City' and our mission is to promote architecture, design and Scotland's creative industries. We create public, business and learning programmes that celebrate the talent within Scotland and bring the best from around the world to these shores. We believe that architecture and design are of major social, cultural, political and economic importance and our programmes aim to engage both professionals and the public in the debates surrounding these issues. Our belief is, quite simply, that a country that supports and embraces quality design and architecture is a happy and successful one.

Since opening in July 1999 we have welcomed over 1.2 million visitors and staged around 200 exhibitions. Not one of these exhibitions had been dedicated to interior design, until February 2007 when we hosted 'Thinking Inside the Box' an exhibition and conference by Interiors Forum Scotland. Of course interior design had appeared in other exhibitions, especially ones that award student work. The 2006 Glasgow 1999 Design Medal, for example, was won by an interior design student from Glasgow School of Art.

Interiors Forum approached us in Spring 2006 and our first questions were: why do you want to do this and why do you want to do it in The Lighthouse? Their answer: so people can understand what interior design is and because The Lighthouse hasn't devoted a project solely to this discipline. We couldn't say no. Like Interiors Forum Scotland, The Lighthouse is concerned by the perception that design is something that we don't really need, that it is a fashionable or luxurious extra. Yet design that is good should be embedded within all that surrounds us in the unnatural world. Good design and good architecture improve all our lives – they are not about just about decoration.

Interiors Forum Scotland wanted to create an exhibition to help define interior design and where it belongs. The design professions classify interior design as part of architecture and the public think it is to do with lampshades and wallpaper. The exhibition 'Thinking Inside the Box' – from which this book developed – successfully explained that it can be both these things plus a whole lot more. Interior design is a vast and complex discipline that requires intelligent and intensive academic courses. Interior designers create environments in which we work, live and play. These can be interiors in the traditional sense but they can also occur in outdoor spaces like bus shelters; they can be temporary or mobile as part of theatre, film set or exhibition design or they can be virtual digital environments.

Many misunderstand interior design but the exhibition 'Thinking Inside the Box' and the related conference presented a strong case: that we need good interior design, it benefits us all and we need visionary teachers to inspire the next generation of interior design students. That case is restated in this reader. This is not a 'how to' manual of interior design, or a glossy coffee table tome, but a 'why?' sort of book, designed to provoke students, thinkers, academics, and anyone else involved in the world of interiors into thought, and to help them explore those thoughts further. There are contributions that discuss the definition of interior design, its history, its body of theory, and its modes of education. None of these provide definitive answers, but are designed to stimulate debate, argument, and further thought. Eventually we hope these debates will feed back in to a more thoughtful, challenging, and rigorous discipline.

Ed HOLLIS and Alex MILTON
Edinburgh College of Art

Andrew MILLIGAN
Duncan of Jordanstone College,
University of Dundee

Drew PLUNKETT
Glasgow School of Art

THINKING INSIDE THE BOX: AN INTRODUCTION

Interiors is an evolving yet slippery discipline. Whilst the interior is everywhere, it is nevertheless ephemeral and difficult to define. The interior domain is itself saturated with the everyday artefacts of consumption; it's a platform in which to project lifestyle; a place to benchmark fashionable social mores, to test patterns of behaviour and ritual; and the place of dwelling, sanctuary, memory and association. Interiors is becoming an increasingly diverse field of spatial design enquiry which – through education at least – operates without that familiar artefactual framework so common to partner disciplines of art, product and fashion. Interiors education operates within, and is limited by, paper space abstraction of *visualising* rather than *doing*. Whilst others have identifiable notions of disciplinary craft, what is the craft of interiors? Within education and practice, interiors occupies multiple identities, yet its historical, theoretical and contextual framework remains patchy, and is frequently contested and unclaimed territory in comparison to those of other disciplines. How, therefore, might we speculate about the role, validity and purpose of interiors in the twenty-first century?

Thinking Inside the Box: A Reader in Interior Design for the 21st Century is an interior theory reader designed to enable students, academics, researchers and practitioners to access the broad and evolving nature of interiors thinking today. This collection of essays, by prominent thinkers, practitioners and key authors in the field from Australia, the UK, Italy, New Zealand, Turkey, Canada and the USA addresses an eclectic range of issues: doubleness of image and the emergence of the interior; the slow home; textiles and feminism; branding the discipline; the relationship between the interior and the enclave in the contemporary age of terror; the regulation of the profession of interiors and deregulation of education; rereading theories of interior space; Hertzian interior space describing the lived traces of use, occupation and environment, amongst many others.

This publication emerged initially from the international interiors conference and exhibition 'Thinking Inside the Box: Interior Design Education in the 21st Century: New Visions, New Horizons & New Challenges' at the Lighthouse, Scotland's Centre for Architecture, Design and the City held in March 2007, and organized by the Interiors Forum Scotland. Established in May 2005, the IFS comprises the leading Scottish interior programmes at Duncan of Jordanstone College of Art (University of Dundee), Edinburgh College of Art, Glasgow School of Art, Glasgow Metropolitan College and Napier University in Edinburgh. This reader resulted from continued discussion and a shared concern and passion for the field of interior design. Like the earlier conference and exhibition, this reader is designed to provoke within the international community of interior designers and interior architects a desire to rediscover, reframe and perhaps reclaim the field of interior design; and, through the IFS, to establish an annual conference platform which places interior design and/or interior architecture firmly at the centre of critical debate, rather than on the margins of other design disciplines. In reading this publication one may sense that interiors, for all its diversity and indeed doubt, is re-emerging as a dynamic spatial activity with shared concerns and challenges: identity, anxiety over unregulated expansion, challenging perceptions, sharing good practice across an international interior community, advocacy, philosophy, reflecting and rethinking our discipline and issues of gender, amongst others.

Very early on the IFS explored thinking *inside* rather than outside the metaphorical box as a vehicle for an event for the interiors community. Thus began a number of free-ranging discussions about the nature, theory and practice of interior design, about the educational vision driving our institutions, the international dimension, the impact radical practice may have on visionary teaching, the emerging of recent interior research and theories, and how we might best promote, support and advocate excellence within this unique discipline. What we all shared, to some extent, was a feeling that, when compared to many design disciplines, interiors is somewhat hazily defined, perhaps undervalued and yet, as a result, full of possibilities.

What has made both the IFS and *Thinking Inside the Box* possible is the relative intimacy of scale of the higher education interiors sector within Scotland, within which there exists a surprising diversity of programmes. Scotland supports six honours degree courses in interiors, compared to some two hundred in England and Wales combined. This meant that it was relatively easy for the Interiors Forum Scotland to get started, to get talking and to get doing. However, it would be wrong to mistake small numbers for uniformity. The interiors degree courses of Scotland, situated as they are in different institutions and different cities, represent a wide range of viewpoints on the discipline. Post-industrial, style-conscious Glasgow, where interiors is driven by retail and hospitality, is a world (and fifty minutes on the train) away from staid, bourgeois Edinburgh, where museology, conservation and heritage are only now giving way to other disciplines. The Fine Art traditions of Duncan of Jordanstone, Glasgow School of Art, and Edinburgh College of Art have a very different pedigree to the more practical and professional focus of the former polytechnics. And of course, staff and students, attracted by these combinations of place and ethos, serve to reinforce and exaggerate these characteristics.

The upshot of the initial meetings of the Interiors Forum Scotland was the decision to extend our own discussions into a wider arena. On the one hand we decided to hold a joint exhibition, in which we could explain our individual and common approaches to the education of the interior designer. On the other, we decided to stage a conference, in which the questions to which we found ourselves returning in our own discussions might be addressed by the wider world. A call for paper presentations was issued in July 2006 and, to our delight, some fifty proposals were returned, from which we selected twenty-four for presentation at the conference. Not only was the range of subject matter impressive, but also the geographical spread of respondents. There were proposals from Turkey, Australasia, Canada and the US, as well as the UK and Europe. It was clear that, out there, there were a lot of people worrying away at the same things we were. The conference took place over an intense two days and was attended by 100 interiors academics, students, practitioners, and writers. Feedback from delegates praised – and expressed concern – over the sheer intensity of the programme, but most agreed that the presentations and discussions left them with ample food for thought and provocations to further action. Following its success, this initial event is to be followed by another IFS conference event in the summer of 2008.

One of the keynote speakers at the conference, the New York interior designer Shashi Caan, called for a consensus about interior design to arise from the present confusion that clouds the discipline. While it would be untrue to say that the opinions published in this reader represent any sort of consensus, it would be equally untrue to detect in them a miasma of confusion either. It might be more true to say that many interiors academics are, in the words of T.S. Eliot 'united by the conflict that divides them'. Several clear debates appear in these pages again and again. There are several ghosts at the feast and several absences, all of which lend any theoretical discussion of interior design a certain consistency.

Chief among the debates that dominated the discussion was the question of point of view: should interiors be discussed and visualized from the inside, or the outside? Mark Taylor and Mark Burry's explorations of Hertzian space, for example, discuss the interior as a 'third skin', an extension of the body; while Lois Weinthal's 'Towards a New Interior' visualised the discipline as a series of skins, whose validity is derived from what they contain. In contrast, Graeme Brooker and Sally Stone discuss the interior from outside, from the point of view of the building that it inhabits and 're-reads'.

Another key debate that emerged was the definition of interiors: should it be regulated and strictly defined, as are some other design disciplines (or as it is in many places outside the UK), or should it be allowed to maintain the flexibility of a 'non-discipline'? Chalmers and Close's chapter 'But is it Interior Design?' celebrates interdisciplinarity, for example; and Susie Attiwill's 'What's in a Canon?' exposes the vast range of points of view that can be held about the discipline of interiors. On the other hand, Patrick Hannay's 'A Regulated Irregularity' calls for a tighter definition of the profession, in order to combat sliding educational and professional standards, while Shashi Caan argues that interiors is not interdisciplinary, but a discipline in its own right.

If there were two ghosts at the feast that seemed to lurk behind every discussion, ready to pounce, they were architecture and interior decoration. Teresa Hoskyns' 'Not Cushions and Curtains' seeks to slay the monster by inverting their relationship, proposing an architecture made of fabric, in contrast to the 'architectural' hardness of the contemporary minimalist interior. Andrew Stone's 'The Underestimation of the Interior' explores the contrasting ways in which architects and interior designers have addressed the nature of their respective disciplines. Time and time again, the independence of interiors from either architecture or decoration was stated, to the extent that one was led to wonder whether the discipline doth protest too much. Curiously, there was a notable absence from that same feast: namely the discourses of product design, which seem to have made little impact on interior design theory and practice.

It was always the intention to publish some of the contributions to the conference, and *Thinking Inside the Box* as a reader derives from some of these. An additional section has been appended, in which the members of the Interiors Forum Scotland outline their own approaches to the education, the theory and the practice of interior design, setting the subsequent chapters in context.

The reader is organized into five main sections:

- 'Educating the interior designer', in which the members of the Interiors Forum Scotland outline their approaches to interior design

- 'What is interior design?' Debates on the identity, the profession, and the regulation of interior design

- 'Why do we do interior design?' Essays on the relationship between theory and practice in interiors

- 'Histories of interior design' – stories from the practice of interiors; and meditations on the history of the discipline

- 'How do we teach interior design?' Case studies and reflections upon the education of the interior designer.

Thinking Inside the Box is not a 'how to' but a 'why?' sort of book. It is not a textbook, but should be regarded as a provocation to speculation, a book designed to start arguments rather than to conclude them. We at the Interiors Forum Scotland believe, from our own experience, that out of such debates interiors will become a more rigorous, robust and challenging discipline.

Educating the interior designer

Ed HOLLIS and Alex MILTON

Edinburgh College of Art

INHABITING A WARREN OF ROOMS: INTERIORS DESIGN AT EDINBURGH COLLEGE OF ART

Introduction

Edinburgh College of Art, located in the shadow of a medieval castle, perched above the steep crow-stepped gables of an ancient town, does not possess the attributes of a crucible of modernity. Edinburgh's last cultural revolution was the eighteenth-century Enlightenment; and the College of Art is the child of that now somewhat aged parent, having been conceived originally by the municipal board of manufactures in the 1760s. The College building, completed in 1907, twenty years before the Bauhaus (and a decade after Glasgow School of Art), opened by the then Prince of Wales, stands for everything that modernity sought to overturn. Its strict use of the orders and its high mansard roofs refer directly to the Ecole des Beaux-Arts, and at its heart is a sculpture court, designed specifically to house plaster casts of the Parthenon, donated to the college upon its foundation by the man who stole the originals, Lord Elgin. Indeed, when Shashi Caan, one of the keynote speakers at 'Thinking Inside the Box' came to speak to our students, she noted their perception that the college was a traditional sort of place with one foot placed firmly in the past.

Interiors: the queen of the crafts

That past extends a covert as well as an explicit hand over the day-to-day running of the college, and in the individual programmes it teaches. The college is divided in a rather Beaux-Arts way into several schools, whose general groupings may be defined as the three traditional fine arts (painting, sculpture and architecture) and the more modern (to the nineteenth century at least) grouping of the Applied Arts, into which is lumped the newfangled dark art of Design.

Figure 1: *Edinburgh College of Art and the Castle*, John Macgregor, from the archives of Edinburgh College of Art

The School of Design and Applied Arts is, whether of Arts and Crafts or Bauhaus provenance, a school whose courses were originally about the manipulation of materials. Jewellery and silversmithing taught students to engage with metals; the printed textiles, tapestry (now, curiously in the school of painting), fashion, and performance costume courses were about the manipulation of fabric; glass, architectural glass, and ceramics (now defunct) were just that; and the furniture course was, until recently, very much about the working of wood.

The odd one out, ultimately and historically, in this school of the crafts was, of course, interior design: its subject is empty space and its material of manipulation, once the rotring and trace, is now the immaterial pixel. In the Bauhaus Manifesto it was stated: 'the ultimate aim of all the arts is... the building'. That might have been true for the fine arts of painting, sculpture and architecture at Edinburgh College of Art; but once upon a time, the ultimate aim of all the *applied* arts at ECA was... the interior. Still, when applicants to the course are asked what interests them about interior design they most often cite its interdisciplinarity. That is to say that they imagine interiors to be the *arrangement* of metalwork, fabrics, glassware, ceramics and furniture, and it is this art of *arrangement* which remains the most accessible and engaging feature of the discipline.

Such a view has a long history, and echoes everywhere. Upon recently visiting the State University of Arkansas in the USA, where interior design was located in the School of Agriculture (along with the rather marvellously named apparel studies), it was explained that the School of Agriculture had been established to teach young American men how to be good farmers, and young American women how to be good farmers wives able to throw a home together – and to knock up their own clothes as well. If one thought that they were old fashioned, they said, one should take a look at the course down the road in Kansas, where the degree show project every year was to design... a wedding. Foreign as all of this might have seemed, the underlying rationale was the same as the historic position in Edinburgh College of Art: that the art of *arrangement* was the key skill of the interior designer.

If interior designers are there to arrange, then what is the purpose of their arrangement? Again, we turn to our own students (or those who are applying to become so) for advice. They almost all state that the purpose of interior design is to make people feel good, to help people. Again, the example of the Kansas degree show is enormously helpful, in expressing, in extremis, this attitude: what is a wedding but an arrangement of 'stuff', activities, and people, designed to affirm society's values, and to make people feel good?

Such values genuinely distinguish interior design students from others at Edinburgh College of Art. The artists, applied or otherwise, still make things (though fine art has recently moved towards the art of arrangement considerably) rather than arrange them. The architects design rather than make, but they would never admit to stooping to the lowly art of arrangement. The architects and the artists, rather loftily scorn the ideal of making people 'feel good', placing more emphasis on the critique of society rather than its affirmation. One cannot imagine any of them designing a wedding, unless it involved considerable upset to the mother of the bride. So interior design at Edinburgh College of Art is, historically, an odd one out. She is queen of the applied arts, rather than princess child of architecture; a course in arrangement rather than designing or making, in pleasing people rather than challenging them.

Or thus was it once conceived.

Interiors: a portfolio of courses

If the place of interior design in Edinburgh College of Art has a history, so does the way it is taught. All programmes in the School of Design and Applied Arts share a course structure that is, at root, deeply traditional, and derives ultimately from the education of the applied artist. There is studio practice, in which all aspects of design are taught and assessed, including technical skill, aesthetic judgement and creativity; professional practice, in which students learn about the profession they are studying to join; critical and theoretical studies, which used to be 'history of art'; and then, because this is an art college, there is what is now known as 'supporting studies', but used to be called 'portfolio'. This area used to comprise life drawing, studies of the classical casts and self-motivated artwork – in short, what used to be the common currency right across any art college.

Things have changed, and an examination of interior design reveals just how much.

What used to be history of art is now visual and cultural studies: a menu of courses about all manner of subjects from which students select ones that interest them. The common currency of these is reading and writing – and the sense of critical scepticism essential to any degree-level liberal education. Thus is interior design grounded in the liberal arts rather than for instance, the sciences, as it might be elsewhere, especially on the continent.

Professional practice is, in the crafts and the applied arts, a guide to constructing, costing, and publicising exhibitions and the like; but in interior design it has to be, nowadays at least, much more about getting a job. This is not as simple an affair as it might seem. Being the slippery discipline it is, interior design offers – in Edinburgh anyway – an ever-changing range of opportunities. When the course was founded, most of the work on offer for graduates would have been small scale, domestic, and decorative. Ten years ago it was very largely architectural – Edinburgh at that time was oversubscribed with approximately two or three hundred small (i.e. fewer than two people) architecture practices, all undertaking the small domestic conversions and bar/ restaurant jobs that interior designers would be doing elsewhere. Since then, mainly by historical accident, Edinburgh has become a global centre for lighting design, with practices like Speirs and Major, LDP, and David Brown Associates mopping up lucrative contracts and graduate students alike. The growth of a café culture in Edinburgh has spawned a generation of 'classical' interior designers, such as Kerr Blyth Associates, whose work revolves around cafes, bars, and hotels. And Edinburgh's sustained role as a global finance centre has resulted in many graduates working in the design and planning of offices. The purpose of professional practice then, is to help students find their own niche in this kaleidoscope. Each year, every student on the programme makes a presentation to everyone else, quite simply entitled: 'what is interior design?' It is taken as a given that there is no one, or correct answer; and the point of the exercise is to raise debate – and professional expectation – among students. On the basis of this debate, lists of fantasy employers are drawn up, CVs and covering letters addressed directly to them are concocted, and students begin to articulate the confusing world of interior design practice for themselves. The validity of such an approach is evidenced by the exceptionally high employment rate for our graduates.

Drawing – what used to be 'portfolio studies' – is perhaps the greatest challenge facing interiors education. What sorts of work should the portfolio of an interior designer contain; and, more critically, how do we draw/represent the interior? At Edinburgh College of Art a well-provided workshop and a strong relationship with furniture and product design students, through shared facilities and staff, ensure that the 2D is always accompanied by the 3D, and that physical modelling is a core element of the course. Whether in making conceptual models at 1:200 for architectural type proposals, portions of constructional detail at 1:1, or large scale, realistic, lit, 'models as hats' of interior spaces at 1:20, in which the viewer can immerse themselves, the 3D experience is made anterior to its 2D representation. In addition, the 'art college system' encourages our students to value sketching, observational or developmental. In a world in which the 3D-rendered CAD image is becoming as ubiquitous (and commonplace) as the word-processed document, these two last skills, modelling and drawing, make our graduates valuable and give them a competitive edge over students whose sole means of expression is the clicking mouse.

The interior design studio: three rules

So that leaves studio practice, which is the most important of all of the four generic 'subjects' the students undertake in their time of study. At ECA we apply three 'rules' to projects.

The language of architecture

The first of these rules is that all our sites or conditions are, literally or analogically, architectural. Almost all the sites and briefs we set are addressed to buildings – and very particular types of buildings at that. Edinburgh is a city of nineteenth-century buildings with stone walls at least two-feet thick. These buildings last for hundreds of years, and Edinburgh is a city that has not changed substantially in appearance for a century. Those evanescent sheds of steel frame and aluminium cladding, those paper-like plasterboard walls and suspended ceilings, ubiquitous as they may be everywhere else, are in short supply in Edinburgh. Architecture, from a Scottish point of view, is an art that unfolds over rainy centuries rather than the rapid turning of the page of a magazine. As such, it provides a strong and dominant frame for interiors that it might not in more disposable architectural environments.

Figure 2: *Glasgow Headquarters for the RIAS*, Lynne Semple, final year project 2005

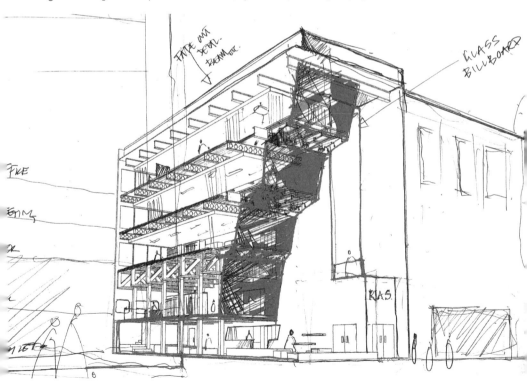

At one level, then, the language of architecture is a language our students must learn. Whether they are prototyping at 1:1, or masterplanning at 1:500, they are always working within a repertory of scales that are, ultimately, derived from architecture: 1:1, 1:5, 1:20, 1:50, 1:100, 1:200, 1:500 and so on. The conventions of orthographic drawing, constructional detailing and the architectural procurement process are crucial.

Rooms

The second rule is that, while we may practise interior design at the scale of accessories (from ashtrays to furniture) or at the scale of the masterplan for an entire building (and sometimes maybe more), these are the outer limits of a spectrum, and the centre of that spectrum is something that, whether you call it a cave, a painted interior, or Hertzian space, is, at root, a *room*. Importantly, this term 'room' differs significantly from architectural discourse, whose centre is the *building*.

Edinburgh, stuck as it is somewhere in the nineteenth century, is a warren of rooms. There are the garrets and the turnpike stairs, the subterranean howffs (drinking dens) and the vaults of the Old Town; the gilded saloon bars, banking halls and drawing rooms of the New Town; the outdoor rooms of High Street and Park. In addition, the climate's primary condition is dark, wet and windy which militates against the open plan, the merging of inside and outside, the exploded corner and the virtual cloud so beloved of Modernism and after. When it is cold and wet and windy, you drink underground, you close your timber shutters, and you retreat into interiors well wrapped up from the storm outside.

Figure 3: *Constructed Perspective, Vermeer's Milkmaid*, Louise Graham, first year project

Spotlights.
grubby wooden floor.
wooden & leather furniture.

Figure 4: *The Human Be-Inn Bar: sketch*, Rory Robertson, second year project

It is the task of the interior designer to create such rooms, to be the mistress of space and sensation; and this is their core task and their field of expertise. At all levels students undertake projects that require them to devise, to articulate, resolve and stage rooms. This means that, unlike architects, or product designers, who occupy either end of the spectrum of interiors practice, our students have to learn to think in spaces, not objects, places and events rather than things.

The room suffered something of a reversal of fortune in the twentieth century. Modern Architecture's advocacy of the free plan, planar glazing, and the explosion of the box, attacked the enclosed room as the hiding place of bourgeois hypocrisy. The circulation ramp of the Villa Savoye, the complete transparency of the Farnsworth House and the Barcelona Pavilion's *architecture as object*; furniture that floats above the ground on chrome legs, the iconic hi-fi and the signature designer lamp have turned the room into a notionally blank canvas upon which the treasures of the modern consumer can be displayed as art.

But somehow closets, garrets, parlours, salons, chambers, cabinets, *wunderkammeren*, antechambers, robing rooms, dining rooms, vaults and kitchens are smelly and evocative in a way that 'breakout space', 'waiting area', 'meeting pod', 'lift lobby', 'level 3' and 'living space' just aren't. They conjure sensations of light, temperature, humidity and smell, as well as function and configuration. We all know, subconsciously, the smell of a cellar, the humidity of a kitchen, the sound of a chamber or the texture of a closet. Rooms are the site of ways of behaving, special clothes, appropriate furniture and products, and above all a sense of place and occasion (rather than, in the words of Aldo Van Eyck, space and time).

All of which places interiors fairly firmly outside the eternal oblivious present and the glorious or apocalyptic future of Modernist architectural theory, which admits no history. However, it would be dangerous to place our students so far outside such a discourse that they were trapped in a tweedy world of heritage and history, unable to engage with contemporary practice and theory elsewhere, in less-traditional contexts than Edinburgh.

The art of telling a good story

And so we have a third rule. Our students learn right from the start that they are always altering things that already exist, rather than inventing them anew. In this respect, the architectural practice of Richard Murphy is a crucial influence on the teaching of interiors in Edinburgh. Murphy's researches and monographs about the work of Carlo Scarpa, written while he was lecturing in architecture at the University of Edinburgh, formed a powerful argument for the creative re-use of historic buildings as opposed to their slavish conservation. His work in practice, which is evident all over Edinburgh, is an exposition of this philosophy. The influence of his work has encouraged planners, conservation bodies, and architects themselves to be more adventurous in addressing the historic stones of Edinburgh. This, in turn, has elevated the art of alteration to a status that it might not possess in a city less blessed (or cursed) with ancient stone buildings, and a spokesman with the rhetorical force of Murphy.

In this respect, Graeme Brooker and Sally Stone's idea that interiors involves a 'rereading' of architecture is crucial; and at Edinburgh College of Art we take the difference between reading and writing, rereading and rewriting, very seriously indeed.

The interior designer is not the author of a work of art, but its 'teller', in the same way that a storyteller or an actor takes a script and reinterprets it in order to perform or narrate it. Cinderella's slipper turned from fur to glass in translation, and every folk tale alters as it is handed down from generation to generation. Shakespeare, Wagner and Monteverdi spent their lives re-staging stories which already existed, while the rapid operations of the internet have accelerated and exaggerated the development and dissemination of myth. Because it deals with the alteration of given states, every act of interior design is itself an act of historical research and exegesis; an act of memory and of forgetting that is analogical to these 'compromised' situations of authorship and interpretation.

The rules and the context

The choice – or rather the unconscious development – of these rules has been driven, above all, by the context of Edinburgh: an ancient stone warren of rooms, whose survival is only guaranteed by endless alteration and re-alteration. This context provides a strong architectural frame for interiors which are themselves defined spaces, or rooms, the very strength or presence of which admits and calls for creative reinterpretation.

Every August, Edinburgh is invaded by about a million visitors who come to perform, spectate or critique some two thousand acts that constitute the Edinburgh Festival. For four weeks, every room in the city is appropriated: single bedroom flats accommodate ten or twenty in sleeping bags on the floor; church halls become the setting for cabaret performances that would outrage the stern Presbyterian elders who built them; pubs become concert halls, or the scene for the telling of ghost stories; forgotten vaults under the streets, suburban parks and dark alleys host promenade performances; and rooftops become the setting for installation art. The city grinds to a halt under a tide of discarded flyers, plastic beer mugs and broadsheet reviews, and when the party leaves town in September, the residents of Edinburgh are inevitably left with a terrible flu, a hangover, and a sewage system on the verge of collapse.

But is it the Edinburgh Festival's medium and message – of creative reinterpretation and reuse of the city itself – that sustains the city, culturally rescuing it once a year from provincial respectability and a conservative, albeit highly successful, financial sector that now drives a twenty-first century capital city edging towards even greater independence from Westminster. If a clear metaphor for the role of interiors in a city like Edinburgh is needed, let the world's largest and arguably greatest arts festival be it.

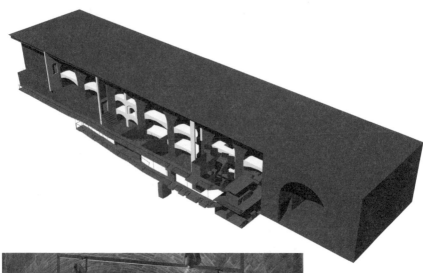

Figures 5 and 6:
*Performance Space,
the Vaults, Edinburgh,*
Margrete Landro,
schematic and
perspective showing
junctions between old
and new construction,
final year project

Conclusion

This returns us to that traditional perception of interiors as arrangement, out of which the modern discipline has grown, and which still informs potential students in the discipline.

What interior design students study in their studios next to the castle, in the shadow of plaster casts of the Parthenon, is unapologetically and clearly un (if not post) modern: they design rooms in old (or at least existing) buildings. But this is not to say that the way interiors is practised is the way it was conceived a century ago. We are no longer in the business of finishing young ladies and helping them to design their weddings, no longer in the business primarily of arranging things to please people. Interior design has changed, and so have the people who are studying to practise it, and the people who are teaching it.

As lecturers and students have come and gone, interior design has reflected their interests, becoming at one time subservient to furniture, at others closely wedded to set design, at others more of an 'architecture lite'. What is clear is that arranging things and pleasing people, laudable aims as they are, are no longer enough, either to be the foundation of a higher education degree course, or to prepare people for the realities of professional life. The ability to design and perhaps make – or at least to resolve design work so that it can be made – has become very much more important than it once was. Architectural modes of drawing, product design development methodologies and the critical stance of the fine artist have all crowded in as necessities on the young interior designer.

However, in the rush to answer these needs (and to cast off the notion of the course as a finishing school for nice 'gels') it is arguable that the simple desire to make arrangements to please people has been lost. Students who apply are often shocked by their immersion in architectural drawing practice, postmodern cultural theory and building things in the workshop. It would be fair to say that they do not receive enough teaching (or learning) in those essential skills of the interior designer: shopping and specifying. In not having these skills at their elbow when they leave, for all their spatial, constructional, theoretical skill, they may have lost an essential competitive edge on their 'designer' colleagues. Something we at ECA intend to rectify through rehabilitating the notion of taste. Madame de Pompadour's objet du goût, the first conscious expression of consumerism, was contemporaneous with the birth of the college, and is perhaps justification for the staff feeling less guilty about reintroducing retail therapy and aesthetic classification into the curriculum.

Interior design at Edinburgh College of Art has been subject to a dramatic environmental shift since the conference's initial conception 18 months ago. We have been rehoused in a £20 million contemporary flagship office building adjacent to the classicism of our old studio accommodation. Trading paint-splattered cells, marble staircases and cups of tea in the canteen for the modernity of vast open-plan studios, Otis lifts, frappuccinos and wi-fi. This has made the staff and students of interior design even more committed to remaining connected with its history, something which the discipline at large may also benefit from.

'Thinking Inside the Box' has been one way in which it has attempted to do just that: to develop new modes of thinking out of existing ones – rather than trying to (re)invent them anew. And as such, all the temptations of radical innovation, of thinking outside the box, may well be a distraction interiors could do well without.

Andy MILLIGAN

Duncan of Jordanstone College, University of Dundee

Roland ASHCROFT

College of Art, Science and Engineering,
University of Dundee

INTERIOR DIVERSITY *IN* AND ENVIRONMENTAL DIVERSITY *OUT*?

Introduction

In March 2002, a chance conversation led Interior and Environmental Design at Duncan of Jordanstone College of Art and Design to initiate a new partnership. Interior programmes within the Scottish Higher Education sector, including Edinburgh College of Art, Glasgow School of Art, Napier University and Glasgow Metropolitan College (with Glasgow Caledonian University), formed a new academic body, the Interiors Forum Scotland [1]. The IFS aims to provoke and promote debate amongst interior educators, researchers and practitioners who share a passion for, and concern with, the development and future of interior design and interior architecture. It exists to generate critical debate on the past intentions, present dilemmas, and future challenges affecting interiors and to focus upon leading research in this diverse environmental field. Establishing a regular conference platform is essential. Whilst confused by its slippery origins, the discipline seldom takes charge of its possible futures, having very few frameworks in which to build upon, particularly within the UK.

However, the IFS is also part of a resurgence in the intellectual and theoretical scope of interior education, discourse and practice. Recent publications have shifted from pragmatic *construction*, toward strategies for re-reading interior architecture [2]; provocative interior design theory readers celebrating interior design and/or interior architecture's multiple personalities and perspectives [3]; the radical theories of Rice's doubleness within the spatial and visual aspect of home; and the critical debates on interior education in IDEAS in Australian and New Zealand interiors institutions. These developments indicate a growing international re-emergence of interior pedagogy, theory, strategy and practice.

This critical re-emergence may be timely, and could bring a new critical focus to interiors higher education in the UK which has seen a dramatic increase in new 'interior' programmes. Against this critical re-emergence of the interior and exponential growth, there is an erosion, discomfort or neglect in how to frame and promote interiors, and the erasure of 'interiors' entirely from the RCA's MA programme.

Roots and risk

Interiors, it seems, remains in denial over its feminine roots, uncertain how to integrate, celebrate or position this against an architectural direction. Yet gender in student recruitment is a recurring issue which is itself bound up in perception; female students in predominantly male academic teams offer interesting territory for further debate beyond mere statistics. Yet from emerging statistics, hard facts are now being established, both from BIDA (the British Interior Design Association) and informally, from the newly formed Interior Educators group in the UK (previously the AIDDC, Association of Interior Design Degree Courses). Whilst gender in recruitment is a concern, other related issues which refer back to interiors' domestic/feminine origins are also worth revisiting. Interior programmes seem happy to avoid links to pattern, surface, decoration and the transience of skin, rather than evolving them, and coming to terms with the relative transience of the subject. Interiors seems content to survive (but seldom thrive) on history and theory 'hand-me-downs' from other disciplines, rather than seek to redefine them in its own image. Luiz Diaz's thought-provoking chapter, 'Discourse, History and Interior Architecture' [4], offers distinct theoretical models rooted in Modernism for interior architecture; whilst Mark Taylor and Julieanna Preston's excellent book *Intimus* offers fascinating insights into the feminine legacy and domestic heritage of interiors, reflecting important contextual frameworks often missing from so many of our programmes.

In an increasingly pressurised educational 'industry', it is creative experimentation, risk taking and disciplinary diversity (so long at the heart of dynamic interior education within the Scottish art and design experience) which may themselves be at risk, and which have been the focus of recent conference debates on creativity [5]. To what extent might interior educators defend intellectual freedom? How might disciplinary boundaries be challenged, and how can we engage learners with a disinterested interior industry? Does this industry exist in the way we imagine, or has it evolved into multi and interdisciplinary practice? However, interior educators also need to reflect on where new risks lie. In seeking to redefine our discipline, we identify territory; and in articulating territory we define limits, not limitlessness. It is precisely those limits and boundaries we should seek to challenge and cross. In an era of educational accessibility, flexibility and openness, how progressive, or retrogressive, is it to limit horizons?

Ownership and guardianship

Ownership has particular currency in design education and new initiatives within the UK higher education sector will continue to drive this agenda in coming years. Ownership is a key element within Interior and Environmental Design culture at Dundee, where intellectual and creative ownership leads students toward informed, independent and often cross-disciplinary perspectives on interior design practice, research and teaching. Creative ownership is central to a Deconstruct–Reconstruct environmental project, in which the design process is enriched through a more visceral and fluid creative response to found products, materials and objects from local waste streams, and which underpins the crucial nature of making within a discipline normally confined to paper-space speculation [6].

There is also a public sense of ownership 'of' interiors through domestic, lifestyle and decorative formats, fed by the pervasive popular culture of TV 'make-over' shows – often fronted by people who are not the interior designers we think 'we' are. To what extent though might the global phenomenon of TV make-over shows motivate applicants to select interior design as the career of choice? Ownership may also be problematic. The exerting of ownership and authority 'over' interiors, through architecture, has been a recurring issue affecting our, and others', perception of the discipline, disciplinary self-confidence and self-belief. What happens if we take architecture out of the agenda for once? Very few disciplines would relinquish creative and intellectual ownership so easily to another 'related' discipline en-masse; but in the past, guardianship of interiors has been 'directed', and sometimes dominated by, architectural academic teams, rather than diverse interior or environmental teams. The message this sends students, keen to pursue this as a serious interiors career, is clear and unfortunate. Many disciplines, including architecture, certainly would not accept the reverse scenario. Why indeed should they?

This goes some way towards explaining the seductive attraction, insecurity, and recurring debate about the positioning of interiors toward architecture. It also exposes a discipline lacking self-confidence, confused over its direction and anxious for affirmation. Whilst there may indeed be a market for interior architecture courses, particularly where there is a close correlation between the course and that of an architecture school – a common first and second year for example – the prerogative of art schools may be to expand the creative and conceptual boundaries of disciplines outwith any sense of external industry approval, which could enhance the intellectual potential of interiors.

Interior and Environmental Design

Interior and Environmental Design (www.dundee.ac.uk/design/bdes-interior-design. php) is a dynamic spatial discipline with ambitions well beyond its pro-decorative or co-architectural role. It co-exists with, and operates across architecture, design and art. Its future may involve spatial psychology, virtual and digital environments and conventional interior/architectural practice, but it is also concerned with re-energising and recycling redundant architecture. It can explore a wide range of inhabited spatial contexts, from the interiority of home, to the exteriority of bus shelters, to community centres, to the physicality of architecture (interior architecture), toward the formlessness and ambiguity of digital environments. Equally important are the expressive and emotive contexts of installation and theatre. Ritual, process, behaviours and context are as important as pragmatic concerns.

This four-year programme views the discipline of IED as a vehicle for experimentation and reinterpretation. It leads students towards very diverse career opportunities, from mainstream design, such as architectural and interior practice (with students migrating into formally recognised architecture professions), lighting design, exhibition, theatre, TV, film-set design, graphics, animation, the computer games industry, landscape design, environmental management, interdisciplinary design, school, college and university teaching, psychology, museum and exhibition design, museum curators, social work, as well as disciplines of a more sensorial or expressive nature, such as installations and sound-scapes. Installations, in this context, are seen as part of an environmental trinity including exhibition and theatre set. The programme explores process within the context of practice, designing for behaviours before bricks and mortar. Individuals use the undergraduate experience as a vital creative spark defining their own response to the discipline, something which helps individuals find their own identity and roles within the creative industries.

New alliances and auld enemies

Irrespective of how partisan we may feel, interiors is relational to architecture; but what new alliances are now being forged with these old enemies? Within Dundee, old tensions are giving way to new visions through cross-disciplinary teaching, exploring themes of poetic ekphrasis. Although this term applies primarily to poetry and, in turn, to how poets re-present the visual arts through written structure, many contemporary artists (though very few design disciplines) have conceptually inverted this by deconstructing and then reconstructing poetry or painting into new 2D images, 3D 'spaces' or objects which interpret the literary arts within an art context [7]. The artist Calum Colvin is one such example. This literary ekphrastic theme developed in a design context where teams of interior and architecture students were asked to reinterpret architectural illustrations intuitively and analytically, and to translate these into objects for sitting on. Occurring within a neutral space, 160 diverse students were split into thirty teams, and supported by IED and architectural staff over a five-day workshop. New research partnerships are being forged, focusing on spatial narratives. Indeed, the experimentation, cross-disciplinary working and diversity which IED has been pioneering at Dundee, is now being embedded within architecture. Just as interiors education seems set to discuss the future, UK architectural education is itself contemplating fundamental change within its own educational format [8]. Within the European dimension, interior design programmes working in partnership are responding to the Bologna Accord, and establishing new International Masters in Interior Architectural Design, Edinburgh College of Art being a leader within the Scottish scene.

Diversity in and out

Whilst Interior and Environmental Design aspires to maintain a *diversity in, diversity out* ethos, diversity is becoming increasingly difficult to fund and to manage. The in-house IED staff team working throughout the four-year programme includes architects, interior designers, artists, illustrators, theatre set designers, sound artists, multi media and furniture designer/makers. The student group are increasingly female, with increasing numbers of mature students, and a surprising proportion are dyslexic. Maintaining a diverse agenda is increasingly difficult within continually decreasing budgets and shrinking teaching time. The imposition of modules promises flexibility, whilst simultaneously limiting it. Diversity places pressures on an ever-decreasing staff team, making them the sole, rather than co-specialist; and the impact of the RAE (which in Dundee is individually focused, rather than driven by the discipline) places further pressure to pursue independent research. This dilutes deep research into interior education, practice and theory.

With diversity comes dynamic and provocative learning, capable of transforming a discipline; but it also brings with it consequences. Yet within this, the *diversity in, diversity out* approach at Duncan of Jordanstone offers an effective, if increasingly challenging, model leading graduates towards very broad career routes: from architects and interior designers to artists. Diversity reflects the eclectic nature of interior design and suggests a viable approach to educating interior designers who bypass the architectural Modernist agenda. Do new interior courses signify a healthy disciplinary diversity, or reflect an unregulated and unprotected discipline which remains open territory? Theory of interiors is itself defined as being particularly diverse and multifaceted, whilst others speculate further that interiors' historical origins predate the emergence (rather than follow in the wake) of architecture [9].

Artefacts, images, language

To what extent does the interior educational experience equip students to create and test ideas physically? We may obsess about constructing interiors physically, but drawing restricts this to imaginal visions in paper space; we very rarely deal with actual build space or place that can be experienced. There are no actual representational artefacts, no real settings, and indeed no 'real' interiors which define interiors to its audience directly and which could enable interior design learners to make the leap of faith from theory to practice. IED at Dundee has been addressing this through overtly making and building tasks for many years, whilst research into experimental low-fidelity artefacts, objects and spaces can carry significant meaning for interior design education [10]. Whilst painters may paint, sculptors sculpt and textile makers weave, neither interiors nor architecture truly makes. Both operate within an odd, visually dominant paper-space abstraction.

The authors speculate whether this 'reality of limits' is replicated globally across the bandwidths of interior education. Whilst the visual tends to dominate the spatial narratives which emerge, do we really engage with these visual aspects beyond the merely prosaic, practical or pixellated context of drawing? Indeed, our dependence on the visual makes less sense when we consider the deeply sensorial realities of what we do as interiors people. Our images are curiously fixed, frozen, lacking motion or scent. Equally, our drawings are rather dumb, existing without any auditory quality; yet these crucial sensorial elements need to be addressed through a deeper intellectual exploration of images.

Conversely, we may invert this and reframe how we explore sound. This latter approach has been the subject of a two-year experiment at IED, run by the sound artist Pete Nixon, entitled 'Swapping Senses'. This project explores how interiors students create sonic responses to inhabited and experienced space using sound equipment and software to help develop more holistic awareness of sound within interiors, and also explore alternatives to AutoCAD presentations. Indeed, we could then explore the relationship of language, text, writing, verbalising and encoding or decoding of spatial narratives. Language needs to be transformed beyond the prosaic 'specification' of working drawings, or indeed, escape from the academic straightjacket of dissertation writing. A classic theoretical exploration of the interconnected relationship between drawing, architectural space and language is Adrian Forty [11].

A recent collaboration between Interior and Environmental Design and Interior Design at the University of North Texas offers insights into the ambiguity of language, the ubiquity of socialising software – MSN, chat rooms and email technolgies – and the roles these play in private, social and professional interiors thinking. It sought to digitally simulate the real-world scenarios, tensions and conflicts between Texan and Dundee interior students. The students each alternated between roles as *proxy designer* and/or *surrogate client* virtually, and produced physical personality sample objects of their 'clients'. At the very end of the task they met face to face in a virtual conference room [12]. Through the designing and interpreting of questions (rather than interior spaces), students in Texas and Dundee simultaneously established personality profiles of one another, without meeting in the flesh – instead corresponding remotely, and without exchanging images of each other. The project explored the relationship between the text, context, visual thinking and dealing with clients, and culminated in a virtual conference exchange of the 3D personality sample objects of each other. This was the first, and last, time students would meet face to face. The concept represented a development of a further international collaboration, exploring ekphrastic, poetic and spatial experiments between interiors at Dundee and the University of Groningen's Word and Image department, initiated by the Irish Artist and Illustrator, Brigid Collins.

Interiors and power of description

What might distinguish interiors education from other artefact-driven creativity? Perhaps what interiors has at its disposal is the potency and power of description; that's it. But it's a 'power of description' which is in itself diverse, fluid, context-dependent and focused on multiple levels of communication and persuasion of visual, verbal, poetic, textual, sonic, sensorial, material or how motion effects our emotions. This multifaceted aspect to 'description' also allows us to reflect upon the experiential, multi sensory and multi modal (rather than visually dependent) potential of future interiors education, and to rethink how we approach designing for interiors, environments, spaces and places. Juhani Pallasmaa's seminal book, *The Eyes of the Skin: Architecture and the Senses*, is particularly valuable in this regard. However, in exploring our disciplinary relationship toward the visual, we need to address a potential banality within digital imagery, affecting interiors and many other digitally dependent design fields. Whilst we continue to define this as a 'professional' necessity, the profession itself has mixed, and, often contradictory, views on the effectiveness and requirement of CAD, or on learners' deficiencies in sketching, and education's inability to prepare graduates adequately.

Sketches, however, don't crash; computers do. So to what extent, and in what way, does CAD affect, influence and direct what we do within this theme of 'description'? The authors speculate that the bulk of what emerges through engagement in CAD is a pastiche, giving unwarranted authority to weak ideas, and seldom evolving beyond the predictably slick, yet superficial veneer of ordinary, rather than visionary thinking and expression – rarely the intellectually rich digital theatre of thinking we need. From a pedagogic perspective, too much learner dependency or departmental reliance on CAD may lead students to become prematurely satisfied with their thinking – or to expect a spoon-fed, hands-held approach to learning software. Concerns over poor analogue drawing skills, and over reliance and predictability of digital execution, are themes which design educators are becoming increasingly concerned with [13]. Future conferences need to debate this pervasive issue; but rather than merely react to the whims of industry (and again, which industry do we mean?) educators need to explore this as an ambiguous and deeply 'internalised' environment in itself, rather than a mere technological armature in which to hang a pixel-thin image.

Some time ago, the sociologist Manuel Castells speculated that we were moving from an age in which we lived in recognisably fixed spaces (e.g. home, work, university) toward spaces of virtual flows [14]. If home is also the place of work and, consequently, of distance and e-learning, what will home morph into, and in what way are progressive interiors programmes engaging with this important area? If spaces are indeed within virtual flow, is interior education digitally flowing in the way we imagined, or in a state of flux?

Domestechtopias?

A paradox of the contemporary 'private' interior is that in certain situations [post 9/11] its design forces the behavioural expectations of others on to us… subjugates the individual's will to that of the group… paving the way for domestic designs that imprison 'free' inhabitants in alarmed paradises…

What is it that makes today's home so different, so appealing, and yet so ignored by interiors programmes? The relationship between home, domesticity and technology has had a considerable impact on the evolution of interior design, but how are interiors programmes re-examining the potential of the digitally enabled smart home in the context of post 9/11? How might the emergence of new technologies within the smart home allow us to reframe home as place of dwelling, working and escape? Aristotle defined space as a 'container of things', like a succession of all inclusive spatial envelopes, (or nesting Russian dolls), but the spatial territory of home is layered, both in terms of the tangible depth and distance into its more private heart, and the intangible psychological depth in terms of the protection, sense of belonging and security it offers its occupants. It is multi dimensional, multi faceted, but seldom the sum of its significant structural parts – or indeed, the interactive domestic products and smart technologies which now seek to occupy it. Here, the space is more than its fabric. Home is a place to 'be', rather than merely occupy.

We may think of home as essentially rooted to a plot (as a washing machine is perhaps rooted to its water supply), but in a way which a TV, telephone and PC, due to their ability to migrate effortlessly within the home, are perhaps not. How then might interiors practice, theory and education reinterpret Manuel Castells' concept of home as no longer a domain of fixed spaces and distinct places, but in a space of digital flow, forcing new ways of envisaging the relationship between society and spaces? As a counterpoint to digitally driven ideals within domestic space, to what extent are the more ethereal, poetic phenomenological perceptions of home and dwelling (George Perec and Gaston Bachelard are significant in this philosophical context) still fertile symbolic, psychological and philosophical territory for interior design?

Home has perceptual thresholds with implicit territories, explicit boundaries, and physical (outside/threshold/inside) and metaphysical polarities. The latter was defined by Bachelard as the Oneiric Axis, represented conceptually as a vertically stacked trinity of distinct domestic realms: the lower cellar, with its allusions toward nightmare; the inhabited formality of the 'middle kingdom' of the house; and the elevated dream space of the attic. Bachelard's exploration of the poetic phenomenology of home touched upon emotive aspects of domestic space which celebrated the capacity for home to become a place bound up with memories, associations, dwelling and of dreaming.

Today, our relationship toward home, and the role new technologies may offer within it, suggests an inevitable redefinition of home, but in what way can interior education seek to advance this? There has always been conflict, uncertainty and suspicion when new technologies migrate into new territories and provoke new contexts, and this is particularly important within the domestic territory of the family home. Both Bachelard and Heidegger shared a mutual mistrust, and resistance toward encroaching urbanism and new technology, but both also shared a sentimental fascination for the suburban, the ordinary, and the provincial contexts of home. Paradoxically, interiors programmes often seem keen to distance themselves from this familiar and ordinary domestic landscape; but given the pervasive (and invasive) impact of digital technologies, how are we responding to this hybridised domain? Whilst interactive products have examined the everyday nature of home, ritual and behaviours with considerable success (RCA's Equator project), research by interiors in this regard seems patchy. Given our experience today with technology, what will happen when the house, like the PC, crashes? Whilst the internet-enabled microwave communicates with the wirelessly enabled cooker, the dysfunctional, but digitally enabled, family will have few incentives to talk!

This informal marriage between the home and technology has a long pedigree. The writer and architectural theorist Reyner Banham explored anti-monumental but pro-consumer ideas through his *Un-House* in 1965. This explored an optimistic fascination for the car and services, offering consumers a visionary new mobile home, with core services and facilities. Futuristic and interactive interiors, such as Archigram's automated *House for 1990* (exhibited at Harrods in 1967), and the spatial narratives of the French interior designer Olivier Mourgue, in his film sets for Stanley Kubrick's *2001: A Space Odyssey* in 1967, share a connection with the reframing homes of the future.

Michele Foucault's interests in themes of surveillance within 'Of Other Spaces, Utopias and Heterotopias' [15] explored a very particular strain of spatial typologies, several of which are neatly interconnected with issues of home, security, homeland, colonies and the paranoia of insecurity post '9/11'. Foucault defines these as 'heterotopias', as extreme, and often deviant 'otherness', defining spatial typologies which are forced to fit the normative shell of civilised society, such as the highly controlled environments of prisons, insane asylums and ships. These illustrate a dystopian view of how societies may view the spaces they create, and the potentially deviant roles technology may play within them.

Interiors and interdisciplinarity

Over the last three years, Interior and Environmental Design has led the interdisciplinary agenda at Duncan of Jordanstone College of Art and Design, which has also been the subject of collaborative research [16]. These projects integrate *experience prototyping* (research by Jane Fulton Suri at IDEO) and explore intellectual risk and creative uncertainty, through Eddie Obeng's design paradigms of *fog*, *quest*, *movie* and *paint-by-numbers* [17]. Prada, for example, is designed on the risk and uncertainty of Obeng's *fog* principles; Starbucks however, is *paint-by-numbers*. Interdisciplinarity is helpful in provoking disciplines to re-examine perceived boundaries, sense of identity, and exposes disciplinary limitations and attitudes (it's equally good at exposing an institution's resistance to risk).

However, interdisciplinary working also lets us tentatively cross and challenge imaginary disciplinary boundaries; in sharing our imaginations we transform our horizons. Over the three years, projects have explored themes of 'experience design', 'mapping', and this year 'defining design'. In these projects, 155 students, from interiors, products, interactive media, graphics, textiles and jewellery worked within 19 teams over five intense days within a neutral, and rather exposed, studio space and in response to a neutral design brief. An interdisciplinary staff team act as 'producers' (working discretely in the background), student teams are the 'actors' everyone comes to see perform, and the 'audience' are the assessors. Yet in seeking to define design we immediately limit it; and whilst the task revealed a consensus amongst staff and students that *design* has multiple, overlapping and continually shifting identities and definitions, why do we remain particularly anxious when we fail to finalise a definition of interiors? Interiors educators are not the only group to express anxiety in this case: the design professors who happily confirm that defining design is elusive are also sceptical when interiors refuses, like design, to be pigeonholed.

Discussion and conclusion

- Diversity is an important aspect to interior education and needs to be protected, but educators need to debate the consequences of this

- Interior diversity may also dilute identity

- Interior educators, practitioners, researchers and supporting organisations at home and abroad need a regular conference platform in which to debate the future of interiors

- Both interiors and its closest relation, architecture, are exploring changes to their respective education formats – but what opportunities exist for joint discussions, and sharing of good practice?

- Interiors is leading interdisciplinarity and diversity at Dundee

- How can interior educators re-engage with the home, given the rise of new technologies within the smart home?

References

[1] www.interiorsforumscotland.com
[2] Brooker, G. and Stone, S. *ReReadings: Interior Architecture and the Design Principles of Remodelling Existing Buildings* (London: RIBA Publications, 2006).
[3] Taylor, M. and Preston, J. *Intimus: Interior Design Theory Reader* (London: Wiley Academy Publisher, 2006).
[4] Diaz, L. 'Towards a History of Interior Architecture', Interiors Forum Scotland: Thinking Inside the Box Conference, the Lighthouse, Glasgow, 1–2 March 2007.
[5] 'Creativity or Conformity: Building Cultures of Creativity in Higher Education', University of Wales Institute, Cardiff, Wales, 8–10 January 2007 (www.creativityconference.org).
[6] Milligan, A. and Nelson, J. 'Dysfunction, Deconstruction & Reconstruction: Exploring Sustainable Thinking Through Design Making', 4th E&PDE Conference, Educating Designers for a Global Context, Salzburg, Austria, 6–8 September 2006.
[7] Collins, B. and Robillard, V. 'The Poetics of Installation; the Poetic Revolt', SWIG, the Scottish Word & Image Group Conference, University of Dundee, March 2006.

[8]   Taylor, D. 'Class Acts', *Blueprint: Architecture, Design, Culture*, no.236, November 2005, pp.74–9.

[9]   Conway, H. *Design History: a Students' Handbook* (London: Routledge, 1994).

[10] Badke, C. and Walker, S. 'Contextualising Consumption', 3rd E&PDE Conference, Crossing Design Boundaries, Napier University, Edinburgh, September 2005.

[11] Forty, A. *Words and Buildings: A Vocabulary of Modern Architecture* (London: Thames & Hudson, 2004).

[12] Mohr, C. and Milligan, A. '"Throwing Pebbles Across the Pond", Creativity or Conformity: Building Cultures of Creativity in Higher Education', University of Wales Institute, Cardiff, Wales, 8–10 January 2007.

[13] Lambert, I. 'Sketches Don't Crash', 4th E&PDE Conference, Educating Designers for a Global Context, Salzburg, Austria, 6–8 September 2006.

[14] Massey, D. 'Reinventing the Home', edited from 'The Intimate Space: Reinventing the House', *Blueprint: Architecture, Design, Culture*, no.159, March 1999, pp.24–5.

[15] Foucault, M. 'Of Other Spaces, Utopias and Heterotopias', 1967, and published in *Lotus International* 48/49, October 1984.

[16] Milligan, A. and Rogers, J. 'Experience Design & Artefacts after the Fact', *CoDesign: The International Journal of CoCreation in Design and the Arts, Special Edition: Crossing Design Boundaries*, vol.2, no.2, Taylor & Francis Publishers, 2006, pp.89–96.

[17] Anusas, M. 'Creativity in Mass Education Contexts', 4th E&PDE Conference, Educating Designers for a Global Context, Salzburg, Austria, 6–8 September 2006.

Drew PLUNKETT

Glasgow School of Art

FINDING A WAY

Shared understanding of the conventions and mechanisms of everyday existence gives interior designers and those who use the places they create a shared sensory language. It is the particular responsibility of designers to enrich the vocabulary of that language, to give their audience something that it neither realised it wanted, nor knew it could have.

Effective interiors must be practical, must function, but the idea of 'function' should not refer only to utility. Whenever humankind has achieved something more than the most basic level of subsistence it has aspired to embellish the expediencies of its shelters, to add elements, whether applied or integral to the processes of construction, that satisfy its collective aesthetic appetite.

It is comparatively simple to apply the formulae which deal with the physical expectations and limitations of the human body. It is more difficult, and ultimately more significant, to bring to utilitarian spaces resonances that satisfy the sensuous and cerebral expectations of those who use them. The obligation to provide such satisfaction is so fundamental to the creation of successful interiors that it must be perceived as an essential component of 'function'.

At Glasgow School of Art we believe that students learn to design by intense, challenging experience of the design process, guided and supported by collaborative tutorial discussion. We believe that inventive orchestration of aesthetic ambitions and practical priorities is the key to making a successful interior. We do not believe that this necessarily requires a grandiose gesture. Creative use of colour will transform a space as effectively as extravagant spatial remodelling.

We try to do all our teaching within the context of projects, because we think the subject must be treated holistically. The creative application of practical skills is best taught and best learnt in studio practice. We do not presume to teach students to be creative. It is our responsibility to select those with the most acute instinctive creativity and to help them express it through the cultivation of appropriate intellectual and practical skills. The course offers a structure within which they can prepare for the demands of the increasingly specialised and competitive world of professional interior design, in which conceptual flair must be complemented by practical capability, and precisely tuned, balanced skills are the only reliable means of survival. Our comparatively small year groups are cohesive, dynamic communities which allow students to see themselves as individuals, with personal responsibility for the direction of their own creative development, and allow staff to form a clear perception of individual abilities and aspirations.

All full- and part-time staff are actively engaged in professional practice and the department maintains close links with progressive practitioners who advise on course development and contribute to its delivery. Lectures, seminars and reviews promote understanding of theory and practice and help cultivate essential verbal skills but the ability to conceptualise, evolve, refine and bring ideas to fruition is recognised as the core skill and *that* is learnt in the studio.

Our conviction is that students can only properly find their own creativity when they have discovered and perfected mechanisms for exploring and expressing it, in two and three dimensions. Visualising ideas in drawings and models – sometimes made by hand, increasingly by computer – is our fundamental activity but only as a means to the essential end of creating beautiful interior spaces. Nevertheless we value the beautiful image and model because we believe that everything a designer produces should be aesthetically tuned and that the impulse to achieve should be nurtured.

Figure 1: *Action Replay and Office*, Naemhi Prahm, year 1

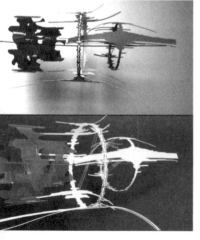

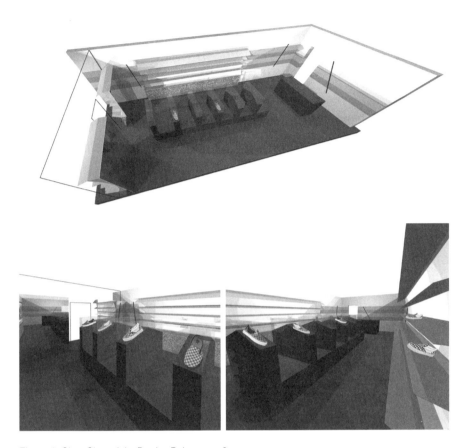

Figure 2: *Shoe Shop*, Jake Powley Baker, year 2

In the beginning, first-year students learn how to explore and explain ideas. The projects are a little oblique. There is no rush to deal with the specialist demands of designing interiors. The intention is that students should begin to understand how to define and develop ideas. As the year progresses they begin to think more about the reality of buildings. They make simple plans and sections. Practical considerations are identified and discussed, but the emphasis remains primarily on the definition and expression of an aesthetic ambition.

In second year the focus is firmly on interior design. Students do short projects, two or three weeks long, which demonstrate theory in practical contexts and stress the importance of coherent conceptual thinking. We believe that there is little to be gained from stretching students' necessarily limited skills over too long a time; that it is better to move on and experience the process of designing in the fresh perspective of another

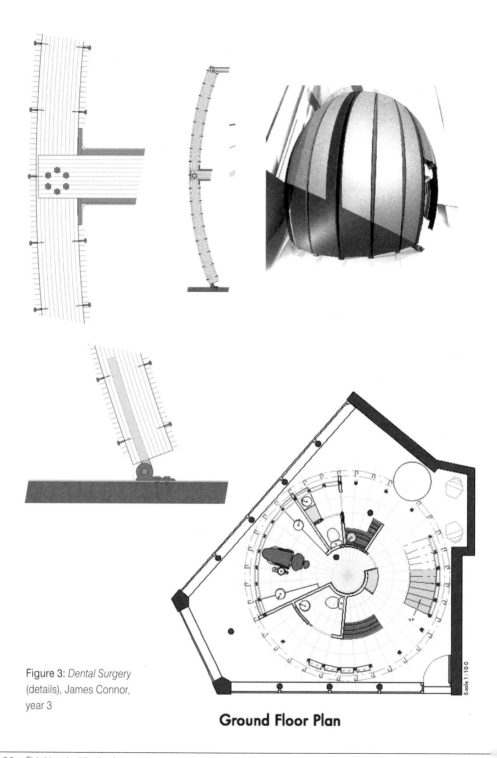

Figure 3: *Dental Surgery* (details), James Connor, year 3

Ground Floor Plan

Scale 1:100

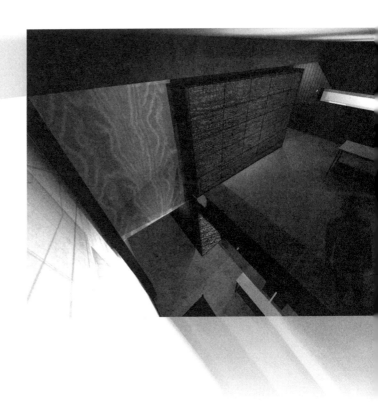

Figure 4: *Men's Clothes Shop*, Richard Smith, year 4

project. Aesthetic quality remains the paramount criterion but increased importance is placed on the precise practical resolution of ideas. Model making becomes a means of understanding and explaining complex spatial ideas but digital drawing is the primary visualising tool, precisely expressing and explaining volume, surface, detail. Diversity of projects gives experience of the range of specialist activities, from the comparatively prosaic work space to short abstract animations that explore the poetic potential of new media.

Third year encourages holistic understanding of design with an emphasis on increased precision and resolution of detail, on learning how to build without compromising aesthetic intention. As students begin to discover and develop their mature voice so they represent their ideas with increased personal intensity, demonstrating conclusively the synergy which exists between conception and expression, expression and realisation.

Students entering final year refine this personal aesthetic, and the practical skills that support it, in more complex projects that they bring to comprehensive completion. They

Figure 5: *Digital Art Gallery*, Olga Reid, year 4

also develop projects from second year. These often have extraordinary conceptual ambitions that are worth editing and making buildable. This reprise closes the circle of students' educational experience, offering them an opportunity to reflect on the nature and development of their creativity, and positions them to move with enthusiasm, and a few nostalgic regrets, into practice.

When they graduate, we try to follow their careers. The great majority find their niche and cope comfortably with the demands of the profession. A few push its boundaries a little further forward. Occasional mavericks apply their bedrock skills on the margins and beyond.

Frazer HAY

Programme Leader, Interior Architecture,
Napier University, Edinburgh

INTERIOR ARCHITECTURE

Interior architecture is a part of a larger group of professionals referred to by Tony Fretton, Chair of Architectural and Interior Design at the Technical University of Delft in the Netherlands, as 'The Interiorists'. This group primarily comprises of interior designers, interior decorators, interior architects, exhibition designers, lighting designers, stage designers and architects.

Although part of a relatively new 'interiorist' movement, interior architecture has strived for a recognised identity and method of approach whilst creating successful spatial solutions to a brief.

Interior architecture's roots loosely began with the Arts and Crafts movement of the nineteenth century, where architects were joined with artists and paid just as much attention to the interior of the building as to the exterior. Interior architecture has evolved in earnest however over the last few decades as a response to the void which arose over the last 20 to 30 years between architecture and interior design.

After the Second World War there was a rise in the number of large corporate architectural firms, mainly as a result of the massive reconstruction required by a war-torn society. Due to the scale of these corporate architectural firms, specialisation became a matter of course. There became a general shortage of architects and designers prepared to show the same commitment to the interior of a building as they would to the exterior. Unsuccessful attempts were made to bridge the gap by combining the educational requirements of both professions, allowing students to specialise after three years of architectural education in order to create architects specialising in interior design.

> Studio at the school of Architecture: Lord Llewelyn-Davies has described this course at the Bartlett School of Architecture at London University where: 'The first three years of the course would need to be so broadly based and generalised as to make it

extremely difficult to cram the essential technical content of the course into two final years and secondly the tendency would inevitably be for the most brilliant students and the tougher personalities to opt for architecture of the building industry, leaving only the less self-assured to the study of interior design.' This was the fact conceded by Lord Llewelyn-Davies who, when he took charge of the Bartlett School, closed down the course in interior design in 1963, planning that it could be more comfortably accommodated in an Art School [1].

Although a good idea, the resulting failure to combine the two disciplines alternately led to a greater division in both professions. This growing separation was the catalyst needed for interior architecture to evolve as a separate discipline catering for the increasingly diverse interior demands of modern society.

As a practical and environmental solution to the increasing demands of an ever-growing high-tech modern society, interior architecture evolved yet further –specifically to deal with existing buildings architecturally, whilst remaining respectful to their context and integrity. A skill that the more established professions of interior design and architecture are struggling to execute successfully.

> Interiors are the transformation of a building – from distant, gleaming object into a rich experience of spaces, resonances, light. The interior is where a building embraces a person [2].

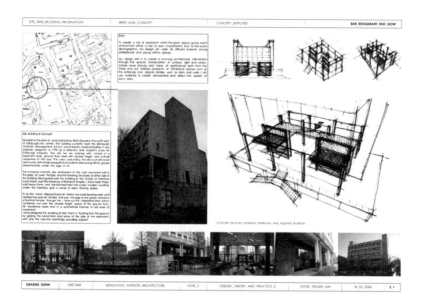

Figure 1: Graeme Dunn, second-year student project, Napier University, Edinburgh, Scotland [student's presentation, board one, highlighting the structural, contextual and environmental aspects of the project's host building]

Interior architecture is the spatial manipulation of an existing building whilst engaging with its structural DNA, history, context, orientation and proposed programme. There are a number of architectural approaches and a variety of skills to facilitate these structural and spatial changes.

Interior architecture employs three systems or strategies:

> The three types of strategy are classified according to the intimacy of the relationship between the old and the new. If the existing building is so transformed that it can no longer viably exist independently and the nature of the remodelling is such that the old and new are completely intertwined, then the system is *intervention*. If a new autonomous element, the dimensions of which are completely dictated by those of the existing, that is, it is built to fit, is placed within the confines of the existing, then the system is *insertion*. The final system, that of *installation* includes examples in which the old and the new exist independently. The new elements are placed within the boundaries of the building. The design or the grouping of these elements may be influenced by the existing, but the fit is not exact and should the elements be removed then the building would revert to its original state [3].

These systems depend on the architect's analytical ability with which to make sense of the host building's structural, historical and contextual information. This information is not unlike human DNA in that it dictates character, build and physical ability. It is this ability to decode a building's makeup which underpins the architect's choice of system from which to remodel an existing structure successfully. It is therefore essential that architects and designers learn the skills required to analyse and explore structural DNA as soon as possible. Uncovering the DNA can prove complicated, so it is therefore split into four key analytical strands: the composition and form of the host building; the historical and functional factors; the building's context and environment; and finally, the building's future function.

In order to understand the building's DNA more clearly, designers are encouraged firstly to analyse the building's structure (**analytical strand one**) by modelling the building digitally (using the latest CAD Package) and physically (using traditional methods such as card and timber).

Exploring:

- Exterior and interior dimensions
- Column grid spacing, floor and ceiling heights
- Location and dimensions of exterior and interior openings
- Location of interior bearing and non-bearing partitions
- Composition of structural frame, floor, ceiling and roof systems
- Composition of exterior walls and interior partitions
- Survey of vertical transportation systems

- Survey of capacity of floors and roof

- Orientation.

The historical and functional factors (**analytical strand two**) are often overlooked; however, it is these factors that directly contribute to the building's initial design and use. Exploration of the materials, and construction techniques used can determine the approach regarding the redesign, whilst remaining sympathetic to the existing architecture. Material and construction methods are only part of this analytical strand. Equally important to considering the host building's past is to understand how the building functioned in terms of the circulation, services and spatial hierarchy which are also woven within the fabric of analytical strand two.

The structure's context and environment (**analytical strand three**) play a key role in the building's makeup and continue to play a major part when creating a new design solution for a building's re-use. Considering and questioning the relationship established with adjacent structures, public spaces, the natural elements and landscape help establish a clearer representation of the structure to be remodelled. How does the structure engage with the street, the city and the area's demographic? How has the site and its orientation influenced the original design?

The future function intended for the host building (**analytical strand four**) has an enormous impact on the redesign. Programmatic requirements of a new function require exploration to ensure compatibility.

Tectonics and the ability to facilitate the interior architecture created are vital to a cohesive and successful design solution. Understanding and appreciating the fundamentals of detail design in regard to architecture and interior architecture is without a doubt important: it is not until the architectural elements are brought together through sensitive detailing (junctions and service interfaces for example) that a space becomes wholly believable and creditable. All the architectural greats (past and present) understood the importance of quality detailing. It is clear therefore that a fundamental grasp of horizontal or vertical surfaces, architectural furniture, construction materials, connection techniques, specification methods, service interface and finishes contributes to the success of an interior project.

Lighting plays an integral role in creating successful interior environments, capable of separating areas, suggesting circulation, manipulating mood and creating atmosphere within a space. The correct use of light is a complicated process, not only in managing the desired effect but also in handling the detailing issues in regards to its interface with the host architecture. Natural light has got to be one of the most important elements of an interior environment and requires a serious level of engagement from the earliest stages of the project's design process. In many cases the success of an interior relies on the clever and sensitive use of light both artificial and natural.

Interior architecture is an exciting and relatively new approach to dealing with existing buildings. It has become especially important as the construction industry struggles to justify the impact it has on the environment: in the UK alone, the building industry is currently responsible for 70 million tonnes of construction and demolition waste every year, most of which is sent to landfill.

Recycling or remodelling buildings can be a thrilling, dynamic way to breathe new life into our tired and strained cities.

The Installation System

Figures 2, 3, 4: Sverre Fehn, the
Archbishopric Museum of Hamar

Sverre Fehn's project, the Archbishopric Museum of Hamar, shows an example of *'installation'*, in which the old and the new exist independently. The new elements are placed within the boundaries of the building. The design or the grouping of these elements may be influenced by the existing, but the fit is not exact; should the elements be removed then the building would revert to its original state. Below is an example of a final-year student's work. The Old Post Office on Edinburgh's Princess Street has been redesigned to house a market space that nestles beneath a key high-street store. These new elements sit within the host building; however, the new and the old exist independently.

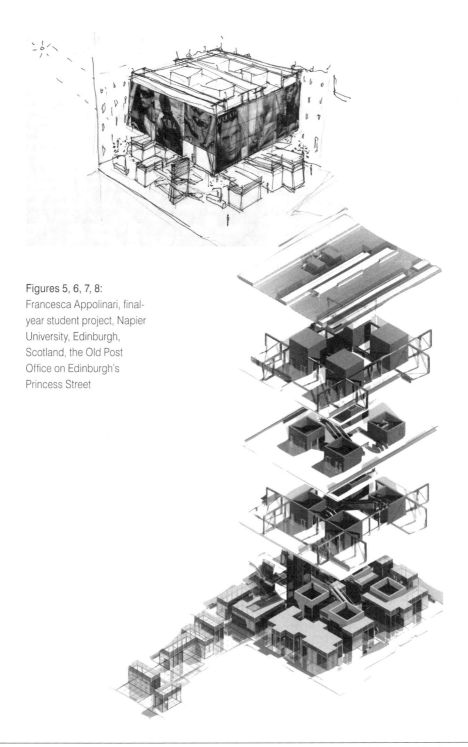

Figures 5, 6, 7, 8:
Francesca Appolinari, final-year student project, Napier University, Edinburgh, Scotland, the Old Post Office on Edinburgh's Princess Street

The Intervention System

Figures 9, 10, 11:
Richard Murphy,
Fruitmarket Gallery

The above project is Richard Murphy's Fruitmarket Gallery. If the existing building is so transformed that it can no longer viably exist independently and the nature of the remodelling is such that the old and new are completely intertwined, then the style is *'intervention'*. Below is an example of a final-year student's work. A warehouse on Brick Lane in London has been redesigned to accommodate a white-goods recycling industry. The student has intertwined the new architectural elements with the fabric of the existing structure, manipulating light and circulation.

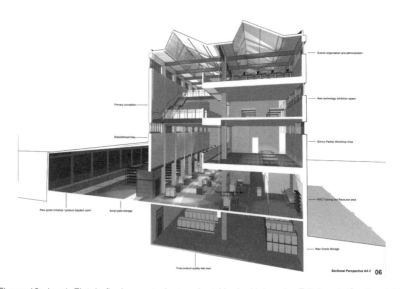

Figure 12: Jacob Fintch, final-year student project, Napier University, Edinburgh, Scotland, White goods warehouse, Brick Lane, London

The Insertion System

Figures 13, 14, 15: Aparicio
and Fernandez, Architectural
Documentation Centre in
Madrid

The above project is Aparicio and Fernandez's Architectural Documentation Centre in
Madrid. The final classification is that of a new autonomous element, the dimensions of
which are completely dictated by those of the existing; that is, it is built to fit, is placed
within the confines of the existing, and so the category here is *'insertion'*. Below is an
example of a second-year student's work. No.6 Bristo Square has been redesigned to
provide the area with a restaurant and bar that reflects the demography of the local
area. The student has inserted a sleeve of timber within the existing structure which
holds the new design, whilst creating an interesting tension between new and old
materials and structure. The timber sleeve also serves to discretely facilitate all services
required.

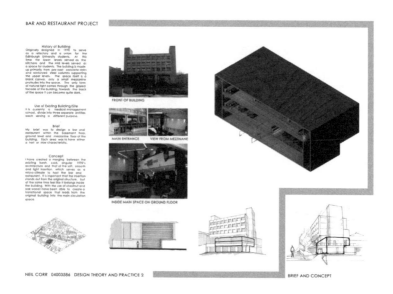

Figures 16 and 17: Neil Corr, second-year student project, Napier University, Edinburgh, Scotland, No.6 Bristo Square, Edinburgh

References

[1]   *AR*, special number: Inscape 05/1966, p.365.

[2]   Rebekah Hieronymus, Int. Architecture, Foster+Partners.

[3]   Brooker, G. and Stone, S. *Rereadings: Interior Architecture and the Design Principles of Remodelling Existing Buildings* (London: RIBA Enterprises Ltd, 2004).

Joyce FLEMING

Glasgow Metropolitan College

GLASGOW METROPOLITAN COLLEGE

We teach interior design – that specialist branch of architectural design, which is not covered adequately in any architectural course. It is a vocational programme, supplying the needs of a growing and increasingly professional industry. The sector's main clients fall within the commercial, retail and leisure industries. The industry and its client base are well established in Glasgow. Although interior design is a specialist course, it has a broad educational application. Students are expected to be independent learners, undertake extensive individual research, and use analytical models and investigative process to develop conceptual ideas into imaginative resolutions. The interior design course at Glasgow Metropolitan College is further enhanced by links with Glasgow Caledonian University, which provides articulation to its Honours Degree course.

Interior design is a complex process. It is not easy. It is not self-indulgent, or flippant as portrayed in some TV shows, but it can be witty, fun, and very rewarding. The practitioner has to balance form and void, colour and texture, proportion and scale, light and comfort, material and construction, cost and programme, to accommodate a particular set of functional and sensual human requirements. The articulation of these, their cohesive whole, becomes manifest in the visual 'style' of the completed work. This 'style' is a simple way of saying very complicated things. At its best it evokes memory, delight, and elicits an intellectual response. It is widely supposed that 'visual style' is inherent or intuitive in an individual; however, we believe that this intuition becomes more acute and articulate with practical experience. This philosophy underlies our teaching program.

Three areas are important: creativity, communication and practice. The designer's role is to identify and solve problems. Combining pragmatic functionalism with an idea of quality and aesthetic ingenuity is the main objective. Original imaginative and conceptual solutions are sought. To facilitate the communication of these ideas, free-hand and orthographic drawing is taught, together with computer-aided drawing and the usual ICT packages. Direct, verbal communication is encouraged, to supplement the visual and to engender confidence. Building construction and interior detailing are taught in a variety of ways. An understanding of the statutory and business framework in which an interior designer works is also important, so requirements such as building regulations, together with procurement and contracting, are covered in the latter stages of the degree course.

Teaching methods are customised for the further education student. Tuition is intensive in the early stages of the course. Students are challenged. The apprentice model is widely used, the tutor showing 'how to', or showing examples of solutions to similar problems, and the student applying the acquisition of learning to a given brief. Most learning is organised around and integrated into a design project, and will normally be carried out in a wide variety of progressively more onerous applications to reinforce the acquisition of a variety of skills. This layering of experience, in constantly producing solutions to different design briefs, expands horizons, enables the student to become adept at handling increasing levels of complexity and hones visual articulacy.

There is no such thing as a typical interior design project. We use real live projects, collaborative projects, group projects, projects built on stage plays, projects on boats, as well as exhibitions, centred round poetry, and self-selected projects. Some projects are based on national competitions, such as the RSA project. There has been considerable success in competitions and a great sense of achievement attached to this.

Students occasionally work in teams. Peer-group competition is an underlying feature of this type of learning. The class is studio based and strong relationships are formed between groups of students and ownership by a class tutor. This engenders a creative atmosphere for apprentice-style teaching. Although some classes are taught by the 'chalk and talk' method, they are the exception. Group tutorials are used to emphasise a particular method or skill, or to instigate brainstorming exercises. We consider our teaching to be supportive: a hard-working student is never left to flounder.

Inspiration and understanding of the design process is covered in several ways. We do not attempt to be visionary, except that we believe that the future is inherent in the design of the present. Further, we believe that 'to be modern is not a fashion, it is a state. It is necessary to understand history, and he who understands history knows how to find continuity between that which was, that which is, and that which will be' (Le Corbusier). Therefore a continuous programme of history of design classes is included in all courses. These are supplemented by architectural visits, and assignments. Broadening experience is a prerequisite for teaching interior design. Access to other cultures, other perceived 'class' based activities such as theatre, have a profound impact on some students' understanding. Study tours are organised to internationally renowned architects and designers' studios, such as EMBT, Estudio Mariscal, Ron Arad, and Fernando Salas. This access gives our students a privileged and inspirational insight into the work of such designers. Talks are frequently given in college by outside practitioners, manufactures and contractors. Sometimes they agree to take part in crits.

Feedback and assessment of work is given verbally to the individual on a regular basis in the studio. These discussions around the design process offer both student and tutor a type of sounding board. Critiques of work are given at stages throughout the projects, and always on completion. They present the student with a barometer of the level of their work, indicating the areas that require improvement, and try to provide a positive assessment of progress.

The college policy allows admission to 'access' courses without any formal qualification. It is possible in some circumstances for a student to begin an 'access' interior design course and through hard work, determination and that intuitive 'style' to gain an Honours Degree in interior design. Most of our students are school leavers, who grow before our eyes into accomplished designers; a few are mature students with work experience, looking for a career change; some are single parents training to return to the workplace. The majority are committed and focused on the rewarding opportunity that they have within the course.

Scratch the surface of any interior design practice in the West of Scotland and you will find at least one graduate of Glasgow Metropolitan College. Our alumni are well thought of, competent, creative, motivated and confident individuals, with the training and personal resources to make a real contribution to the interior design industry in particular, but also to make a positive impact on society as a whole.

What is interior design?

Shashi CAAN

Shashi Caan Collective, New York City

CONSENSUS OR CONFUSION

Introduction

Interiors is a slippery discipline. Among all designed artefacts, interiors themselves are uniquely ephemeral and hard to define. The practice of interiors is relatively unregulated. The history of interiors is patchy and contested. The theoretical basis of interiors is largely unexplored in comparison to those of other disciplines. How, therefore, might we speculate about the role, validity and purpose of interiors in the twenty-first century?

IFS – Thinking Inside the Box: New Visions, New Challenges, New Horizons

This descriptor introducing the questions for the 2007 Interiors Forum Scotland conference captures the plight of the interior design discipline in the United Kingdom. However, these questions are not just limited to the UK but pervade the world and represent the state of affairs for interior design today – as demonstrated by the participants who came from around the globe. What is interior design? Why is it necessary? How do we best do it? What constitutes its history, substance, value, content, distinction, theory, practice, etc.? These are crucial issues that require substantial answers. As interior design becomes ever more fashionable and popular with the general public, many of those involved with its education and practice look for ways to distance themselves from the common misconceptions and seek to establish a more intellectually respected, artistic and perhaps more cerebral educational process and practice.

This chapter, 'Consensus or Confusion', is partly a response to the intense and very full debate which has been provoked by 'Thinking Inside the Box'. This ranges from a proposal for re-branding, finding new impetus from the decorative beginnings and legislating what we have, to rethinking the why, what and how. The other part of my response seeks to offer my own point of view as it was influenced and further honed by digesting this diversity of critical thinking.

Perhaps the most encouraging aspect of this debate was the intensity and the focus of the educators, in their desire for an interiors theory that seeks not only to improve the quality and content of education but also to enhance the respect and seriousness in which the field is held. To achieve this, many of the presenters saw a need to improve the definition of interior design, or even to redefine it, by proposing a new vision, new beginnings or underpinnings. Some expressed the desire to re-invent the discipline by broadening its content or by searching for an impetus in other related practices (architecture, furniture design, painting, drawing, sculpture, technology, etc.). In this context, the variety of new descriptors proposed for interior design, such as interiors, interior environments, interior architecture, etc., demonstrated a desire for distance from the title 'interior design' and all of its connotations. It also highlighted the lack of a universal agreement about the existing content or substance of the discipline. This is perhaps one of the reasons for the continued fracturing of the interior design discipline and the cause for the ever-increasing inter-disciplinary confusion; which brings us back to the fundamental questions that we have to address.

Two general outcomes are worth mentioning: the one expected and one less so. Not so expected but very encouraging was the diversity and high quality of the theoretical and critical propositions offered. These can help to increase the substance of interior design and to facilitate its further evolution. The other somewhat expected outcome was that most educators, when considering the essence of interior design, wanted to turn the discipline into more of an abstraction; whilst those focused more on the practice wanted to address the discipline with a 'nuts and bolts' practicality, an almost trade-like emphasis. Education and practice seemed to have little in agreement; yet they must find a consensus for the benefit of the field at large.

In my view, abstract interior design lives without clients/users, constraints or any limitations of materiality or industry; and if focused only on design, creates fictional environments. If the common purpose is to educate better and more comprehensively – in part to stimulate expanded and ongoing critical thinking but also to produce a better-considered, more thoughtful execution of the discipline – then educators must identify a set of core criteria for a cohesive and broadly accepted academic springboard. Also, our common language needs to be refined and the process of design, specific to interior design, needs to be better understood by the educator, practitioner, user and researcher alike. This will actualize the elevated quality that will convert conceptual thinking into real, tangible environments that can be used and experienced by all. Under the theme of this book, 'thinking inside the box' has resulted in a rich, provocative and insightful discussion and made the conference successful in fulfilling its aspiration to speculate and explore the spectrum of issues haunting contemporary interior design. However, more is required to help the field coalesce, to seek better-defined objectives for explorations at the outset and to mandate the formulation of a specific and well-balanced list of actions that forces the discussion beyond *just* discussion.

Since all the conference presentations have been included in this book, this chapter will not attempt to summarize their content but rather attempt to expand the discussion into areas that were not addressed.

Interior design origins

A sometimes hotly contested but critically important aspect on which common agreement must be achieved is the historical underpinning of interior design. While a symbiotic relationship with building has always existed, the act of constructing architecture has always been seen to make the interior a secondary consideration. From an interior design perspective, the position has to be reversed and making the interior must become primary. Decorating, on the other hand, is an important aspect. Although it cannot alone be the impetus for twenty-first century interior design, we must acknowledge its importance as a human need and we are required to rethink its value. Placing interior design within art may be the most appealing for many since it offers latitude for poetic and theoretical development. Without question, there is a great art to interior design, and 'spatial manipulation' is intrinsic to the making of an interior. An artistic or conceptual interior created for the sake of artistry or as a social commentary remains limited in its purpose and is often just a stylistic interpretation devoid of any real purpose or use. Business, the social sciences, psychology, the perceptual, the behavioral science and social anthropology – among others – are additional and important considerations that have to be more fully incorporated and integrated to achieve a holistic and comprehensive discipline.

While there is a consensus amongst educators and practitioners alike that a substantial, academically and publicly well-respected interiors discipline is needed, historical precedents continue to provoke the age-old arguments that have resulted in the formation of different factions and turf wars. With that much dissent within the discipline, we cannot possibly expect the general public to have a clear understanding of what interior design is and why it is so important.

It is curious that in history interiors are primarily defined within the context of highly cultured and rationalized fields such as architecture, art, decoration, etc., where they are identified with values that debase the body, sensate exploration and the realm of emotion. Yet human response to interior environments is far more basic, just as visceral as it is rational, and shapes the resultant behavior. Interiors ask to be seen not just in the context of art and culture but also through a clinical and keen understanding of experience (through the senses); and this in turn requires a knowledge of comfort, wellbeing, support, meaning, psychology, perception, etc. To this end, anthropological and scientific underpinnings need to be explored and integrated. The interior designer is, after all more than anyone else, the keeper of human wellbeing.

In looking for compelling arguments for this construct, simply identifying and exploring the first ever interior has considerable merit. The first ever interior was not built, it was found. It was an existing space, a cave. It existed prior to any form of rationalized structure or other intellectual consideration and thus predated engineering, building and architecture. The purpose of the cave was primal and essential and it was simply to provide shelter. However, there is more. Human history has recorded that the primitive cave dweller quickly incorporated other activities, such as making pictures on the cave walls, which were not essential to surviving... or were they? These interiors exemplify essential human needs that have not fundamentally changed, only evolved. They remain intrinsic to the nature of an interior. Interestingly, to this day interior designers work with 'found' space – within new or existing building – which is appropriated for a myriad of specific functions. Since the cave predates architecture and art, perhaps by a more thorough examination of this beginning we may obtain knowledge that can help to give new impetus and a larger sense of purpose to establish a clear and unique distinction for interior design.

What is interior design?

The interior is a contextualized backdrop for all human engagement and is much more than just the sum of its parts. In Lao Tse's words 'The reality of the building does not consist in roof and walls but in the space within to be lived in'. Interiors have at their core people and space. These two words – people and space – are key to interior design and are often used in discussions about interiors. However, these words primarily evoke generic and abstracted qualities – for instance the 'non-specific body' (as in robot?) as explored by Diller and Scoffidio in their work, or 'space' as an abstraction, whether literal, virtual or cyber – and are discussed as formalized and intellectualized interpretations. If human wellbeing and the care of the intimate is the direct purview of the interior designer, then interior considerations need to transcend abstractions and generic interpretations of human scale and the generic body, and acknowledge the holist person. We must address human intimacy and who/what people become within the environments we design. Interior spaces have to become actual places for human interaction and activity. This does not mean that they cannot be explored as abstractions. It does imply, however, that it is important for the interiors discipline to define the idea of the body and space in ways that are more intrinsically connected to interiors and with a clearer expression of how they relate to people, function and wellbeing.

The following is an itemization of criteria – both those discussed and those omitted in this book – which attempts to provide a list of considerations to be included in the efforts to define interior design, to provide a basis for agreement leading to a smarter, more substantial and unified interior design discipline, while allowing latitude for individual interpretations.

Interior design is:

- Shelter
- An essential need

- Habitation and the occupation of an inside (which does not have to be fully enclosed)
- More than a given set of conditions, envelope or container
- Transformative (it can happen by any means such as renovation, intervention, adaptation, re-use, completely new, etc.)
- Tangible and experiential
- Emotive and evocative
- About human wellness and support for all human activity and behavior
- Interpretive but context and site specific
- About place making and not about the abstraction of space.

Interior design must:
- Incorporate the decorative, beauty and address aesthetics, which are essential human needs regardless of the level of acquired literacy and regardless of what some earlier philosophers may have had to say about these issues
- Define its essence and must first integrate itself before it can integrate with other disciplines
- First acknowledge and celebrate its own legitimacy before it seeks a greater public recognition and formal legitimization. As a discipline, interior designers are working very hard at convincing themselves that the discipline matters and is important. Interior design is an essential need and is important. This belief needs to become a conviction and must be devoid of any inferiority complex or apology.

As an aside, interdisciplinary engagement and collaboration are very important aspects of the twenty-first century. It takes a large diversity of expertise to design and build an interior. It goes without saying that we are required to cultivate a culture and practice of collaboration and interdisciplinary engagement, but this is not to be confused with finding interior design roots in other disciplines. Interior design is quite specific and we need to know and operate from our unique 'roots'.

Interior design ideally:
- Is poetic and touches the human soul
- Uses all knowledge to stimulate the senses and inspire human response
- Causes discovery and delight
- Makes manifest dreams and aspirations
- Evokes the sensual, luxurious, the magical and the efficient.

Interior design has:

- An identity crisis

- A low self-esteem

- A considerable lack of professional self-confidence

- A confused image in the public perception.

Given the reality of these last four bullets, I think that re-branding is not an antidote; but rather that a more appropriate solution is to re-position the field with a deeper understanding of its essence, personality and characteristics, and an emphasis on the sensibility of the interior designer. Of course, this is work that is to be done with a general agreement between those that research, those that teach and those that put into practice that which we call interior design. This is less about how the public perceives the discipline but first and foremost an identification of who and what that discipline is, which is subsequently presented to the public in a clear and concise manner. This will also require addressing the prevailing culture – both good and bad – around interiors.

The issue of who can practise interior design is intimately connected to this and needs to be addressed. Just as not all people want to be mathematicians, there are particular individuals who aspire to become interior designers. We need to understand and support this sensibility in the broadest terms. There is nothing wrong with requiring that anyone wishing to design interiors must study interior design in order to practice; on the contrary, it is an important requirement. While currently we allow anyone to practice who has studied art or design (in general), engineering or architecture, regardless of their personal interest in the interior or whether they have an adequate understanding of interior design and its specialization, it is illogical to assume that they know what they are doing. We accept the fact that most Hollywood film actors do not have the aptitude, expertise or temperament for Broadway stage acting regardless of the fact that these are all actors. So how is it possible that without specialized knowledge, other disciplines automatically understand the interior?

Adrian Forty has said that space:

> allowed architects to rub shoulders with the socially superior discourses of physics and philosophy in so far as architecture had always suffered the slur of being no more than a trade or a business, [and] the claim to deal with the most immaterial of properties, 'space', allowed architects decisively to distinguish themselves as dealing with the mental rather than the manual.

I wonder why we continue to play turf games with architecture when our parallel is not physics or structure but psychology and the behavioral sciences. In some ways it can be argued that the interiors discipline is to the built world what psychology is to the world of science. This similarly unique distinction allows us to make a tremendous contribution to the world at large, in as far as interior design is also required to be 'of the mental' rather than the manual. The psychological, physiological, sensory and the emotional must not be ignored. To this end:

Interior design can:

- Be literal and metaphorical

- And ought to make important cultural, social or political commentary

- Be cerebral, theoretical, reflective or provocative

- Be privileged and wealthy or be concerned with the more mundane and assume an idealistic social stance.

Most importantly, as a holistic discipline, we must quickly strive for a unity of voice and get beyond our self-created confusion pertaining to the core of interior design. We must strive for a consensus of the most important and fundamental attributes so that we are in a position of being able to articulate why we do what we do, how we do it and why it is so unique and great – and show what interior designers can best do… design interiors.

Suzie ATTIWILL

School of Architecture and Design,
RMIT University

WHAT'S IN A CANON?

Introduction

Portable Corner is just that – a portable corner which can be placed in various locations to create a space within a space, a personal space, an interior. While the drawing expresses the provocation for Interiors Forum Scotland's (IFS's) conference 'Thinking Inside the Box', the main reason for including it here is to refer to a forum titled 'What's in a canon? The state of interior design at the beginning of the 21st century.' *Portable Corner* was the image used on a postcard promoting the event. This forum shares with IFS a similar impetus – a desire to focus a discussion on interior design. To pose the question of thinking inside something, the box or canon provides a space to gather and analyse what can be said and thought. For some, this might suggest an opportunity to overcome the slipperiness of the discipline of interior design and to search for answers which can claim a degree of certainty and truth; for others, it becomes a provocation and a momentary pause within slipperiness where it is possible to consider potential trajectories. Both offer up material in terms of what can be actually said and thought in relation to interior design.

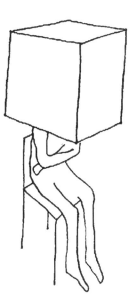

Figure 1: *Portable Corner,*
Shelley Penn, 1999

Pandora opened her box, curious to see what was inside and in so doing, let loose chaos on the world. Only hope remained, clinging to the side of the box. Boxes are good for keeping things contained but they can also be reductive and static – a butterfly pinned inside a museum box is a different thing to a butterfly in the world. Curiosity and thinking tend to open things up and, in so doing, offer lines of flight, creativity and the potential for the new.

This chapter will begin with a discussion on the concept of the canon, followed by an analysis of the forum in terms of what was offered by each speaker. Potential trajectories in relation to histories and theories as well as practices of interior design emerge and produce openings at the end of the chapter – or, one could say, open the box. A methodology described by the philosopher Gilles Deleuze seems useful here: 'we have to untangle the lines of the recent past and those of the near future: that which belongs to the archive and that which belongs to the present; that which belongs to history and that which belongs to the process of becoming' [2].

The/a canon

The term 'canon' within the field of design has particular affinity with architecture. Architects and architecture students are familiar with the architectural canon as something that is part of their field of practice. Outside of architecture, the term is not used explicitly. The concept of an interior design canon raises questions and debate as distinct from reference to a set of canonical examples. In the twenty-first century, the term has lost a lot of currency; feminism, postcolonialism and poststructuralism rendered visible the exclusionary, authoritative and absolutist qualities of canonical thinking; and, in the process, pluralised history as histories and the canon as canons.

Architectural theorist Peter Downton writes: 'In architecture we speak of The Canon as if it exists. ...Etymologically there are two dominant senses of 'canon' that are both of religious origin: 1) as consisting of a collection of sanctioned works and 2) as being a dogma-derived set of principles, rules or standards of judgement'. He continues and defines a third sense with reference to the canon in music which involves the imitation of a theme by subsequent voices. For Downton, this third sense is the most useful in relation to architecture: 'imitative purpose underlies the very idea of a canon as a collection of works in architecture: canonical works are exemplary works exhibiting characteristics deemed worthy of emulation or possessing attributes deemed valuable to understand by an architect who might reuse or reinterpret aspects of the knowledge embodied in the work'. As such the canon 'comprises works deemed significant at a point in time' [3]. While some may argue for an absolutist idea of judgement in relation to what's in a canon, Downton and others emphasise the canon's relation to contemporary cultural discourse. Gusevich writes: 'the significance and status of a building as architecture is not dependent on some pre-established set of attributes, on some essential features, but on its status as a cultural object established through critical discourse' [4].

Journals, exhibitions and teaching are vital to canons as vehicles of dissemination but they also contribute to the formation of the canon through selection, recognition and publication. In architecture, according to Downton, 'images are the predominant conveyors of the canon. Hence they are major conveyors of the knowledge embodied in the canon. They substitute in journals, books, exhibitions and lectures for the actual works and for many people replace those works entirely, for the image has a greater audience than the original' [5]. Downton argues that there are in fact two parallel architectural canons – the canon of actual buildings and the canon of images.

In the context of thinking inside the box, it is interesting to note that canons are often described in box-like terms as containers or holders of things. 'The canon serves two epistemological functions: as a cumulative cultural repository it is a means for storing a number of different kinds of architectural knowledge and it is the vehicle for the propagation of this knowledge.' The works within a canon are also described as containers in that they embody knowledge. 'Architects produce knowing through their designing. This is embodied in their works. The collection of canonic works, by making architects' knowing available at a public, collective level is an embodiment of design knowledge' [6].

One of the motivations for convening a forum posing the question 'what's in a canon?' was the intense debate stirred at any mention of an interior design canon. Those for a canon argue that all practices and practitioners have canons; that interior design's is implicit as distinct from explicit and therefore it would be interesting and valuable to articulate it. Those who dismiss the idea argue that the practice of interior design requires other kinds of evaluation than the architectural canon with its emphasis on a collection of 'cultural objects' – to use Gusevich's term – and dependency on the visual image for dissemination.

The experiential nature of interior design does distinguish it from object/artefact-based practices and requires other processes of collection and documentation than a photograph. The multidisciplinary nature of interior design also renders problematic any effort to identify significant works which are significant for all. In Australia, a distinction is made between interior design and interior architecture where the former is understood without implicit reference to architecture. Hence interior design as the design of interiors is a different proposition to the architectural interior in that the inside/interior is not a given. The question of 'what's in a canon?' provokes many questions for the discipline of interior design.

What's in a canon?

Portable Corner was used on the invitation to the forum because it opened up the question. It did not define what is in a canon by offering an image of what could/should be in it; instead it suggested relations. It opened the possibility that what is in a canon for interior design may be about the individual's spatial experience as distinct from a published object. As a drawing, it suggested practice, process and projects as well as artefact and outcome. As an interior, it suggested that the interior may not be the inside of a room but an interior which is in relation to the person's inhabitation of that room, space, landscape – an interior inside a room. It also expressed the idea that some interiors are ephemeral/events. As an inside of a box it suggested the private and personal, with a quality of intimacy in its gentle humour.

The question posed 'what's in a canon?' could be read in at least two ways: as an invitation to identify examples of interior design which are significant to the field of interior design and therefore could be placed in the canonical repository; and also, as 'what's in it for interior design?', i.e. to question and evaluate the value of a canon for the field of interior design with the view to opening other possibilities. The forum included practitioners, academics, students, editors, writers, critics and curators. Seven speakers were given ten minutes to respond to the above provocations. Each speaker was invited because of the relation between their practice and interior design, and their role in the production of a canon: magazine editors who evaluate and select works for publication and thereby contribute to the establishment and transmission of canons; academics and curators through processes of selection and publishing/disseminating via teaching, research, exhibition and publishing; a recent interior design graduate and her encounter with precedents during her education; practitioners who produce work which could become canonical and who shape canons through influence, recognition and transmission.*

The aim of the forum was to produce a pause, a moment in time and space with a number of people gathered together discussing interior design – and from this, to note what could be said and thought 'to untangle the lines of the recent past and those of the near future: that which belongs to the archive and that which belongs to the present; that which belongs to history and that which belongs to the process of becoming' [7]. What follows is an attempt to untangle some lines of the recent past to distinguish lines of becoming.

The question of 'what's in a canon?' in terms of what's in it for interior design yielded diverse responses. Some speakers identified useful qualities in a canon and what it

---

*   The speakers were:
- Cameron Bruhn, editor, *Artichoke. Interior Design and Architecture*, the Design Institute of Australia publication
- Peter Geyer, strategic director, Geyer (established in 1970s, Geyer is Australia's longest running, dedicated interior design practice)
- David Clark, editor of *Vogue Living*, a magazine of interior decoration
- Eliza Downes, recent RMIT graduate
- Professor Leon van Schaik, academic, curator, writer (author of *Design City Melbourne*)
- Caroline Vains, interior designer, PhD student (UTS, Sydney)
- Andrew Mackenzie, editor-in-chief, *inside (Australian Design Review)* and *Architectural Review Australia.*

Note: any quotes without reference are transcriptions from the forum.

could offer the discipline of interior design; others dismissed the canon as particularly un-useful and anachronistic; 'mercurial and dangerous'; possibly irrelevant in the twenty-first century. The former considered the canon as 'a collective communication tool' which unites a profession; as a collection of significant works which articulated the discipline; as 'a library of ideas' where everyone interprets those ideas in different ways. Existing canons such as the architectural, decorative arts and fine arts were discussed in terms of the relation between a canon and an area of practice. They become references which may be emulated or rejected. In contrast, interior design's canon is not explicit, if there is one.

The potential of a canon is to collect together significant examples of practice. The emphasis here on practice is not to distinguish from theory but to emphasise activity, i.e. the making of interiors. The shift from a history of interior design to a canon of interior design would still engage with establishing an archive yet with an emphasis on practice. It could shift from the unquestioned assumptions of history, in terms of its methodologies of classification and establishing linear chronologies, to pursue lines of significance, lines of practice, lines of affiliation.

Offerings

During the forum, different lines were proposed and examples offered, each based on a different way of thinking about interior design: 1) A collection of interiors, all architectural (and incidentally done by architects), deemed to be significant because of their impact on the profession of interior design. This collection was organised according to types of interior designs – workplace, retail, library and museum/galleries. 2) A proposition that a canon of interior design consists of canonical experiences where interior design concerns the experiential and relational, the phenomenal and emotive. 3) Interior decoration as the practice of interiors – concerned with the aesthetic, atmospheric, personal expression and intimacy. 4) A reconceptualisation of interior as a horizontal connective surface in a dynamic relation with exterior.

Peter Geyer, an interior designer, focused on the profession of interior design and significant works which challenged and changed the nature of that practice. The emphasis here is on the collective aspect of the profession motivated by a desire for there to be something which is shared by a community of practitioners. Briefly, some of the examples he gave included: under 'workplace' – Gaetano Pesce's 'TBWA/Chiat Day', New York, 1993. 'This project communicated the principle behind the open workplace; if we did not have this project, which took us out on that limb, I doubt that most of the projects we have today would have occurred.' Libraries – Domed Reading Room, British Museum, 1850, which 'transformed a library into a knowledge forum' and, for Geyer, finds culmination in Toyo Ito's 'Sendai Mediatheque', 2001. Retail Design has metamorphosed mainly through Koolhaas's Prada store in New York, 2001. Museums/galleries – Frank Lloyd Wright's Guggenheim, 1959; Gehry's Bilbao, 1997; Herzog and de Meuron's Tate Modern, 2001.

Magazine editor, Cameron Bruhn suggested that a canon might contain interiors that are not canonical in themselves, on the basis of the experiences they give us. 'In this schema, we would canonise the phenomenal and emotive aspects of interior design. In this way of thinking, Charles Garnier's late nineteenth-century Paris Opera could stand for the social drama played out in the act of seeing and being seen rather than simply Second Empire Baroque. Adolf Loos's interiors could stand for the reconciliation of modernity and domesticity – the interior as a casing of self rather than an example of the beginning of the Modernist project. Or Michelangelo's vast dome at St Peter's could stand for the awe-inspiring power it communicates – the unseen made visible, not Mannerism- or the Renaissance-in-transition.'

Eliza Downes, a recent interior design graduate, took this line further and defined interiors as a subjective experience. Without citing interiors inside of architecture, she cited an underground cave in a remote part of the Australian desert, Blur Pavilion (Diller and Scofidio, 2001) – 'Blur is not a building, Blur is pure atmosphere' – and Roden Crater (James Turrell, begun 1975). With these examples, the interiors and exteriors are not clearly defined by boundaries of walls. Each is an example of 'the power of interiors; that by manipulating space and spatial conditions we have the power to change the way that people see the world.'

David Clark, editor of *Vogue Living*, in his introduction showed a collection of images downloaded from the internet under a search titled 'a history of interior design'. He observed it was a history of architecture and not interiors, and that the forum had focused on things which are more architectural than interiors. For Clark, decoration is critical to any conversation about interior design; and his presentation made it apparent that the distinction between interior decoration and interior design was perhaps not a desirable one to sustain, creating an allegiance between interior design and architecture where interior design can no longer be separated. Clark presented two interiors, both domestic spaces – one by artist Dale Frank, who lives in the house with his family, and another by Hecker, Phelan, Guthrie, a Melbourne-based interior design practice. Each room had a palpable sense of an interior as something separate from the architectural inside. Clark defined this as having to do with 'aesthetics, mood and feeling'.

The concept of interior reconceptualised in relation to issues of horizontality and urbanism rather than the verticality of architectural walls was proposed by interior designer, Caroline Vains. Pointing to 'the phenomenon of the connective horizontal surface' evident in contemporary architecture and landscape projects, Vains proposed that such a phenomenon is:

significant to the practice of interior design in three ways:

1) it liberates interior space from architectural confinement and urban invisibility; the veil is removed and the boundaries between inside and outside become indeterminate

2) now thrown dynamically into each other, inside and outside exist as inseparable whole and may occupy each other

3) and consequently this connective surface allows interior affordances such as participation and occupation, contemplation and community, rest and repose, shelter and place-making.

Examples offered by Vains were: the International Port Terminal, Yokohama by Foreign Office Architects completed in 2002; New York Highline by Field Operations with Diller, Scofidio + Renfro, due for completion in 2008.

Lines of becoming

This tangle of lines and plethora of ways of thinking about interior design could be understood as confusion and a discipline in crisis, triggering a process of reduction and identification; or alternatively, it could be celebrated as provoking experimental connections and lines of flight. The opened boxes of the interior and the canon produced chaos for some and hope for others. The value of the discussion was apparent in its vitality and the fact that it drew people from practice and the academy, as well as associated disciplines. It became apparent that this is the potential of a canon for interior design – to frame a discourse, to provide a site for debate, to value ideas and address them with seriousness; and to do so by evaluating their implications and encouraging lines of potential so that they can be shared, debated and evaluated by practitioners, academics and students.

Some trajectories which emerged included: decoration as a potential trajectory in relation to interior design and, along with this, concepts of the domestic. A relation of hierarchy and Modernist values has dominated the relation between decoration and interior design together with a positioning of the domestic as an already given condition. In discussing decoration, what became apparent was its independence from architecture rather than its application to the surface of architecture and also the process of making relations between people; to the inside and outside (one of the rooms in the Frank house is called the Storm Room and the family sit on a couch made of entwined grey tubes and watch the storms); with light; with the past (a carpet has reference to Frank's grandmother's house). This trajectory finds resonance with Charles Rice's thesis on the emergence of the interior:

> with conceptual specificity in the context of bourgeois domesticity. It is not simply architectural, but borrows on the enclosure provided by architecture to be articulated through decoration, the literal covering of the inside of an architectural 'shell'. In this sense the interior is also not simply spatial, but is equally an image-based phenomenon [8].

And further, a conjunction can be made with a rethinking of 'domestic' – from a description of a kind of interior such as a house to interior design as a process of domestication: of taming the wild, of bringing an outside in.

Another trajectory emerged in a shift from thinking about canonical interiors, i.e. interiors as artefacts, to interiors as composed of relations, phenomenal and emotive.

While resonating with observations above, the emphasis here was on relations between a person and space in the production of interiors. Instead of noting styles and imaging existing inside spaces, diagrams which visualised interior programs, ways of viewing and circulation could capture interior experiences. The experiential and subjective were discussed. Geyer defined interior design as an inside-out practice with the person at the centre. He used the metaphor of an onion where 'architecture is of the outer leaves, the closer you get the more it is interior space and then very close is psychology'. Van Schaik introduced the concept of spatial intelligence as something which each person carries with them and is produced from their history in space: 'What we in the spatial professions hold in custody for everyone is the ability to put them back in touch with their own spatial intelligence. We cover the universe with drawings we have lived.' There are connections here to other discussions such as that accumulated in the inaugural interior theory reader *Intimus*. In the introduction, interior design is described as an intimate profession concerned with the 'specifics of inhabitation and bodily presence' [9]. Similar trajectories can be found in other areas of contemporary discourse, for example Nicholas Bourriaud's concept of 'relational aesthetics' which has extended beyond the field of curatorial practice into ways of thinking about various practices which involve collection, arrangement and encounter [10].

While entangled with lines above, it is possible to distinguish other kinds of relations: relations between interior and exterior, insides and outsides also ran through much of the discussion. Vains' proposition of interior affordances and 'moments of interiority' within an environmental urbanism gave momentum to a trajectory of thinking about interior design outside the architectural box. It is interesting to note that when interior design does move out of the box, it is usually met with concern that it's becoming everything (i.e. the inside of anything – a room, a city, a building, a pocket) and the implication that this isn't possible – or perhaps more precisely, that such expansiveness is not allowed and people/professions need to know their place. One can appreciate the threat of this trajectory when such a proposition is put next to the definition of interior design John Pile offers in his book, *The History of Interior Design*: 'interiors as an integral part of structures that contain them – in most cases buildings. This means that interior design is inextricably linked to architecture and can only be studied within an architectural context' [11]. Yet it is apparent that such a definition is limited as those in the field of interior design continue to seek other ways of speaking of and designing interiors without the dominance of architecture. Architecture has been the creative constraint for interior design to emerge as a distinct profession during the twentieth century. However, as a practice architecture is also changing, particularly in terms of structure, and provision and division of inside and outside can not be assumed as a given. Terms such as 'flux', 'fluidity', 'emergence' and 'flow' inflect contemporary architectural, as well as social and cultural, discourse. Deleuze claims that 'all environments of enclosure are in crisis' [12].

How then does interior design respond to this? Architecture – the box – has provided a creative rub for the discipline of interior design to emerge during the twentieth century. In the twenty-first century, the box as a given is in question. A rethinking of the concept of interior has potential to engage many fields of practice and offer up new ways of thinking and doing. To be able to do this, however, involves giving value and seriousness to the lines of becoming.

To finish with one more trajectory: a poignant and challenging observation made by van Schaik was the fact that most examples cited by the speakers were by architects – 'I don't see how you can claim for interior design, works which are clearly the product of architectural processes and architecture as a professional practice.' Perhaps this comment says more about the limitations of the architectural canon than the examples given, in that the canon must include products and outcomes. Nevertheless the nerve that it touched for me was the active relation between a canon and a practice and hence the question of interior design as a practice and its manifestations.

Reflecting on the forum, this is what it offered to all those who attended: various lines of practice to be considered, debated and evaluated. The forum, in posing the question 'what's in a canon?' made apparent the potential of canons in that they give value to an area of practice. The different ideas are treated with seriousness and evaluated within a context of that practice. They become pedagogic tools. As an articulation of practice, the different connections made to past practices are different to those that history makes. Canons are sites where practitioners, theorists, academics, historians, students, curators can share a platform for discourse and debate. In contrast to history's linear composition, canons can be composed of diverse juxtapositions where seemingly diverse types, different time frames and cultures can be brought together as a singular concept. The above trajectories which emerged in one evening express the vitality of interior design as a practice and the value of a discourse which engages people to evaluate what is significant. It is also apparent that interior design is a practice which is situated at a point of intensity at the beginning of the twenty-first century – not just professionally but socially, culturally and historically. The concept of the canon could be reinvented from the canon to canons, becoming multiple and dynamic; as an intensity of a gathering, an assemblage composed of tangled lines; canons of interiorisations where it may be more useful to pose questions in relation to practice – asking 'how' as distinct from 'what is interior design?' or 'who is an interior designer?'

References

[1]   Gusevich, M. 'The Architecture of Criticism: A Question of Autonomy' in Kahn, A., ed. *Drawing, Building, Text* (New York: Princeton Architectural Press, 1991) p.11.

[2]   Deleuze, G. 'What is a dispositif?' in Armstrong, T., trans. *Michel Foucault. Philosopher*, (Hertfordshire: Harvester Wheatsheaf, 1992) p.164.

[3]   Downton, P. 'The Canon: a site of architectural epistemology' in *Firm(ness) commodity de-light?: questioning the canons*, (Society of Architectural Historians of Australia and New Zealand, 1998) p.43.

[4]   Gusevich, op. cit., p.11

[5]   Downton, op. cit., p.46

[6]   Downton, P. 'Theory's Cupboard: myths of knowing, form, memes and models' in Ostwald, M. and Moore, R.J., eds. *Re-Framing Architecture: Theory, Science and Myth*, (Sydney: Archadia Press, 2000) p.52.

[7]   Deleuze, op. cit., p.164

[8]   Rice, C. 'Rethinking histories of the interior', *The Journal of Architecture*, 2004, 9(3), pp.275–87.

[9]   Taylor, M. and Preston, J., eds. *Intimus. Interior Design Theory Reader*, (Great Britain: Wiley–Academy, 2006) p.6.

[10]   Bourriaud, N. *Relational Aesthetics*, trans. Pleasance, S. and Woods, F. (France: Les Presses Du Réel, 2002).

[11]   Pile, J. *A History of Interior Design*, (London: Laurence King, 2000) p.9.

[12]   Deleuze, G. 'Postscript on the Societies of Control' in Leach, N., ed. *Rethinking Architecture. A reader in cultural theory*, (London: Routledge, 1997) p.309.

C. Thomas MITCHELL

Chair, Interior Design Program, Indiana University, Bloomington

Steven M. RUDNER

President, The Streetview Group, Inc., Indianapolis

INTERIOR DESIGN'S IDENTITY CRISIS: REBRANDING THE PROFESSION

Introduction

In the United States, at least, the interior design profession faces an identity crisis. This mistaken perception has many effects and implications for university-based interior design programs. Students enroll in programs expecting to learn what they've seen on TV. It often takes several semesters to convince them what the design profession actually is, causing related problems for these students who then must redirect their studies to other areas (often with costly tuition consequences), as well as for interior design educators who must painstakingly 'weed out' students not making the grade.

University administrators are likewise often confused and influenced by popular culture and television programming. Not understanding the rigor and methodology of professional interior design, they form a dismissive attitude toward programs, starving them of support and resources. Perhaps most importantly, the many skills interior designers have to offer are often hidden from the public – the potential client base for designers' services. To the broader public, the interior design profession is misunderstood and undervalued. As a brand, it is considered to be far inferior to architecture.

In order to explore these issues more fully, a 'rebranding exercise' was organized with a variety of representatives of the design community. Brainstorming exercises were conducted to determine the current state of the 'interior design' brand and to explore ways of bridging the gap between largely negative or dismissive public perceptions, and the reality of a rigorous academic discipline and professional training. The results of the brainstorming sessions were analyzed and a strategy for closing the perception–reality gap – at least provisionally – is presented.

The branding process

Depending on your perspective, brands can be defined in many ways. Some think of a brand as a firm's logo or graphic identity. Others consider a brand to be a company's advertising slogan, while others may define a brand as a firm's reputation or set of values.

A brand is all of these things and more. Yet the branding process is not limited strictly to corporations and institutions. We all maintain impressions and opinions about professions, so in reality, professions have brand identities as well.

For example, we may hold preconceived notions about professional athletes as being overpaid. Or perhaps we hold the clergy in high regard because of our respect for this profession. Our opinions and ideas shape perceptions of these professions and establish a general brand identity in our minds.

Branding is a conditional training process in which individuals, corporations and professions establish and mold opinions about themselves, their firms or their industries in order to influence and produce specific behaviors from targeted audiences. They may want us to buy a specific product, select their firm's services over another, or regard their profession in a positive manner. The resulting behavioral patterns exhibited by target audiences in response to stimuli put forth in these efforts are based upon their experiences with the brand.

The conditional training processes used in brand development efforts are not new. Conditional reflex training was widely heralded in the late nineteenth century through famous experiments conducted by Ivan Pavlov, who manipulated auditory and visual stimuli in order to produce reflex responses in a dog. The dog's responses to these stimuli, such as salivating in anticipation of food upon hearing a whistle, only occurred conditionally upon the dog's specific previous experiences. The more often the dog heard or saw the stimuli and then received the resulting food, the more conditioned it became to salivate upon experiencing these stimuli. Pavlov's research on conditional reflexes greatly influenced psychology and science, as well as popular culture. Today, the commonly used phrase 'Pavlov's dog' often describes someone who merely reacts to a situation or stimuli, rather than using critical thinking.

Similarly, brand identities are created when visual, auditory and written messages are sent consistently and repeatedly over time by individuals, corporations and professions. When target audiences encounter communications delivered consistently in understandable language, they will form or change their opinions of a brand, and establish a perception in their minds of what the brand means to them.

As a result, a brand is what consumers remember about a product, corporation or profession after being exposed to marketing stimuli. Through repeated encounters with the communications, people will form an opinion of a brand and then take action based upon what that brand means to them. It's at this point that they may buy a product, call a company for more information, or choose one firm over another.

Some brands have clear, unmistakable identities. Starbucks, for example, is known for its coffee products and ubiquitous retail presence worldwide. Nike athletic shoes are regarded for their technical ingenuity, with the implied perception that wearing these shoes will improve your athletic performance. The Volvo vehicle brand is built on a premise of family safety. These identities were all built over time, through repeated consumer exposure to marketing messages, and from personal experiences with these products by target audiences.

Brands are built upon experiences and perceptions. These perceptions are what drive the reality of brands in the minds of consumers and other target audiences.

The interior design brand: today's conundrum

In a world then where 'perception is reality', the 'reality' of the interior design brand has become confused, misunderstood and distorted. There is a genuine disconnect between the general perception of what the profession is and does, and the reality of today's professional interior design services and expertise. This confusion is widespread – not just among consumers and corporate end-users of interior design services, but within the profession as well.

As witnessed by the Starbucks, Nike and Volvo examples, the value of a memorable and easily understood brand is a powerful asset for any organization or profession. The interior design profession's brand is lacking in strength, and indeed, faces an identity crisis that poses serious consequences for professional practitioners, educators and the industry as a whole.

Through results of focus group research with interior design industry professionals, educators and students, we believe the interior design profession's identity crisis, particularly in the United States, results from three primary factors:

1. Its perception among many as being an 'inferior' design profession to architecture.

2. The proliferation of numerous, popular television programs which are labeled as 'interior design', but are in fact glorified exercises in decorating. These programs create an image and perception of interior design as something that is easy and that 'anyone can do', thus trivializing the profession.

3. The inconsistency of post-secondary interior design curricula, which results in a lack of consistent academic standards for interior design graduates entering the profession.

If the interior design profession fails to address these issues, it will continue to be misunderstood and the profession's reputation will suffer. A new, clear brand for the profession should be established and communicated in order to shape, or in some cases change, the behavioral patterns of the industry's targeted audiences.

By applying the conditional training processes utilized by successful brands worldwide, the interior design industry's identity will improve and its true characteristics, strengths and features will become more evident. This new perception will thus become the new reality for the interior design profession.

Architecture's perceived weak sibling

As a profession, architecture has clearly defined, strong features that help shape its brand identity. Our focus group used terms such as 'structure', 'buildings', 'columns', 'stone', 'cities', 'formal', 'inspiring', 'art', 'historic' and 'strength' when asked for words associated with this profession. Architecture has a perceived sense of solidity because there is typically a concrete manifestation of this design process that everyone can identify and form an opinion of: a building or structure.

When asked for terms to describe the 'interiors' profession, this same focus group used such words as 'layout', 'space', 'movement', 'style', 'comfort', 'safety', 'warm' and 'supportive'. These words are softer and much less concrete than those used to describe the architectural profession, thus supporting a more ambiguous definition for the profession.

Translating into the professional marketplace, architecture has a much stronger, established stature than interior design. The general public understands what architecture is, what architects do and the value they contribute to society. The same cannot be said for interior design or designers.

Builders and contractors frequently perceive interior designers as 'decorators' or 'creative types', rather than professionals with extensive technical training and skills who can dramatically influence a building's design and ultimate success or failure.

Corporate clients do not always understand the interior design profession, and hence may involve a spouse in interior design processes because they believe interior design is simply a matter of selecting colors, textures and finishes for a room or facility.

Pop Culture influences

In the United States, television shows featuring residential interior 'design' and do-it-yourself decorating have become hugely popular in the past five years. Through the widespread proliferation of cable television programming with hundreds of channel options, consumers can view dozens of programs focused exclusively on interiors topics.

One network in particular, Home & Garden Television, or HGTV, is at the leading edge of this type of programming. HGTV has approximately 85 distinct shows dedicated to design and decorating topics, not including special program presentations. While we presume HGTV's producers do not intend to trivialize the rigor of the interior design profession, the fact remains that their entertainment-based programming creates a skewed perception of the realities of the design discipline. When an entire house can be remodeled in a one-hour television program, many details behind the design methodology are left on the editing room floor.

Through such television programming, interior design has been transformed from a serious design discipline requiring academic and practical expertise and skills, to a pop culture activity that anyone can do. For example, these television shows do not promote the fact that in 23 states in the United States, as well as Puerto Rico and Washington, D.C., practitioners must meet certain requirements to be registered or licensed as interior designers. In many of these states, you cannot label yourself an interior designer unless you meet or exceed a certain level of accredited education and, in some cases, pass the qualifying exam administered by the National Council for Interior Design Qualification (NCIDQ).

The mistaken perception created through television programming has also produced corresponding effects on post-secondary interior design programs. Whether they attend a vocational school, community college or university, many students enroll in academic programs expecting to learn what they've seen on HGTV shows. It often takes several semesters to convince them what the design profession actually is, causing related problems for students who then must redirect their studies to other areas (often with costly tuition consequences), as well as for interior design educators who must painstakingly identify, counsel and, ultimately, flunk students not meeting academic requirements.

University administrators are likewise often confused and influenced by popular culture and television programming. Not understanding the rigor and methodology of professional interior design, they form a dismissive attitude toward interior design academic programs, starving them of support and resources.

Academic consistency issues

Regardless of their location or size, U.S. law and medical schools utilize relatively common curricula and academic approaches to train future professionals. Graduates must also pass standardized testing (bar exams and medical boards) in order to practice. A result is that these professions have strong, well-established brand identities for professional excellence.

Conversely, post-secondary interior design programs in the United States do not share similar common approaches. Aspiring interior designers can receive their education from art and design schools, vocational institutions, four-year universities, online programs and two-year community colleges. The academic rigor and curricula of these post-secondary programs vary greatly. Yet regardless of where they attend or the divergence in curricula, students graduate with the same degree name: interior design. There is not a single standard to which interior design graduates are held. As a result, this further confuses the value of the profession and the interior design brand.

While national accreditation processes help ensure a baseline of academic standards among a limited number of university programs, there are widely disparate approaches to interior design education, particularly in utilization of design technology. The Council for Interior Design Accreditation, the non-profit accrediting organization for interior design education programs in the United States and Canada, currently accredits only 150 interior design programs, serving approximately 20,000 students.

Compounding the situation, there are truly no barriers to entry into the profession. According to the Bureau of Labor Statistics, there were 60,000 interior designers employed in the United States in 2002, yet the American Society of Interior Designers (ASID), the nation's largest professional organization for interior designers, only counts 38,000 members, of whom 20,000 are practicing designers. Further, only 18,000 people have successfully completed the NCIDQ examination.

With or without an academic degree or interior design licensing accreditation, anyone can call himself or herself an 'interior designer', thus muddling the discipline's professional stature even further.

Identifying the brand perception–reality gap

Our focus group brainstorm analysis identified multiple target audiences for interior design branding messages, including:

- Potential consumers of interior design services
- Corporate and institutional clients
- The general public
- Architects, contractors and builders
- Current and potential interior design students
- The interior design industry itself.

These audiences' identified perceptions about interior design today are diverse, as exemplified in perceptual responses from our brainstorm group. The group indicated that *target audiences* view interior design as an industry in which:

- There is just a residential focus
- The creative talent aspect of the profession overshadows its practicality/ education components
- There are cultural differences affecting respect levels for the design profession; for example, design and architecture are more respected when they're part of the culture, as in Europe
- There is little differentiation among designers
- There is not a design process

- Design is an add-on to a building, rather than a primary element of its development
- There is not a problem-solving function
- There are not firm benefits
- There is less academic rigor than in architecture.

Yet the designers in our group held these views about *themselves* and their profession:

- Designers understand human interaction in space; as an example, they said designers know how to address the needs of an aging population in designing buildings and homes
- We are more in touch with clients than given credit for
- We roll up our sleeves and get to know how people work
- We deliver creative talent and technical skills to support facility development
- The need for interior design services/expertise is growing because of increasing complexity of buildings and spaces
- We are highly educated
- We understand technology
- Our technical expertise is important; we are not just creative types with a good eye for color and where furniture should be placed in a room
- We're problem solvers and solve how things work/interact in a space
- We communicate and listen
- We take client ideas, but figure out how to make them work
- We manage design processes
- We are research-oriented experts
- We offer a higher level of thinking than other design professions
- Interior design is a discipline with established methods, yet also a creative function
- We understand business issues and clients' business requirements.

Clearly, there is a tremendous difference between these internal and external perceptions of the profession. The target audiences' perceptions are driven by the three underlying factors noted earlier: architecture's perceived superior position, pop culture, and academic preparation inconsistencies. The designers base their self perceptions on their actual experiences and academic training.

These differing viewpoints create a gap between how people perceive interior design and the profession's true realities. This perception–reality gap feeds the profession's identity crisis, and as a result, the brand suffers.

A rebranding of interior design would help to solve these problems and more effectively align the perception and reality of the profession.

Closing the brand perception–reality gap

When there is confusion over a brand in business environments, 'rebranding exercises' take place to solve these issues. Through these initiatives, a company, product or service can be re-examined, assessing its strengths and limitations, and presenting it to target audiences in a new, more readily understandable and positive way.

The interior design profession is ripe for such an exercise.

Through our focus group effort, we identified three primary underlying causes for the interior design profession's misperceived brand identity. To close this gap, we must return to the example of Pavlov's dog, and develop methods for conditioning target audiences to think of the interior design brand differently. By doing so, we can close this perception–reality gap and create a truer, clearer perception of the industry in the minds of the public, clients, students, academic leaders, suppliers and interior designers themselves.

Potential solutions for closing this gap and addressing the profession's identity crisis include:

1. **Curricula changes** – Readdress post-secondary interior design curricula to ensure they not only provides design students with requisite technical and creative training, but also develop business-oriented skills, such as communications, leadership training, writing, economics, marketing and business practices. Establish more consistency in education across schools through greater standardization of curricula.

2. **Self perception** – Through professional associations, university courses and corporate settings, seed the identity of interior designers as business people in a creative field, not vice versa.

3. **Technical expertise promotion** – Create greater awareness of the technical aspects of the interior design field to address misperceptions among many target audiences that designers only possess creative skills, such as fabric selection.

4. **Problem solver identity** – Build the identity of interior designers as creative problem solvers.

5. **Training** – Establish more opportunities for designer training beyond post-secondary education programs, such as with certificate programs and professional education courses. Create more training through professional design societies.

6. **Professional–educational interaction** – Develop more opportunities for interior design's professional and educational communities to interact, particularly through greater practitioner integration in classrooms. Promote the 'real-world' aspects of interior design to students and aspiring designers so their perceptions are more attuned to the profession's realities.

7. **Internships** – Establish greater internship opportunities for students to gain practical field experience before entering the profession on a full-time basis.

8. **Research** – Conduct research that conclusively proves how interior design impacts the building process, including post-occupancy evaluations, and share it with industry colleagues in the architecture and building/contracting fields to help dispel their misconceptions of the interior design profession.

The ideal brand

Brands develop over time and through consistent application of messages. Further, a brand's target audiences must also experience positive results when utilizing the brand in order for them to develop and maintain a positive image of that brand.

The interior design brand of 2007 has tremendous opportunity for transformation and improvement in coming years. By closing the existing perception–reality gap, the brand's identity can move from its current state to one in which:

- Target audiences consider interior design to be a necessary profession whose practitioners possess unique skill sets

- Target audiences understand the process interior designers deliver through their services

- Customers will consider their lives, businesses and work settings to be unquestionably improved by working with an interior designer

- Interior designers are perceived as capable of improving a client's bottom line through their professional expertise

- Interior designers are perceived to provide unique talents, skills and services not available through decorators who haven't received applicable training and education

- Interior designers will be recognized for adding aesthetic value to projects; with the end result being a better product than if clients did not use a designer.

Through this transformational rebranding process, the interior design profession will gradually assume an identity as a solutions-oriented industry, while interior designers will be perceived as highly skilled professionals who provide value-added, unique design solutions.

Acknowledgements

The authors gratefully acknowledge the participation of Eric Rowland, AIA, Chairman of Rowland Design who hosted the focus group brainstorming session, and those who participated: Abigail Clark, Tricia Trick-Eckert, Brenda Gerst, Tom Graham, Darrell Nickolson, Denise Wilder and Barb Young.

Lynn CHALMERS and
Susan CLOSE

*Department of Interior Design, Faculty of
Architecture, University of Manitoba*

BUT IS IT INTERIOR DESIGN? – CONSIDERING THE INTERVENTION OF THEORY INTO DISCIPLINARY PRACTICE AND EDUCATION

Introduction

...but to make your fortune... you have to leave home and travel a long way.
Jonathan Culler [1]

As literary theorist, Jonathan Culler [1] has acknowledged that in order to make your way in the world it is often necessary to leave the comfort of the familiar and move into new and sometimes uncharted territory. This is true for the emerging discipline of interior design as it strives to be taken more seriously as an academic discipline and an intellectual pursuit. This chapter examines the application of interdisciplinary theory to interior design education and practice. Specially, it argues that interior designers should use theory to enrich both its disciplinary education and its practice. This argument is built from a dialogue between two interior design educators, Susan Close who has a background in cultural analysis and Lynn Chalmers who has a background in practice, and draws on their common concerns.

The format of this chapter is slightly unconventional. It is written in the form of a conversation that considers some of these key questions related to the intervention of theory into the practice and education of the interior designer.

Susan Close: We have been asked to start out by giving some biographical background information to contextualize our conversation about interior design and theory. Can you talk a little about yourself and your research interests?

Lynn Chalmers: My background is in interior design practice in Australia, and design education in Australia and Canada. I did my Masters of Design at the University of South Australia, after working in design practice in Melbourne and Adelaide. My research focus is privacy and identity in work environments and I am currently undertaking PhD studies at Ryerson University in Communications and Culture. I teach studio and graduate seminars in the Masters of Interior Design program at the University of Manitoba.

LC: And you?

SC: My background is a hybrid of photography, art history and critical theory. My PhD is from the Amsterdam School of Cultural Analysis, Theory and Interpretation at the University of Amsterdam where I did my dissertation on how women use photography as a social practice to establish identity. My current research looks at photography and design culture as well as gender and identity. The focus of my teaching in interior design has been the development of curriculum and seminars related to the integration of critical and cultural theory and design practice.

SC: Why do you consider interior design as a delimited practice?

LC: Interior design, as a discipline, is caught between the structure and self-importance of architecture and the laissez-faire and self-indulgence of interior decoration. In trying to define itself it has tended to emulate architecture through self-regulation and the creation of defined boundaries to disciplinary knowledge that ultimately act as walls or barriers against collaboration. Instead of protecting the profession and its knowledge, interior design has constrained its own healthy development and evolution. As more design projects defy disciplinary boundaries, the traditional view of the design professions is challenged. Interior design has lacked a rigorous intellectual framework and a critical discourse since its inception.

SC: Why do you think interdisciplinary theory is important to the practice of interior design?

LC: Interdisciplinarity is the lifeblood of the practice of the design professions, allowing complex and multidimensional problems to be understood and elegantly and economically resolved. In firms such as IDEO, anthropologists and social scientists are part of the design team, demonstrating the creative benefits of pooling divergent knowledge. Theory gives designers the language and capacity to slip into interdisciplinary dialogues. We can engage in critical discourse with artists, planners, architects, social scientists and others bringing intellectual legitimacy to interior design and, possibly more importantly, bringing interior design knowledge to the notice and benefit of a larger community. The language of theory is disciplined and rigorous, creating a springboard for intellectual vitality.

LC: How and why should the connection be made between theory and practice?

SC: The place of theory is significant in design education as it engages students to think critically about the creative design process. It is not enough to merely consider what to make but it is necessary to reflect upon how and why it is made. My training in cultural analysis draws on critical theory so as to allow the design object, in Mieke Bal's words, 'to speak back'. A good design education should also allow the student to gain a thoughtful voice in order to be an articulate member of the design community. To date, there is no actual canon of design theory. Like art and architectural theory, most design theory is drawn from interdisciplinary sources that include pertinent issues such as gender identity, performativity and privacy. The future relevance of design theory is to inform designers of such key concepts related to contemporary society.

This argument about involving theory in design is not new. It began with the integration of interdisciplinary theory into art and architecture.* However, this is only recently being recognized by interior design in North America and being led by design programs taught in universities. There is logical connection between theory and practice in interior design that involves content, context and narrative. Semiotics and phenomenology have a long history of informing spatial writing. Two prominent examples are Gaston Bachelard [2] and Jean Baudrillard [3]. A sociologist as well as a theorist, Baudrillard argued convincingly about the place of cultural theory in interior design. His writings are more accessible to designers as they explore interior design concepts like colour and style. Bachelard's poetic offering challenges designers to think more metaphorically. Understanding theory is part of the visual literacy that needs to continue to be developed in future design education. Interior design, particularly in North America needs to be less insular and consider ideas from outside the 'profession'. Pertinent issues such as: space, place, globalization, gender identity, branding, migration, performativity and privacy that are significant areas of theoretical study are all transferable to the more revisionist study of interior design being constructed in the twenty-first century.

LC: Can you give us an example?

SC: My own methodology is informed by the practice of cultural analysis as defined by Mieke Bal. To read an object or an interior one accepts that it can be viewed as a visual text. The object or space must be examined closely and a detailed analysis made of the information or signs it contains. Then it can be considered in relation to related concepts and theory. It must be stressed here that the object or space is allowed to have its voice as part of the interaction with the theory that is used to analyse it. This is a significant step of the practice of cultural analysis as described by Bal who explains:

> As a professional theorist, it is my belief that theory can be meaningful only when deployed in close interaction with the objects of study to which the theory pertains. Close, detailed analysis established a kind of intersubjectivity, not only between the

---

*   For example, see books designed specially for introducing theory to architecture and art history: Nesbitt, K., ed. *Theorizing A New Agenda for Architecture – An Anthology of Theory*, 1965–1995 (New York: Princeton Architectural Press, 1996) and Emerling, J. *Theory for Art History* (London: Routledge, 2005).

analyst and the audience, but between the analyst and the 'object.' The rule that I have imposed on myself, and which has been the most exciting productive constraint I have ever experienced, is never to just 'theorize' but always allow the object 'to speak back' [4].

SC: How is the connection between theory and interior practice framed?

LC: Increasingly, a good place to make this connection is through education. As they move forward as academics and practitioners, young designers revitalize and reinvent the discourse of interior design. This parallels the development of contemporary theory in architecture as it moved practice away from 'functionalist, empiricist, foundational ways of thinking' in the mid-sixties (Hays) [5].

Avenues such as conferences and journals allow for the continuing development of a critical conversation about interior design and philosophy. Such venues assist in the evolution of an appropriate language and provide confidence around the establishment of this tentative and amorphous body of theory that designers try on and discard or embrace as useful to the profession and the discipline of interior design.

Significantly we also have publications such as Mark Taylor and Julianna Preston's *Intimus: Interior Design Theory Reader* [6] that establishes legitimacy for those of us who are committed to bringing theory into the interior design curriculum and encourages an open-ended exploration of theoretical writing rather than the establishment of a canon.

SC: Which brings us to why.

LC: The nature of interior design practice is intrinsically commercial, embedded in the capitalist hegemony of contemporary society. The consideration of philosophy and theory allows for an inversion of the monolithic materialist foundation of design allowing for other stakeholders' perspectives to be understood, facilitating a critical view. As a result students, practitioners and educators challenge the status quo and expose a diverse social context with ideas more widely applicable in society that address both community and individual welfare.

An example is the phenomenon of the everyday as represented in the writing of Michel De Certeau [7], working from a Marxian celebration of the value of rituals and habits of working class people. It is in the everyday that culture and cultural heritage most powerfully reside for most of us. Design has traditionally been available to the wealthy and privileged few. Critical theory and social anthropology give us methods for observation, analysis and discourse around daily living and its rituals and practices. This perspective allows interior designers to acknowledge and honour the small gesture. It is in the interpretation of the artefact, through methodology such as semiotic analysis, that the designer can seek out and uncover subtle subversive actions that inform the ways in which we design.

LC: What are the challenges in teaching theory to visual thinkers?

SC: One of the greatest challenges is the perception of theory itself. Culler lists the characteristics of theory to be: interdisciplinarity; analysis and speculation; a critique of common sense; and reflection, thinking about thinking [8]. As a result, he concludes that theory is often intimidating. Many design students and professional designers share this fear of theory. They are often not certain what it really is and tend to avoid its integration with their work. At best, they agree to a light dusting of theory like chocolate sprinkles on an ice cream sundae. Instead, students need to discover specific theory appropriate to their project and integrate it as part of the essential framework. Learning to employ certain concepts and ideas drawn from cultural and critical theory is part of establishing 'one's own methodological toolbox' [9].

LC: So what can be done to alleviate this anxiety?

SC: I have been using a strategy in my theory seminar that is derived from cultural theorist and educator, John Tagg. This is particularly effective for teaching theory to non-theory majors. Tagg writes:

> As far as the students go, I would not expect studio students to come into the theory seminar that I do for art history students. In their case, I'd start from the other end, as I have done in a course called 'Looking Aloud'. Behind this lies the recognition that in any studio programme, I am never the only one teaching theory. There are all the other people who teach about form, perception, a belief in beauty, a notion of creativity... So far from bringing 'Theory' to the studio, I want them to get the students to first speak the theories they already have [10].

Tagg thus acknowledges the importance of validation of the students' prior knowledge. Most of the interior design students in the Masters of Interior Design (MID) program in which I teach intuitively practice semiotic analysis but they may not call it by this name. My challenge is to unpack this theoretical approach in a non-threatening and pragmatic manner. This form of analysis seems to make the most sense to the MID students, for the reasons I have discussed earlier.

In the curriculum at the Masters level there is a movement away from the teaching of traditional history of design to an analysis of design culture. My course reading list contains writings by such design theorists as Guy Julier [11], Tiiu Vaikla-Poldma [12], Mark Taylor, Julianne Preston [6] and Elizabeth Grosz [13]. I have observed that graduate students embrace the readings from writers who have design knowledge. The use of what Bal calls 'concept-based methodology' [4] allows pertinent concepts such as perfomativity, privacy or gender identity to assist in making theory more accessible and understandable. Additional problems occur when students have little background or exposure to theory, little time for reading, and weak critical skills.

To elaborate briefly, we have supervised graduate projects relating to the nightclub and the public washroom informed by Judith Butler's notion of performativity [14]. Gender identity has been explored with regard to gay retirement communities and issues of privacy considered in a study of the death rituals related to funeral homes.

SC: How does this carry over to inform the design studio?

LC: In the development of the graduate design studio project, various methods are employed to provoke creativity and to look beyond obvious answers to design issues. Theory is one of these techniques. By engaging the students intellectually with perspectives from outside the design disciplines, from philosophy and cultural theory, prejudices are often circumvented. This takes time away from concept development and there is no doubt that juggling reading, writing and drawing often extends or short circuits the design process. Finding the right balance is challenging.

Conclusion

If indeed Walter Benjamin was correct when he wrote that 'to live is to leave traces' [15], it is essential that designers be taught to be visually literate in order to interpret just what these traces mean. Theory thus provides an intellectual framework for the discipline of interior design. This framework allows for the very esoteric and ephemeral nature of the design and creation of interior spaces to be the subject of analysis and rigorous exploration. Through phenomenology and semiotics we are able to reveal the essence of light, colour, poetics, texture, and atmosphere. Theory allows interior design to address gender, race and culture; the dilemma of technology; the making of meaning through design; hegemonic structures and the culture of consumerism. Directly and in an unflinching way theory speaks to a critical and challenging generation of learners. We trust these minds to challenge the status quo.

References

[1]   Culler, J. 'Philosophy and Literature: The Fortunes of the Performative', *Poetics Today*, 2000, 21(3), pp.48–67.

[2]   Bachelard, G. *The Poetics of Space* (Boston: Beacon Press, 1994). First published as *Poetique de l'espace* (New York: Orion Press, 1964).

[3]   Baudrillard, J. *The System of Objects*, trans. James Benedict (London: Verso, 1996). First published as *Le systeme des objets* (Paris: Gallimard, 1968).

[4]   Bal, M. *Looking In: The Art of Viewing* (Amsterdam: G & B Arts International, 2001).

[5]   Hays, M. 'Foreword' in Baudrillard, J. and Nouvel, J. *The Singular Objects of Architecture,* (Minneapolis, MN: University of Minneapolis Press, 2002) p.ix.

[6]   Taylor, M. and Preston, J. *Intimus: Interior Design Theory Reader* (Chichester: Wiley-Academy, 2006).

[7]   de Certeau, M. *The Practice of Everyday Life* (Berkeley: University of California Press, 1984).

[8]   Culler, J. 'What is Theory' in *Literary Theory, A Very Short Introduction* (Oxford: Oxford University Press, 1997) p.15.

[9]   Bal, M. *Travelling Concepts in the Humanities* (Toronto: University of Toronto Press, 2002) p.5.

[10] Tagg, J. 'Practising Theory: an Interview with Joanne Lukitsh' in *Grounds of Dispute: Art History, Cultural Politics and the Discursive Field* (Minneapolis, MN: University of Minnesota Press, 1992) p.69.

[11] Julier, G. *The Culture of Design* (London: Sage, 2000).

[12] Vaikla-Poldma, T. *An investigation of learning and teaching processes in an interior design class: an interpretive and contextual inquiry* (Montreal: Magill University, Unpublished PhD Thesis, 2003).

[13]. Grosz, E. *Space, time and perversion: essays on the politics of bodies* (New York: Routledge, 1995).

[14] Butler, J. *Gender Trouble: Feminism and the Subversion of Identity* (London: Routledge, 1999).

[15] Benjamin, W. 'Paris the Capitol of the Nineteenth Century' in Tiedeman R., ed. *The Arcades Project* (Harvard: Harvard Press, 2002).

Teresa HOSKYNS

University of Brighton

NOT CUSHIONS AND CURTAINS: TEXTILES, ARCHITECTURE AND INTERIORS

Introduction

The debate surrounding architectural interiors and textiles can be viewed in a new light as the interdisciplinary practice of the two is becoming one of the most fashionable activities in architecture. Many leading architects are starting to work with textile design to create new architectural materials. It is in this context that this chapter aims to explore the relationship of textiles with the discipline of interior architecture. Whereas textiles have a long history within interior design or interior decoration, their relationship with interior architecture can be seen to be problematic.* This, of course, is very different in different institutions. When I left London Metropolitan University, where the emphasis was on concrete and glass, to go to the Royal College of Art our first project was to design a cushion. But when I started teaching at the University of Brighton, the interior architecture course was described to me as 'not cushions and curtains'.

There are a number of factors influencing why interior architecture could be seen to be defined as 'not soft furnishings'. I will describe three.

The first is the modernisation of the interior away from preconceived or traditional notions of interior decoration. Early Modernist writings like *Towards a New Architecture* by Le Corbusier and *Ornament and Crime* by Adolph Loos, have been described by Christopher Reed as the 'anti-domestic tenor of avant-garde architectural theory.' [1]

---

*   This comment comes from personal experience at some institutions. Of course, the attitude towards soft furnishings is very different in different institutions.

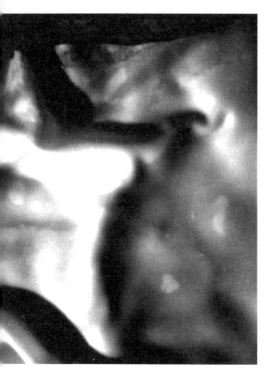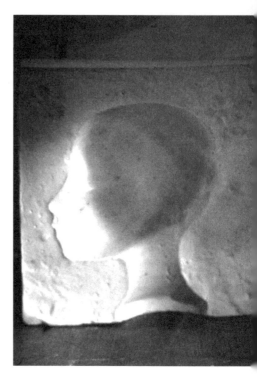

Figure 1: Cushions, Teresa Hoskyns, 1997

For example, Loos argues that the more refined man is, the less inclined he is to decorate, so primitive or native man is more likely to decorate himself than modern man. For Loos, ladies were therefore behind in their development because of their long skirts and decorated textiles [2]. The decorated domestic interior was seen as equally problematic. For Loos, the interior designer only came about during the course of the nineteenth century; before that, people were untroubled by style. He claims that the interior designer is really an upholsterer who adds cosiness to the room with curtains, door curtains, carpets, net curtains and portieres, catching dust and creating rooms with a lack of light and air [3]. For Corbusier, men travelled from the rational workplace that was designed with what he describes as the engineer's aesthetic, an aesthetic deriving from mathematical calculation and natural law, to the 'sentimental hysteria' of the home with rooms too small and a conglomeration of useless disparate objects; and that this contradicted their real existence [4].

Anne Boddington argues that historically textiles can be found in the earliest building types but, during the industrial revolution, they began to distinguish the domestic interior from the workplace. The division between the domestic interior and the workplace reinforced gender stereotypes and power relations, which began to establish themselves in specific locations, between the factory where the textiles were produced, and their application within the domestic interior – the latter created and inhabited predominantly by women. 'Textiles and the interior became the sites of production for women, whether it be embroidery as part of social grooming, or to more practical ends through making clothes and furnishings for use, exchange or sale.' [5]

It could be argued that the practice of interior architecture was created as an alternative to the 'criminalised' practice of interior decoration and embraced the modern architectural movement through the stripping away of the decorative or clothing typical of the nineteenth century [6].

The second factor is the temporal and the ephemeral: the word 'architecture' in interior architecture associates the discipline with the monumental or eternal rather than the ephemeral. I argue later in this chapter that this definition of architecture is changing; architecture is becoming lighter and today, partly through its relationship with textiles, is even weightless. Textiles are associated with transient changing interiors that symbolise the identity of their users; the interwoven patterns embody cultural identities, histories and myths, linking the interiority or privateness of the subject to the interiority of the space. Boddington argues that this is achieved 'through the manner of construction, such as knotting or weaving, as well as within the patterns and symbols themselves'. This argument is also explored by Victoria Rosner. Through her examination of the work of the Bloomsbury artists, she compares the interiority in their literature to the furnishings of their homes and examines how, in their writing and their art, the 'interior' is both the inner nature of their personality and a particular space. 'Human subjects and material objects constitute one another and what remains outside the regularities of that constitution that can disrupt the cultural memory of modernity and modernism.' [7] Textiles therefore symbolise the ephemeral, subjective and changing identity of the user.

The third point concerns the relationship of textiles to the human body. Textiles have a continuous relationship with the body, protecting it from the external environment. This relationship is shown clearly in the work of Paris-based artist Lucy Orta of Studio Orta and her work collection entitled 'Body Architecture', which was a response to human distress in social environments [8].

Other than in very controlled or particular conditions, like a bathroom, textiles are always present between the body and the hard fabric of the building or the city, either in clothing or through furnishings. For interior architecture not to include soft furnishings is to strip the discipline of its relationship with the body, positioning it with the building rather than the body.

However, recent advances in textile technology mean that textiles as a material are shifting from furnishings to construction materials and this has the effect of breaking down the relationship between the building and the interior. Here I want to examine how interior architecture can regain one of its greatest assets, textiles, and look at how textiles can re-enter the discipline in a contemporary way that takes advantage of the new and exciting advances in textile engineering and research.

Figure 2: Body Architecture, Lucy Orta, 1995

Body Architecture-Collective Wear Soweto, 1997
Tent membrane, second hand clothes from Soweto, 1
telescopic carbon armature, 5 aluminium poles, 6 copper
joints.
50 x 200 x 200 cm
Photo J.J.Crance
© Galleria Continua, San Gimignano – Beijing

Refuge Wear – Survival Sac with water reserve
incorporated, 1994
Microporus laminated polyester, PU-coated
polyester, meditative objects, folding aluminium
structure, translucid PVC, transport bag.
Photo Philippe Fuzeau
© Galleria Continua, San Gimignano – Beijing

Nexus Architecture x50
– Nexus Intervention Köln,
2001. Original Lamda
colour photograph,
laminated on Dibon
150x120cm
© Galleria Continua, San
Gimignano – Beijing

Textiles in the new millennium

Textiles as materials have become one of the newest and most expanding areas of research in many subject areas as well as architecture. To give examples both of the contemporariness of the subject and of the breadth of material it covers, I will describe a number of major exhibitions and publications that have occurred in the USA and the UK in the past few months.

Extreme Textiles in August 2006 showed how textiles are now so highly engineered that they can be used as high-performance materials in many products where there is a need to perform in extreme conditions. Old techniques such as weaving and knitting, combined with new advances in science and engineering, are producing textiles that are more dynamic and versatile than ever before, not only in architecture but in many disciplines such as medicine, engineering, transport and aerospace [9].

Skin and Bones: Parallel Practices in Fashion and Architecture opened in November 2006 at the Museum of Contemporary Art, Los Angles. The exhibition examined the similarities between fashion and architecture since the early 1980s [10]. In the *LA Times*, Christopher Hawthorne claimed that the parallel practices arose out of the joint interest in deconstructionist literary theory of Jacques Derrida, which sparked new creative energy in both fields. These parallel practices occur between architects such as Zaha Hadid, Foreign Office Architects, Office dA and Bernard Tschumi, and fashion designers including Alexander McQueen and Issey Miyake. These practices have broken with the backwards-looking practices of postmodernism and are using theory to create something new [11].

These parallels have now developed into collaborations. For example, the fashion designer Issey Miyake has collaborated with architects Frank Ghery and Jean Nouvel and the Museum de Quai Branly that opened in the spring.

The types of research reflected in the recent publication of *AD – Architextiles* edited by Mark Garcia, November/December 2006 – cover a wide range of materials and history but also show students' work and projects from the RCA, which gives a pedagogic idea of how there is a merging of the two disciplines, hence the title 'Architextiles'. The Royal College of Art has been one of the leaders in interdisciplinary research through collaborations between the textile department and the architecture department under the professorship of Nigel Coates [12].

Robotic Membranes, a collaboration between architect Mette Ramsgard Thomsen and knitter Toni Hicks, opened in January 2007 in the School of Art and Design at the University of Brighton. The collaboration developed out of teaching between architecture students in Copenhagen and textile students in Brighton and the product of the teaching work has become a research project in itself.

These exhibitions and publications express a twenty-first century new chapter in the story of architecture and textiles. This could be explained by elements coming together from many different angles, from high theory to new developments in textile technology and textile engineering, combined with far more advanced CAD computer modelling tools.

The advances in engineering stem from the quality of the yarns, which are made from a variety of materials like carbon fibres, metals, Kevlar and Teflon. These are combined with new developments in fabric technologies such as ultrasonic welding, fabric setting, and countless other fibre technologies that offer new spatial possibilities. Textiles are then subject to coatings giving fire resistance or can be stiffened through heat forming. Garcia even argues that forms that look like textiles but are in fact conventional materials such as ceramic and glass can be described as textiles. For example, Norman Foster's Swiss Re Tower in the City of London or the new glass roof of the British Museum courtyard would then be described as textiles.

Microscopic strands of stainless steel can be added to the weave or knit to transform the textile into smart materials that can respond to actions or commands through an electronic circuit. An example of this type of smart material can be seen in the new uniform of the US army that records and responds to movements made by army personnel [13].

Architecture and textiles

Textiles and architecture have a long history that dates back to the origins of architecture. Boddington argues that for centuries textiles are one of the earliest-traded commodities and have been at the leading edge of economic and cultural development. She argues that textiles have therefore played a role in shaping cities as merchant cities grew out of economic trade.

Textiles are also one of the earliest man-made shelters, as woven huts and their use form part of an age-old nomadic tradition and a hunter-gatherer existence. Nomadic roaming over the earth's surface in response to seasonal and climate change, or in search of food, has been predominantly exchanged for permanent settlement and the subsequent evolution of an urbanised landscape [14].

It is through temporary structures that I became interested in textiles. Textiles imply an architecture that responds to event and performance. With my partner Mat Churchill we designed and built the Mamaloucos Circus Tent first used to tour the Royal National Theatre's production of Joan Littlewood's *Oh What a Lovely War*. Joan Littlewood had refused to allow the production to be performed at the National Theatre as she saw it as elitist, whereas for her 'theatre should be free like air, water or love' [15].

Here it could be argued that textiles are performing the same task in the circus that they perform in traditional interior decoration. The circus coming to town brings with it a new identity and subjectivity, recognised by the colour and patterning of the textile. The square or public space is transformed by the outsiders who, like the Bloomsbury group, provide a new interiority through combining their interior space and their art, this time with performance instead of writing. The public enters into the otherworldly interior of the performers, an interior that is not real because most of the time it is a pile of

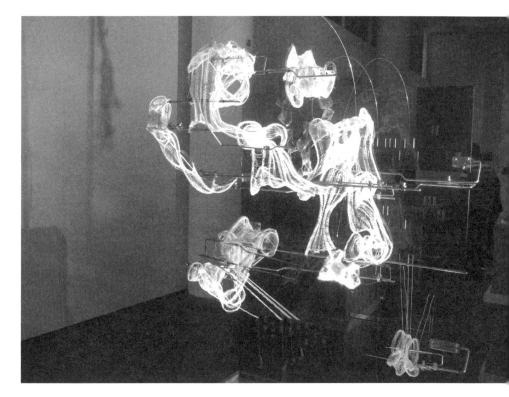

Figure 3: *Robotic Membranes*, Mette Ramsgard Thomsen and Toni Hicks, University of Brighton, 2007

plastic on a lorry, but when it is hung in tension in the air the 2mm thickness of plastic becomes a delineation of interior space.

Textiles are now being used for permanent architectural projects and I will give two examples, one from each side of the Atlantic. One is by the California-based architect Peter Testa and the other is by UK-based architect Will Alsop. Both show the possibilities for textiles but, I would argue, they are moving in different directions.

The first example I will give is Will Alsop. Alsop concentrates on fabric's ability as an external skin able to take on different qualities of light and be patterned. He uses standard building structures, for example steel frame, and stretches textiles over the frame to create the skin. To describe the use of fabric in his projects he uses terms from fashion or the interior such as dress, shawl, skirt and table cloth, and he exploits fabric's ability to be decorated. In the case of West Queen West, Toronto, Canada, Alsop skinned the building with a double skin to break down the barrier between the inside and the outside. For the outer skin he used a sheer fabric, cut holes into it and lined it with foam. This was then wrapped over the stripped exterior of the building [16].

In contrast, Peter Testa's work explores the structural and spatial qualities of the fabric itself. His Carbon Tower, a proposed 40-storey skyscraper, replaces steel structure with a carbon-fibre lattice that is several times stronger and lighter than steel. This lattice is interwoven with a carbon-fibre embroidered lace [17]. Testa's work marks a shift away from modern building practice with structural members and skin and proposes a building construction that is 'woven like a cocoon' [18].

Alsop and Coates appear crude in comparison to Testa's Carbon Tower, where their use of coloured and patterned textile skins is reminiscent of postmodern architecture. What Testa shows is not a building skinned in fabric and patterned but a fabric building, where the form has a material integrity derived from textile processes like weaving, lace and embroidery, relating to structure and construction.

Despite the often-traditional approach to fabrics in interiors, in architecture fabric couldn't be more like the modern world, and its displacement of Vitruvius' ideal of an architecture as monumental and eternal into an embrace of change, movement and newness. Jonathan Hill in his latest book *Immaterial Architecture* shows how architectural thinking has changed and he uses the Reichstag in Berlin as an example of the desire for immateriality. Foster's glass roof and Christo's wrapping both give a heavy gravity-based monumental building a sense of impermanence. Hill uses fabric as one of the materials that describe an immaterial architecture, which includes glass, mirror, bamboo, aluminium and cloud [19].

Philip Beesley and Sean Hanna describe how the desire behind fabric architecture is for an 'interwoven floating new world'. They use a phrase from the *Second Communist Manifesto* – 'all that is solid melts into air' – to show how modern visions of weightlessness are becoming an architectural truth [20].

There are some key concepts that are unique to textiles and which mean that the notions of immateriality, weightlessness and floating architecture are a reality. The first is that textile structures work in tension as well as compression, meaning that the forces pull both upwards and downwards, making fabric structures weightless in comparison to gravity-based stone, brick and steel construction.

The second is the concept of synergy, a concept developed by Buckminster Fuller and explored by Testa and Weiser in their research into extreme networks. Synergy can be described as 'the behaviour of whole systems unpredicted by the separately observed behaviour of any of the system's separate parts' [21]. This means that the structure is viewed as a whole with each part playing an equal role. Synergy allows the building to behave not as a set of elements which each perform different tasks, but as a network where the qualities of the building come from its performance as a whole and not from the properties of the individual members. The possibilities for the future research and development of this concept are endless as they not only free us from columns and posts, but also allow for construction to become interactive and responsive. If the structure is working as a network, rather than a collection of individual elements,

Figure 4: The Theatre Tent, Mat Churchill and Teresa Hoskyns, South Bank, 1999

and some of the elements move, then others can respond. 'Form and structure are emergent properties of extreme networks and have no pre-established topology or morphology' [22] – implying that one day we could have an architecture that doesn't have a fixed form, but like cushions and curtains, is constantly able to change and respond to different users.

Textiles and interiors

As described above, textiles have become popular materials in architecture, but I would argue that the possibilities for textiles and the interior are much larger. The new developments described above mean that textiles have become more architectural and can be used in the types of architectural adaptations that are expected of interior architects, such as to skin buildings or replace roofs, for textiles are stronger,

Figure 5: Carbon Tower, Peter Testa, 1994
Carbon Tower (2001–4)
© Testa & Weiser Inc.

Figure 6: Matthew Adams, Studio 3, University of Brighton, 2006

lighter and smarter than any other materials. Textiles are no longer relegated to soft furnishings, but textiles have always had a natural link with the body and inhabitation, a layer between the building and the body, or the city and the body. The work of Design Research and Development (DR&D) shows how the building and the interior can merge into one through what they describe as the performative textured surface. The building becomes inhabitable and performative as the textiles respond to its use [23].

Breaking down the separation between the architectural and textile layers can break down the separation between the architectural and the body. The layer can almost be seen more clearly by the ability of textiles to create outside interiors. This has been one of the starting points for the work of Studio 3, where for a time we removed the architecture and looked purely at the interior through inhabitation.

In Studio 3 in Brighton we have been working with textiles since the beginning of the year. The students arrived at the start of the course with a piece of fabric and then deconstructed it to discover the processes involved in its making and its material properties such as translucency. They then reconstructed the fabric to make their own structural fabric. The idea was that through using textile processes such as knitting, weaving, folding, pleating, knotting, the students could design in the properties they wanted. For example, the students would decide the types of light quality, or how tactile the material is through the construction of the textile, or changing the scale, including structure through developing the weave or adding pleats.

A knitting workshop with Toni Hicks and Mette Ramsgard Thomsen also allowed the students to start making 1:50 three-dimensional conceptual models that expressed the types of qualities inherent in textiles such as flow and weightlessness. We discovered that using textiles as model-making materials allowed the students to create forms that would normally be very difficult to draw or model.

Research in Brighton University between architect Mette Ramsgard Thomsen and knitter Toni Hicks examines 'textile architecture shaped by its own inherent movement patterns'. It includes the merging of architecture, textiles and robotics to produce responsive architectural elements showing how the concept of synergy can include social, as well as physical networks.

My experience of teaching textiles in an interior architecture course is that student feedback is positive: students say that they are doing what they thought they would be doing, rather than arriving at college to find that what they thought interior architecture was is actually excluded from the course. Interior architecture no longer has to define itself against the excluded and criminalised 'other' of interior decoration.

Interior decoration contains many of the tools and materials key to the discipline of interiors – and not only through textiles, for decoration and patterning are key processes in the interiorisation, inhabitation and subjectivity of a space. Rather than exclude these processes we should unpick them, transform and reclaim them as contemporary practices for the new millennium.

I would also argue for an end to the divisions between interior architecture, interior design and interior decoration and for combining them under one title: interiors.

References

[1]   Reed, C., ed. *Not at Home: The Suppression of Domesticity in Modern Art and Architecture* (London: Thames and Hudson, 1996) pp.7–17.

[2]   Loos, A. 'Ladies Fashion' in *Ornament and Crime* (Ariadne Press, 1998 [1898/1902]) pp.106–11.

[3]   Ibid., pp.51–6

[4]   Le Corbusier, *Towards a New Architecture* (New York: Dover Publications Inc., 1986 [1931]) pp.13–20.

[5]   Boddington, A. 'Textiles and Space', internal paper and lecture, University of Brighton, Department of Fashion and Textiles, 2004.

[6]   Wigley, M. *White Walls Designer Dresses: The Fashioning of Modern Architecture* (Cambridge, MA: MIT Press, 2001).

[7]   Rosner, V. *Modernism and the Architecture of Private Life* (New York: Columbia University Press, 2005) pp.127–75.

[8]   See http://studioorta.free.fr/lucy_orta.html, accessed January 2007.

[9]   Chang, K. '"Extreme Textiles" Come of Age', *New York Times*, 12 April 2005.

[10] *Skin + Bones: Parallel Practices in Fashion and Architecture* (Thames and Hudson, 2006).

[11] Hawthorne, C. 'MOCA's "Skin + Bones" ends up feeling thin', *LA Times*, architecture review, 17 November 2006.

[12] Garcia, M. ed. *Architextiles, Architectural Design*, vol.76, no.6, November/December 2006.

[13] Chang, op. cit.

[14] Boddington, op. cit.

[15] Littlewood, J., cited in a BBC obituary, 'Theatre's defiant genius', 21 September 2002, http://news.bbc.co.uk/1/hi/uk/1628351.stm.

[16] 'The Pull of Black Velvet, Latex, Tights, Quilts, Tablecloths and Frocks: An Interview with Will Alsop (Mark Garcia)' in Garcia, op. cit., pp.36–41.

[17] Chang, op. cit.

[18] Miodownik, M. 'Carbon Culture', *Materials Today*, vol.9, no.6, June 2006.

[19] Hill, J. *Immaterial Architecture* (London: Routledge, 2006) pp.107–11.

[20] Beesley, P. and Hanna, S. 'Sean Hanna: lighter: a transformed architecture' http://www.sean.hanna.net/publications/lighter.htm, accessed 2007.

[21] See the Buckminster Fuller Institute website, http://www.bfi.org, accessed 2007.

[22] Testa, P. and Weiser, D. 'Extreme Networks' in Garcia, op. cit., pp.42–3.

[23] Richter, D. 'Camouflage as Aesthetic Sustainability' in Garcia, op. cit.

Tara ROSCOE

STUDIOS Architecture, New York City;
Associate, Pratt Institute of Art & Design;
Visiting Instructor, Department of Interior Design

IMMATERIAL CULTURE: THE INTERIOR ENVIRONMENT REPOSITIONED

Introduction

Over the past twenty years, Western society has become reliant upon, defined by, and realised in a variety of non-physical loci. The introduction of advanced electronic and digital technologies, ubiquitous computing, wireless global networks, and real-time communications has effectively transformed how society takes place. Professor of architecture and urbanism at Princeton University, Christine Boyer reminds us that the resulting consequence of the digital era is that 'reality is increasingly immaterial' [1].

Interior design relies on material culture for its manifestation and effect. The premise of an expanding immaterial culture should be of primary concern to those who deal with the design of physical environments. Important questions arise, such as: what does an expanding immaterial culture imply for the physical properties and composition of the physical spaces we inhabit? What does an immaterial culture determine for the future identity and status of the interior environment?

Increasingly ubiquitous technologies such as the internet, wireless networks, mobile gadgets, real-time global networks and smart environments introduce a number of complex states of digitalia into a growing number of physical locations. Architectural theorist Elizabeth Grosz argues that this is bound to affect our perception of space, materiality, and boundary, and will inevitably alter how individuals come to understand habitation and the built environment [2]. How are interior designers contending with the impact of these technologies?

Professor of Design History at Southampton Institute, Anne Massey reminds us that interior design 'is concerned with all the elements of the interior spaces of the architectural shell' [3]. This would seem to imply that interior design is, by definition, bound solely to the physical realm, through the material containment and demarcations set by architecture. As we move further into the digital era, this axiom imposes great limits on interior design to effectively contend with the more abstract and complex identity of contemporary space [4].

Science journalist and cyberspatial theorist Margaret Wertheim claims that cyberspace is typically not considered a genuine space [5]. She challenges this common acceptance of assuming that physical artefacts and spaces are the dominant sources of experience. Wertheim asserts:

> [Cyberspace] is no less real for not being material... Just because something is not material does not mean it is unreal, as the oft-cited distinction between 'cyberspace' and 'real space' implies. Despite its lack of physicality, cyberspace is a real place. I am out there – whatever this statement may ultimately turn out to mean [6].

There are great variations in beliefs on how cyberspace influences our understanding of space. For architect and information theorist Peter Anders, cyberspace is merely an extension of the human senses [7]. Taking a phenomenological position, Anders attests that: 'Space is a medium by which we understand our world, ourselves and each other. And cyberspace is its electronic extension' [8]. For others, the immediacy and speed offered through advanced technology will break down traditional design metrics and some of the more fundamental principles of architecture. Specifically, this challenges the reliance on the Cartesian and Euclidean principles of space.

Dematerialization

In simple terms, immaterial culture is a threat to material culture. Artist and architectural theorist Marcos Novak refers to dematerialization as a process by which technology replaces physical, tangible events and artefacts with digital or electronic counterparts [9]. The equation revealed in this transaction is quite straightforward. For example, as photographic images become digital, composed of bits and pixels, transmitted through networks and stored in electronic files, the traditional paper-backed photograph dematerializes. This simple translation has great consequences beyond the scale of the photo itself. The dematerialized photograph in turn affects the status of corresponding artefacts and systems, such as the photo album and the photo processing lab.

As artefacts leave the physical realm, design theorist John Thackara labels the new vacant space they leave behind as a *cybernetic loss* [10]. Upon further review, dematerialization can sweep out and engulf a variety of artefacts and spaces. Whether it's the photograph, a record store or a meeting room, it becomes clear that nothing is free of being considered as future prey, as potential sites for the act of disappearance. The act of disappearance is not restricted in scale, scope or reach.

This is not to propose that all physical artefacts are about to disappear. Rather, the intention here is to highlight some of the more subversive and perhaps less obvious attributes of a devouring feasting nature or appetite inherent in these technologies. Technology has the potential to eradicate many of the physical artefacts and spaces that have come to define our environments.

Liquid to cybrid

Immaterial culture introduces new structural components to the design process. As atoms translate into bits, new building blocks for architecture become defined by the ones and noughts of computer language. Marcos Novak refers to this as a *liquid architecture* [11]. For Novak, liquid architecture is not defined through the resistance and statics as inherent in physical material, but in contrast is defined through its transmittable and fluid characteristics. Novak explains:

> Liquid architecture is an architecture that breathes, pulses, leaps as one form and lands as another. Liquid architecture is an architecture whose form is contingent on the interests of the beholder; it is an architecture that opens to welcome me and closes to defend me; it is an architecture without doors and hallways; where the next room is always where I need it to be and what I need it to be [12].

Liquid architecture poses to redefine and reconstruct our spatial language. What does the organic nature of liquid architecture imply for the static nature and confined features of the interior? How does a liquid architecture spill into, draw out, overlap and puncture the interior?

Design theorist John Thackara [13] claims that the increasing convergence of cyberspace and physical space proposes a holistic spatial experience. He asserts the digital era is producing a new kind of hybrid space [14].

According to postcolonial theory, 'hybridity is the margin where oppositional cultures overlap. It is the edge where cultural differences clash and conflict, disrupting the stable identities that are constructed around oppositions such as past and present, inside and outside, or inclusion and exclusion' [15]. This margin spawns new generations where oppositional features begin to give in to one another, intertwine, overlap and blur. Hybridity in terms of space encompasses a dual spatial condition. It successfully blurs the distinction between cyber and physical, mental and material, conceptual and tangible.

Hybrid space has no fixed or stable identity. The dynamic state of the hybrid relies upon the continuing evolution of polar identities in order to rebuild and inform its own creation. It relies on the relationship of the physical and the cyber, on their actively engaging one another: to inform and influence, add and subtract, flex and bend as it coalesces into its evolving identity. Through this process, the spatial domains come together to create new definitions, identities and boundaries.

In this view, hybrid space suggests an evolving condition of site and context. Establishing location or 'placing' architecture or architectural components in this view appears trivial. The framework for an interior as defined by the static and stable enclosures of architecture becomes suspect. Hybrid space implies the material shell of the interior is porous, penetrable and, in turn, unreliable or volatile.

Architectural theorist Ole Bouman provides additional comment when stating that, in the digital era, architecture:

> becomes a migrant. Rather than creating a place, designers stage-manage movable situations. The relation between the individual and object becomes the relation between dynamic places and (sometimes manipulated) states of mind. This architecture belongs in neither the physical nor the virtual domain; it is a hybrid. Space becomes genuinely fluid; it forms the link by which the digital space can flow into the real space of daily life. And vice versa [16].

As more sophisticated technologies become embedded into a greater number of places, hybrid spatial conditions are bound to proliferate. This raises significant questions as to who will be responsible for the overall choreography and execution of the future hybrid. Who will study the multi-spatial phenomena in order to discern where the domains are compatible, how they are oppositional, and how they will ultimately unite? If, as some suggest, convergency is the inevitable future outcome for the domains, who will decide how this occurs [17]?

Professor and Executive Director of the Claremont Information and Technology Institute, Thomas Horan identifies the overlapping point of convergency between the domains as a threshold connection [18]. For Horan, the success of a hybrid relies on the careful design and construction at the threshold connection. The design objective becomes one of unification and seamlessness.

Similar to the crafting or joinery of a material-to-material connection in the physical realm, the design of the threshold requires a different yet equally important level of attention to detail. The threshold between cyberspace and physical space becomes an area for careful study of complex joinery; it is an emerging area of design craft and detailing.

Cybrid

Expanding further on the notion of hybrid space, Peter Anders defines this morphing of spatial domains as *cybrid space*. According to him, cybrid space is 'an environment or artefact that incorporates both physical and cyberspaces' [19]. Examples of cybridity can be found in everyday settings such as an office, a retail store or a contemporary library. In the example of the contemporary library, its collection is defined by the physical books as well as the endless streams of online sources found in cyberspace. The domains of cyberspace and physical space, together, define the contemporary library collection.

Anders notes that the cybrid design model contends with objects and experiences that essentially straddle both modes of being [20]. This suggests that the site of a cybrid design is located in a distributed spatial sphere. How can interior designers consider objects and experiences that cut across both domains?

Case study: cybrid design process in studio

Currently, very few firms or individuals appear fully equipped to tackle the multispatial phenomena as outlined in this chapter. Architecture has catalyzed most of the discourse and theory on the cybrid today, yet the sole responsibility for its future design and creation is not limited to this trajectory. The design and development of the future cybrid is a multi-displinary exercise and endeavour. Design teams may include individuals from a variety of professions and backgrounds, such as video game programmers, graphic designers, phenomenologists, interior designers, urban planners or interface designers.

In his book *Envisioning Cyberspace,* Anders [21] explains the methods used to introduce cybrid design problems to his graduate architecture students. His students developed a problem-solving approach that engaged both spatial domains. Students had to critically assess and identify the benefits and shortcomings inherent in both spatial domains and, as Anders notes, 'employ each mode of space to its best advantage' [22].

Design instructors Sally Levine and Warren Wake of the Boston Architectural Center have introduced their students to similar design problems. Using what Levine and Wake call 'Siamese sites', their students were challenged to grow a single and independent design program into a dual-realm design project. As explained by Levine and Wake, 'students considered the unique characteristics of each realm as well as the connections between the two' [23].

To support deeper inquiries into cyberspace, Levine and Wake's studio used a variety of sophisticated computer software programs. Experimenting with what they call complementary virtual architecture, the students were able to explore a virtual environment and a physical environment simultaneously. The students developed interactive virtual architectural models, defined multimodal design principles and created avatars to construct complementary identities. Students studied how experience and activities translate from physical space into cyber experiences and vice versa. Ideas such as movement, navigation, communication and spatial sequence were effectively translated into the cyberspatial design realms.

During my instruction of a third-year undergraduate environmental design studio at the University of Manitoba, I introduced elementary design principles of cybridity to the students. I developed student project criteria to redesign the existing fine arts and architecture slide library on campus. The library housed the entire physical slide collection on-site. The objective of the project was for students to consider the repercussions of relocating the slide collection off-site and gaining primary access to the collection via electronic, digital and wireless technologies.

I encouraged students to engage in a dialogue about what activities, artefacts and experiences should be considered for deployment to cyberspace and which should reside in physical space. The discussions highlighted how the act of engaging one domain (i.e. the removal of the physical slides from the site) introduced a new sequence of spatial conditions that would affect both domains and would inevitably need to be resolved by the students' design solution. As the digital collection became accessible via cell phones and PDA catalogue searches, interesting discussions emerged as to how and where individuals could 'access' the slides.

The ideas developed in the studio had a clear association to the ideas of recombinant architecture as defined by William Mitchell [24]. According to Mitchell, designers and architects can effectively dissolve and then reformulate spaces into new innovative typologies through the integration of advanced technologies. He explains that:

> The spatial linkages that we have come to expect are loosened. The constituent elements of hitherto tightly packaged architectural and urban compositions can begin to float free from one another, and they can potentially relocate and recombine according to new logics [25].

The recombinant features of the slide library offset the apocalyptic views one might first assume of dematerialisation and disappearance. One of the most valuable lessons from the study highlights that dematerialisation has benefits and merits. Through the act of digitizing the collection, the physical space could be considered, designed and realized in innovative ways. As physical space became available, students embedded other types of non-programmed space such as student resource materials, a lounge, a café and student team meeting areas.

Although the students at the University of Manitoba were asked to execute design solutions limited to the physical realm, the design analysis did not ignore the influential features of cyberspace. The design solutions successfully embraced a dual-site condition by creating an interior solution that was complementary and an active agent of its cyber counterpart.

Conclusion

As technology evolves, its ability to influence how space is perceived and experienced will intensify and remain in a constant state of flux. Interior design will need to expand its discourse to remain actively engaged and conscious of the conditions of this changing paradigm.

The effects of an evading material culture should also become a central area for further study. It is important to understand whether or not human beings are losing anything of value through this process of dematerialization. What becomes of the tangible, the sensual and intimate physical spatial experience? As nostalgic as this may sound, it becomes crucial for designers to ascertain what is actually leaving, what is remaining and what has become available for redefinition.

Earlier in this chapter, I referred to interior design as defined through the containment, enclosure and limits set by architecture. As this boundary is in a state of flux, so the status of the interior shifts in tandem. Solving future spatial issues will require designers to consider the study of elements that traditionally have lain beyond their scope, realm and perhaps their understanding. This may force designers to venture beyond the safe and familiar territory of the interior. In the end, keeping interior design 'inside' may prove to be an unnecessary constraint.

As technology can support anytime–anywhere activities, the functional need to go to a place comes into question. For example, banking activities can occur at an airport, in a taxi or on a porch – so why would one need to go to the physical bank? Mitchell claims that 'if you can locate anywhere... you will locate where it's particularly attractive in some way.' [26] This may come down to a good cup of coffee, a lively social setting or a beautifully designed interior space. Mitchell refers to this as the 'revenge of place' [27].

As more experiences become immaterial, that which remains material may actually attain a new status as the exotic, the rare and, perhaps, the more meaningful. Thackara explains: 'physical spaces have the opportunity to become islands of salvation of the real in a sea of endless streams of information, media and digital saturation' [28]. In response to our overexposure to digital objects and environments delivered through immaterial culture, that which remains tangible, tactile and material has the power to potentially 'root us to the ground, as human beings.' [29]

References

[1]   Boyer, C.M. *Cybercities: Visual Perception in the Age of Electronic Communication* (New York: Princeton Architectural Press, 1996) p.11.

[2]   Grosz, E.A. *Architecture from the Outside: Essays on Virtual and Real Space* (Cambridge, MA: The MIT Press, 2001).

[3]   Massey, A. *Interior Design of the 20th Century* (London: Thames & Hudson, 2001) p.6.

[4]   Space in this context refers to the understanding of the 'location of being', and character grounded in contemporary architectural theory and active in the discipline of interior design. Space in this context embraces space as social, political, and active – as well as the physical material properties of architectural space. This definition derives from Henri Lefebvre's notion of an all-encompassing spatial experience, where the realm of material space (comprised of atoms) and the realm of cyberspace combine to define the perception of space (*The Production of Space*. Oxford: Basil Blackwell, 1991).

[5]   Wertheim, M. 'The Pearly Gates of Cyberspace' in Spiller, N., ed. *Cyber_Reader; Critical Writings for the Digital Era* (London: Phaidon Press Limited, 2002) p.300.

[6]   Ibid., p.301

[7]   Anders, P. *Envisioning Cyberspace: Designing 3D Electronic Spaces* (New York: McGraw Hill, 1999).

[8]   Ibid., p.217

[9]   Novak, M. 'Liquid Architecture in Cyberspace' in Benedikt, M., ed. *Cyberspace: First Steps* (Cambridge, MA: The MIT Press, 1991) pp.225–54.

[10]   Thackara, J. 'Beyond the Object in Design' in Thackara, J., ed. *Design after Modernism: Beyond the Object* (New York: Thames and Hudson, 1988) pp.11–33.

[11]   Spiller, N. 'Introduction' in Spiller, N., ed. *Cyber_Reader; Critical Writings for the Digital Era* (London: Phaidon Press Limited, 2002).

[12]   Ibid., p.153

[13]   Thackara, J. 'Designing the Space of Flows' in Antonelli, P., ed. *Workspheres: Design and Contemporary Work Styles* (New York: The Museum of Modern Art, 2001).

[14]   Ibid., p.40

[15]   Macey, D. *The Penguin Dictionary of Critical Theory* (London: Penguin Books, 2000).

[16]   Bouman, O. 'Quick Space in Real Time, Conclusion: Architecture Online', *Archis,* 1998b(7), p.79.

[17]   William Mitchell, Convergency/Asymptote Convergency, TBD.

[18]   Horan, T.H. *Digital Places: Building our City of Bits* (Washington, DC: ULI – Urban Land Institute, 2000).

[19]   Anders, op. cit., p.195. It is important to move beyond the term hybrid, and so the relevance of the term 'cybrid' cannot be overlooked. It 'marries together the actual and the virtual in one term, rather than resting in the ambiguity of "hybrid space", "mixed reality" and "augmented space"' (Sam Kinsley, 'Cybrid: Reaching a Common Lexicon', 5 April 2004, www.samkinsley.com/archive/000022.html) and so reinforces the relevance of the connection point directly at the overlapping intersection between domains.

[20]   Anders, op. cit., p.199

[21]   Anders, op. cit.

[22]   Ibid., p.195

[23]   Levine, S.L. and Wake, W.K. 'Complementary Virtual Architecture and the Design Studio', *Journal of Architectural Education*, 2002, p.19.

[24]   Mitchell, W.J. *City of Bits: Space, Place and the Info Ban* (Cambridge, MA: The MIT Press, 1995).

[25]   Ibid.

[26]   Mitchell, W.J. 'E-Bodies, E-Building, E-Cities' in Leach, N., ed. *Designing for a Digital World* (London: John Wiley & Sons, 2002) p.51.

[27]   Ibid.

[28]   Thackara, J. 'Cultural Engineering' in Mitchell, C.T., ed. *New Thinking in Design: Conversations on Theory and Practice* (New York: John Wiley & Sons, 1996).

[29]   Ibid., p.119

Patrick HANNAY

Cardiff School of Art and Design, UWIC

A REGULATED IRREGULARITY

The UK interiors education system has been in exponential expansion mode for over a decade. The national source of information on all UK higher education courses, the UCAS website, lists 228 courses under 'Interiors' for the UK [1]. Ten years ago there were 31 degree-level interiors courses in the UK with final years of between 15 and 20 students. Now there are, at a very, very conservative reading of the UCAS data, 55 courses at that level (a 70 per cent increase), each with a third year of say 25–30 students. That could mean an increase of final year output onto the market from 620 students per year to 1,375 per year – a 110 per cent increase. There are also 15 foundation degrees (two-year courses) created in the last two years and growing, and four long-standing HNDs. Add those in and you could have a 150 per cent increase. Given that each of these degree courses is probably having a 50 per cent increase in intake numbers compared with ten years ago, do we think that employment opportunities within the UK interiors industry have expanded at an equally exponential rate? No single practitioner I have spoken to thinks so. Some would then argue that we are providing designers for the global economy. So, are we all happy with the quality of education this huge annual cohort is getting?

We all know that staff–student ratios have risen dramatically. Moreover, while we may have tightened up on our delivery techniques, we have all witnessed the erosion of content and substance, at least in England and Wales, through the stretching of too few tutors over too many students. And all this while studio space is cut from beneath our feet. Sadly, short memories exacerbated by frequent staff turn-over undermine that coherence of perspective. (This is not a bleating nostalgic refrain from times past.)

Do we care about all this? Should we care – and even if we do, has any educational economy or profession ever successfully regulated HE intake to fit it neatly to industry demand? After all, the last attempt by the architectural profession to regulate HE numbers in the UK, in Lord Esher's 1984 report, was roundly rebuffed as unworkable and, for some, politically unacceptable [2]. (Of course, the lawyers have been at it for years.) It was the same for Colin Stansfield-Smith a decade later. But then you have to ask how many new courses in architecture have come online since 1984? Very few. Living up to the intense scrutiny of the RIBA/ARB validation system and surviving the quinquennial visiting board regime keeps the HE breeding instinct in architecture in check. There is no such check whatsoever on interiors. Thank God I hear you say.

So in 2006 in England and Wales we have 24 architecture schools, essentially one for every 2.3 million citizens. In interiors however, we have we have one course for every 1.1 million! You may counter that by saying each is a smaller school in interiors, and so this isn't comparing like with like. Well, let's look at some other countries doing interiors education.

In Oceania (Australia and New Zealand) the figure is one for 2.2 million. For Finland it is one for 2.5 million. In France it is one for 4.3 million. In the Netherlands it is one for 2.3 million. In Germany it is one for 5.2 million [3]. Should we be worried that we in the UK seem to be so startlingly out of sync that we have twice the number of anywhere else? Is this wise? Does it matter? Could it be that we are spreading the intellectual icing a little thin on the cake? Interestingly, no interiors course in the UK asks for three A grades at A-level as so many of the architecture courses do. In fact, the opposite is more the case. As the pool of applicants is spread thinner over more and more interiors courses, to keep the course viable and with ever more bums on seats, the intellectual threshold for entry is lowered and lowered. Is this good for our discipline? Is this simply the inevitable outcome of our totally unregulated educational environment? After all, we are quite unique in having such a total free-for-all.

The rest of the Western world tends to have a wide range of national/regional regulatory mechanisms for interiors students, most of them justified by the instinct to protect the client/consumer and in turn the student. The USA has a national examination system [4]. The Netherlands have a five-year educational system and a proper protected-title registration tied in with it [5]. In France, the state schools for interiors are all regulated and visited by national panels [6]. In Germany and their current four-year courses, they have recently been instrumental in the Association for the recognition of Studies in Architecture and Planning (ASAP, which absorbs interiors as well), committing themselves to aligning with the UIA minimum five years of consecutive study. Interestingly, they set up ASAP partly 'as a result of university deregulation' [7]. They will have visiting boards. They have protected title.

None of us may relish the stuffy over-zealous investigatory system of UK architecture. Many would say that such a professional invasion into a modern university environment is distrustful and disrespectful of what, assumedly, are the proper internal academic quality verification procedures. We value our academic freedom and some say it has served generations of interiors students well [8].

But is not the UK's Chartered Society of Designers (CSD) the polar extreme of all this, as a professional society? It has no panel of validated external examiners; no panels of professionals available as university course validation external verifiers; no national exams on professional competence. It simply has a portfolio interview for those wishing to join the society – which most do not. (In this it is not much different from Germany, for example, where 15–20 per cent of students join [9].) The CSD has no oversight whatsoever on any educational matter, no policy initiative or even vehicle for intellectual debate about the teaching of the discipline. When universities want to merge 'interiors' with 'architecture' or 'product design' or to hot-desk space usage, or suggest that interiors could be allied to pastry cooking, is there any national body with clout for educationalists to turn to, to protect their intellectual integrity? When the Royal College of Art in London, the supposedly top postgraduate environment in design, lopped off the word 'interior' from their former jointly titled MA course with architecture, did the CSD rush to object or even comment? There was utter silence. The initiative to object has had to come from elsewhere, from educationalists and those practitioners in the past who have devoted a sizeable chunk of their time to teaching [10]. More of that later.

Is your response to all this simply 'Thank goodness' – let a thousand flowers bloom… and die. Is this Darwinism of modern UK education really doing the industry and its respect amongst its clients any favours? Do we all see a rising qualitative tide in the output of students' work, or are we all locked up in our insular distinct contexts, focused on short-term survival and simply shuffling nervously when we review our end of year shows?

At one level, of course, this rapid and uncontrolled expansion of interiors courses could all be seen as a triumph of New Labour's 'access to HE' expansionism – that infamous target of 50 per cent. (But of course there is no national body of interiors education to receive Blair's congratulations, nor is there any national monitoring of this expansion's impact on the student experience.)

Universities may monitor teaching practice and check curricula relevance by counting bums on seats, checking retention rates and employment records; but is this really all we need to do to ensure maintenance of standards? Do any of us believe those employment returns – particularly when in so many cases they simply ask is the student 'in employment'… in Debenhams? Are we silently complicit in the erosion of what used to be a much-respected design degree culture in the UK?

Are we on the edge of making our educational output a laughing stock of mediocrity? There are rumblings in the undergrowth that suggest we might be.

In the practice of interiors, a sizeable section of output is wedded to conspicuous consumption, the boundaries of who practices it are utterly indefinable, and the public is conveniently – but seemingly happily – confused. Is an utter laissez-faire education ethos simply an inevitable extension of this situation? Does this matter to the students, their practitioner–employers, clients and the public? Do we all thrive on complete deregulation? Do students benefit from the smokescreen of imprecision?

More importantly, do other cultures with a more regulated professional environment for interiors secure higher-quality outcomes and, if so, should we follow suit?

Just at the moment when RIBA, under pressure from SCHOSA (The Standing Conference of Heads of Schools of Architecture), is potentially decoupling the monitoring of architectural 'graduate' studies from its supervisory procedures, and in turn tightening the final entry gate and focusing any curriculum definition and examination criteria on postgraduate courses, interiors education is potentially a laughing stock of deregulated anarchy or a joyful free for all (depending on your perspective). This is all just at the moment when EU regulatory fever is on the horizon for interiors. (Conveniently some might note that the UK, Portugal and Denmark are the only three European countries not signed up to the European Council of Interior Architects (ECIA) [11].) Shouldn't we get our own house in order before it is done for us, and in the wrong way? And if we do, who would be best constituency to do it, and what mechanisms would be the most creative?

Some will hesitate about this. They should reflect on the fact that, once graduate architecture is decoupled from any institutional supervision by RIBA, there may be a surging proliferation in BA Architecture (Interiors) courses – whereas, for the moment, the University of Westminster offers the only one. The very thin icing on the cake will disappear dramatically.

The German BDIA (Bundes Deutsche InnenArchitekten) could be seen as the polar opposite interiors culture of our own in the UK. There is a highly active professional body (in contrast to CSD interiors) and firm regulatory educational frameworks – even a regulation which limits the floor area of a project which an interior architect can legally handle on their own, without legal oversight by a qualified and registered architect. (How very Germanic I hear you groan.)

Interior architecture at UWIC has had a ten-year student exchange with the interior architecture course in the Mainz Facchocschule. Through questionnaires and interviews with former students from Mainz and their teacher–practitioners, it becomes clear that a very heavily regulatory environment in every aspect of the building industry – and their increasing binding of the BDIA into a European framework – does mean that students coming into the UK educational environment find its studio-centred teaching attractive and a spur to their design skills, when contrasted with their lecture-dominated curriculum in Germany. But equally, they are disturbed by what they see as a somewhat unprofessional environment in terms of a serious engagement with the technical complexities of the discipline, and also the proper protection of competence. It should also be noted that they come as part of a four/five year course, entering the second year at UWIC when they are actually either third or fourth year students. So they hugely thrive, having such a solid foundation of knowledge [12].

It is curious but not surprising that the lightly ringing alarm bells in the UK interiors environment are coming from educationalists and a few concerned teacher–practitioners. There is as yet no detectable outrage about competence from clients, but anyway who would they turn to, to complain? There is no formal body. Maybe the revolt from students and parents is temporarily restrained because there is no YouTube-style web space yet for them to cross-correlate their experiences on the ground. It will come.

If some of what I have set out above does strike a chord, then is it better that it is acted on by those on the ground, conducting the teaching? I would suggest so. There has been a call for a loosely creative monitoring body for the UK run by educationalists. This was the proposal of the recent forum of educationalists that met in interiors in Manchester (now named IE) [13] which is in turn based on observations of the IDEA initiative (Interior Design Educators Association) in Australia and New Zealand.

This book and the conference that preceded it, in their clear attempt to raise the intellectual temperature within the discipline, are also another signal that the smoke screen of the free-for-all in interior education UK is in need of treatment. There are also several texts in production and recently published which will hopefully push the intellectual thermostat up a notch or two. This of course flies in the face of the general intellectual dumbing down, as Wikipedia becomes a mass substitute for a proper reading of a substantial book.

For some, the necessity of national examinatory, regulatory, frameworks and mechanisms with gateways, professional practice exams and CPD, are tempting protection methods for interiors clients and students. However, at this juncture, we might all be better served in our history of interiors education by a rigorous and robust ongoing debate through exhibitions, online journals, books, one-off talk events, and conferences, organised through such a body as IE.

I would also personally be seeking, through IE, a national panel of course validators for UK universities to call upon, and a mechanism for external examiners to keep in close touch with each other through IE on shared issues of concern. A national panel of external examiners (hopefully mostly teacher–practitioners) run by IE would also be helpful in creating some sense of a shared raising, or at least protection, of standards. The body should also be responsible for producing literature and websites that accurately give students and parents useful, fair and concise advice about the boundaries of our discipline and where it is best practised. There should be a web-space for students to cross relate their experiences. Maybe even external examiners reports would be available nationally. The body would be there to protect the undermining of the discipline by those with a purely philistine pecuniary agenda in universities. It would start to tackle the moribund formulaic processes of Craft Design and Technology (CDT) teaching that have such an iron grip on our schools curricula. It would remonstrate with Professor Christopher Frayling for allowing interiors at the RCA to evaporate. It already has done.

We have seen a steady remorseless attempt by UK governments, since the early years of Thatcher, to enforce business culture and the competitive market as the dominant mode of thinking on university education. The competitive free-for-all that should supposedly send the weak to the wall and protect and reward the highly competent, so that 'consumers' (students) can make informed choices, might work creatively – providing that students could gain real comparative information and have the discernment, based on decent accurate feedback from former students, as to which courses could accountably be said to be delivering what they said on the tin. But expecting this to occur with no structure in place to collate and disseminate it is pie in the sky. A regulated irregularity is necessary.

References

[1] The UCAS website is www.ucas.ac.uk. Given that a recent fashion is for an interiors team in a university to join a language or, for example, property development to an interiors BA, it is difficult without an awful lot of extra research to ascertain what size of cohort are within each of these components. So I have tended to count only one BA per educational institution.

[2] *Facing the Future: a Report on Advanced Courses in Architecture of Higher Education in Great Britain.* 'The Group' chaired by Lord Esher, London, 1984.

[3] For information on Oceania go to www.idea-edu.com. For Finland go to www.lamk.fi. See [5] and [6] below for further national organisations.

[4] For information on interiors in the USA go to www.ncidq.org.

[5] For information on the Netherlands, see www.bni.nl. Also, contact Ingeborg Holtman at Stichting Bureau Architectenregister, Nassauplein 24, 2585 EC Den Haag, Netherlands. 070 3467020. e-mail: info@architectenregister.nl.

[6] For information on France go to www.fnsia.org or write to FNSAI, 14 rue Fontaine, 75009 Paris, France. e-mail: info@fnsai.org. Also look for Conseil Francais des Architectes d'Interieures (CFAI) 5 rue Saint Anastase, 75003, Paris, France. 01 40 27 91 24. e-mail: cfia@wanadoo.fr.

[7] Information on the Association for the recognition of Studies in Architecture and Planning (ASAP), in English, from Elke Kaiser at the BDIA Kaiser@bdia.de.

[8] November 1991 conference under auspices of AIDDC (Association of Interior Design Degree Courses) 'What is Interior Architecture?' at the Mall Gallery, London. Fred Scott and many others spoke out strongly for the retention of the 'Interior Design' title and more critically not to become involved in the RIBA educational regulation system.

[9] Information supplied from Erich Weiler, international liaison officer on the interior architecture course at the Facchoccschule Mainz, Germany.

[10] Letters have gone from IE (Interiors Education) to Frayling; and from various practitioners (Fred Scott, Ben Kelly, Julian Powell Tuck, Dinah Casson, Lumsdens etc.). The RCA claim nothing has changed, simply the title. IE has argued for a distinct course in interiors not one absorbed into architecture.

[11] For information on the European Council of Interior Architects (ECIA), see www.ecia.net.

[12] Interviews and questionnaires have been conducted with eight former Erasmus students who attended the interior architecture course at Cardiff.

[13] Interiors Education (IE) formed in November 2006 out of the former AIDDC. It held its first meeting at Manchester under the chairperson Graeme Brooker. The second is Wednesday 28 February 2007 in Glasgow.

Lois WEINTHAL

Parsons, The New School for Design,
New York City

TOWARDS A NEW INTERIOR

Introduction

Interior spaces can be found at a range of scales, from the clothing we wear to the city we inhabit. Between these two scales is an array of layers that can be pulled apart and further investigated, often revealing an identity with which we surround ourselves. Adolf Loos believed in *Gesamtkunstwerk* (total work of art); Le Corbusier, the *objet-type* (typical object). Both recognized that parts contribute to a complete whole. Their perspective informs design at every scale, whether it be that of clothing, furniture, architecture or details and colours. If we were to take inventory of the objects we use everyday, we would find that multiple design disciplines have played a role in their design and production. From clothing to the closet to the concept of domesticity, interior design can be seen as the stage set on which we act out our lives as we move fluidly between these layers. At the larger scale, we can also look to related disciplines of film, fiction, photography, art and politics that similarly address and rely upon interior spaces in order for their works to become realized. Focusing on these layers in an interdisciplinary light addresses a discourse on interiors that does not isolate itself from its surroundings, but rather references them in order to understand how one affects the other.

The discipline of interior design has separated itself from architecture, but it still remains secondary. It has yet to pick up the pieces that define a discipline that is not insular, one that places itself in the same scope of criticism that references history, representation, fabrication, theory and the interdisciplinary. The following sections investigate the layers that constitute interior, from body to city, both conceptually and pragmatically, in order to contribute to the under-represented topic of theory in interior design. Unlike architectural theory, which seeks to harness other disciplines and translate them into architecture's language, this proposal for a theory of interior design seeks to investigate related disciplines as a way to better understand the ways in which interior design can learn from them and expand its scope. References are made to critical writings that act as a base for furthering the dialogue in order to broaden the lens of interior design.

The interior realm is rich with phenomena, poetry, life and order – order in two senses, one being that by which we experience phenomena, and the other being that of tectonics supplying the rules and systems by which we physically construct spaces based upon conventions [1]. These two principles, the phenomenal and the physical, rely upon one another as the phenomenal is the senses responding to the physical components of the world. The phenomenal is also associated with being ungrounded and temporary, and is therefore viewed as subjective. In contrast, the physical is associated with being grounded, permanent and therefore objective. Art and science are often thought to represent these two camps. In the search for a theory of interior, the desire is to keep one foot grounded in conventions and tectonics required to construct the interior space, while having another foot grounded in the phenomenal.

These two camps stem from Christian Norberg-Schulz's essay 'The Phenomenon of Place', where he attaches the words 'character', 'atmosphere' and 'identification' to understanding the essence of a place. To expand his point, he uses a poem by Georg Trakl that describes a house in a winter setting located in a forest. Within the house is a dinner awaiting its recipient. Wine and bread, amongst other savouries for the feast, are laid out on the table. A flicker of light is revealed to the exterior as the guest approaching the house hears the tolling of bells in the distance on the cold winter night. We can decipher those elements that are nameable, but they gain their character by determining '*how* things are' [2]. This transition between spaces that reveals more than their physical attributes but contain character is what Norberg-Schulz defines as having atmosphere and essence. Character is what gives identity, not only to our immediate self, but to the things that surround us. The following sections focus on character and essence in related disciplines that address various layers related to interior while grounding them back into the tectonics.

Unravelling the first threads: body and clothing

How the body occupies the interior can be found in historical and contemporary representations. In an essay titled 'Body Troubles' by Robert McAnulty, the body is explored under a number of themes. The iconic Renaissance image of Leonardo da Vinci's Vitruvian man acts as a starting point for representing man's centrality as inscribed proportionally within the circle and square. With evolving socio-economic classes, codes developed by society become the norm with an example seen through the behaviour of soldiers as representative of mass identity and through literature as seen in Franz Kafka's 'The Penal Colony', amplifying the extremities by which codes are scribed onto the body [3]. McAnulty leads us to contemporary examples of anthropomorphism in architecture and objects through the works of John Hejduk and Diller & Scofidio. Hejduk's animated characters are seen as a hybrid of body and architecture, whereby the body is allowed to scribe its own animations on architecture, in turn, acting as a mirror of ourselves. The body's ability to see, reach and move is scribed onto architecture, thereby inventing an architecture that exists somewhere between body and building, no longer one or the other, but now contained in the realm of object. 'Hejduk's work renovates the body and in doing so, it renovates architecture.' [4] Taken further, the works of Diller & Scofidio address the body both through analogue and digital technologies:

> Diller and Scofidio's projects do not attempt to replace the Vitruvian figure with another figure. …by confining their focus to a limited number of peculiar spatial relationships, Diller and Scofidio shift attention from the figural presence of the body acting within a world of objects, to the conditions under which the body comes to embody certain social definitions [5].

Diller & Scofidio's works address the social realms within our constructed spaces, making architecture secondary to the role of social norms, which are then played out on the interior. This by-product, the social norms–body dichotomy, is the palette by which they shape architecture, but an architecture that is closer to the body, between clothing and room.

One can find the iconic forms of Le Corbusier's 'typical object' in the works of Hejduk and Diller & Scofidio, used as a base upon which to make a start. In doing so, conventions, such as those found in the interior are allowed to deviate from their origins in order to apply new concepts. As architecture has its iconic forms, so clothing and photography also rely upon iconic foundations within their disciplines. The word 'coat' brings to mind what most people would see as a collar, buttons down the front, perhaps a dark colour such as grey. It is a coat that ties Wim Wenders, the German filmmaker, and Yojhi Yamamoto, the Japanese clothing designer, together in a documentary titled *Notebook on Clothes and Cities*. Wenders agrees to film this documentary for the Pompidou Centre once he tries on a coat by Yamamoto, which makes him recollect memories of a similar coat owned by his father. The ability for the coat to transcend time and fashion is similar to Le Corbusier's acknowledgement of the typical object, bridging the notion of recognizable objects for their utility and conforming aesthetics from mass-production. Wenders remarks: 'We spoke of craftsmanship and of a craftsman's morals: to build the true chair, to design the true shirt, in short, to find the essence of a thing in the process of fabricating it.' [6] To recognize the 'essence of a thing' is what can be shared amongst different disciplines.

Within this concept rises the issue of nostalgia. Although Yamamoto's designs are of the present, he refers to the past through images by the photographer August Sanders, from his book *Menschen des 20. Jahrhunderts (Citizens of the twentieth century: portrait photographs)*. These images are used as references for synthesizing the person in the photograph, their expression, and what can be gathered about who they are and what they do in life based upon the clothing they wear. Yamamoto looks at the photographs as Sanders intended, as a documentary of citizens. Simultaneously, Wenders is questioning the role of nostalgia as he uses a new digital camera rather than his film camera. He searches for the links between the two as they similarly capture images with different outcomes. Although film and fashion are different disciplines, we see Yamamoto and Wenders sharing common questions about design and their representation. This sets an example of an interdisciplinary dialogue that includes questions about technology, representation and nostalgia among different disciplines. Interiors, in particular, often succumb to nostalgia through historic styles as clients yearn for a fashion of a previous era, which they never experienced. What is it that makes one long for a style from an era long past? Is there safety in residing in a familiar style even though it wasn't part of one's own past? How is identity affected by nostalgia? Could it be this stagnant position that keeps the discipline of interiors from furthering itself in other directions?

In the search for embedding essence into the layers we inhabit, the word 'essence' is often excluded in the discipline of interior and tends to default to architectural theory.

Gender and the domestic interior

Fiction allows for a story to be made vivid through the description of a setting. The nineteenth century early feminist writer Charlotte Perkins Gilman relies upon the setting of an interior to provide not only a visual location in which to situate characters, but assigns the interior itself a role just as significant as that of the characters. Transforming the pattern in wallpaper, Gilman's short story 'The Yellow Wallpaper' uses the latent element of wallpaper to convey issues surrounding the secondary role of women in society [7]. The characters, a young couple, are vacationing in a rented country house. Their first child having just been born, the vacation is meant to ease the main character's nerves after the stress of childbirth and depression. Medical treatment is prescribed by her husband and brother, both doctors, that includes assigning her a children's room in the attic, away from her family so as not to be disturbed, and for its lightness and cross breezes. In addition to this room, she is kept from her writing, seen as unnecessary by the men and only a deterrent to her healing, but which she sees as her treatment to recovery. She expresses her first impressions of the wallpaper, writing that 'I never saw a worse paper in my life. One of those sprawling, flamboyant patterns committing every artistic sin.' Soon after, she begins to assign human characteristics to the wallpaper. 'There is a recurrent spot where the pattern lolls like a broken neck and two bulbous eyes stare at you upside down.' [8]

We are made to waver back and forth between the character's healing and depression. We understand her capacity to make sensible decisions and her desire to write, whilst her husband and brother attempt to take this pleasure from her. She begins to understand that she has little more control over her life than the children who occupied the same room before her. As time passes, she begins to see the wallpaper as animated: 'I never saw so much expression in an inanimate thing before, and we all know how much expression they have! I used to lie awake as a child and get more entertainment and terror out of blank walls and plain furniture than most children could find in a toy store.' [9] As the character identifies with the wallpaper, she sees women trapped behind the pattern of the paper trying to escape, symbolic of her own situation.

Another world is set up between the interior of the room, the wallpaper, and what lies behind it. It is within this thin layer of the interior that the story develops. The setting of the room allows Gilman to build upon the tangible elements of the house in order for her character to reach a state of either enlightenment or madness or both.

Previously, the difference between genders and the need for privacy led to the emergence of the boudoir in eighteenth-century France [10]. Related to 'The Yellow Wallpaper', women and their desire for education would lead to the need for a private room assigning equality in programming the home in upper classes by providing the feminine boudoir and the masculine cabinet or library. These new room types appear within the shell of architecture, forcing the interior to reassemble itself in order to make room for the gender split. The boudoir was a place where wealthy women could retire for a variety of reasons. Partly, it was a place for her to retreat during her menstrual cycle; also, it was a place for her to read and be educated, which was preferably not to be seen publicly by men. As Ed Lilley writes in his essay on the boudoir, 'why did women in the eighteenth century develop the need of a room in which to sulk? Or maybe, why did men think that women needed such a space?' [11]

Parallel to 'The Yellow Wallpaper', the space of the boudoir is twofold: it is a place that allows men to believe that women remain secondary to them, whilst being used to a woman's advantage and giving them a private space to do as they wish in, whether nap or read.

Miniature and full-scale representations

Paintings from the seventeenth century Netherlands preserve the domestic interior, as in the works of Vermeer, whose use of light, perspective, colour and characters depicts a potent interior setting as if a narrative is being told. In addition to paintings depicting interior life, the Dutch sought models of their homes, similar to the ship models which their proximity to the sea made familiar. 'The Dutch affection for their homes was expressed in a singular practice: they had elaborate scale models built of their houses. These replicas are sometimes referred to as dollhouses… They were built like cupboards which did not represent the exterior appearance of the house.' [12] The ways in which interiors are represented finds conflict when it comes to the model, a tool most commonly used in architecture with success because of the abstractness by which the absence of detail is accepted. The role of the model in interior design has the potential to fall into the realm of the dollhouse because, without detail, it becomes an empty space. What is the model for interior design? Is it digital? If so, how is the loss of gravity through the weight of materials and objects still translated into the tangible weight of our everyday?

The physical, tangible, three-dimensional model, is often made of foam core, chipboard, basswood, or other materials depending upon the aesthetic of its builder. Although the small-scale model is not the thing itself that it is representing, we understand the translation of the projected outcome to the miniature model. A shift in scale takes place.

Details found at the final constructed scale are lost at the small scale, mostly due to the reduction in proportion of space that limits finer detail in the model's production. The interior is often represented with a few walls and columns in order to give an overall basic spatial understanding, but the shift from abstract to liveable is usually not undertaken, for fear of the model turning into a doll's house. Mark Wigley addresses this issue through James Casebere's photographs. The photographs act as a lens for Wigley to investigate the role of the model as a representation of a convincing space that requires little transition between the final image (a photograph) from the model and the ability to imagine oneself inside the model. Wigley writes: 'The unique atmosphere of these images is produced by the removal of detail. If each model begins as a realistic approximation of a building, details are progressively taken away until the critical sense of haunting suspension is approached. If the sensitive point is passed and the model looks too much like a model, something must be added.' [13] Casebere's photographs rely upon the conventions of architectural model making, but show a direction that opens up the potential for what the interior model could be. Although the final product is not the model itself, but the photograph of the miniature model, the photograph shows the interaction of light, colour, space and gravity. If the goal of the model is to show the onlooker the closest example of occupying a space, then perhaps the model for interiors is not that which latches onto examples in architecture, but one that learns from photography.

At the opposite scale from Casebere's work, Gordon Matta-Clark and Rachel Whiteread address domesticity, nostalgia and interior representations that one often finds at the scale of the model and drawing, but now realized at full scale.

Gordon Matta-Clark's cut sectional houses treat built construction as a further investigation of the drawing. The orthographic drawing is normally seen as a cut section or plan, and allows us a view never made possible by cutting through the conceptual picture plane in order to better understand the construction of architecture. Whilst the drawing often comes first and architecture follows, Matta-Clark reverses this, treating the already built as a drawing, making it seem effortless to cut through a house as one would simply cut through the section of a drawing. As a result, we see the lives that have already occupied the home, rather than the sterility preceding occupation found in the drawing. At one time, the Beaux-Arts tradition of rendering shade and shadow was seen as sufficient in the understanding of depth in the drawing. What Matta-Clark's cuts reveal is the true depth of space [14].

Whiteread's *House* project in the East End of London forms a dialogue with Matta-Clark's work, in the sense that we are allowed to see remnants of the lives that were part of the house, now seen on an exposed skin. Filling the interior of a row house with concrete and peeling away the existing exterior shell as formwork affords a view to inner details from the remains of wallpaper, paint and the crevices formed by the offset of windows and doors [15]. As we normally look at the outside of a house and see the exterior skin, the skin is now removed and we view the interior void as solid. Where brick once stood as the protective layer, our eyes now stand in that poché, trying to look through the solidity of what is normally a room filled with objects and transparent air. It is now solid, and we begin to understand the quietness and patience of brick. The layer of joists and beams separating the floors similarly gives us a view of the edge of the floor–ceiling relationship we never usually experience. This structural thickness is hidden between the finished surfaces we know as floor and ceiling.

The role of looking into the already occupied, lived space challenges the conventions by which designers work. We often seek to begin with a clean slate and then insert our ideas. But Matta-Clark and Whiteread remind us of the lives already lived, not just through the colour of the walls or leftover wallpaper, but in the sense that the wood with which the houses are constructed has been carrying the physical weight of the house and the lives of those within. Physical matter also contains memory. It makes us recall our own childhood, the rooms we called home, the smallest details such as the height of a table or the materiality of a chair. Our memories might even go so far as to envision family members that occupied these spaces and the conversations that took place. Nostalgia can be defined as longing for something past. This does not require the interior to transplant styles from another era, but to consider the ephemera of an interior in future years even before it has begun, to prescribe longevity to it.

Interiors on the exterior

The objects and furniture one places in an interior become a reflection not only of oneself, but of the political and economic regime under which one lives. A case study of East Germany under Soviet control after World War II reveals a direct link between domestic interior products and a larger political agenda. The need to reserve natural materials for heavy industry throughout the Soviet Bloc led to propaganda in support of plastics as the new material for the domestic interior. Plastics were seen as the answer to fabricating furniture, dishware, domestic electronics and interior finishes. Promoted as a surface that could be wiped clean, and therefore as more hygienic, plastics would rival wood, metals and ceramics throughout the domestic interior. Because the ideals of the Soviet Bloc were built upon the sharing of resources, the German Democratic Republic would become the leader in designing plastic products that were then transported throughout the rest of the Soviet Bloc, thereby contributing to homogeneous interiors, not much different than the current trend of IKEA furniture. Similarly, housing constructed after World War II throughout the Soviet Bloc relied upon pre-fabricated concrete panel systems assembled into housing blocks that can be found throughout Eastern Europe. Building efficiently and supplying housing with modern amenities such as indoor plumbing and radiant heating as opposed to coal ovens were seen as achievements in housing solutions at the time. With the goal of building enough apartments to accommodate population needs, the immediate public spaces were neglected [16].

Witold Rybczynski focuses on details found in a number of cities that engage us at a personal scale, reminding us of what is often overlooked in these public spaces. Using similar criteria for what makes a place have interiority at private and public scales, cities also rely upon scale in order to draw intimacy into the larger public realm. Details of the streetscape such as width of streets, heights of buildings, landscape and the overall scale and detail are what make exteriors similar to interiors. The loss of these characteristics or the changing of their proportion can also be found in globalization, contributing to the loss of character and essence of places.

Venice and New York are two cities on different scales; but the proportion of streets/canals to heights of buildings recalls the intimacy of an interior. Cobble stone streets transform into interior floors rather than exterior sidewalks because of the heightened presence from the sound of shoes striking the surface. The fact that these places are densely filled during the daytime reminds us of their public role; yet at night, the facades of buildings waver back and forth between stage sets and buildings, once the cacophony of people and transportation is silenced for the night. Streetlights and lighting from the interior of buildings mask the sky, transforming the city into a stage.

Conclusion

The city, known through its essence, character and identity, is what returns us back to the interior. The discipline of interiors should be responsible and take a position on these words, whether it accepts them or not. The point being that it is time for interiors to take a critical look at itself.

Through examples from various disciplines, shared terms, and the crossover of concepts, a direction can be forged in which interior design can re-position itself outside of its current shell. Issues of nostalgia and definition, along with the essence and tectonics of design as seen in related disciplines, open up the opportunity for interiors to learn, borrow and expand its scope. From the cloak of clothing to the cloak of wallpaper, interior design can fabricate a dialogue with these disciplines. Once realized, we can build a momentum towards a new interior.

References

[1] Norberg-Schulz, C. 'The Phenomenon of Place' in Nesbitt, K., ed. *Theorizing A New Agenda For Architecture: An Anthology of Architectural Theory 1965–1995* (New York: Princeton Architectural Press, 1996) pp.414–27.

[2] Ibid., p.418

[3] Kafka, F. 'The Penal Colony', *The Complete Stories* (New York: Schocken Books, 1983).

[4] McAnulty, R. 'Body Troubles' in Burdett, R., Kipnis, J. and Whiteman, J., eds. *Strategies in Architectural Thinking* (Cambridge, MA: MIT Press, 1992) pp.180–221.

[5] Ibid., p.193

[6] Wenders, W. 'Notebook on Clothes and Cities', *The Act of Seeing* (London: Faber and Faber, 1997) p.89.

[7] Lane, A.J. 'The Yellow Wallpaper' in *The Charlotte Perkins Gilman Reader* (The University Press of Virginia, 1999) pp.3–19.

[8] Ibid., p.7

[9]   Ibid.

[10] Lilley, E. 'The Name of the Boudoir', *The Journal of the Society of Architectural Historians*, June 1994, 53(2), pp.193–8.

[11] Ibid., p.195

[12] Rybczynski, W. *Home: A Short History of an Idea* (New York: Penguin Books, 1987) p.62.

[13] Wigley, M. 'Inside the Inside' in *The Architectural Unconscious: James Casebere + Glen Seator* (New York: Distributed Art Publishers, 2000) p.17.

[14] Diserens, C., ed. *Gordon Matta-Clark* (London: Phaidon Press Limited, 2003).

[15] Lingwood, J., ed. *House* (London: Phaidon Press Limited, 1995).

[16] Weinthal, L. 'Postcards from the German Democratic Republic', *Space and Culture: The International Journal of Social Spaces*, 2005, 8 (3), pp.325–31.

Acknowledgements

The author gratefully acknowledges the participation of students over the years in the seminar, 'Towards a New Interior', where the dialogue and ideas have contributed to the development of this essay.

Why do we do interior design?

Graeme BROOKER

Manchester Metropolitan University

Sally STONE

Manchester School of Architecture

FROM ORGANISATION TO DECORATION

Interior architecture, design and decoration is a growing intellectual discipline. As the subject has become more accessible and highly visible, so it has become more respectable – to the extent that it is now considered as a subject in its own right rather than an adjunct to architecture or an extension of decoration. The study of the discipline is often dogged with issues of decorative finishes and cut MDF. Interiors are frequently regarded as the forgotten elements within a much larger theoretical discussion, as the spaces left over and produced merely as a consequence of building an exterior. It has been regarded as a superficial practice that lacks a particular set of distinct design theories or principles. However, there are more than 100 interior design and interior architecture courses listed on the UCAS website in Britain, as well as the subject specialism within architecture. It is extraordinary that there is very little academic writing on the subject.

Interior architecture, interior design and building reuse are very closely linked subjects. In varying degrees, all of them deal with the transformation of a given space, whether it's the crumbling ruins of an ancient building or the drawn parameters of a building proposal. This alteration or conversion is a complex process of understanding the qualities of the given existing building while simultaneously combining these factors with the functional requirements of its new users. Traditionally this subject has been associated with interior design/decoration and has been seen as peripheral to the central subject of architecture. Recently, several large and high-profile projects designed by eminent practices have changed this perception of interior architecture.

Issues of sustainability have forced architects, who had predominantly shunned remodelling work, to appropriate it for themselves. The existing building is regarded as a legitimate target for high architectural practice. The reuse of existing buildings is a subject that is central to the evolution of the urban environment and issues of conservation and sustainability have become vital to the development of cities. As the manner in which the urban environment is viewed has changed, so the prevailing attitude towards building reuse has also altered.

The study of interiors is now seen by many as an independent intellectual subject, although it has yet to attract the sort of respect and attention that it deserves. This is slowly changing and it is apparent that the question of exactly how distinct the subject is, is being addressed and readdressed. One of the problems is that the actual practice of interior architecture and design is difficult to categorise, being positioned somewhere between architecture and decoration.

Interior design is a term that has traditionally been used to describe all types of interior projects. This would have included everything from decoration to remodelling. However, in view of the fact that building reuse has become such a highly regarded practice, it has clearly become necessary to divide the main subject and define more clearly its individual specialisms.

This would be a good point at which to clarify the precise nature of each area. The exact disciplines inevitably overlap but, by and large, the differences seem to concern the magnitude of change to the occupied space.

Interior decoration is the art of decorating interior spaces or rooms to impart a particular character that fits well with the existing architecture. Interior decoration is concerned with such issues as surface pattern, ornament, furniture, soft furnishings, lighting and materials. It generally deals only with minor structural changes to the existing building. Typical examples of this practice are the design of domestic, hotel and restaurant interiors.

Interior design is an interdisciplinary practice that is concerned with the creation of a range of interior environments that articulate identity and atmosphere, through the manipulation of spatial volume, placement of specific elements and furniture and treatment of surfaces. It generally describes projects that require little or no structural changes to the existing building, although there are many exceptions to this. The original space is very much retained in its original structural state and the new interior inserted within it. It often has an ephemeral quality and typically would encompass such projects as retail, exhibition, domestic and office interiors.

Interior architecture is concerned with the remodelling of existing buildings and attitudes towards existing spaces and structures, building reuse and organisational principles. It bridges the practices of interior design and architecture, often dealing with complex structural, environmental and servicing problems. This practice encompasses a huge range of project types from museums, galleries and other public buildings, through office and other commercial buildings to domestic developments.

It is obvious that the practice and study of interiors has breadth and depth, from the light touch of decoration through to the forceful restructuring of an existing building. Working with existing buildings is viable and economically sustainable; and this

Figure 1: Glenlyon Church, Victoria, Australia. Multiplicity, 2004. The new elements of the house sit within the confines of the original building.

has allowed interior architecture to move into the domain of the architect, who now regards it as legitimate and viable practice. However, their approach is often neither discriminating nor sensitive. It is not a subject that is regularly discussed in schools of architecture and, more importantly, this lack of dedicated theory has often led to mediocre projects based upon miscalculated whimsy.

Figure 2: Küppersmühle Museum, Duisburg, Germany. Herzog and de Meuron, 1999. Glazed strips interrupt the rhythm of the original façade.

Perhaps we can look back to understand why this situation has come about.

At the beginning of the twentieth century, Modernism and the pursuit of the new meant that the existing building stock was regarded as having little worth; important and fabulous buildings were demolished with what we now regard as misplaced and fanatical zeal. Reuse was not considered as a significant or even respectable activity and architectural practices were unwilling to become engaged with this type of work. The predominant attitude was one of dismissal and discrimination – although of course, the practice of remodelling and reuse has been commonplace ever since the first buildings were constructed.

The Athens Charter of 1931 generally recommended that restoration work should respect the existing building, regardless of the style or period, and that any alterations or additions should be clearly differentiated from the original. They recommended that the evidence of preservation should be clearly obvious. This was drawn up with the best of intentions, to preserve history, while not confusing or compromising it, and emphasised the importance of conservation rather than restoration.

This charter was drawn up in reaction to the then-fashionable procedure of either restoring the monument to its original condition, thus removing any evidence of history or time, or 'updating' the building; that is, restoring or remodelling it in the style of the period. The signatories of the Athens Charter rejected historical pastiche, and insisted upon the importance of interventions within historical areas being made in a modern architectural language.

The problem with this approach is that it led to uncompromisingly modern structures being constructed, often overpowering and diminishing the original building. Carlo Scarpa was really the forerunner of an approach that rejected the Athens Charter and advanced a method based upon a sympathetic understanding of the existing building. His approach was to take all the cues for the remodelling from the existing building, with particular attention to scale, light, form and movement, so his design approach was part archaeology, part analysis and part new construction. This is an approach that is not just restricted to remodelling existing buildings. Colin Rowe and Fred Koetter, who are amongst the most influential postmodern urban theorists, advocated a process of Contextualism within urban design in their seminal book *Collage City*.

This process, with an emphasis upon urban texture, integration and sympathetic renewal has gradually become more prevalent and can be seen in such contemporary works as Herzog and de Meuron's Tate Modern, the Scottish Poetry Library by Malcolm Fraser Architects and even the quite extreme design for The Brasserie in the basement of the Seagram Building in New York by Diller and Scofidio.

Today, remodelling represents a sizeable market that cannot be ignored. The evidence of big-name architectural firms involved in reworking buildings is testimony to the fact that it is a sector of design and architecture that is no longer seen as insignificant. It is important to establish the principles of working with the existing in order to define this field of practice, to demonstrate that this area of work is rich in creative inspiration and packed with some of the best design work of recent years.

It is apparent that although issues such as gender, philosophy and other architectural theories have influenced the practice of interior architecture, the most significant ideas do appear to derive from two distinct areas: urban theory and installation art.

The practice and philosophy of Contextualism is more than a generation old; Carlo Scarpa's Castelvecchio was completed by 1964 and *Collage City* was published in 1976, but the principles that it extols are regarded now, as ever more relevant. There has been a massive change in our attitude towards the existing, from the urban concerns of the city, through the regard for the individual building, to the qualities of distinct spaces and finishes. This approach towards regeneration has as much to do with the change in political attitude as with the revolution in the manner in which we occupy space.

The other significant influence upon interior architecture and design is installation art, especially by such artists as Marcel Duchamp, Robert Irwin, Gordon Matta-Clarke and Rachel Whiteread. Within their work these artists strive to activate a place. Using a process of investigation and recognition, they utilise the properties of the existing to stimulate and provoke a transformation or translation.

The artists believe that a clear analysis of an area can reveal its true consequence or worth. This analysis can be conducted in many different ways, but will reveal certain clues or pointers to the manner in which the space can be changed. Robert Irwin in his essay 'Being and Circumstance: Notes Towards a Conditional Art', described this approach as site conditioned/determined:

> Here the sculptural response draws all of its cues (reasons for being) from its surroundings. This requires the process to begin with an intimate, hands on reading of the site [1].

The installation or intervention made by the installation artist has the advantage of not having to manage such considerations as user, function, accessibility and servicing. This gives the piece a sort of purity; the response is simply towards the space and the revelation or translation of that space. The artist will often apparently do little more than reveal what is already there; but what already exists is only apparent when it can be seen, when the individual parts can be distinguished and an appreciation of how they contribute to the whole is made. This perception and visualisation of their relationships with each other, and their individual strengths, allows the imagination to comprehend the complex connections and associations and to make sense of the meaning of the place. If the solution is to discover what currently exists, to enhance, justify, interpret or adapt what is already present, then surely the desire is to see, to experience and to uncover that presence. Or perhaps as the influential artist Robert Irwin explained, 'There is no there there until you see there there' [2].

It is this liberation of not having to consider these service functions that allows the creator of the intervention the freedom of interpretation not always available to the architect or designer. And yet, the attitude espoused by the artist is highly relevant to the practice of building reuse. Sebastien Marot, in his Manifesto for Sub-urbanism, speaks of '[r]edirecting emphasis from programme to site'. That is, rather than letting the use of the new building dictate the building process or razing everything on a site and starting again, allowing the new to be generated by the old.

It is the lack of clarity that characterizes the familiar, something that is so well known that we can no longer acknowledge its independent existence. We take for granted certain aspects of our day-to-day existence and perhaps only when these artefacts, statements, images, events, things are highlighted do they once again become apparent. Maybe by mentally removing an element from its given context we can see and emphasise its individual qualities.

By combining the theories of contextualism with those from the installation artist it is apparent that a collection of writings that is highly relevant to interior architecture and design can be compiled; that is, theories dealing specifically with the existing and with particular spaces and situations. This connection is obviously not an original concept but these ideas have not been emphasised or given sufficient credence in interior architecture and design theory. They are the ideas that make these practices distinct from architecture. There are definitely a small number of important publications that convincingly discuss in an intelligent and cohesive manner the basic philosophy of the subject, but these are few and far between.

One of the most important was published some 30 years ago in 1976; Rodolfo Machado uses the palimpsest, or 'writing over', as a metaphor for building reuse. When the text of the manuscript has been scraped off and the canvas or parchment used again, inevitably a trace of the original text remains, a shadow that haunts and influences the author of the succeeding inscription. And so with buildings: they are remodelled, reused, rethought and yet a suggestion of the former meaning disturbs and inspires the subsequent design. It is this search for that meaning that is the basis of the analytical chapter. As Rodolfo Machado describes it:

> Remodelling is a process of providing a balance between the past and the future. In the process of remodelling the past takes on a greater significance because it, itself, is the material to be altered and reshaped. The past provides the already written, the marked 'canvas' on which each successive remodelling will find its own place. Thus the past becomes a 'package of sense', of built up meaning to be accepted (maintained), transformed or suppressed (refused) [3].

Some other significant examples are: *Sub-urbanism and the Art of Memory* by Sebastien Marot; *Collage City* by Colin Rowe and Fred Koetter; 'From Contrast to Analogy' by Ignasi de Sola-Morales; *Adaptations* by Philippe Robert; and *Being and Circumstance: Notes Towards a Conditional Art* by Robert Irwin. Obviously, there are others that have been missed from this list, but in comparison with writings on art and on architecture it's a fairly paltry yet significant collection.

This chapter argues that the way forward for interior architecture is a method based upon process rather than function. An approach based upon a perceptive and discriminating reading of the existing can produce both dynamic and appropriate results. The discovery and recognition of the embodied meaning of a place can be interpreted through building. The designer or architect has the opportunity to reflect

Figure 3: Archbishopric Museum, Hamar, Norway. Sverre Fehn, 1979. The brutal walkway is suspended over the archaeological remains.

upon the contingency, usefulness and emotional resonance of particular places and structures through the reuse of existing buildings.

> The most successful building reuse projects are produced when a firm understanding of the original building is combined with a sympathetic remodelling. The existing context, structures, spaces, function and history can offer many significant conceptual opportunities and an appreciation and interpretation of these can provide the inspiration for the redesign. The uncovering of the meaning in the precondition of the building determines the rules or strategies for the subsequent redesign [4].

It is through the understanding of the pre-existing that the remodelled building can become endowed with a new and greater meaning. An investigation of the archaeology of the original can reveal previously hidden or obsolete characteristics that contain the possibility of being exploited. The place can be activated.

References

[1]   Irwin, R. 'Being and Circumstance, Notes Towards a Conditional Art' in Kristine Stiles and Peter Sels, eds. *Theories and Documents of Contemporary Art* (Berkeley: University of California Press, 1996).
[2]   Ibid.
[3]   Machado, R. 'Old Buildings as Palimpsest', *Progressive Architecture*, Nov. 1976, pp.46–9.
[4]   Brooker, G. and Stone, S. *Rereadings* (London: RIBA Publications, 2004).

Gini LEE

University of South Australia

CURATORIAL THINKING: PERFORMANCE SPACE AND THE INTERIOR

Introduction

The theory and practice of interiors is normally predicated upon the assumption that some type of physical design intervention is the generator of the spatial and material qualities of enclosed places. The following investigations into curatorial approaches to (re)making responsive interiors suggest alternative postproduction methods that enable interiors to be conceptualised and realised by ecological and cultural parameters. This design research seeks to transform familiar practice through approaches borrowed and appropriated from other disciplines and sensibilities. To achieve this, the postproduction method aims to demonstrate how the material and ephemeral world is noticed and acted upon when mediated by the reactions to/outcomes of a more performative and ephemeral approach to design intervention. The intention is to move beyond the structures inferred by normative architectural and master planning regimes through uncovering and making explicit, material and ephemeral conditions informed by speculative travelling, peripatetic drifting, dispassionate observation and chance association. The upshot of this may be the production of outcomes such as storytelling, archiving, experimental itineraries, collaborative interventions and exchange events where multiple readings of seemingly familiar concepts enable alternative practices to evolve.

One pertinent concept inquires into what ecological practice offers to design methodologies concerned with postproduction. Stengers describes ecologies of practice as a new political ecology beyond individual concerns, where 'landscapes for thinking and feeling' are the mobile grounds for emerging collective events and collaborative relationships [1]. The challenge is to facilitate forming relationships across boundaries through an ecological approach that recognises the instability of border conditions and works around, and with, the consequences. An ecological approach may be informed through the concepts around the nature of curation. Rugoff, writing on the Museum of Jurassic Technology in Los Angeles explains:

> the word curator derives from the Latin to 'care for', and here (in the museum) caretaking extends not simply to objects, but to our relationship with the past, particularly those portions that have been overlooked, dismissed, forgotten or destroyed. Here a home is provided for the marginal artefact, for things not usually prized or deemed worthy of serious display [2].

Tracing postproduction

The technical term, *postproduction* [3] has been related to practices that (re)work forms that have already been produced to (re)make and (re)configure such works into something else. 'The... question is no longer: "what can we make that is new?" but "how can we make do with what we have?"' [4] Postproduction practices are essentially about recycling existing material into new material to produce the new through adoption and transformation of the existing. Much material is already available for manipulation and (re)presentation if existing forms and objects are acted upon and in a design sense, curated, to enable producing different results. An examination of postproduction practices suggests a range of tactics that prove useful for both design and curatorial interventions. A brief selection of these, below, emerge as useful methods in postproduced works. *Appropriation* of the everyday object and those other forms that are readily available for review and reuse moves beyond fabrication to involve selection and modification of that which exists for insertion into a new scenario. *Between fiction and fact* produces different storylines and alternative narratives to (re)invent the present through decoding existing scenarios and to imply the creation of new ones. *Mise-en-scene* in the physical environment, its actors and scenery in which an event takes place is remade, and uses re-*articulated* forms re-*placed* in relation to one another. *Montage* (the succession of images) involves pictorial work composed by assembling, overlaying, and overlapping many different materials or media collected from different sources, or a sequence consisting of a series of dissolves, superimpositions or cuts to condense time or to suggest memories. And lastly, *Superimposition* of real time and *mise-en-scene* to produce potential scenarios that allow substitution of the real inserted into fictional narratives. This method generates potential projects that may derive from the finished or unfinished state of the forms, incompletion through abandoned jobs and unfinished objects, and/or the repositioning of the audience from passive to active participants [5].

In summary, the two essential attributes of a practice that is concerned with the ethics and aesthetics of postproduction involve firstly the *transforming* of familiar, often mass-produced or discarded, unused objects as devices that contribute to new scenarios and the development of new strategies for intervention into everyday spaces and landscapes. The second lies in the *participation* of passive viewers and consumers in active collaborations, undertaken in familiar yet altered situations and discourses, towards the creation of new communities, albeit ones that may exist only temporarily.

On museums and gardens

Museums and gardens are places where collection, design and curatorial practices implicitly coincide and where examinations into collection and curation practices that exist outside, or on the boundaries of, what is understood as museum space can be fruitfully located. A curatorial approach to making interiors uncovers the discourses of 'new' museology and suggests pertinent attitudes to collecting and archiving materials beyond classification and the repository of 'valuable' objects. What differentiates the 'new' museology from the 'old' is the idea that a museum installation is a discourse [6]. What differentiates traditional gardens from most interiors is that gardens have always acted as sites of discourse; either physically shaped by them, or as generators of new debates, through a compositional attitude to space and artefact intended to convey abstract narratives. For design, examining the works of collectors/curators who manage ephemeral material, and house it in discursive space that is appropriated from some other/original use, assists operations in the margins between conventional and experimental practices, that may be museological or may be 'gardening'.

Museums conceived through an ephemeral conceptual framing exist as sites of coincidence and of postproduction, between the space of the everyday here and now, and of the performative space of theatre. In his fourth principle of heterotopia, Foucault writes that museums operate within a temporal multiplicity because they endlessly accumulate, yet ultimately enclose, conceptually and spatially. He also contends in his third principle that the garden is a heterotopia of superimposition where incompatible space and locality are juxtaposed and where, therefore, distinctions of otherness collapse [7]. The adoption of Foucault's definitions inextricably links the museum and the garden as places that exhibit thematic, yet often incompatible collections, framed through spatial itineraries that unfold over time.

Established design practices operating in museum (and garden) spaces which are framed by strategic mechanisms that project predetermined outcomes, express the desire to plan and fix, to protect and conserve, and to overly explicate underlying narratives. Such predetermination inhibits participation and exploration and fails to notice the subtle and enduring qualities of places. A curatorial approach seeks engagement in the realm of subtle movements in space, time and in what causes things to emerge; this approach counteracts presumptions of obvious alteration to existing physical fabric as outcomes.

The performed interior in two ways

A review of the collection and the auteurial/curatorial founding of the Museum of Jurassic Technology (MJT) through making wandering journeys around the collection, then enables applying this method to a journey around a space that could be, but isn't generally, regarded as museum space; the abandoned Tack Shed on an outback pastoral station in South Australia. The MJT is a museum of postproduction; the Tack Shed is postproduced curatorially.

David Wilson, the MJT's curator/director has employed spatial tactics to make unreliable museum space, reinforced curatorially, in the discursive selection of materials that he judges collectible and displayable. Yet in the MJT its defining quality is the manner/ method in which it invites others in – to experiment, exchange and intervene with the existing physical and cultural fabric, in a very open-ended and generous way. It also exhibits the qualities of both the 'old' and the 'new' museology, and in so doing transcends such dialectical concerns through adopting an interstitial museology, a curatorial perspective where artefacts and discourses coincide; consequently the audience is encouraged to imagine and move beyond what is in front of them.

Conceptually, the collection is elemental to postproduction practice, and it is also a hedge against forgetting. Introducing speculative work done at the MJT, Morton writes 'collecting is inherently a culture of fragments, a sticking together of material bits that stand as metonyms and metaphors for the world they may refer to but are not.' [8] From the collection, the material and data from which new works and new interactions are produced are drawn. The collection is a go-between, between the visible in objects and the invisible world of meaning; it also allows recall of things present and absent [9]. Wilson collaborates with his borrowed and donated collections, and his friends, to make new exhibits, while at the same time collaborating with his motley collection of buildings as he shapes them into a labyrinth of passages and dead ends in a journey through an idea of the Jurassic. The MJT is universally regarded as a 'high' museum where the connoisseur has arranged his collection, yet this place has a touch of the 'low' about it; a quality that adds to its curiosity value for tourists and also allows room for other(s)' interventions. Simultaneously immersed in factual and fictional realms, the tourist is asked to expand their imagining of what is going on. And to do this you must tour through labyrinthine space, to backtrack spatially and visually, to become lost, and never to take the same path and draw the same conclusions.

The MJT is an interior of narrative montage, where taking a wandering tour following a successive path sees each display unfold an intriguing theme and a narrative explained through text, image, sound recording and an object-based tableau. Within these seemingly informative assemblages, sensations of spatial and narrative disassociation occur. Pools of light draw the visitor into webs of ideas conveyed through objects arranged in vitrines or ordered as in a stage set; each one a distinct display, but juxtaposed as a cabinet of curiosity, where one's searches for the factual are confounded at every turn. Visitors and writers who have attempted to substantiate the veracity of the collections have been confounded by half-truths and dead ends. Rugoff says that the MJT isn't what it says it is, or, at least, is an unreliable narrator where fact and fiction collide and the curator makes 'use of information that lies on the edges of our cultural literacy'. [10] This reflective thinking is what the MJT asks of its visitors through presenting with great seriousness and theatricality, information and artefacts that lay no claims to greatness or fame. The MJT embraces exhibition materials as the site for metaphor and superimposition in both narrative and in spatial forms. In making each *mise-en-scene*, it leads us into a theatrescape between reality and metaphor, where the boundaries between the two are dissolved.

It is a challenge to convey the multiple itineraries explored in the MJT as tours that can be re-presented to capture experiences; so to suggest possible tours through museum spaces that could take three hours or three days and that post-curate the already curated. Through appropriating a method from Sir John Soane, I experiment in making an itinerary for the MJT. Soane wrote his *Crude Hints* as a series of writings and annotations on an imagined history of his house [11]. His graphic method is one that represents spatial thinking in a narrative form and suggests a performative movement around his future dreams for the house-museum. This method of layering many collected parts together in chance juxtaposition reveals a collector's and curator's ethic of the accumulator and subsequent re-arranger to see what comes up; a practice antithetical to design training where strategies based upon systematic analysis of describable data are the underlying security for master planning and constructing interventions. The fragment below of my 'Raw Hints for the MJT' draws upon noticing that what exists is in constant transition and is influenced by future curatorial aspirations. These 'Raw Hints' could expand indefinitely, each time they are read and overwritten.

museums include Noah's Ark
and the Alexandria museum
arranged according to
scientific tradition
relics and curiosities
surface, texture, alcove,
moulding, wood,
darkness

*that morning in the tack
Shed
when the sun warmed,
cracking, clicking
birdsong

flute, eastern,
music/curtain/images
projected as floating

Here, an ecology of practice encompasses both the space and the material of a postproduction practice, through operations that embrace making do with what is offered. Inclusive attitudes to reprogramming museum spaces as zones of activity enable space, artefact and curatorial collaborations, in turn to be (re)interpreted through diverse itineraries. The MJT is imagined as a paradoxical theatrescape where paradox refers to a situation that seems to be absurd or contradictory, but in fact is or may be true; theatrescape infers a metaphorical intent towards spatial design populated by compositions of representational objects. The *mise-en-scenes* produced demand the attention of the audience to interpret enacted events. The paradox and the theatre that direct the MJT implicate the audience into its ongoing life and the institution works beyond its physical boundaries to invite new collaborators.

The abandoned, but not unused, Oratunga Station Tack Shed is a relic of pastoral station life in a remote, arid landscape of South Australia. It is a remnant archive space that provokes design exploration within the margins of that which is material and therefore physically malleable, and that which is ephemeral and therefore open to abstract and performative actions; both contribute towards the making of event spaces. In experimenting with dissolving space and time in making a visual montage to enable viewers, who may never experience this place, to imagine the events that

have shaped it; the intent is for the montage image to travel beyond the located space and its collection. In theatrical montages, objects and spaces are subsequently made meaningful through the adoption and acting out of imagined narratives. In such spaces fact and fiction coincide in temporal space, yet often the audience is detached from the action and positioned as witness to unfolding events. However, certain experimental productions invite audiences into abstract worlds where the boundaries between reality and fiction dissolve and are transgressed, and the passive spectator is insinuated into the event.

The old Tack Shed remains virtually intact since its inception and gradual accretion. The challenge of making a curatorial intervention in such places where 'rubbish' has accumulated over time, either through lax management or through intent, is enabled through applying a postproduction intent where layers of dissimilar data are reconfigured as interconnected collections. This approach to artefacts/objects encountered and/or collected recognises that they do not 'fix' space. Rather, they act as points or moments to move with/against and scale relationships dissolve where the interior may be experienced and occupied through the curated tour, over the course of three hours, three days or any other temporal interval.

The performed garden in two ways

Curatorship that involves walking, recording and then reframing spaces of collection such as done in the humble Tack Shed is one of itinerary making that can be performed indoors and outdoors. The act of walking to (an interior) plan defines a conceptual spatial enclosure populated by associative objects. Walks framed by an intended itinerary, mediated by points of departure and arrival, involve peripatetic travelling to explore and immerse in the fabric of places. Such an altered walking methodology enables chance detours, interruptions and losing one's way framed through a collector's practice of picking up things material and visual as one proceeds.

Two experiments in walking as a method of spatial curating came about by chance. The curatorial project made around navigating and recording the Valamanesh Garden in suburban Adelaide, over the course of a grey spring afternoon in 2003, invited a gathering of artists, writers and designers to mark the surface of a paper torn from a notebook. On the top of the sheet was hand written, 'While walking (in the garden) you may notice…' and asked the gathering to react materially, immaterially, literally and laterally, to the garden, and then to give the papers to the studio table. The idea was to explore through others' eyes and feet, how the [conceptual] garden exposes spatial mutability within an enclosure that is both porous and immersive. The other journey was made with a friend as an attempt to (re)discover the eighteenth-century Alticchiero garden near Padova in Northern Italy. Some years ago I heard of a garden where its owner and maker, Angelo Quirini, had invited Justine Wynne, an English woman living in Italy, to curate and to write the garden, to show it to others and to translate it into narrative voices other than his own. His auteur entered into collaboration with her curator, and in the process, narrative itineraries were written; itineraries that could take three hours or three days to experience. The indeterminate spatial design of the garden, suggested by this temporal itinerary, inspired the contemporary tour.

The journey to Alticchiero involved a circuitous route that firstly involved finding Justine's original text on the garden in the British Library and transcribing in pencil the text from the French. The translation conveyed just enough to imagine snippets of Justine's unfolding examination as she journeyed through each section of the garden and her endeavour to share every detail of her lyrical review of the spaces, the elements and the activities experienced during her time spent at Alticchiero. Inside the book, the 1784 engraved plan enabled the new walk around the garden on the banks of the Brenta River with the intent to record what now exists of the described feature gardens – searching for, among other things, the altar of friendship, the pigeon house and sailing ship, the altar of the fury and the charmingly named forest of the young [12]. In this brief excerpt from the translated text, Justine introduces 'the general idea of this house in this countryside' in praise of its owner and maker Angelo Quirini.

> Our friends reject with indignation the flattering reputation of Tusculum, of Laurentian, of the carefree... Imagine a plain without hills, without water sources, without fountains (the absence of water has its own beauty and mystery that add to the imagined and lack of water but adds to the beauty of the rest of nature and the garden). Also Mr. Quirini said one day with a proud modesty of his successes; this place does not have any other merits that it does not leave to chance.

Justine's account reveals a range of itineraries and narratives woven around the philosophically engendered features that are apprehended each time. Williamson notes that:

> Wynne's text is an itinerary that purposefully distorts time and space in favour of a sequence of experience tied to a rich narrative. She leads the reader through the house and garden, not only describing, explaining and interpreting the sights along the way, but also making occasional suggestions about the conversations and behaviour that are appropriate at each stop. Her tour through the house and garden, an area whose perimeter could be walked in an hour or so, takes two days, with pauses for meals and rest [13].

Over the course of a winter afternoon some two-hundred-plus years later, we rambled, backtracked and became lost in a peripatetic wandering with increasingly forlorn intent, as we were unable to find the physical traces of the once rich narrative. During the time spent in the contemporary Alticchiero landscape, as we became more certain that we would not find the garden's remnants, the immediate landscape was recorded photographically in order to construct a new imagination for the garden once it was left and to test such a method to inform what could constitute an ephemeral garden-making practice. An approach that delves into the topographical layers of a site, subject to regular inundation and successive waves of settlement over hundreds of years, where the material details are absent, but hints of the qualities exist, should usefully inform a performative curation methodology. Recalling the moments where imagined fragments and traces appeared – in the ruined house, the line of trees, or the winter vegetable garden – we retraced our steps and asked for directions that proved fruitless dead ends. This walking itinerary coincides with the original only in the imagination, but at some moment we probably followed Justine's footsteps.

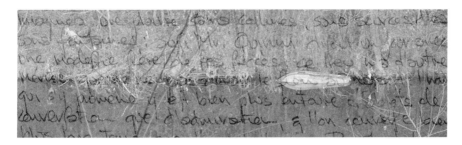

This composite imagining juxtaposes the surface detail of the plan and the spatial qualities of the elevational panorama; this is mediated again by Justine's transcribed narrative ghosted over the contemporary image as a successive memory layer. The doubling effect in this work moves across time and space zones to reconfigure the original garden as a contributor in a new garden narrative, seeking out what Justine might have meant and acted out in her itineraries. Travelling to Alticchiero and finding only traces of the garden now enables strolling through Justine's text, at leisure, in any place that is not her place. And in not finding Alticchiero beyond its ruined state, another itinerary is performed in the footsteps of Justine – one that departs from the physical route in 'real' space, to the space of juxtaposition of many leads: physical, narrative, textual, translated and imagined.

The Valamanesh Garden is both a 'real' garden and an in-between space; physically it provides the locus between home and studio, between creative living [the domestic] and creative making [work]. It facilitates the work and yet sits beside the work as a place of respite and of another making; that of gardening and responding to site and the circumstances of such elements as weather and visitors. Yet while physically positioned as an in-between space, this garden is where collaborative thinking coincides. In the space of that spring afternoon these coincidences were made material through the marking of paper as a record of conversations engaged upon while walking. In the garden, the notebook pages became the medium for collaboration between maker and site, and maker and maker, simultaneously. Through marking the sheet, and then passing it on and then a reworking and a re-noticing through the act of walking around and around, the garden becomes a more practised place. The invitation to contribute is also an invitation to exchange ideas and transformations of initial readings, as well as opinions about, and of, a place. A review of the pages reveals multiple voices; yet those voices fade materially as the authors' initials become obscure, or were never there. Authorship is not the primary concern here, where marking, collecting, rubbing, writing and watering result in postcards, in a place, in a time to be remembered fleetingly.

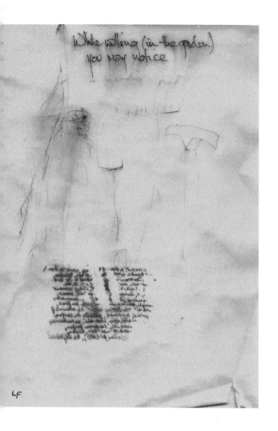

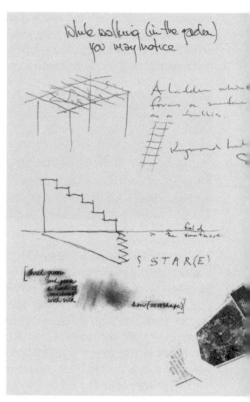

Rather the collaboration is with place and a space of exchange across disciplinary boundaries that transcend location and co-author.

The act of appropriation of other people's ephemeral space and work, has added in a slight way to the archive of performative garden spaces – not to any particular end, but to see what turns up and what occurs when we engage in open-ended conversations with (interior) landscapes.

Curated interior practice(s)

This work contends that curated interiors constitute an expanded description of interior design practice; one that embraces performance space and narrative movement as essential methods in the making of interiors wherever they emerge in an ephemeral world. Beyond seeking comfort in a contextual design position, this work looks towards acceptance of points of departure in ways that allow for future intervention, rather than towards a place where absolute knowing is the desired aim. Confronted by the paucity of representational theories and tools to support and convey such departures – perhaps because they tend to exist in the ephemeral and performative world rather than in the everyday and are hard to pin down and make enduring – this research experiments with visual and itinerary-making tools to reflect and draw upon existing conditions and situations for a wider audience. Exploring postproduction theories and practices that build upon, translate and often overturn the normative assumptions of design and curatorial practices (that are not open to chance events and outcomes) is one method that reinforces an ongoing experiment with collaborative ephemeral practice. I now recognise that for artefacts, collections, archives, museum spaces and their associated narratives to endure, they require being collectively reworked and then left open ended, to allow for chance occurrences and inexplicable actions to do their work in everyday spatial situations.

References

[1]   Zournazi, M. *Hope: new philosophies for change* (Annandale: Pluto Press Australia, 2002) p.244.

[2]   Rugoff, R. 'Beyond Belief: the Museum as Metaphor' in Ray, M.A. and Mangurian, R. *Wrapper* (San Francisco: William Stout, 1999) p.103.

[3]   Bourriaud, N. *Postproduction: Culture as Screenplay: How art reprograms the world* (New York: Lukas & Sternberg, 2002) p.7.

[4]   Ibid., p.11

[5]   Ibid., pp.19–51

[6]   Bal, M. *Double Exposures The Subject of Cultural Analysis* (New York: Routledge, 1996) p.128.

[7]   Foucault, M. 'Of Other Spaces: Utopias and Heterotopias' in Leach, N., ed. *Rethinking Architecture, a reader in cultural theory* (London: Routledge, 1997) pp.354–5.

[8]   Morton, P. in Ray and Mangurian, op. cit., p.7.

[9]   Ibid.

[10] Rugoff, op. cit., p.99

[11] The Soane Gallery, p.60, Fig. 22, Pages from the *Crude Hints towards an History of my House in L[incoln's] I[nn] Fields* MS. (ff.30–31).

[12] Wynne, J. *Alticchiero*, self-published, 1780 and 1787.

[13] Williamson, R. 'Giustiniana's Garden: an Eighteenth Century Woman's Construction' in Szczygiel, B., Carubia, J. and Dowler, L., eds. *Gendered Landscapes, An Interdisciplinary Exploration of Past Place and Space* (Pennsylvania: State University, 1999) pp.48–57.

Gennaro POSTIGLIONE

Facoltà di Architettura e Società,
Politecnico di Milano

Eleonora LUPO

Facoltà del Design, Politecnico di Milano

THE ARCHITECTURE OF INTERIORS AS RE-WRITING OF SPACE: CENTRALITY OF GESTURE

Centrality of gesture

> He looked at the bedroom furniture placed in the garden... Everything was arranged just as it had been in the room: side-table and lamp on his side, side-table and lamp on her side. ...The chest of drawers stood near the foot of the bed. Beside the chest of drawers was an electric stove. At the foot of the bed there was also a small bamboo armchair with a print cushion. The gleaming aluminium kitchen furniture occupied the path, instead. The table was covered by a yellow muslin tablecloth. The cloth, too big, hung down at sides almost to the ground... He had also brought an extension wire into the garden and all the household appliances were connected to electricity. It worked, just as when they had still been inside the house [1].

Within a specific tradition of interiors studies, from the very early beginning of my teaching activity in architecture, I have always tried to identify and focus on some characteristic elements of the interior discipline that I could use when working within other frameworks – such as my course in architectural design, where there was no express requirement for interior themes. With this specific task in mind, I tried to transform practice into methodology, identifying design behaviours able to give deeper meaning to architectural space and bringing in what I had always thought to be the core of interiors.

A fundamental parameter for recognizing whether a project is characterized by an approach from the field of interiors is the evidence of human presence in the design

Figure 1: *Annunciazione ad Anna*, Giotto, 1303–4

process: not only the use of human-scale metrics, from inches and feet to the more sophisticated golden section and so on, but also the capability of the project to show existing relationships with the space – what we prefer to call place, gesture, use and meaning. Space is an abstract term coming from the ancient Greek word *stadio* used to define the parameter for measuring. Therefore space is objective and abstract and never related to the subject: it is a quantitative way to count the world.

On the other hand, place is a subjective way to refer and describe spaces: it is always related to the subject. There is no place without a subject, while there is always a space [2]. With this knowledge in mind, practice and teaching of architectural design have to recognise the subjective dimension of life: abstract geometric compositions aren't in themselves interesting, because a correct project always involves use and gesture, objects and subjects, defining/describing places.

This also explains why, when working with interiors in an academic context, the self-dimension is often called in evidence: the reflexive action of involving 'yourself' in the design process is almost the only strategy for both avoiding extreme generalization and giving depth of meaning to design choices.

According to these statements, interiors own a specific character that connects buildings with life, the needs and desires of the people for whom they have been designed and realized [3]. Shape and gesture in the interior are strictly connected and this topic represents the basic specificity of interior culture.

Therefore, interiors represents, rather than an operative field in itself, an approach to design focused on the relevance of gesture, considered as the action building the place [4].

Moreover, in opposition to the aesthetic and technological drift towards spectacularisation of some contemporary architecture, the architecture of interiors overcomes the concepts of dimension, context and building typology: no matter whether you are inside or outside, in an open or closed space, in a room or in a shopping mall – these are all considered a 'place of the gesture', produced and signified by the action of inhabiting [5].

Interiors as a discipline makes architecture concentrate on the crucial question of 'dwelling through actions', transforming the abstract space into a 'place-to-be' [6]. This theoretical interpretation underlines the role of interiors in contemporary architectural debate as the discipline whose validity lies in the methodology of shaping spaces, building relations and meanings between people's needs and the places where they live.

Figure 2: Verdens Ende Art Gallery Project, Sverre Fehn, 1988
(Courtesy of Sverre Fehn)

Around objects

There is a semantic polarity between the physical nature of objects and their capacity to nullify themselves in deference to the activities to which they are linked; and even more drastically, between their features and the settings that their simple use creates.

This is a dichotomy that shifts attention from the product to the spatial phenomenon produced by its use: it determines a new semeiological figure in which the object, its use and the space generated by this use, appear indissolubly linked to one another. And so, despite the fact that product is the locus of designing and exchange, it is elsewhere that the significance linked to the goods appears: for instance, in that spring from the way in which the objects are used, from their intrinsic capacity to construct precise spatial situations.

In his *La filosofia dell'arredamento*, Mario Praz called them *Stimmung* [7]. He notes with scrupulous precision that a discourse on the subject of furnishing – and on its indispensable complements – cannot be held without grasping the presence of a broader, more complex phenomenon that, starting expressly from objects, arrives at the spatial dimension determined by them through the way in which they make themselves available for use.

The character and the quality of an ambience are defined by the system of objects and of actions this system can give rise to: they construct precise settings, suggest models and lifestyles, support cultural endeavours. This is the reason why everywhere we go, museums of material culture are obliged to mend the fracture that always exists between objects and context, through hypothetical reconstructions, through a plethora of information, through communication strategies, through – in a word – the 'exhibition setting up'. That is again a discipline within the field of interiors. All those efforts are due to the attempt to close the gap that makes objects mute once they have been torn out of their space, of real life: the only place where they have and keep a meaning.

The same silence, the same privation, is at times the fate of a contemporary furnishing product when, uprooted from its settings and its use, it becomes incapable of any performance that is not self-referential and autistic, whether it relates to performance, to aesthetics, to technologies, materials or something else.

The practice of interiors, in this view, is addressed and suitable both to new design and to intervention on/around existent spaces since it takes care of relationship between gesture and space, with the help of objects. However, 'working on the existing' is paradigmatic for the discipline: already-existing construction is the place where space has to be thought around the subject, where new gestures need to 'find home'. It is the place where investigation between actions and shapes are more deeply developed because of the reduced freedom connected with the existing boundaries.

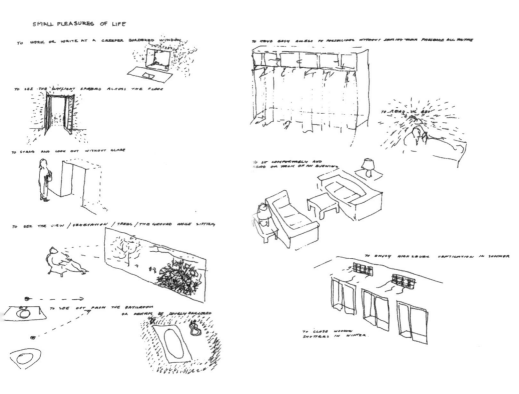

Figure 3: *Small pleasure of life*, Alison and Peter Smithson
(From: Smithson, A. and P. *Changing the Art of Inhabitation*, London: Artemis, 1993)

Working on/around the existent as a re-writing of space

Working on/around the existent has to be considered not only as 'building on existing buildings'. Even when we recognize a tradition in this field, with a specific value, our interest directs us to the more extensive definition, 'working on/around existent', which involves more possibilities: 'building on existing buildings' is only one amongst many.

The extension of meaning, that is also an extension of opportunity, is rooted in the very primitive condition of recognizing every act of design as an act taking place within a given context – from the hyperbolic crowded Tokyo city centre to the extreme emptiness of a desert [8].

Taking the self-evidence of context as the starting point of any design process is the only possibility we have, if we are to avoid self-referential shapes and projects: no other discipline more than interiors develops a sensibility towards the existent read throughout its several layers, from the philological (and objective) to the phenomenological (and subjective).

Figure 4: Superstudio, Camp: fundamental acts, 1971–2
(from *Area: designing actions*, 2005(79+), p.25)

It is also the extension of a methodology developed from the 'human dimension' to 'being-things': the attention devoted to gesture and use can be easily extended to context, to what is on site when/where we are going to work. Design turns into the art of negotiating realities through built form: everything is taken into account and needs to find a place. That place is the project's answer, the final construction.

In this concern, Roland Barthes' theory about text product and production [9] can be very helpful for throwing light on the typical process underlying every well-planned piece of interior design work. If we take his assertion 'every meaningful activity can generate text' and metaphorically transpose it from the field of literature to that of architecture, we gain a possible operative method.

However, we should define the scope in which this model could be useful and valid. Although the equality between the reading and the writing of a text appears a clear and logical fact in literature, it is much more complex to transfer the procedure of decoding/creating to the field of architecture where we immediately encounter the physicality of the matter, the weight of the third dimension and the oddity of the concept of void. Of course, every text contains a specific physical dimension, since it is written (or printed) on 'physical' pages; but it establishes a different relation with the user. It is the book, we might say, that enters and inhabits the reader when, by reading, fragments of text temporarily move 'into' the user. On the other hand, every act of understanding or 'reading' an architectural artefact implies the action of entering/inhabiting a physical space. Nevertheless, with all the diversities of the case and with a (necessary) specific knowledge of the discipline, the comprehension of an architectural work is the result of a 'reading' that is produced through a constant process of separating/rejoining. Reading a building implies 'deconstruction' in order to recognize the fundamental elements and seize the design principles to achieve new level of understanding.

In the same way as in the textual practice of language, the point is not to discover the meaning which that text/work is supposed to contain – a univocal meaning crystallized into the work/product – but the production of a new 'significance' that 'emancipates the signification's statute and makes it plural'. There's no actual distinction between the identity of the author and that of the reader, and it is precisely this need to define the two roles that falls off in the practice of text, refusing a 'metaphysic of the classic subject' as sustained by traditional philology. This way of understanding things doesn't discharge or deny the traditional scientific methods; rather, it considers them as a starting point for the production of significance. When dealing with projects that are related to 'the existing', this new approach produces a positive and powerful effect whose consequences overcome those of simple comprehension.

Figure 5: Le Corbusier, Besteguì Apartament, Paris 1929–31 (from *Rassegna: Cemento*, 1992(49), p.34)

Every act of building, by evidence, deals with an existing condition which it must establish a dialogue with, for all the reasons that provoked the act itself. A careful analysis and reading of the existing context enables the architect to recognize and underline the elements characterizing the form and the space which the new structure will be put in relation with. This process of knowledge shouldn't try to discover or 'unveil' hidden meanings but rather remain a semantic activity that becomes, therefore, 'production'. By breaking off the 'mono-logical state' of the architectural work, the comprehension becomes wider and the authenticity as unique/original can start to be dismantled. This idea arises from a profound critical revision of the Kantian aesthetic where the artwork and the spectator are counter-posed and strange to each other. In textual practice, and then in thinking about 'difference', subject and object lose their 'stability' and the same borders that used to mark their ambit become uncertain, as transitory elements, introducing a 'practice of representative perception that presupposes the mutual imbrication' [10] of the one and the other. In a similar way, Bhabha talks about the 'third space' as a new semantic and relational place that originates from the impossibility of defining in an exact and fixed way both the object and the subject as well as their reciprocal boundaries.

> This implies an inevitable weakening of every abstract interpretation of the idea of the authentic. The pure and uncontaminated concept of the other (the work) has been crucial for the anti-capitalistic critic of the cultural economy of the Western world in modern age. ...But who can define authenticity then? Once again (someone) stands for the observed assigning him a position... [11]

and a universal value in accordance with the Western order of things.

In this way the idea of a 'moving significance', immersed in the circumstances, originates and demolishes the basis of the monolithic authenticity that was traditionally accepted. A fuzzier notion focuses on the productive action of the subject and on the productive condition of the object, introducing an intermediate space where subject and object overlap and where their meanings become plural. Although it is more difficult to define, this concept is not reliant on the (counter-posed) idea that used to build a system of power and justify the action through the invention of the authentic and the original. In this way, the reader becomes profoundly responsible; the old beliefs provided by the myth of the authentic are left behind and a new relationship with the work is established. The reader is eventually a direct and active author in that productive process of significance he has always been excluded from. As 'discoverer', or even just 'spectator', the designer becomes, as well as the author, 'craftsman' in a continuous confrontation with his work that, as we stated before, evolves from product into production.

Moving the discussion into the specific field of the architectural, it is necessary to remark that working on 'what is built', acting within a given space, reveals the role of place in providing hospitality. Every project that 'finds its home' inside an existing realm measures and challenges the ability of that space to welcome the gestures and the structures necessary to its new use. Researching to what extent a place is able to host these is a fundamental passage in a design process that is not willing to be a 'colony' of space, but a guest [12]. This way of designing could, ultimately, occur as the simple insertion of furniture and objects into a space – which might be the perfect challenge for the designer's ability to understand the hospitality of the built matter and to perform in a built environment [13]. There's no dwelling (inhabiting) without hospitality and dwelling is – to say it with Norberg-Schulz – an existential phenomenon more than a physical need.

There is no gesture without a place willing and available to receive it; and place has always welcomed gesture and life. Some places – either natural or artificial – have been destroyed by intense exploitation or abandoned to decay through someone's ineptitude at inhabiting them. Some places are 'colonized' by the aggressive violence of univocal gestures. Many places have been built with no care for their distinctive characters, with no interest for their specific fundamental elements, with no concern for their form, but only with the stubborn superimposition of an alien, foolish design act. This was true every time the architectural process was carried out by 'running after' the myth of the authentic, as an ontological legitimisation of the design, through a continuous search for the origin and the primitive state.

It is not possible to 'get back home'. We must now deal with progressively more complex negotiations and interactions that are dissolving and hybridising the original state of works – works which survive only in the movement, in transit, in their incapacity to stand still.

Conclusion

Freed from the obsession with authenticity, and from the utopia of 'returning to the roots'; driven by a healthy will to research, read and understand an existing space as it is (with its imperfections, with its history of transformations and transitions), Italian architects of the second generation of the Modern Movement managed to attend to context without giving up the necessary productive attitude that should sustain every project. To these architects – and to those that successfully followed their path, in Italy and abroad – we should look today.

The work as text, the space as a place for gesture, the project as 're-writing' and the search for hospitality – these then are the fundamental elements of a praxis that expresses itself through a conscious manipulation of the existing, which is continuously transformed as its authenticity is disintegrated.

References

[1]   Raymond, C. *Perché non ballate? In Da dove stai chiamando?* (Roma: Minimum Fax, 1999) pp.178–9.
[2]   Farinelli, F. *Geografia* (Torino: Einaudi, 2003) pp.16–21.
[3]   Cornoldi, A. *L'architettura dei luoghi domestici* (Milano: Jaca Book, 1994).
[4]   De Certeau, M. *L'invention du quotidian* (Paris: Gullimard, 1990).

[5]   Basso Peressut, L. and Postiglione, G. 'Il progetto di Interni' in Cornoldi, A. *Architettura degli Interni* (Padova: Il Poligrafo, 2005).

[6]   Norberg-Schulz, C. *Dwelling* (New York: Rizzoli Int, 1985).

[7]   Praz, M. *La filosofia dell'arredamento* (Milano: Longanesi, 1981).

[8]   Banham, R. *Scenes in American Deserta* (Cambridge, MA: The MIT Press, 1982).

[9]   Barthes, R. *Le Plaisir du texte* (Paris: Èd. du Seuil, 1973).

[10]   Bhabha, H.K. 'The Third Space' in Rutherford, J., ed. *Identity, Community, Culture, Difference* (London: Lawrence & Wishart, 2003).

[11]   Chambers, I. *Paesaggi migratori* (Genova: Costa & Nolan, 1996) pp.16–19.

[12]   Flora, F., Giardiello, P. and Postiglione, G. 'Legittimità degli interni', *Area*, 2000(50), pp.2–3.

[13]   Jabés, E. *Le livre de l'hospitalité* (Paris: Gallimard, 1991).

Acknowledgements

The authors gratefully acknowledge the participation in this research of both the PhD Course in interiors and the one in design at Politecnico di Milano.

Mark TAYLOR

School of Architecture,
Victoria University of Wellington, New Zealand

Mark C. BURRY

SIAL, School of Architecture, Design and Fashion,
RMIT University, Australia; Visiting Professor, School of
Architecture, Victoria University of Wellington, New Zealand

HERTZIAN SPACE

Introduction

In the paper 'Syncopated Space – Wireless Media Shaping Human Movement and Social Interaction', Teri Rueb observes how in the brief period before the snowmelt, a carpet of snow provides the opportunity to subvert or reorder the terrain. She suggests we have an opportunity to rewrite the physical and social landscape of the city according to a different logic of movement and interaction. The expanse of white evenness, Rueb suggests:

> invites us to cross lines, improvise, detour and play in places forbidden or ignored in our everyday lives. We traipse across manicured lawns, walk straight down the middle of streets and invent lanes on the snow-covered freeways [1].

This effect of snow alters our conventional perceptions of surface, space, movement and interaction. We are no longer bound by conventions and practice, rules and behaviour but cross and connect in a more fluid overlapping manner. Rueb suggests that we can understand this space of overlapping fields and frequencies as Hertzian space, 'characterised by connectedness as opposed to the discrete boundaries and territories suggested by physical architecture and visually based constructions of space.'

Hertzian space is a term used in the wireless industry and is increasingly becoming of interest due to the expansion of mobile phones and communication systems including radio waves. Research suggests that material space (the physical hard stuff) has an effect on the electromagnetic intensity of signals, and that the introduction of a new signal (using a mobile phone) changes Hertzian space because the phone becomes a transmitter of microwaves. Anthony Dunne and Fiona Raby propose that:

> Whereas 'cyberspace' is a metaphor that spatialises what happens in computers distributed around the world, Hertzian space is actual and physical even though our

senses detect only a tiny part of the electromagnetic spectrum. Images of footprints of satellite TV transmissions in relation to the surface of the earth, and computer models showing cellular phone propagation in relation to urban environments, reveal that Hertzian space is not isotropic but has an 'electroclimate' defined by wavelength, frequency and field strength. Interaction with the natural and artificial landscape creates a hybrid landscape of shadows, reflections, and hot points [2].

Taking clues from this proposition, the aim of this design research is to read interior space as connected space, bounded not exclusively by 'construction' but as a spatial delimitation that contributes to the making of surfaces. Such surfaces are not necessarily dependent on exterior form, nor are they 'universal' in a Modernist sense. That is, the research seeks differentiated spaces providing for individual occupation, use and preferences of inhabitants – space informed directly by intended occupational activities. It is an alternative to Modernist universal space and seeks equal opportunity for inhabitation. These latter spaces, according to Michael Hensel and Achim Menges, are largely homogenised Modernist interior environments, perpetuated through open-plan arrangements [3]. Against this, they note that contemporary architectural discourse has tended to favour heterogeneous architectures, manifested as either generic shells that are modified to suit the inhabitants, or 'exotically shaped buildings that are, from their outset, varied in expression and spatiality.' [4] Our research concurs with Hensel and Menges' conclusion that 'homogenised interior environments simply cannot satisfy the multiple and contrasting needs of its inhabitants.' [5]

We also observe that design practice tends to exclude or at least ignore the generation of a specific interior environment from particular bodies, occupations and activities unless it is deemed to be exceptional – such as in the automotive industry or hostile climatic environments. Rarely are everyday occupational activities elevated to this status; more often they are held within homogenised space that can accommodate change through the repositioning of furnishings, décor and occupational activity. Moreover, boundaries or the physical delimitations of space tend to define territories that are based on visual constructions of space.

Studio design research

Our approach has been to suspend belief in design dependent on 'concepts', 'metaphors' and other idealised notions at the outset of the design process. Instead, we have looked to data-driven environments in which topography and levels of activity are informed by varied dynamic systems associated with the occupants. The methodology is more closely aligned with bottom-up thinking allowing for complex interactions between parts, whilst bringing together disparate entities. It is a flexible system able to respond to and influence its own effects. Such methodology runs counter to traditional systems in which the linear process of hypothesis, analysis and intervention are understood as being less adaptive and responsive to data input.

Working from metric and observational data, specific spatial and surface descriptions are generated in response to a field of data that affect, interfere and overlap, creating intensities that are responsive to the changing nature of information. Importantly, the process realises multiple virtual potentials generated from the lived traces of inhabitation and occupation. For example, these might include a kinetic response to shifts in activity or occupation, or connections realised through interference and interaction.

In this process, the problem of excess information is very real and at times seems to overwhelm design decision making, opening data and material 'to intuition, interpretation and evaluation as architecture.' [6] That is, different forms of data whether 'read' through photographic images, measured on site, or obtained through focused group interviews need evaluating and actualising through architectural modelling. And since there is no traditional 'concept' acting as partí, data is not edited until all relational constructs are explored, thereby allowing for architectures that are unknown and impossible to preconceive.

Early analysis through site observation and documentation of variable and changing data on such things as the body's(ies') occupation of space, placement of artefacts, operational requirements, environmental factors and so on, are used to re-describe an interior lining that is specific rather than general spatial envelopment. The opportunity to experiment with unstable spatial and topological descriptions of form by developing an underlying structure of stable characteristics (parameters) is provided by understanding a particular type of syntax: parametric design (also referred to as associative geometry or relational modelling). Moreover, the methodology encourages parametric thinking, as a means of finding connections or associations between data, form generation, activity and occupation.

To engage with design at an early stage the students are encouraged to model ideas as though they were real, rather than a representation of something yet to appear. The intention being to test whether the ambiguity of traditional conceptual models can be overcome by engaging directly with modelling as process. That is, can the process provide 'real-time' feedback on effects and outcome such that they inform decision making, enabling students to move beyond their traditional reliance on sketches and verbalisation to communicate concepts and ideas? With emphasis on learning through researching properties, effects, combinations of form and material, and software programming, modelling is understood as an iterative process rather than finished 'presentation'.

Project work

The work discussed here emanates from a design research studio offered to senior undergraduate architecture students that, given the studio title Hertzian Space, explored issues of collaborative design and design through modelling. An emphasis on digital and/or physical modelling was placed across the programme in an effort to understand modelling as an active component of design thinking rather than as a scaled representation of the thing to come.

The studio was divided into three exercises. The first, an individual component, invited students to identify a physical property of skin/surface, and find ways of mapping, documenting and representing it as a digital and/or physical model, and extending that into areas unknown or unfamiliar. Traditional notions of solid structures were tested against overlaps, plications, and laminates where density, thickness and absorbency came into play. The intention was to expose the way surfaces might change, or be understood differently through connections, links and overlaps; some of which might not be physically readable. For example, Yi Wen Seow's realisation that transparency can be registered through shadow was in keeping with the studio intentions of Hertzian space. Working through a series of physical experiments with folded and shaped clear plastics, the overlap of self-similar material forced the appearance of shadows whilst still allowing transparency. As light shone through the plastic, shadows were cast signalling a new relationship between material, light and transparency registered as a virtual surface. As shadows fell on a person they signalled a relationship to transparent surface, such that the project generated a narrative of shifting from one effect to another. A second example by Diana Chaney was generated from a 'sensitivity map' of the human back. Using two needle points simultaneously pressed onto the skin, a map was made of where both points were felt as distinct pressure marks. Further development led to a three dimensional string model that was affected by pressure, demonstrating that shape change due to an effect or action is co-dependent. That is, the form model transcended the physical limitations revealing connections between parts that are visually non-apparent.

Some students initially invented a scenario or situation to contextualise their surface, suggesting it is associated with a form or situation rather than being an entity in its own right. Moreover, their traditional understanding of the model as a scaled version or concept rather than being real and full-scale inhibited progress. Feedback from the studio suggests that the assignment was too abstract, in that some students could not understand how to conceive or make a thing independent of any architectural setting. This might be taken as evidence of the need to undertake design research of this nature as the perceived abstraction is as likely to be the result of the students' unfamiliarity with working in this way as for any other reason.

For the second exercise, students worked on their own design project with a brief derived from semi-professional service industries such as hairdressing, barbers, beauty therapy, tattoo and massage parlours, podiatrists, pregnancy massage, and sports medicine (massage, physiotherapy). Some of these services have a high profile, generated by both the cult of 'perfection', and society's desire to promote strength, fitness and beauty. Style magazines and 'make-over' television programmes conspire with this to re-shape the body, promote youthfulness and disguise evidence of aging. However, such observations are cultural concerns – our objective was to examine spaces designed to accommodate these activities and respond to the architectural position outlined above. The intention was to examine programmes and environments that have a close and clear relationship of activity to the body and that are beyond the domestic setting.

Site visits are important to gather data and understand how existing activities use the space provided. Taking part in the chosen activity is also beneficial but although some students did engage with the activity, personally experiencing wet shaving, full body massage etc., others chose not have a tattoo, lose a lower limb or get pregnant for the sake of a studio exercise.

Site data was gathered and recorded through photographs, sketches, notes, and audio/video interviews. Photographic documentation revealed many places to be simply furnished generic commercial spaces, with the equipment necessary for their specialisation organised in an add-hoc manner that is incredibly rich for the dissonance between space and function. For example, the wet-shaving barber's premises reflected the accumulation of objects and artefacts normally associated with a domestic setting. Notions of comfort and familiarity are difficult to design at the outset, but can be allowed for in the longer term. Other premises were less 'homely', including the full-body massage parlour captured in a series of extraordinary covert images depicting the starkness of uncontrolled accumulation of equipment and paraphernalia. With little space to change or place clothes, the client's body is literally forced onto the only remaining free space – the massage table. Any sensuality of the naked body or intimacy between form and materials is lost. This observation was made in other projects, leading to the conclusion that interiors are generally conditioned by the existing environment and 'generic commercial space' function-neutrality rather than by operational requirements.

With the individual projects, the students' traditional design methods, including reliance on conceptual models, drawing and verbalisation, tended to overshadow modelling as process. Moreover, as projects grapple with complexity of information rather than follow a simple 'conceptual' proposition, the difficulty of realising ideas through modelling became apparent. To overcome this several projects returned to the researched data. For example, Elizabeth Chaney's Botox clinic focused on spaces of self-administration and how the presence of another self-administrator interferes with and alters the environment, creating a tension between the parties. A further but undeveloped idea emanated from realising that the temperature sensitivity of the product and user could inform the space. This notion was taken up in exercise three (group work) where temperature-based spatial descriptions led to form. Such an approach examines how shifts in temperature, occurring when two or more bodies are present in the same location, might affect a description of space.

The final exercise involved students working collaboratively in groups of three to four, on a selected project from exercise two. For each proposal the original designer was excluded from the group, thus offering space to critique and refine the project at a level of 10:1 detailing [7]. This is not to suggest that further development is purely technical; but rather, it concerns refinement of ideas against realisation. Projects were selected for their potential, difficulty of design proposition and (to some extent) how they understand notions of Hertzian space. For this part, all design refinement was conducted through virtual and physical modelling making use of physical materials,

Further design data came from considering massage practice itself and the position of the masseur relative to the client's body, rather than any pre-existing homogenous space. Two students of differing physical stature simulated massaging a client, documenting the process through a series of digital images that were used to generate a description of the body moving through space that could be mapped. Head, shoulders, lower back and feet position were imported into a Sketchup™ model (Figures 1 and 2). These parameters were used to define tolerance volumes accommodating data from both students' simulations (Figure 3). The final digital model was generated from a series of U-lofts made from vertical/radial sections through the bubbles (Figure 4).

To account for membrane transparency and determine deformable surface areas from areas of rigidity, the team returned to the positions of both 'masseurs'. From this data the enclosing membrane followed the profile of the inner (smaller) body, and stretched to accommodate the larger figure. That is, when the head, lower back and feet press into the membrane the surface expanded. Elasticity was achieved by reducing the thickness of material and introducing cuts and folds.

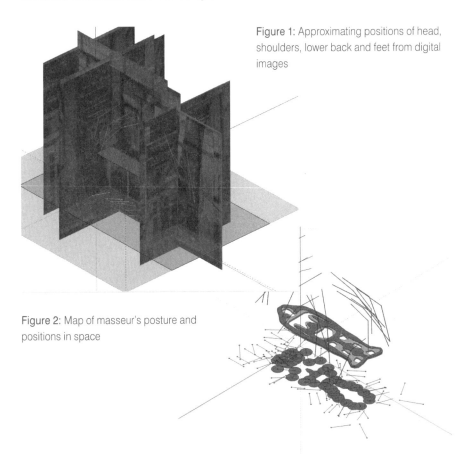

Figure 1: Approximating positions of head, shoulders, lower back and feet from digital images

Figure 2: Map of masseur's posture and positions in space

Figure 3: Tolerance volumes applied to posture, extremities of head, shoulder and lower back

Figure 4: U-loft made from vertical/radial sections through bubbles

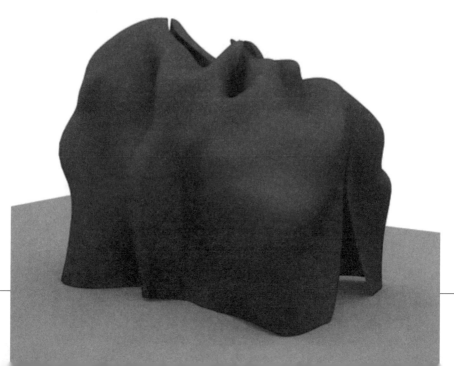

Outcomes

In the introduction we suggested that a principal motivation for engaging with Hertzian space is the possibility that another definition and construction of interior space allows for greater interaction between the space itself and the activities that it accommodates; what we might regard as connected space, without the usual hard and fast physically manifested boundaries evident in visual constructions of space. Our objective was to see whether such thinking can alter our understanding of space in favour of a continuum of bodily presences, a continuum that interferes and marks out spatial terrains. The outcomes as designs were taken to be test-pieces that might reveal barriers that limit design to known conceptions from the outset. That is, they begin to dismantle conventional ways the interior is conceived and understood, and refigure the way we are conditioned by and condition space.

Of course, as an architectural proposition, such Hertzian space is far removed from its observance in telecommunications systems where for example 'the radio scanner enables new urban maps to be made, revealing normally hidden structures of the visible and conventional.' [9] But to undertake an exercise of this type is clearly important not only 'because it reflects back on our own understanding of a relationship of self to other but also to the world around us.' [10]

To work with concepts of Hertzian space and connectedness is difficult in a discipline which has, in the Western tradition, concerned itself mainly with 'permanent' physical constructions. However, there is the possibility of destabilising this tradition and extending our understanding of architecture through speculations and projections on the way space influences and is influenced by the body, occupation and activity. This approach integrates data analysis with speculations, such that form is an outcome rather than a preconception and precursor to broader design enquiries. The process described here merges traditional understanding of 'substantial' structures with more fluid bodily movement and occupational activities leading to unexpected and provocative new readings of interior space and its associated human activity.

References

[1]   Rueb, T. 'Syncopated Space – Wireless Media Shaping Human Movement and Social Interaction', http://www.receiver.vodafone.com/10/articles/06_page02.html, (accessed on 22 June 2006).

[2]   Dunne, A. and Raby, F. 'Tunable Cities', *Architectural Design*, 68(11/12), 1998, p.78.

[3]   Hensel, M. and Menges, A. 'Differentiation and Performance: Multi-Performance Architectures and Modulated Environments', *Architectural Design*, 76(2), 2006, pp.60–9.

[4]   Ibid., p.61

[5]   Ibid., p.63

[6]   Kolotan, S. and MacDonald, B. 'Lumping', *Architectural Design*, 72(1), 2002, p.79.

[7]   See Burry, M. 'Homo Faber', *Architectural Design*, 75(4), 2002, pp.30–7.

[8]   See Burry, J., Maher, A., Burry, M.C., and Taylor, M., 'Experiments in Sublimation in Design Education' in Newton, C., Kaji-O'Grady, S. and Wollan, S., eds. *Design + Research: Project Based Research in Architecture*, ISSN: 1449 – 1737 (Melbourne, Australia: Association of Architecture Schools of Australasia, 2003).

[9]   Dunne, A. *Hertzian Tales, Electronic Products, Aesthetic Experience and Critical Design* (London: Royal College of Design, 1999).

[10] Teri Rueb in conversation with Sabine Breitsameter: http://www.swr.de/swr2/audiohyperspace/engl_version/interview/rueb.html#bio (accessed on 25 November 2006). See Burry et al., op. cit.

Acknowledgements

The authors gratefully acknowledge the ARCH 412 students and research assistants Matthew Randell and Elizabeth Chaney. The original author of 'Full body massage suite' was Yijing-Xu. The collaborative design team: Diana Chaney, Matthew Randell, Yi Wen Seow.

Histories of interior design

Luis DIAZ

University of Brighton

DISCOURSE, HISTORY AND INTERIOR ARCHITECTURE: NOTES ON A POSSIBLE HISTORY OF INTERIOR ARCHITECTURE

Introduction

The ideas considered in this chapter are part of a conversation concerning the possibility of a dedicated history and theory programme for the interior architecture programme at the University of Brighton. As in many other schools, the history and theory programme at Brighton is shared between the architecture and interior architecture programmes. While there are practical benefits to this arrangement there are also problems, not least of which is the tendency to focus on architecture. This is not necessarily caused by prejudice or lack of interest. There is a comparative shortage of literature focusing on interior architecture, not to mention an absence of a comprehensive historical overview of the field. The challenge of conceiving a history and theory programme for interior architecture is seen as an opportunity, not only to begin the process of assembling an overview, but also to raise questions about the nature of the discipline itself.

This chapter seeks to introduce and raise issues around which various debates could take place. The work here is tentative and suggestive of areas for further research. The main purpose is to identify weaknesses of various historiographical approaches and to suggest general ground rules for future work. These thoughts are formed by a review of architectural historiography; this is based on the idea that while interior architecture may be defined as a distinct practice, it is nonetheless closely related to architecture.

In these notes a number of limits have been set to simplify the inquiry – for example, the emphasis here is on history as a taught subject rather than theory [1]. There is, nevertheless, a need to use theory as a critical tool for questioning various historiographical frameworks. In addition, the history in question is primarily the history of the modern period. In my view the problems raised by the history of Modernism are different to those raised by general history. The relationship between the history of interior architecture and history of architecture may be compared to the relationship between art history and the emergence of architectural history at the end of the nineteenth century. Many of the ideas here are provoked by this analogous condition in the hope that with the hindsight of this earlier development, the history of interior architecture might avoid the most common pitfalls. The problem of the definition of interior architecture itself as a field, discipline or practice is closely related to the problems investigated here and cannot be altogether avoided; the issue of definition is raised where necessary but not addressed in depth.

Discourse and critical history

Banham's black box

In his 1990 essay, 'A Black Box: The Secret Profession of Architecture', Reyner Banham proposed an obvious but controversial definition of architecture. Doing away with any attempt to provide an objective definition Banham suggested that architecture is no more than a certain way of working which is primarily defined through a particular way of drawing. Banham drops a tautological teaser: 'What is it, in other words, that architects uniquely do? The answer, alas, is that they do "architecture".' [2] This is not a tautological conceit, since it is 'doing' that Banham is highlighting; that is, architecture is distinguished by a method and not a product. Banham sets aside questions of quality as well as distinctions between architecture and building:

> So why do we not admit that what distinguishes architecture is not *what* is done – since, on their good days, all the world and his wife can apparently do it better – but *how* it is done [3].

This 'how' of architecture is centred on a certain way of drawing which reflects a particular approach to design. This approach is neither systematic nor transparent, and hence it remains mysterious to the uninitiated. It is coherent only in the fact that it is transmitted by the education process through which nearly all practitioners must pass. It is a process where, as Banham notes, inconsistencies are openly displayed – for example, by the fact that resolving a design brief is never sufficient. Although Banham does not invoke Foucault, he is defining architecture as a discursive formation. That is, it is a particular way of doing things, a way of speaking, and a set of inclusions and exclusions. These formations, as Foucault notes, do not need to display coherence or unity [4].

There is, in the end, no objective logic to architecture, at least not in any terms that would distinguish it from engineering or other modes of designing or building. This is one reason why architecture has taken a defensive posture against inroads from engineering and other design practices. But if there is no objective core, this does not mean that it does not have specificity. This specificity, however, can only be based on theory. As for history, which is at stake in Banham's essay, its subject comes to be seen as a construction (in other words, it is a discursive formation). There is nothing natural or objective about what can be included or excluded:

> We could recognise that the history of architecture is no more, but emphatically no less, than what we used to believe it was: the progression of those styles and monuments of the European mainstream, from Stonehenge to the Staatsgalerie, that define the modest building art that is ours alone [5].

This does not make history arbitrary or traditionally determined. When Banham suggests a tradition that runs from Stonehenge to the Staatsgalerie, there is a theory behind this formation, which in his case revolves around a mode of design. We may not agree with Banham's suggestion, but if we conceive of architecture as a discourse, then we can replace it with another (perhaps better) one – but never with an objective 'essence'.

Foucault and discourse

I do not intend to rehearse the whole of Foucault's thoughts on discourse, or even to reflect its complexity. I want only to suggest that even a cursory understanding of his ideas is useful when thinking about the problems of history and in particular a history of an emerging field. To begin with, Foucault proposes that we both acknowledge discontinuities, ruptures and breaks in a discourse and still work towards understanding its specificity. This double role is important as it frees us from having to artificially fill in gaps, holes, or fissures in our conception of interior architecture, but still challenges us to work towards identifying the unity of the discipline. Foucault also suggests a number of procedures which are particularly useful in this case where one discipline (and its discourse) is related to and partially based on another. Though existing discursive unities may be challenged they can be used as temporary supports. Unities or categories can be temporarily accepted in order to interrogate their logic [6]. This means that we do not have to invent the history of interior architecture from scratch. The key proposition here, picked up by Banham in his 'Black Box' essay, is that a shift in focus needs to be made from objects to the space in which they emerge: 'the problem arises of knowing whether the unity of a discourse is based not so much on the permanence and uniqueness of an object as on the space in which various objects emerge and are continuously transformed.' [7] For interior architecture this raises the question of where the field is primarily emerging: is it in practice or in academia? And if it is both, what is the specific relationship between the two in the formation of its specific terms and identity?

Foucault also suggests practical tasks that can be carried out in the identification of discourses and their history. Some of these entail mapping how formations are recognised by particular societies, describing relevant authorities, analysing how objects are classified, analysing what is included and excluded by statements and recognising who is making them. These activities may seem self-evident, but I reiterate them here within the context of Foucault's thought in order to prevent these tasks from being seen as the definitive or only work necessary for understanding the discipline.

Tafuri and critical history

If we treat interior architecture as a discourse rather than an objective field (or a set of objects) then various forms of absolute or total histories can be avoided. We still have the question of what history does apart from recognising the contingent nature of the discipline.

Having emerged out of art history and the shadow of Heinrich Wölfflin [8], architectural history was for many years concerned with the development of styles. As late as 1961 Vincent Scully was tracing stylistic motifs:

> Taking a view of the Willitts House, of 1902... we may concentrate upon the linear pattern and derive a Van Doesburg of 1918, and more remotely a Mondrian, from it. Ignoring the lines and focusing upon the advancing and receding volumes, we may derive a 'construction' by Vantongerloo, of 1921. Taking the process a step further and reading the planes as forming hollow, interlocked boxes, we may arrive at a Neo-Plastic house project by Rietveld and Van Doesburg, of 1920. Going only one step beyond this and separating some of the planes further, we can come to Reitveld's demonstrations, of 1924 [9].

By the end of the 1960s such histories were no longer tenable. If aesthetics were considered they were now examined in more complex ways under the influence of structuralism and later poststructuralism. At the same time new priorities were emerging, such as technical, material, social and environmental concerns. However, not all histories were descriptive, and even Scully's contribution ends on a political note.

Many early texts were operative, that is, they used history to support a particular interpretation or approach to contemporary architecture. Many of these histories were in support of modern architecture, such as Nikolaus Pevsner's functionalist interpretation of Modernism in *Pioneers of Modern Design* [10] and Giedion's spatial interpretation in *Space Time Architecture* [11]. Watkin's more recent survey of Western architecture is upfront about its support for a particular kind of architecture. After quoting the American architect Alan Greenberg, in which he advocates the continued use of classical architecture on the grounds that it has successfully endured for 2000 years, Watkin admits that 'it will be the principal aim of the present book to tell the exciting story of that (classical architecture's) success.' [12]

The Italian historian Manfredo Tafuri was critical of such operative histories [13]. For Tafuri, it is not the role of history to support a discipline or to prop it up; instead it should aim to critique it. History must be analytical, its focus not on objects but on 'the mental structures of any given period.' [14] This does not mean that history is neutral or benign since the laying bare of situations and conditions has potential for political significance.

In Tafuri's view it was history and not architecture which retained the possibility of being political. In terms of the history of Modernism it was important to show the relationship and complicity that modern architecture had with the development of capitalism. Operative history is distorted by the application of attributes which were not necessarily significant in its contemporary context. As such, any possibility of understanding the critical potential of the object of history and of history itself is lost in distortion. Carla Keyvanian has shown that Tafuri himself was not immune to this tendency, specifically in his earlier works [15]. His awareness of this problem led him to the idea of microhistory, a notion borrowed from the historian Carlo Ginzburg. This approach gives up on the idea of reconstructing larger tableaux in favour of focusing on fragments of history. These fragments do not necessarily have to be major or significant ones. The idea is that even obscure or everyday fragments are capable of revealing, under close scrutiny, the larger conditions and problems of their historical context. Keyvanian shows how Tafuri was able to question key and widely held assumptions about Renaissance architecture (e.g. unity and agreement of ideas) through a discreet study of four projects by Jacopo Sansovino – not the first name to come to mind when thinking about key figures of the Renaissance.

These ideas and approaches liberate us from forcing unity and coherence where none may exist. They do not, however, relieve the historian from specificity, from the necessity to deal with precise quality, form and content of things; they are not licence to practice endless relativity, which in most cases serves no useful purpose.

Recent histories: essentialism versus specificity

It is generally accepted that many histories of modern architecture have focused on the nature of space as a key feature of the period. The emphasis on space, while operative (e.g. Siegfried Giedion and Bruno Zevi), can also be seen as ontological or essentialist in that they claim to identify the defining aspect of architecture. This is difficult territory for interior architecture, and for what I am proposing here – that is, that history can contribute to our understanding of the nature of the discipline itself. The problem is to avoid using history for purely essentialist purposes. This can be achieved by understanding the difference between the specificity of a discourse and a search for essentials.

It is interesting to note that in the last 20 years only one major survey history in architecture has been written (Colquhoun, 2002). The 1980s saw four key texts by Frampton (1980), Curtis (1982), Tafuri and Dal Co (1986) and Watkin (1986), while Scully's text (1961) was in at least its tenth reprinting and Benevolo's (1971) in its fifth printing by 1982. The last two decades have seen a shift from history to historiography. This reflects not only changes in historical methodologies, but also a loss of faith in the idea of total histories, meta-narratives or other kinds of synthetic historical summaries. During this absence of history, useful methodologies have been introduced such as various forms of cultural and literary theory, gender critique, and postcolonial theory. These have served to break up what was seen as a monolithic history of Modernism.

These new methodologies tend to focus on and emphasise differences. The result, however, is that history begins to appear like a collection of infinite contingencies, making the suggestion of categories, similarities, sets and other groups nearly impossible or, at best, negative practices. This produces a tendency to reduce history to a description of differences. But if history is an attempt to understand how things occur and how things come to be made then connections need to be identified as well. If we follow Tafuri's interest in wanting to understand the 'mental structures of any given period', then it is necessary to identify similarities as well as differences. And where differences are noted these should not be taken to automatically suggest that conditions are purely contingent since Foucault reminds us that breaks, ruptures and differences can be part of the unity of a discourse. From this point of view it is still possible to conceive of a broad historical narrative; that is, to write an historical overview or survey.

Though the critiques and correctives which have been levied on historical surveys were and are necessary, these have tended to become an end in themselves. The pendulum has swung from one extreme, the dominance of meta-narratives, to another, the fear of connective narratives altogether.

Preliminary notes towards a programme

Given this overview, we can establish some 'ground rules' and limits, and take note of danger areas in the search for history. For starters, if we propose that interior architecture has been recently formed, we can suspend a search for a historical origin. This might seemingly make the idea of constructing a history of interior architecture nonsensical. However, discourses do not appear instantaneously and wholly formed; instead they coalesce, amalgamate, and emerge over time. So although interior architecture may be emerging and gaining coherence and recognition as a practice, its various strands and characteristics may be traced over time.

Next, linearity and chronology need to be questioned [16]. For example, while the notion of style is in itself not problematic, the presentation of style in linear and chronological schemas can suggest that progress is a natural agency. By setting aside such assumptions, other explanations for style, or any other issues at stake, are made possible.

We can also suspend objectifying categories such as style, typology, and function as unifying and essentialist criteria. Again, this does not mean that these categories are unimportant – the question is whether there is a real argument for inclusion, and if so, where it is that such categories exist. Are they objective qualities or are they discursive properties? Are they actual or perceived? Are they categories that belong to the making of things or to the analysis of things?

So how then might a history be structured and investigated? One idea for an organisational structure is a reverse chronology. This has the benefit of responding to the newly formed nature of the discipline. Such an approach could begin with general statements on various parameters concerning interior architecture and then work backwards through moments, events, statements and objects (projects) that trace their formation. For example, one can start with contemporary notions of space which inform interior practices and work through their historical evolution. Such a strategy would recognise the 'constructedness' of both the discipline and history.

Another approach is the 'pebble in the pond' approach or what Richard Sennett calls a 'postholing technique' [17]. This technique does not try to cover all areas or to explain everything but to investigate different places and times where one can 'excavate' deeply – that is, it sets up a series of microhistories.

This would also begin with a general introduction but then be followed by mini-series of lectures on different themes and debates critical to interior architecture. For example, one mini-series could focus on culture versus mass production debates covering *l'art decoratif* in France, the Werkbund in Germany and the Arts and Crafts movement in England. (Examples of other themes that could be presented are: profession versus artistic practice; author versus user.) These in turn could be complimented with mini-series focusing on formal or practical issues such as spatiality, performance, tectonics, materiality, etc. This would allow personalities, buildings or ideas to re-emerge in different contexts thus preventing an approach that pigeonholes each person and thing into single categories.

This method takes existing debates and issues and presents them in terms of their significance to an understanding of the practice of interior architecture. For example, a figure like Ludwig Hilberseimer, who is normally seen as a background character, might be foregrounded for his approach to architecture and urbanism which related the cell (and its interior) to the city.

A variation on this bases the themes around methodology. This idea is demonstrated in a little-known book by Dora Crouch, *History of Architecture, from Stonehenge to Skyscrapers*, published in 1985 [18]. The book is not without its problems, such as its focus on so-called 'monuments' and 'masterpieces' of architecture. It does, however, provide some interesting models on other fronts. Each historical period is explained through a different theoretical framework. This is presented as a pedagogical decision: 'In this book, to simplify learning, one question will be matched with one monument.' [19] So, for example, while Stonehenge is discussed in relation to the concept of time, the pyramids are discussed in relation to surplus economy. Each period introduces a new framework – tradition, social order, materials, prototypes, uses of history, style, and so on. To make this approach work Crouch makes clear from the outset that every question can and should be asked of each period. The book ends with an example using the World Trade Center in New York analysed across various frameworks.

There is another unique twist in that while certain historical periods or buildings are engaged with expected categories – Stonehenge and time, Gothic cathedrals and structure – others introduce unexpected combinations – Christian architecture and adaptive re-use or Minoan palaces and social order. There is a problem in that some of the pairings suggest the early appearance of concepts that are in fact modern concerns; but what is gained is a less 'unified' history, since none of these categories are ever presented as the essence of any of the periods in question.

Ideally, what is needed is a combination of the last two approaches, recognising that it is not just the object in history that can be discussed, but the frameworks of history itself. What should be avoided here is the common schema of delivering an 'objective' history, or a history of objects, in the first year or two, followed by a shift to theory in the following years of a programme. The suggestion here is to present history together with its theory and a declaration of the historiographical methodology.

Historical snapshots: interior architecture, space and Modernism

The following sketches are meant to illustrate some of the problems discussed above as well as suggesting how one might start the process of proposing a history of interior architecture. If one were so inclined, an historical origin for interior architecture could be conceived. Some historians point to the building of the Roman Pantheon (and the Roman period in general) as a moment when the concept of interior space and representation took precedent over exterior expression [20]. It would not be difficult from this starting point to trace a line of development citing the interiors of Gothic cathedrals, Renaissance palaces and Baroque churches, through to the Brighton Pavilion, John Soane's house and then into the familiar territory of modern architectural space. This would replicate the problems already mentioned – such as positing origins, emphasising space as an essential concept, suggesting linear development or invoking the notion of progress as a natural agency. We might instead look for discursive statements which propose the notion of space from an interior perspective. August Schmarsow's essay of 1893 (published in 1905), 'The Essence of Architectural Creation' [21], could be a starting point. However, what would have to be recognised is that the essay was not immediately influential. While many of its sentiments were shared by modern architects there was little direct reference to the essay. This does not mean that we would have to dismiss it, since it is, in fact, an important document: it can be argued that it is in contemporary debates, however, where one can locate its impact particularly since its publication in English in 1994. Similarly, Paul Frankl's restructuring of stylistic periodization based on his emphasis on spatial configurations [22] has not stopped the traditional demarcations of style from being repeated. Both are important and significant for their suggestion of the experiential aspect of space and evocation of the body and inhabitation. However, the significance of their ideas is not to be found automatically in their contemporary contexts. It is also to be noted that these two significant texts belong to the world of art history. Architects were busy with their own thoughts about space – the formation of their distinct discourse.

Frank Lloyd Wright's notion of the destruction of the box is another key moment in the history of interior space. The intent and statement by Wright is significant, but its context is complicated. H. Allen Brooks has shown how the development of the 'destruction' was first a decomposition of interior space, before the container, the box itself, was opened up [23]. What complicates the evolution of this idea is the well-known disparity between the European and American reception of his work. Furthermore, it was not until 1942 that the first English language book on Wright appeared. And while Wright discusses the idea in his autobiography, the essay 'The Destruction of the Box' does not become widely available until 1960 with the publication of *Writings and Buildings* [24]. The idea, as a discursive statement, needs to be seen in its various contexts: as an influential concept on the work of de Stijl artists and architects; as a set of buildings which explored and developed the idea; as an idea discussed by Wright; as an essay; as a concept elaborated by commentators, other architects, critics, educators, theorists and historians. Where we situate this concept within the set of ideas elaborating interior architecture requires careful deliberation.

This is admittedly an extremely sketchy outline, but one that I hope is suggestive of how this approach might develop. There are numerous topics that can be interrogated, from the significance of the Parker Morris Report's identification of the importance of storage space in light of a growing consumer culture to the significance of the *Maison du Verre* by Pierre Chareau as an anachronistic modern project [25]. Some topics will more easily link up, others will not – but this is not a hindrance if we understand, even schematically, Foucault's concept of discourses and their formation. Banham's essay was a parting shot, a warning to architects, critics and historians about the crisis of identity that the profession has been grappling with for more than a century. Discourses are slippery, ephemeral, and changeable but are, in the end, more concrete than objective definitions, unified classifications or sets of rules. Notions of interior architecture defined by rules (they must work with existing structures) or objects (it must be an inside) will ultimately limit the practice and shed little light on the discipline. Tafuri suggested that history was about understanding the 'mental structures' that are behind things. This, I think, is the most interesting way of thinking about interior architecture: a mental structure, nothing more or less than *our* own way of thinking about things.

References

[1]   For this reason the research material for this chapter consists primarily of survey history texts. The same process and questions raised here could be paralleled in a study of theories of interior architecture.

[2]   Banham, R. 'A Black Box: The Secret Profession of Architecture', *A Critic Writes* (Berkeley: University of California Press, 1997) p.296.

[3]   Ibid., p.294

[4]   Foucault, M. *The Archaeology of Knowledge* (London: Routledge, 1995).

[5]   Banham, op. cit., p.297

[6]   Foucault, op. cit, p.26

[7]   Ibid., p.32

[8]   Heinrich Wölfflin is generally credited for popularising the notion of cyclical development

of style. His method was applied to both art and architecture in his *Principles of Art History* (New York: Henry Holt, 1932).

[9]   Scully, V. *Modern Architecture* (New York: Braziller, 1961) p.24.

[10]   Pevsner, N. *Pioneers of Modern Design, from William Morris to Walter Gropius* (Harmondsworth: Penguin, 1968).

[11]   Giedion, S. *Space, Time, Architecture, The Growth of a New Tradition* (Cambridge, MA: Harvard University Press, 2003).

[12]   Watkin, D. *A History of Western Architecture* (London: Lawrence King, 2000) p.8.

[13]   See, for example, Tafuri, M. *Architecture and Utopia* (Cambridge, MA: MIT Press, 1976), *Theories and History of Architecture* (New York: Harper & Row, 1976) and 'There is no criticism, only history: Richard Ingersoll interviews Manfredo Tafuri' reprinted in *Casabella*, Jan–Feb 1995.

[14]   Tafuri, M. 'There is no criticism, only history', p.97.

[15]   Kayvanian, C. 'Manfredo Tafuri: From the Critique of Ideology to Microhistories', *Design Issues*, vol.16, no.1, Spring 2000. The following notes on Tafuri and microhistories are primarily derived from this article.

[16]   To be clear, questioning or suspending concepts does not mean discarding them. Chronology, for example, is pedagogically useful in providing students with an organisational structure. What should be avoided is the idea that chronology necessarily or automatically explains things.

[17]   Noted by Harvey Cox in his introduction to Sennett, R. *The Fall of Public Man* (London: Faber and Faber, 1993) p.xvii.

[18]   Crouch, D. *History of Architecture, From Stonehenge to Skyscrapers* (New York: McGraw-Hill, 1985).

[19]   Ibid., p.2

[20]   For example, Boethius, A. and Ward-Perkins, J.B. *Etruscan and Roman Architecture* (Harmondsworth: Penguin, 1970) and Crouch, D., op. cit. See also MacDonald, W. *The Architecture of the Roman Empire* (New Haven: Yale University Press, 1982).

[21]   Published in Mallgrage and Ikonomou (eds.) *Empathy, Form & Space, Problems in German Aesthetics, 1873–1893* (Santa Monica: Getty Research Institute, 1994).

[22]   Frankl, P. *The Principles of Architectural History* (Cambridge, MA: MIT Press, 1968).

[23]   Allen Brooks, H. 'Frank Lloyd Wright and the Destruction of the Box', *The Journal of the Society of Architectural Historians*, vol.38, no.1, March 1979, pp.7–14.

[24]   Wright, F.L. 'The Destruction of the Box', *Writings and Buildings* (Cleveland: World Publishing, 1960).

[25]   The notion of its anachronism comes from its relative notoriety but general absence in history texts. During a lecture at the Berlage Institute (1991) Kenneth Frampton admitted to the difficulty of fitting the project within the accepted narratives of modern architecture. The project does not appear in his *Modern Architecture: A Critical History*.

Charles RICE

*School of Architecture, University of
Technology, Sydney*

FOR A CONCEPT OF THE DOMESTIC INTERIOR: SOME HISTORICAL AND THEORETICAL CHALLENGES

From art history and architecture through to literature, sociology and material culture, studies of the domestic interior have traditionally struggled in having a conceptual understanding of the interior. It is generally subsumed within concepts and objects proper to each discipline: the interior as artistic representation, as part of domestic architecture, as the setting for social and familial life, as constituted through practices of consumption and identity formation. While these perspectives are crucial for understanding the domestic interior and the events that take place there, the interior needs to be recognised as a modern formation that is not reducible to any one discipline, nor even to the simple combination of different disciplinary perspectives. Rather, the domestic interior's historical emergence renders problematic many of the ways in which its study is framed.

The domestic interior emerged as a new and distinct concept at the beginning of the nineteenth century. From the point of this emergence, it had significance as both a spatial condition, and an image-based condition. Semantically, it was only from the beginning of the nineteenth century that the interior came to mean 'the inside of a building or room, esp. in reference to the artistic effect; also, a picture or representation of the inside of a building or room. Also, in a theatre, a "set" consisting of the inside of a building or room.' There is a similar pattern of meaning for the French *intérieur*, a term which is also taken up in German from the beginning of the nineteenth century. The meaning of 'interior decoration' corroborates the idea of the interior's deliberate fabrication, its staginess, and its distinction from architectural construction: 'the planned co-ordination for artistic effect of colours and furniture, etc., in a room or software, 3D scanning and rapid prototyping equipment, where appropriate. There was no prescription regarding representation and individual group members were invited to work in any medium, virtual or physical in any combination.

To be effective, the sharing of information involved collective conceptualisation of the design when there was both partial knowledge about the design and the mode of representation. It therefore required a communication environment supportive of design collaboration. In previous projects of this kind where no studio environment exists, or where the collaboration was between students in two universities, a web-based project site was used as a portal, with online chatting, a 'wiki' editable information space, web cameras, and an ftp site [8]. However, for this project there was a dedicated studio space, regular group meetings, and a student culture of communication via email.

Of the three selected projects, one is particularly worth describing here as it illustrates how quality of thinking is informed by design process. Clearly what is important is the role of 'idea' at each stage, and how shifts in thinking inform development. Importantly, the example illustrated here demonstrates the contribution that a creative group can apply in their own right. The project was a full-body massage centre with individual 'booths' located inside an existing building. The original author offered the notion that the body, on an activated massage table, could be rotated inside the booth thus allowing the masseur to remain in a fixed location. The enclosing membrane was soft, translucent and partially transparent, such that any activity would be registered from without, and between booths. There was little understanding of how this was to be achieved or what its effect might be.

Approaching design through collaboration and modelling as the primary instrument of enquiry, rather than representation, had an impact on working methods. Of importance to the groups was to move away from more traditional approaches of creating a design before testing it through construction and materials, as this method reduced potential for creative input. We found that to test open ideas through modelling required shorter, more frequent iterations, a process that demanded more frequent communication between collaborators. This process led to a more cohesive understanding of the issues by all members of the team.

The group confronted this by seeking to inform form through registering the body's movement in space as the massage is performed, and mapping how space/surface is changed when the masseur's body presses against it. Initial physical experimentation with plaster of Paris and textile materials was conducted through full-size modelling against the body. This included stiffening the textile to provide a solid form where it comes in contact with the body leaving other material loose, and vice versa. At the same time a simple 3D Studio Max™ model was used to simulate deformable surfaces and their interaction with a digital body. But despite the realistic rendering appearing tangible, there was no material possibility nor any physical experience associated with this representation. This type of testing forces the limitations of the various software to be revealed, set against the backdrop of the difficulty that comes with full-scale physical modelling conducted in a studio setting.

building.' [1] The first use given is *Household Furniture and Interior Decoration*, the title of Thomas Hope's 1807 book, which, along with Charles Percier and Pierre Fontaine's *Receuil de décorations intérieurs* of 1801, marked the domestic interior as a site of professional struggle between architects and upholsterers. Indeed, the interior emerged as the newly articulated entity at stake in this battle, properly belonging to neither profession [2].

Doubleness is the significant feature of the emergent interior: the sense of its physical, three-dimensional spatiality, as well as its existence as an image, whether it be a two-dimensional representation such as a painting, a print in a portfolio of decoration, or a backdrop that could conjure up an interior as a 'scene'. This image-based sense also encompasses the interior as an imaginary or projected condition, one which could conjure the spatial from flat representations such as architectural plans, or which could transform a given spatial condition into something other [3]. Ultimately, the interior's doubleness has to do with the interdependence between image and space. Yet one manifestation is not simply transparent to or prior to the other. Both have particular effects as interiors, and a consciousness of the interior has been produced out of their often-disturbing interdependence [4].

None of this is to say that furniture and its arrangement, or indeed domestic habits and mores, did not exist before the interior's emergence. Rather, the interior conceptualized a developing consciousness of and comportment to the material realities of domesticity, realities which were actively formed with the interior's emergence.

With this conceptualization, the interior problematizes the notion of being framed as a ubiquitous and passive context for domestic life, always having existed throughout history, transparently evidencing a progressive evolution of style and ways of living. In order to investigate this problematization in some detail, this chapter will look at some examples of historical studies which concentrate on the interior's visual representation. The first step is to consider how the emergence of the interior relates to several conventions of image making. In relation to its image-based meaning, the interior emerged as a type of representation separate both from the conventions of architectural drawing, and from fine art genres. From the early nineteenth century, the interior view emerged in a practice of professional and amateur watercolour painting, and in engravings used to publish interior decoration schemes, the key examples here being the folios of Percier and Fontaine, and Hope. This mode of representation emerged outside of fine-art easel painting, and in a tense relation to architecture and the techniques of representation proper to architecture.

In pursuing this relationship between architectural techniques and the representation of the domestic realm, Robin Evans has investigated how the 'room' became a new subject for architectural drawing from the mid-eighteenth century. This occurred with the emergence of what he calls the developed surface drawing, one which shows all of the inside elevations of any given room folded out relative to the room's depicted plan. Evans notes that this was a more comprehensive representation of internal decorative schemes than could be achieved through the conventional architectural section drawing, which could only show in detail one inside elevation of any given room at any one time [5]. Developed surface drawings do not partake of the interior's doubled sense, where the interior as a spatial ensemble is understood consciously, and is accompanied by representational techniques that double this spatial sense. As Evans argues, the developed surface drawing maintains a sense of the decorative treatment of internal walls as flat surfaces, making the space between them void-like. Including moveable furnishing that might give a sense of spatiality to such decorative treatment was a problem for this flat representational technique; furniture tends to sit anchored to the wall, or float awkwardly in the void between walls [6].

For Evans, the interior emerged in a spatialized sense in the early nineteenth century when the distribution of furniture became linked to the idea that there was a variety of ways of occupying a room, where previously, differently decorated rooms joined in plan were each to be occupied in one particular way. Humphry Repton was the major figure in this shift: 'It was the call for variety *within* the social landscape of the room that broke the hallowed ring of peripheral furnishing.' [7] Such a shift in distribution, both for furniture and for a room's occupants, began to outstrip the ability of the developed surface drawing to represent this condition adequately. What emerged as a response to the inadequacy of the developed surface technique were representations that showed that 'the *furniture* occupies the room and then figures inhabit the furniture.' [8] These emerging representations were, in a historically specific sense, interiors.

What is most surprising about this argument is that it is so little utilized within studies of the interior that are concerned with its visual representation. Another way of stating this is to say that, while representations such as developed surface drawings, and interior watercolours and engravings are known as historical artefacts, their link to the emergence of the interior is not established. The way in which a new conceptualization of the domestic realm emerges in their difference from representations such as sections and fine art paintings is not recognized. For example, the prominent historian of the interior Peter Thornton understands the separation at the turn of the nineteenth century between architecture on the one hand, and the emerging professions of upholstery and later interior decoration on the other. Yet his book *Authentic Décor: The Domestic Interior, 1620–1920*, covers a broad span of time, utilizing a range of representational types and considering all to be of equal value in providing evidence for a history of the domestic interior. For Thornton, this has to do with establishing the historical veracity of actual domestic objects and the way they are depicted in use. Mario Praz, perhaps the 'founding father' of the historical study of the domestic interior, goes as far back as there exist representations in his seminal book *A History of Interior Decoration from Pompeii to Art Nouveau*. Both Thornton and Praz treat all manner of representations as providing transparent access to ways of living in times past. More recently, scholars of art history who have an interest in the representation of domesticity have noted problems to do with treating paintings, whose purpose was not simply the representation of domesticity 'as it really was', in this transparent way [9].

This issue of the historical treatment of the interior in terms of visual evidence would only be of minor interest if it wasn't so pervasive in more popular accounts of the history of domesticity and the home. Popular wisdom has it that the Dutch seventeenth-century interior is its most recognizable, modern form. This claim offers further insight into the way images of interiors are read as historical evidence of spatial practices. In his book *Home: A Short History of an Idea*, Witold Rybczynski, largely drawing on the work of Praz and Thornton, has identified in paintings by such Dutch artists as Gerard Dou, Pieter de Hooch, Emanuel de Witte and Jan Vermeer the recognizable qualities of home, crucial to these being a sense of intimacy or what Praz identified as *Stimmung*, 'a characteristic of interiors that has less to do with functionality than with the way that the room conveys the character of its owner' [10]. Home develops from this sense in being demarcated as a private world, and Rybczynski finds Dutch domestic arrangements exemplary in managing this demarcation. He allows a universally dominant idea, or rather a fantasy, of home to claim historical credence through the authority of fine art. In addition, it is a fine art that has broad appeal through its supposed realism and association with the domestic. But as Heidi de Mare has shown, these paintings only gained their 'domestic' appeal in the nineteenth century, the time when 'bourgeois family life became a nucleus around which the [Dutch] nation was formed.' De Mare argues that concepts such as privacy, intimacy, comfort and home were nineteenth-century sentiments that 'were then projected into the past and applied to seventeenth-century paintings, books and houses. Thus was born the wide-ranging, homogenous concept of domesticity.' [11] The popularity of these images was related to the mechanism of their availability. De Mare notes that Dutch paintings were sold abroad in the nineteenth century, especially in the United States, the newly associated ideas of domesticity being exported along with the physical artefacts which supposedly originated these ideas [12]. Associated with this export was a strain of art-historical analysis which emphasized the social content of the paintings, this perspective still informing those who would read a recognizable domestic meaning and content into the paintings [13].

In a very different interpretation of Dutch genre painting, Martha Hollander relates their visual enticements not to recognizable characteristics of home, but rather to compositional techniques and associated constructions of meaning which were historically and culturally specific to sixteenth-century Holland. Hollander focuses her investigation on the way space was manipulated in the paintings. Their compartmentalization, drawing on and extending the compartmentalization of rooms and the nesting of vistas, mirrors and other images within rooms, 'makes for a remarkably complex play of meanings'. She locates this development in terms of a 'diagrammatic arrangement of images across a flat surface' [14] that underlies the development of Western image making. She notes:

> Dutch artists integrated religious allegories of an earlier era into their secular images of modern life, [and] they adapted a traditional visual formula for their depictions of realistic space. In fact, their interest in perspective co-existed with the diagrammatic structure of earlier pictorial media. The resulting tension between the associative organization of signs and naturalistic perspective is one of the most fascinating and challenging qualities of Dutch art [15].

For Victor Stoichita, these are examples of meta-paintings, whereby the painted subject offers a comment on the constitution of, and possibilities within, painting itself. The paintings offered a dialogue with the idea of the frame, particularly in the treatment of doors as openings between rooms. This meta-commentary is what defined easel painting [16].

These interpretations reinforce an understanding of what Hollander calls Dutch art's 'depictions of realistic space', rather than its realistic depictions of space [17]. What was being painted was not, as Rybczynski would have it, 'the material world as he [in this case, Emanuel de Witte] saw it'. Rybczynski's idealism substitutes post-nineteenth-century fascination for historical fact. He writes:

> This love of the real world – 'realism' is too weak a word – was evident in many details. We can enjoy the way that the shadow of the windows falls on the partly open door, the red taffeta curtains that colour the light in the room, the shiny brass of the chandelier, the rich gilt of the mirror frame and the matte texture of the pewter jug [18].

Rybczynski is taken in by the actual subject of the paintings, which was the enticement to looking itself, an enticement Hollander captures in the title of her book: *An Entrance for the Eyes*. Rybczynski is unable, or unwilling, to be critical about the specificity of such enticements in their historical context, their meanings apart from his pre-ordained and naturalized narrative of home.

It is established that such paintings, and associated forms such as miniature houses and illusionistic perspective boxes, were made for the Dutch bourgeoisie as furnishings for the houses in which they lived. As visual images, they doubled the domestic space of their reception, setting up a play of relations within this doubled situation, not to mention a play of relations between any one painting and what Stoichita calls 'transposed' paintings within it [19]. Yet this compelling play of doubles, and its domestic content, does not mean that these paintings belong to the concept of the interior. Stoichita's argument about meta-painting is compelling in its own terms, that is, as an argument about the emergence of easel painting, but it does not contribute to an understanding of the specificity of the interior as a type of representation. As the work of Evans shows, the interior does not simply emerge from easel painting, let alone being present in a continuous history of Western image making, as Praz would have it. If these Dutch paintings can be considered interiors it is only by association, and through the construction of a history of the interior that has little bearing on elucidating the historical emergence of the interior.

There seem to be two basic tendencies at play in these conventional histories of the interior. A historian like Thornton seeks to reconstruct how things really were in the past, often using paintings to verify material artefacts and their authentic uses. Rybczynski on the other hand seeks to establish a continuity between present desires about home, and the affirming light historical images might cast on those desires. Even though these tendencies differ from each other, the issue of authenticity underlies them both. Images are subjected to a kind of reality test, where they are made to bear witness either to a supposed past truth of domestic life, or to present expectations about how that past might confirm a current fascination with the interior, and the way it figures in identity formation through the commodification of domestic life. The introduction to Rybczynski's book reveals this latter tendency most forcefully, beginning as it does with a lengthy description of a Ralph Lauren homewares display.

In this light, the transparent reading of various paintings and representations can be seen to be based on a consumerist impulse, one that sees all possibilities to be equally available at the level of style. On the one hand, this is an effect of the interior's emergence, that it is understood consciously as simultaneously an image-based and spatial condition, the idea that a spatial display is read as an image. On the other hand, however, that one can consume visually a Dutch painting in the same way as a Ralph Lauren interior setting produces a historical account of the interior which occludes precisely the formation of this very doubled condition historically. What is common in the histories of the interior that have been considered so far is that they attest to a post-nineteenth-century way of seeing. This way of seeing authorizes a general historical retrospection which is itself not appreciated within a historical context. This situation approaches what Michel Foucault terms traditional history:

> We believe in the dull constancy of instinctual life and imagine that it continues to exert its force indiscriminately in the present as it did in the past. But a knowledge of history easily disintegrates this unity, depicts its wavering course, locates its moments of strength and weakness, and defines its oscillating reign [20].

Foucault's effective history, designated above as arising from a 'knowledge of history', is a history of discontinuity, for the sake of breaking tendencies for recognition and 'rediscovery of ourselves' [21] in the construction of history. In Foucault's terms, the emergence of the interior, in its doubleness, can be cast as an event in the schema of effective history, an event that, when perceived, enables a 'reversal of a relationship of forces' [22]. Traditional history, on the other hand, wants to overcome precisely the eruption of the interior into historical consciousness. It wants to overcome the difficulty of the interior's doubleness by offering a range of historical images for an easy and relativistic consumption. An effective history of the interior would have to fight the interior's very mechanism of doubleness, it would have to lay it bare rather than extend its hold over the consumption of historical images.

Walter Benjamin's work offers the clearest example of what an effective history of the interior would be. In his notes on the interior from *The Arcades Project*, Benjamin recognizes that the problem of history as Foucault would later define it is embedded within the very subject matter of the domestic:

> The difficulty in reflecting on dwelling: on the one hand, there is something age-old – perhaps eternal – to be recognized here, the image of that abode of the human being in the maternal womb; on the other hand, this motif of primal history notwithstanding, we must understand dwelling in its most extreme form as a condition of nineteenth-century existence [23].

Benjamin is proposing that the interior's emergence is bound up with an idea of history which renders problematic the smooth progression of historical time. For Benjamin the interior is both a modern phenomenon – 'a condition of nineteenth century existence' – as well as appearing to be age old. Yet crucially his idea of primal history severs the interior from having a direct link to present experience. Its appearance in this way sets up an ambivalence in its interpretation, this ambivalence being precisely the 'difficulty in reflecting on dwelling': its primal nature can be taken as eternal or unchanging – an essence of the domestic of the kind Rybczynski conjures – or, as Benjamin proposed, as evidence of a rupturing in the very idea of historical continuity. This sense of rupture is precisely what the sort of continuities established in the conventional history of the interior want to repair. Yet evidence of this rupture is precisely given when the techniques of this historical construction are understood, that is, as the nineteenth-century construction of the significance of sixteenth-century paintings. This mutual implication of two time periods suggests something of Foucault's 'wavering course' and 'oscillating reign' of effective history; in other words, it is history not as a linear and progressive development reaching a natural and inevitable point in the present.

In some ways Rybczynski's account makes all of this clear, or at least available to the sort of critical interpretation being attempted here. It is not that he has missed vital evidence that would disprove his case. Rather, he has simply been unable to do anything but affirm a historically formed category – he names it 'home', I would want to name it 'the interior' – as an essential, supra-historical, perhaps even ontological one. The real difficulty in reflecting on dwelling is the difficulty of being critical about something that is so pervasive and 'normal' as simply to be a given. But here again, there is a clue for a 'reversal of the relationship of forces': it is not that the interior is the normal context of our lives, and hence one might like to inquire into the history of this normality; rather, the interior normalizes us at a particular historical moment, as it conceptualizes a particular set of historically inscribed forces. It produces this 'us'. Given this, the critical question is not that we are simply consumers of the interior, and that is the fact of our domestic life. This is not untrue, it is simply not a useful angle on the relationship between history and domesticity. Rather, one might ask: under what conditions did this consumerist impulse also emerge out of mechanisms by which domesticity was formed in the interior? To restate the argument: the consumption of Dutch domestic scenes is not to do with some sort of special emanation from those paintings, some essential characteristic. Rather, it is to do with the fact that those paintings become consumable as interiors only after a particular moment, only after the emergence of a concept of the interior allows them, both conceptually and in practical terms, to become consumable. One effect of this emergence is the idea that one can have something called 'a history of the interior', which, again, does not say anything particularly useful about – and in fact actively occludes – an account of the historical emergence of the interior.

Studies of the interior across a number of disciplines struggle in having a conceptual understanding of the interior because the very concept of the interior is one which acts to naturalize itself. To say that the domestic interior is a concept is not to intellectualize something which is innately averse to such an effort. Rather, it is to de-humanize an area of research which is so pervasively 'human'. As soon as 'we' forget that the interior is where 'we' live, the study of the interior will open up in new and interesting ways.

References

[1] 'Interior', 'interior decoration' in *The Oxford English Dictionary*, 2nd edn. (Oxford: Clarendon Press, 1989).

[2] See Thornton, P. *Authentic Décor: the Domestic Interior, 1620–1920* (New York: Viking, 1984) pp.10–12.

[3] See, for example, Baudelaire, C. 'The Twofold Room' (1862) in Scarfe, F., ed. *The Poems in Prose, with La Fanfarlo* (London: Anvil Press, 1989) pp.36–9.

[4] Vidler, A. *The Architectural Uncanny: Essays in the Modern Unhomely* (Cambridge, MA: MIT Press, 1992).

[5] Evans, R. 'The Developed Surface: An Enquiry into the Brief Life of an Eighteenth-Century Drawing Technique' in *Translations from Drawing to Building and Other Essays* (London: Architectural Association, 1997) pp.200–3.

[6] Ibid., pp.210–14, 222

[7] Ibid., pp.214–15. Emphasis in original. Evans suggests that this was a belated uptake of the example of variety in occupying rooms visible in Paris from the 1750s.

[8] Ibid., p.219. Emphasis in original.

[9] See especially Syson, L. 'Representing Domestic Interiors' in Ajmar-Wollheim, M. and Dennis, F., eds. *At Home in Renaissance Italy* (London: V&A Publications, 2006) pp.86–101.

[10] Rybczynski, R. *Home: A Short History of an Idea* (Harmondsworth: Penguin, 1987) p.43. See also Praz, M. *An Illustrated History of Interior Decoration From Pompeii to Art Nouveau* (London: Thames and Hudson, 1964) pp.50–5.

[11] de Mare, H. 'Domesticity in Dispute: A Reconsideration of Sources' in Cieraad, I., ed. *At Home: An Anthropology of Domestic Space* (Syracuse: Syracuse University Press, 1999) p.14. This argument would also seem to put in dispute the idea that bourgeois culture and society themselves, as particularly 'domestic' manifestations, were born in seventeenth-century Holland. For this perspective, see Lukacs, J. 'The Bourgeois Interior', *American Scholar*, 1970, 39(4), 616–30. The German meaning, derived from the French, for *interieur* as an image references seventeeth-century Dutch painting. See 'interieur' in *Duden. Das große Wörterbuch der deutschen Sprache* (Mannheim: Duden Verlag, 1999). De Mare's argument reinforces the idea that this meaning would have occurred as a nineteenth-century projection of values onto this art.

[12] de Mare, op. cit., p.14

[13] Ibid., p.20

[14] Hollander, M. *An Entrance for the Eyes: Space and Meaning in Seventeenth-Century Dutch Art* (Berkeley: University of California Press, 2002) p.3.

[15] Ibid., pp.3–4

[16] Stoichita, V. *The Self-Aware Image: An Insight into Early Modern Meta-Painting* (Cambridge: Cambridge University Press, 1997) pp.44–53.

[17] See also de Mare, op. cit., pp.20, 26–9

[18] Rybczynski, op. cit., p.69

[19] See Stoichita, op. cit., pp.157–73, and Hollander, op. cit., pp.119–29.

[20] Foucault, M. 'Nietzsche, Genealogy, History' in Rabinow, P., ed. *The Foucault Reader* (Harmondsworth: Penguin, 1984) p.87.

[21] Ibid., p.88

[22] Ibid.

[23] Benjamin, W. *The Arcades Project* (Cambridge, MA: The Belknap Press of Harvard University Press, 1999) p.220 [I4,4].

Terry MEADE

School of Architecture and Design,
University of Brighton

THINKING INSIDE THE BOX – ANXIETIES OF CONTAINMENT

Introduction

> ...in a state of siege order is frozen, yet disorder boils beneath the surface. Like a giant spring slowly compressed and ready to burst at any moment, immense tension lies in strange repose. Time stands still, like the ticking of a time-bomb, and if we are to take the full measure of Benjamin's point, that the state of siege is not the exception but the rule, then we are required to rethink our notions of order, of center and base, and of certainty too.
>
> Michael Taussig [1]

I received the information about the conference 'Thinking Inside the Box' on the same day that my local council delivered two black boxes together with a note urging me to 'Think inside the box'. This note was addressed to the 'occupier' and came complete with appropriate stickers for the boxes, and an admonition to 'separate out' objects for recycling, 'because we love our city'.

This coincidence started a train of thoughts about containment, separation and occupation, and the sort of flows of material and information that move in and out of private space. In this chapter I want to expand on some of these thoughts in an attempt to speculate about what interiors might be in the twenty-first century.

Taken at face value, the conference title has provided something specific to aim at. 'Thinking Inside the Box' is interesting for the issues it raises and those it ignores. The use of the word 'box' suggests a conventional interpretation of interior space as static and contained. It also suggests some sort of imagined border around this academic discipline excluding what might be outside the box. What it ignores are questions about the way spatial boundaries are devised; about the social and temporal context that people move within; and about the presence of people as readers and projectors of ideas about interior space.

As a teacher in this field, I believe students must be encouraged to read widely, and to explore the larger environment they are acting within. They must be aware of the realities of the new century and of relationships between politics and space. Such understanding is indispensable for any sort of practice today and is in fact the source of much creative inspiration. Interiors, concerned as it is with human inhabitation and spatial design, must be open to a range of alternative readings of territory and a range of spatial practices.

Too often in this discipline we encounter students who are content with a restricted vision and narrow horizons. Students who appear happy to produce work that is little better than arranging toy furniture within a shoe-box, with almost no concern about the wider situation.

In this chapter I want to respond to the theme of the conference, 'Thinking Inside the Box', by looking at the wider frame 'Interiors in the Twenty-first Century'.

I have used the word 'anxiety' in my title to describe a condition that seems to be haunting the collective unconscious of Western cities in the twenty-first century – anxiety about a disordered and dangerous world. This condition reveals itself (as Lieven De Cauter has described it) through the spread of a 'Capsular Civilization' [2], a proliferation of walls, boundaries and barricades, that are forming and informing interior spaces today. The first part of this chapter will list some of the forces contributing to the growth of a 'fearful culture' and the defensive measures these have provoked.

The second part (and the more difficult) will be an attempt to unravel notions about the character of barricaded space. This will involve a certain amount of speculation on the irrational and excitable nature of fantasies that may be formed and played out when thought is internalised and distanced from particular objects and events in the world. In the final part, I will briefly suggest some strategies for a way out of this defended view of the discipline, to reassert or recapture the creative and subversive qualities that are, I believe, a major attraction of interiors.

Fear, retreat and exclusion

A number of writers across a variety of fields have noted a sense of threat and insecurity in today's world. A quick shortlist might include: Peter Marcuse, writing about 'The Barricaded City' [3]; J.G. Ballard writing about 'sealed enclaves' [4]; Slavoz Zizek about 'alienated public exchange' [5]; Martin Amis on 'ambient fear' [6]; and Stephen Graham writing about 'Specters of Terror' [7]. Paul Virilio, in his latest book [8], has described 'the great hemming in' and the 'return to the walled city', particularly in America, where gated communities are multiplying, along with the ever-widening net of surveillance. He predicts the rise of the private city and the reversal of notions of inside and outside. This list could easily be expanded. We generally look to writers to provide some sort of insight into the human condition and such a mix of novelists, political commentators and architectural theoreticians using similar themes suggests a broad level of consensus about the current state of collective anxiety [9].

A YouGov opinion poll published in *The Sunday Times* on New Year's Eve, 2006, showed a disparity between people's happiness at home and their despair about the wider world. Fear of terrorism, fear of immigrants, fear of crime, fear of sexual depravity, fear of ecological catastrophes, fear of teenagers, and so on. In an article about fear, Brian Massumi [10] begins by describing the colour-coded terror alert system introduced in the USA in March 2002. He says that life has 'settled, to all appearances permanently, between yellow and orange, (guarded and high alert)'. A similar system has just been set up by MI5, for people in Britain to receive emails about the state of terrorist threat (currently severe). Massumi says 'safe', has fallen off the spectrum of perception, insecurity 'is the new normal'.

> The alert system was introduced to calibrate the public's anxiety. In the aftermath of 9/11, the public's fearfulness had tended to swing out of control in response to dramatic, but maddeningly vague, government warnings of an impending follow-up attack. The alert system was designed to modulate that fear. It could raise it a pitch, then lower it before it became too intense, or even worse, before habituation dampened response. Timing was everything. Less fear itself than fear fatigue became an issue of public concern. Affective modulation of the populace was now an official, central function of an increasingly time-sensitive government [11].

Anxiety has long been part of the human condition and it can be argued that there is little hard evidence to support a new threat. After all, it has been five years since the attack on the World Trade Centre and our lives (in the West anyway) have largely been unchanged.

However, a new element seems to have emerged recently, a sort of 'constructed anxiety' as part of a permanent state of emergency [12]. Richard Jackson, in his book *Writing the War on Terrorism* [13], makes a convincing case about the exaggeration of threat and the construction of myths about terrorism. The purpose, he says, is to 'maintain a certain level of social fear and to justify government's extraordinary measures. Both the British and US Governments have argued that restrictions on civil liberties are necessary for the security of civilised societies. Most poignantly, they both maintain that the threat 'resides within'. Such language is designed to reinforce the idea:

> That 'the home', a place of comfort and security, has been invaded and infected by the scourge of terrorism... [This] touches upon some of our deepest cultural insecurities, and also puts the notion of threat into the mode of disease – terrorism as a cancer or plague – which poisons the body from within [14].

Television, newspapers and the internet have all helped to reinforce the sense of danger, creating constant alert. The sociologist Zygmunt Bauman argues that state power is now built on personal vulnerability and personal protection, rather than social vulnerability and social protection. Politicians have abdicated any responsibility for moderating the impact of the inherent insecurity and instability of the capitalist market so they offer to assuage other types of insecurity, in particular our physical safety [15]. Bill Durodie, director of the International Centre for Security Analysis at Kings College, has argued that people in the twenty-first century, bereft of the moorings of social connectedness and living isolated and fragmented lives, are particularly vulnerable to a sense of insecurity. This is fuelled by the perception that we have lost the ability to make any significant changes in the larger environment [16].

Reorganisation of space

The effects of all this on the organisation of interior and exterior space are quite profound, not least because insecurity often leads to a reshaping of the environment and modification of our actions. An array of walls and borders has emerged recently, all with the intention of isolating, separating and guarding against intrusion. Mike Davis has written about the 'greatest wave of wall building and border fortification in history' [17]. Walls between Israel and Palestine, around the EU, on the US–Mexico and Spain–Morocco borders, on the borders of Kashmir, India, Saudi Arabia, Botswana, Costa Rica – the list could go on. 'Once again, nations are being (re)imagined as bounded, organised spaces with closely controlled, and filtered relationships with the supposed terrors of the outside world' [18]. New laws, rules and regulations in the political sphere, the increased use of surveillance, the militarisation of public space and the use of checkpoints: all point to the rise of a promiscuous surveillance society. Jonathan Raban, whose recent novel *Surveillance* was published last year, wrote:

> Since September 11th CCTV cameras, magnetometers, BioWatch air-sniffers, razor wire, concrete fortifications and all the rest of the machinery of state security and surveillance have become so much a part of the furniture of life in the US that we barely notice them. It has become automatic to remove one's shoes and hat, deposit keys, change and cellphone in the tray provided as one passes the 'No Joking' sign at the airport checkpoint or enters the lobby of a public building. We expect to be intimately investigated in order to prove our good intentions. Year by year the government grows more importunately parental, the citizenry more obediently childish. Of course they log our phone calls – who are we to contradict the grown-ups who wage their hi-tech secret war on our behalf? They know best [19].

Technologies such as those listed above are increasingly employed as preventative measures. Through their intrusive qualities, they dislocate the borders between public and private. Consequently an increased significance is attached to territory, to place and to locality – part of the fantasy about protection offered by the walls and boundaries of protected communities.

Walls, borders and containment

> ...reality, as we know it, is largely an internally generated construct of the nervous system, and once constructed it is projected back onto the world through behavioural

interactions with objects in our local environments. Much of the consistency and logic of external events is, consequently, a property of the 'perceiver' rather than the perceived object [20].

Walls are never inert. Apart from their physical role as spatial dividers, they also have a psychological effect in the way they condition perception, blocking off some scenes from view and allowing others through. Meanings attached to them or that resonate from them are translated as binary opposites to do with inside and outside – public and private; restricted and open; order and chaos; us and them; included and excluded and so on.

In spaces isolated and sealed by walls, the interior world can become intensified. Interiorisation as it has been described, is a 'progressive distancing of thought from the objects and events in the world' [21]. It leads to a separation of thought from any 'here and now' and may enhance notions of retreat and exclusion, acceptance and rejection. This is also the route whereby fantasy enters the interior. According to Jacqueline Rose, Freud considered fantasy to be a psychic field, no less important and no less real than the world we live and move in. However, it is distinguished from that world by the potentially endless transformative capacities of the mind. 'We use fantasy, conscious and unconscious, to explore things that have not happened and never will.' [22] Fantasy is not necessarily a private matter; it can link the 'private' to the world at large, when it plays a part in 'forging the collective will'.

> If fantasy can be grounds for license and pleasure (the popular meaning is not of course completely out), it can just as well surface as fierce blockading protectiveness, walls up all around our inner and outer psychic and historical selves [23].

In Peter Schneider's short novel about the Berlin Wall, *The Wall Jumper*, we read how for those in the West the Wall gradually erased all direct perception of Berlin's other half, and had merely become a metaphor in the West German consciousness. 'The view East shrank to a view of the border complex and finally to a group therapy absorption with the self: for Germans in the West the Wall became a mirror that told them, day by day, who was the fairest one of all.' [24] The narrator of the novel stated, 'I really don't see the Wall any more, time doesn't heal wounds; it kills the sensation of pain'.

Fear needs clearly identifiable enemies. Describing the enormous intrusion caused by the separation wall under construction in Israel/Palestine, Ruchama Marton and Dalit Baum asked: 'What does this wall expose while concealing? What is it supposed to block from our view?' [25]

The stated reason for the wall was defence. But it also acts as a defence against seeing, and to maintain a particular self-image.

> A useful way of understanding some of the psychological mechanisms involved in the wall is the concept of splitting. The power and magic of the splitting mechanism lies in its simplicity. It permits only two extremes: the whole world is split into 'good' and 'bad,' with nothing in between. According to Melanie Klein, splitting is the

psychological defence mechanism that separates good from bad, both in oneself and in the Other: 'Splitting is caused by a high level of anxiety, which offers no options or choice and is considered to be the most primitive kind of defence against anxiety.' [26]

Marton and Baum argue that the wall 'separates the contents of the inner space into two parts: the 'bad', unwanted parts, which are hard to deal with, and the 'good' parts that are in accord with the self-image. The 'bad' parts are externalized – in other words, projected onto the 'other'. This fantasy then gives legitimacy and licence for measures of control and possession over the space of the 'other', the 'bad' parts. In a secluded and heavily defended interior, such distorted thinking cannot easily be communicated back outside for correcting or reworking.

Most designers are aware of the strong emotional charge invested in such symbolic forms as the house. Mark Cousins pointed to the anxiety caused by any perceived damage to the fabric of the home, or indeed, any violation of the private domain. 'At a rational level you might ask why it is that people have a horror, and in certain types an extreme horror, of very minor defects in houses? Why is it that people have an absolute horror of things like stains or very minor leaks, which only require, at that rational level, a bucket under them? You know the house won't fall down, nothing is going to follow from this leak.' [27]

He says that these things operate on powerful fantasies. The house has often been seen as the body's shell, as well as a metaphor for both body and psyche. There is a certain correlation between the anxiety about the elements of the house that go wrong, and the repression about the body.

The fiction that the domestic world is a space of protection against the darkness of an unknown and dangerous exterior has long been accepted and maintained.

In a recent work, 'Family History', Gillian Wearing recreated an afternoon talk-show set and exposed its nature as brightly coloured 'idealised home'. Daytime TV is full of bright lights and colourful furnishings that create a feeling of cheerfulness.

The illusion of security

Zygmunt Bauman argues that the protective capacity of space is now revealed to be an illusion. He says that the attacks of 11 September 2001 demonstrated something that has been evident for some time: that places of escape, retreat or hiding can no longer be viable, no matter how well fortified and protected they are. It does not mean that 'space' is not important, but it does mean that territory cannot be the prime guarantee of security it once was. This, he says, is a reflection of the mobility and speed of global agencies not bound to place. Those who are least space-bound, least tied to (encumbered by) place and who are most free to move, rule.

Writing about a police raid on the home of two Muslim brothers in Forest Gate, South London, in June 2006, Henry Porter predicted that forced entry is going to become a lot more common in Britain. He described it as an attack on that great principle of English law, the 'inviolability of the dwelling house'.

> The right dates back to 1609. A man named Semayne complained that his home had been broken into and his assets seized by the sheriff. The judgement that followed declared: 'The house of everyone is his castle.' It went on to say that if a door is open, a sheriff may enter but that 'it is not lawful for the sheriff, on request made and denial, at the suit of a common person to break the defendant's house' [28].

Porter says that this right has remained more or less intact until recent times. He states that the Serious Organised Crime and Police Act 2005 allows a variety of agencies to obtain a warrant for forcible entry if it is believed that it would not be 'practicable' to issue a notice.

The Israeli architect Eyal Weisman [29] has described more extreme measures used by the Israeli military in their attacks on Palestinian towns. They have developed the tactic of walking through walls, the way a worm moves through an apple, in an effort to avoid circulating in the more dangerous public space of the street. They move through the dense contiguous fabric of the urban structure horizontally through party walls and vertically through holes blasted in ceilings and floors. Before they begin an attack they cut off services (water, sewage, electricity, TV) in order to contain the inhabitants, and then attempt to turn the city inside out, to disrupt its logic. This brings the conflict into the very private domain, into the bedrooms and living rooms of the inhabitants. A Palestinian woman identified only as Aisha described the experience:

> Imagine it – you are sitting in your living room which you know so well; this is the room where the family watches television together after the evening meal. And suddenly that wall disappears with a deafening roar, the room fills with dust and debris, and through the wall pours one soldier after another screaming orders. You have no idea if they are after you, if they've come to take over your home, or if your house just lies on their route to somewhere else. The children are screaming, panicking. Is it possible to even imagine the horror of a five-year-old child as four, six, eight, twelve soldiers, their faces painted black, submachine guns pointing everywhere, antennas protruding from their backpacks, making them look like giant alien bugs, blast their way through the wall [30].

When the soldiers have passed through the wall, the inhabitants are locked inside one of the rooms where they are made to remain – sometimes for several days until the operation is concluded, often without water, food or medicine.

In a bizarre twist, Weisman says that the Israeli army is fully aware of avant-garde urban research conducted in architectural institutions and has reading lists containing many works of critical theory. Works by Deleuze and Guattari, Guy Debord and the situationists, along with contemporary writings on urbanism, psychology, postcolonial and poststructural theory. Even the work of artists such as Gordon Matta-Clark, borrowing terms such as his 'un-walling the wall'. There is a fascination with the writings of Deleuze and Guattari, particularly their writings about Nomad versus Sedentary and smooth versus striated space. A retired Brigadier-General who conducts the Israeli Army Operational Theory Research Institute said the army often uses the term 'to smooth out space' when they conduct operations in Arab towns which are anchored to place and enclosed by fences, walls, ditches, roadblocks and borders.

There is also an extreme reliance on technology in the creation of such brutal chaos. A fantasy that technology can provide answers to complex and intricate questions through control and containment. Technologies of surveillance, creating intricate 3D models of Arab towns, new developments of seeing through walls, and also of shooting through walls, effectively rendering architecture transparent.

Weisman inserts the warning that we can all become victims of this technology. It is not only militaries that learn from other militaries but also large civilian industries. The world is synergetic, inter-connected.

Conclusion

The title 'Thinking Inside the Box', taken at face value, parallels a kind of fortress mentality growing in an over-anxious world. It appears to provide a restricted view of the discipline, and I would argue, it promotes one particular notion of interiors over others – interiors as decoration, applying a sort of cosmetic layer to interior space. The proliferation of interiors supplements and TV makeover programmes such as Changing Rooms are a testament to the success of such perceptions. In work of this kind, it is possible to lose connection with the politics of a particular situation and to engage in a very personal practice, which is not always brought back to the public or political realm.

As part of any conception of interiors, an outside is necessary for communication and connection to various networks and flows. No-one living in a Western city can be unaware of contemporary concerns about major world issues: war, terrorism, security, climate change etc. For those of us involved with interiors, it is impossible to retreat into the confines of one's discipline and not acknowledge the impact of these concerns on our work, our teaching and our thinking.

It has been the intention of this chapter to suggest some of the realities facing or affecting interiors as a discipline in the twenty-first century. The question of the way forward then inevitably arises, of how to operate in such a situation of retreat and insecurity.

Returning to Schneider's novel The Wall Jumper, as a starting point I could imagine operating on walls and borders in a manner similar to the way his characters act as they also strive to get beyond a half-city vision. A novel provides a framework for thinking about things and in this novel, the city is acutely observed. The novelist's intention is to pose questions from various angles and he uses his wall jumpers to this end. For example, as a designer it would be possible to imaginatively assume the character of the boundary walker and be constantly on the move, back and forth through walls and boundaries. Or of Herr Kabe, the wall jumper who repeatedly vaults the wall and in doing so succeeds in overcoming it. Suspended over the wall for seconds at a time, he can view both East and West. These and other characters strive to neutralise the sensory deprivations and distortions caused by the wall by using various ways of passing through it or over it. 'They adopt techniques that on the face of it appear irrational but are attempts to rectify perception of the world on the wall's other side, and make what is half, perceptually at least, whole again.' [31] One could also point to ways of inhabiting walls such as in 'The Wall Game' proposed by Lebbeus Woods, in which two opposing sides playfully act within contested territory. Highlighting the importance of play and games as a method of approach aiming to undermine or eradicate division and containment [32].

Interiors has to operate at the edges and in the margins, in the in-between and unexpected spaces. In fact, this is the very attraction of the discipline, looking and moving back and forth across boundaries with an ability to exploit any gap that allows for a certain amount of play or room to move.

The world is a complex and dangerous place and survival requires vigilance, adaptability and creativity. One of Schneider's characters noted 'It will take us longer to tear down the wall in our heads than any wrecking company will need for the wall we can see.' One has a sense that interiors is much more unsettling and consequently much more interesting in its conception than is implied by 'thinking inside any box'.

References

[1]   Taussig, M. *The Nervous System* (New York: Routledge, 1982).
[2]   De Cauter, L. *The Capsular Civilization, On the City in the Age of Fear* (Rotterdam: NAi Publishers, 2004).
[3]   Marcuse, P. *Walls of Fear and Walls of Support* in Nan, E., ed. *Architecture of Fear* (New York: Princeton Architectural Press, 1997).
[4]   Ballard, J.G. interviewed by V. Vale on 23 November 2004 in *J.G. Ballard, Conversations* (San Francisco: RE/Search Publications, 2005) p.31.
[5]   Zizek, S. *Guardian*, 19 February 2005.
[6]   Amis, M. *Observer*, 10 September 2006.
[7]   Graham, S. *Specters of Terror* in Misselwitz, P. and Rieniets, T., eds. *City of Collision* (Switzerland: Birkhauser, 2006) p.156.
[8]   Virilio, P. *City of Panic* (Oxford: Berg, 2005) p.67.
[9]   Apart from individual writers, there have been conferences, journals and exhibitions devoted to these issues.
[10]   Massumi, B. 'Fear (the spectrum said)' in Birkhauser, I., ed. *5 Codes* (Switzerland, 2006).
[11]   Ibid., p.286
[12]   'President Bush said after September 11th, America is in a state of war. But the problem is that the US is not in a state of war. For the large majority, daily life goes on and war

remains the business of state agencies. The distinction between the state of war and peace is blurred. We are entering a time in which a state of peace can at the same time be a state of emergency.'
Zizek, S. 'On 9/11, New Yorkers faced the fire in the minds of men', *Guardian*, 11 September 2006.

[13]   Jackson, R. *Writing the War on Terrorism: Language, Politics and Counter Terrorism* (Manchester: Manchester University Press, 2005).

[14]   Ibid., p.112

[15]   Bauman, Z. *Society Under Siege* (Cambridge: Polity Press, 2002).

[16]   Bunting, M. 'The age of anxiety', *Guardian*, 25 October 2004.

[17]   Davis, M. 'The Great Wall of Capital' in Sorkin, M., ed. *Against The Wall – Israel's Barrier to Peace* (London: The New Press, 2005) p.88.

[18]   Graham, S., ed. *Cities, War and Terrorism: Towards an Urban Geopolitics* (Oxford: Blackwell Publications, 2004) p.11.

[19]   Raban, J. 'We have mutated into a surveillance society – and must share the blame', *The Guardian*, 20 May 2006.

[20]   Finkel, L.H. 'The Construction of Perception' in Crary, J. and Kwinter, S., eds. *Incorporations* (New York: Zone books, 1992).

[21]   Judge, B. *Thinking About Things – A Philosophical Study of Representation* (Edinburgh: Scottish Academic Press, 1985).

[22]   Rose, J. *On Not Being Able to Sleep, Psychoanalysis and the Modern World* (London: Vintage, 2004) p.55.

[23]   Rose, J. *States of Fantasy* (Oxford: Clarendon Press, 1998) p.4.

[24]   Schneider, P. *The Wall Jumper* (London: Penguin, 2005). See also Garrett, J. '"Teichoscopy" in the Wall Novels of Peter Schneider and Uri Orlev' in Allert, B., ed. *Languages of Visuality* (Detroit: Wayne State University Press, 1996).

[25]   Marton, R. and Baum, D. 'Transparent Wall, Opaque Gates' in Sorkin, M., ed. *Against The Wall – Israel's Barrier to Peace* (London: The New Press, 2005) p.212.

[26]   Ibid. p.214

[27]   Cousins, M. *The First House* (ARCH-TEXT 1, 1993).

[28]   Porter, H. 'How the Englishman's home ceased to be his castle', *Observer*, 18 June 2006.

[29]   Weizman, E. 'Lethal Theory', *Log*, Winter/Spring 2006.

[30]   Segal, S. 'What Lies beneath, Excerpts from an Invasion', *Palestine Mirror*, November 2002. Quoted in Weizman, op. cit.

[31]   Garrett, J. '"Teichoscopy" in the Wall Novels of Peter Schneider and Uri Orlev' in Allert, B., ed. *Languages of Visuality* (Detroit: Wayne State University Press, 1996).

[32]   Woods, L. 'The Wall Game' in Sorkin, M., ed. *Against The Wall – Israel's Barrier to Peace* (London: The New Press, 2005) p.260.

George VERGHESE

University of Technology, Sydney

SENSUAL SPACES THROUGH MATERIAL ABSTRACTION

Introduction

An architectural enclosure captures a volume of material matter within a spatial condition that is called an interior. This elegant yet simple description of an interior space establishes a key issue that is useful for not only reflecting on the path of design over the ages, but for offering a view towards the realignment of methodologies towards solving future design problems. Materiality, in reference to enclosed spaces, is an important concern and the main emphasis of this chapter. However, it is this new materiality that resides in the realm of cutting-edge technology and sciences, resulting in technological developments that adjust our notion of space and place. In order to examine the role that these technological developments play in the preservation of place, I will focus the chapter on its impact on the world of interior design. This is highly appropriate as an interior space establishes a sense of place within a material enclosure.

There has been much written about the sense of place in an architectural framework over the last twenty years but there is limited discussion on interior spaces, and even less on the relationship with materiality. Enclosed space as an idea has a strong relationship to the metaphor of a container, and interior spaces are often viewed as containers for human behaviour. Understanding the behaviour that occurs in these spaces and giving it value allows these spaces to become places. Edward Casey uses the metaphor of container when analysing Aristotle's *Physics* in which he says that 'it rests on the supposition that for Plato "matter and space are the same thing"' (209b12) and thus that place is reducible to matter: inasmuch as 'place is thought to be the extension of the magnitude [of a physical thing occupying that place], it is the matter' (209b6–7) [1]. If place is matter, then new materiality surely prescribes a sense of place in a new manner.

In order to establish a trajectory for the development of interior design's body of knowledge, the emphasis on the spatial and functional programming needs to be reconsidered in light of the shift in design towards new materiality. A wide variety of secondary sources, from philosophical to pragmatic, will be used to frame this shift, and provide a conversation on the interrelationship of the establishment of place-making in terms of new materiality within interior spaces, and its connection to abstraction and change.

Continuity and change

In North America, the National Council for Interior Design Qualification (NCIDQ) definition for interior design is discussed by Guerin and Martin in their research into the interior design body of knowledge. 'Improving the quality of life, increasing productivity, protecting health, safety and welfare of the public' [2] – in short, meeting pre-determined code requirements. All of these concerns are extremely important for designers in their day-to-day activities. These designers are all acting professionally, designing spaces to satisfy the needs of the clients. And if we educate designers to follow this part we will continue the good work of these people. However, regardless of how appropriate the design solutions may be, is continuity the goal?

Heskett discusses the tension and conflicting demands of continuity and change within the discipline of industrial design [3]. Other authors looking at the history of interior design have also echoed these same comments. It will be argued here that the issues of continuity and change belong to a larger debate involving the relationship of abstract thought to design. The challenges that we face with technological developments reside in coming to terms with the balance of these factors.

In addressing the paradigms of the age, modern interior spaces designed in the early 1900s were faced with a dichotomy: to focus either on the past or on the future. The design outcomes either supported conformity, or searched for change. This battle of continuity versus innovation is still active today in the design processes of planning, form-making and material selection, concluding in the finished designed interior. When discussing the polarity of approaches taken in the discipline at the turn of the century, C. Ray Smith describes one direction of interior design as being the age-old approach that looked at historical tradition as the datum point in which gradual evolutionary processes would advance the discipline through constant refinement and elaboration [4]. This led to a conservative approach in which the emphasis was on colour, ornamentation, pattern, texture, furnishing and accessories; an approach extended by the talents of Elsie de Wolfe during that period, and by other decorators today. 'The other direction aimed to explore innovation and invention, the future and the new.' [5] It was with this direction that the term early Modernism applies. The works of Frank Lloyd Wright, Le Corbusier, Walter Gropius, Pierre Chareau and others explored materiality in both construction and structure; they investigated new spatial organizations, shapes and forms, and the integrated use of new materials and manufacturing processes.

Technological change is central to this discussion as it supports 'design to go beyond mass production and into mass customization and so shift[s] design from a strong masculine sensibility based on rationality and efficiency to a feminine one of individualism and sensorial beauty.' [6]

It is clear that the use of new materiality in design today is a form of technology that explores sensory beauty and is driving the design process. One of the leaders in materiality research is Professor Toshiko Mori at the Harvard Design School. When discussing the idea of 'Phenomena' she brings together the issues of sensory engagement and material innovation, and in doing so she firmly rests the new materiality within the domain of change: 'We predict that the development of innovative materials must take place in parallel with new approaches to engaging human senses.' [7] New materials by themselves do not constitute change, or design innovation. It is the application of these materials within a context that issues forth a new era in design, and that new era must coincide with the implementation of new materiality into the process of design and not solely as an aspect of the outcome.

Abstraction

The birth of Modernism did not only see the investigation of new materials but also the development of abstraction. This has helped to explain design as both a process of producing an outcome, and the outcome itself. As abstraction can be viewed as removal of all the clutter to get to the core idea, and could also be considered as constructing anew one aspect of the problem, it is clear that the inductive and deductive reasoning that occurs in the design process is a form of abstraction. 'Architects [and designers] must simplify problems, reduce them to their essential elements. This is a process of abstraction, the exposure of the underlying structure or pattern of a whole system.' [8]

Thomas Kuhn describes elementary transformations in the scientific world as shifts in visual gestalt: 'during revolutions scientists see new and different things when looking with familiar instruments in places they have looked before.' [9] In order to look for change, we need to look at some familiar places. This is precisely what designers do. They are masters of pattern recognition and synthesis of information, which is the art of abstraction – seeing what is not seen in familiar places.

Abstraction is a 'primary human process, one that enables reality or actuality to be codified in a manner independent of its particularity and therefore aids the communication of concepts.' [10] Conceptualising is abstraction; and addressing materiality in the conceptual phases of design will allow for a clear sense of material abstraction to exist. However, there exist two challenges: firstly, the untapped resource of interior designers within the profession who are generally unreflective and view 'abstraction' as something that does not concern them in the 'real world'; and secondly, new materials are often the outcome of scientific developments at sub-particle levels, and their properties are understood through mathematical formulae and not through the senses. A new design methodology is needed to break down these two challenges.

Materiality and Modernism

The world that we live in is a material world made of substances and forms that have a materiality that we respond to through our senses. We construct our world through the interplay of materials and we have 'the ability to see more in a material object than merely its external form. Objects have meaning, carry associations or [are] symbols of more abstract ideas' [11].

As part of the explosion in exploration of materiality in the early years of this century, a Dutch exhibition called Materia® issued a catalogue of their event inviting various critics to comment on materiality. Henk Döll discussed materials in architecture: 'Architecture must touch the senses. Materials stimulate sensory experiences' [12]. '[C]hoosing the materials for a design, we seek those that either strengthen the concept or add nuances to it. Considering unconventional materials may have an inspiring effect to this search as they help to push the boundaries of material options.' [13] This search for the 'new' forms part of the Modernist journey over the last 100 years. Cecil Elliot describes the development of building materials and systems:

> On one hand, new and improved materials made it possible for buildings to satisfy needs that were new to the period, such as larger spans and taller structures. On the other hand, for more traditional functions it was possible to make these materials conform to the standards of propriety and taste to which the bourgeois patronage aspired. This meant that architecture was soon forced to contend with opposing forces: the material nature of the media in which it worked and the visual expectations of the art, whether the latter were founded on historicism or cubistic abstraction [14].

In terms of material technologies, change is an important strategy in the search for new materials as it offers market differentiation that would lead to potential financial revenue in sales, or distinctiveness in non-commercial projects. Novelty, innovation and progress have all been factors in the relentless shifts in technology, and each has had a sociological impact and affected our sense of place. George Basalla clearly states that:

> The diversity that characterizes the material objects of any culture is proof that novelty is to be found wherever there are human beings. If this were not the case, strict imitation would be the rule, and that every newly made thing would be an exact replica of some existing artefact. In such a world technology would not evolve [15].

The search for new technologies and discriminations of the reality of our world allows us to extend it and find comfort in the changed context; these changed contexts would then provide new meanings of place. During the Industrial Revolution, new markets, new materials and methodologies began to appear at a rapid pace, shaping our world, issuing new ideas and corresponding technologies. Technology became the driving force for British industrial growth in the 1800s.

As society grew during the Industrial Revolution, and succeeding ages, the relationship of materials in spatial outcomes fluctuated between the concerns of the inherent qualities of the material and the associated qualities. Malnar and Vodvarka discuss Alberti's reference to the dual nature of materials as having 'qualities of strength and beauty; that is, that materials are needed for the actualization of a structure and are, moreover, subject to aesthetic valuation in the process.' [16] Johnson also quotes Alberti, who seems far more open to abstraction as he states that: 'It is quite possible to project whole forms in the mind without any recourse to the material' [17]. Philosopher François Dagognet eloquently states his views on conceptualising in Ezio Manzini's ground-breaking book on new materiality: 'Our imagination deserves to be freed of its stereotypes, so that materiality can take free flight' [18].

This freedom of flight is aided by the constant development of scientific concepts and corresponding technologies. When considering materiality in this light, we are reminded of David Pye's abstract thought about the essence of matter: 'A single solid thing, after all is merely a slice of space with a few billion separate particles of this kind and that tottering about inside of it.' [19] Our reality is now no longer governed by just abstract explanations 'but with the widespread availability of a new sensory channel: a superview, a remarkable new eye that reaches much further and deeper than the usual range of experiences.' [20] Thomas Kuhn's comments are echoed here again as we are looking at a paradigm shift in the way designers will view the world.

New materials have been constantly shaping our environment and interior spaces for centuries. In the modern interior, a 'parade of new materials came before the public during the 1930s to point the way towards a cleaner, more functionally efficient and healthier world of tomorrow.' [21] Thirty years later in the 1960s, gypsum-board panels revolutionized the construction industry in economical and practical terms [22]. Advances in paint, fabric and polymer technologies have equally offered new products to be used in interior spaces. However, Manzini points out that:

> The term 'new materials' does not merely mean a limited number of sophisticated materials developed in a few advanced applicative areas. We are talking about the entire set of qualities that, to varying degrees are appearing throughout the landscape of materials – including the most traditional and venerable of them – shifting them with respect to manufacturing processes. The term, in short, expresses a new technical and cultural atmosphere, within which the transformation of matter is taking place [23].

Interior designers are currently designing within an outdated paradigm of selecting materials from those that are currently on the market; they are failing to grasp the abstract ideas embedded in new materiality and are thereby relying on the process of specification. Materiality must become a central theme to design. This shift in paradigm shows that materiality viewed in the twentieth century considered the tangible bulk materials, and proceeded by manipulating ways of altering its form, whereas 'the 21st century will be that of surfaces, mono-layers, even single molecules, and the new functionality that these will allow' [24]. Smart materials and nanotechnology clearly fit into this new way of material thought, as do new steel, ceramic and wood technologies.

We will build intelligence into materials and liberate form from matter. Material has traditionally been something to which design is applied. New methods in the field of nanotechnology have rendered material as the object of design development. Instead of designing a thing, we design a designing thing. In the process, we have created superhero materials and collapsed the age-old boundary between the image and the object, rendering mutable the object itself [25].

Application of the new, the novel and ultimately of the untested, requires a degree of risk. Designers have to balance the cost of failure with the likelihood of adding value to the performance [26], and the opportunity to address the character and meaning of the project in ways that existing materials fail to achieve. Bernstein proclaims that the 'revolutionary idea that defines the boundary between modern times and the past is the mastery of risk: the notion that the future is more than the whim of the gods and that men and women are not passive before nature' [27].

Sensuality through new materiality

As advanced technology is becoming more prevalent in society, designers are becoming active protagonists in the exploration of sensuality through the use of new materials in design. An exhaustive survey is beyond the scope of this chapter, but highlights of activities will establish the link between the core aspect of interiors and new materiality presented here.

To explore materiality as a conceptual framework for a design project could prove challenging as the task of materiality is often driven by what exists. To this end, there are companies and organisations like Transmaterial®, Material Connextion®, and Materia® that have developed huge databases for designers of innovative materials. However, there are only a few designers that look at working with material scientists and technologists in the development of new materials. OMA has worked directly with Panelite® to establish new materials and material assemblies for their Prada stores and for projects that range from private houses to embassies. Their polyester foamed panels allow for spatial flexibility but also allude to a tactility that allows for a greater sense of sensual place to be achieved. The work of Chris Van Juijn at OMA also mirrors the passion in which Ron Arad has always approached materiality in his work and the symbiotic relationship that he fosters between material technology and the sensory perception. In critique of his Lo-rez-dolares-tabula-rasa installation at the 2004 Venice Biennale, Lucy Bullivant proclaims: 'Sensuous man-made materials can now be harnessed to new technologies and transformed into unique interfaces for communications' [28]. Arad's unique use of small pieces of Corian® to create a screen that allows the audience to be immersed into the projected images satisfies his desire to create tactile and experiential designs.

As previously discussed, it is not always the new technologies but the new approaches to old technologies that harness the new material or material construction. The Canadian firm, Molo Design, indicates that old can be also new. In exploring flexible spaces for Japanese housing, the firm sought to deal with the realities of tight spaces but also improve the quality of life, and the sensuousness of the space through light and materiality. Stephanie Forsythe of Molo Design clearly indicates the firm's relationship to materials by noting that, '[a]s designers we like to focus on one material and see all that it can do, rather than impose ourselves on the material' [29]. Their paper softwall re-invents a 100-year-old tradition of paper decorations, and clearly demonstrates abstract thought manifested through new material investigation.

Figure 1: Softwall fabrication, Molo Design

Ben van Berkel's design of the Director's Room NAi, in Amsterdam also indicates that the design 'is not derived from the plan analysis or the function analysis of the object but from its material potential' [30]. However, the firm IS.Ar Iwamoto Scott clearly announces the fusion of the concepts of new materiality, place-making, and design process when they comment on their methodology, which 'aims to exploit particular properties and intensities of space and matter by approaching the design process as an ongoing exploration into questions of materiality and perception.' [31]

Sense of place

Early Modernism held a singular world-view and, in its effort to look at abstraction, it favoured formalism in which universal forms and honesty of materials were sought. That Modernist viewpoint has shifted to allow for a pluralistic and often phenomenological approach to be established within the framework of modern interior design, thereby allowing for the development of a sense of place to occur within the modern interior.

> Our preliminary discussion of the phenomena of place led to the conclusion that the structure of place ought to be described in terms of 'landscape' and 'settlement', and analyzed by means of categories 'space' and 'character'. Whereas 'space' denotes the three-dimensional organization of the elements which make up place, 'character' denotes the general 'atmosphere' which is the most comprehensive property of any place [32].

Place-making is the essence of interior design, as spatial juxtapositions and material treatments are aligned with abstract conceptual ideas to expose a desired reaction from the user. The reactions are emotional responses that can be passive, through acceptance, or active through engagement. '"Sense of place" is necessarily a function of people's relationship with specific locations, not a property of them, and for many people it may well have as much to do with intangible memories, associations, scents or other qualities' [33]. Designers present these place-making ideas to their clients through the use of 'mood boards' or 'sample boards'. These boards will undoubtedly indicate materiality; and as clients, for the most part, want to define a point of difference in the marketplace they look at designers as a key to providing that difference. Ultimately, designers respond to this professional request through material manipulation and allocation within a spatial environment.

As the role of interior designers is to provide a sense of character to a spatial condition, in short they aim to improve the quality of life for the users. Quality is created by material manipulations to develop the character of the space. 'The character is determined by the material and formal constitution of the place' [34]. As designers seek to achieve the desired results in their projects, they do so by manipulating materials, either traditional or innovative, to achieve the character and mood for the space. 'The term "place", as opposed to space, implies a strong emotional tie, temporary or more long-lasting, between a person and a particular physical location' [35]. This bond between the user's sensory needs and the place where those needs are met is now clearly addressed by new materials.

As '[h]istorians straddle the gulf between culture and reality, arguing that culture structures, and is structured by, practice over time and that individuals construct their understanding of the world on the basis of reality' [36], we are leading towards an appreciation of the symbiotic relationship between the material and culture. Hubbard et al. describe Haraway's views, on material and culture as changes that cannot be viewed strictly from the outside, as the 'view from nowhere'; and add that 'science is a social and cultural process, so that nature known through science is a cultural artefact, constituted through both the practices and technologies of scientific research' [37]. In his essay, 'Heidegger's Thinking on Architecture', Norberg-Schulz quotes Heidegger's essay 'Art and Space' in which it is stated that '[w]e must learn to understand that the things themselves are the places and that they do not simply belong to the place' [38].

Conclusion

Life is not an outcome, it is a process. As with all things, the *process* of design is essential. We often look at the outcomes of design and forget that there is an action that necessarily precedes that outcome. Similarly, in the design of interior spaces, we must stop seeing material as just an outcome, a noun, an object. We must start to give it character, and consider the materializing of spaces when making places. Just as material culture is an essential part of being human, we must make material thinking an essential part of design. Enzio Manzini clearly catches the essence of this new materiality:

> scientific and technical development – from its beginnings as a simple idea of reality made up of existing and objective material, passive matter awaiting activity – has today attained such complexity and depth in its capacity to manipulate what exists that I offers a vision

of matter (and of our relations with matter) that contradicts all our initial views. And the inadequacy of those initial views has become evident even in everyday life [39].

This chapter aimed at developing a conversation in the discipline so that it could go beyond the stylistic application of materials in spatial arrangements, often selected through habit or necessity, and explore the potentiality of materiality as a core approach to practice. A phenomenological approach to design through the use of materials is needed, and has been addressed by those trail blazers such as Rem Koolhaas and OMA, Herzog and de Meuron, Diller and Scofidio, and Yabu Pushelberg, to name a few. They will be followed by a whole generation of designers who have a tacit understanding of materiality and practise it throughout the process.

References

[1]   Aristotle, translated by Edward Hussey, *Physics* Books III and IV (Oxford: Clarendon Press, 1983) as cited in Casey, E.S. *The Fate of Place – A Philosophical History* (London: University of California Press, 1998) p.52.

[2]   Guerin, D. and Martin, C. *The Interior Design Profession's Body of Knowledge – Its Definition and Documentation* (Toronto: ARIDO, 2001) p.9.

[3]   Heskett, J. *Industrial Design* (London: Thames & Hudson, 1980) p.7.

[4]   Smith, C.R. *Interior Design in the 20th-Century America: A History* (New York: Harper & Row, 1987) p.17.

[5]   Ibid.

[6]   Müller Stahl, J. 'Design: The Art of the Moment' in Müller Stahl, J., ed. *Dish – International Design for the Home* (New York: Princeton Architectural Press, 2005) p.12.

[7]   Mori, T., ed. *Immaterial/Ultramaterial–Architecture, design, & materials* (New York: George Braziller, 2002) p.63.

[8]   Laseau, P. *Graphic Thinking for Architects and Designers*, 3rd edition (Brisbane: John Wiley & Sons, 2001) p.81.

[9]   Kuhn, T.S. *The Structure of Scientific Revolutions*, 3rd edition (Chicago: University of Chicago, 1996) p.111.

[10] Johnson, P.A. *The Theory of Architecture – Concepts, Themes, & Practices* (New York: Van Nostrand Reinhold, 1994) p.332.

[11] Ashby, M. and Johnson, K. *Materials and design: the art and science of material selection in product design* (Boston: Butterworth-Heinemann, 2003) p.1.

[12] Döll, H. in *Future Materials for Architecture and Design* (Rotterdam: Materia, 2002) p.6.

[13] Ibid.

[14] Elliot, C.D. *Technics and Architecture – The Development of Materials and Systems for Buildings* (Cambridge, MA: MIT Press, 1994) pp.2–3.

[15] Basalla, G. *The Evolution of Technology* (Cambridge: Cambridge University Press, 1999) p.64.

[16] Malnar, J.M. and Vodvarka, F. *The Interior Dimension – A theoretical approach to enclosed space* (Toronto: John Wiley & Sons, 1992) p.253.

[17] Johnson, P.A. *The Theory of Architecture – Concepts, Themes, & Practices* (London: John Wiley & Sons, 1994) p.331.

[18] Dagognet, F. in Manzini, E. *The Material of Invention* (Cambridge, MA: MIT Press, 1989) p.13.

[19] Pye, D. *The Nature and Aesthetics of Design* (London: Barrie and Jenkins, 1978) p.24.

[20] Manzini, E. *The Material of Invention* (Cambridge, MA: MIT Press, 1989) p.25.

[21] Smith, C.R. *Interior Design in the 20th-Century America: A History*, p.116.

[22] Ibid., p.33

[23] Manzini, op. cit., p.18

[24] Ashby, M. and Johnson, K. *Materials and design: the art and science of material selection in product design*, p.10.

[25] Mau, B. *Massive Change* (London: Phaidon Press, 2004) pp.140–1.

[26] Ashby and Johnson, op. cit., p.159

[27] Bernstein, P. *Against the Gods – The remarkable story of risk* (Toronto: John Wiley & Sons, 1998) p.1.

[28] Bullivant, L. 'Ron Arad on Interactivity and Low-Res Design' in Castle, H., ed. *4d Space– Interactive Architecture, Architectural Design*, 2005 (vol.75, no.1) p.55.

[29] Forsythe, S. in *Design Secrets: Furniture* (Gloucester, MA: Rockport Publishers, 2006) p.192.

[30] Van Berkel, B. and Bos, C. *Imagination – Liquid Politics* (Amsterdam: UN – Studio and Goose Press, 1999) p.177.

[31] Iwamoto, L. and Scott, C. in Thompson, J., ed. *Young Architects 4 – Material Process* (New York: Princeton Architectural Press, 2003) p.21.

[32] Norberg-Schulz, C. 'The Phenomenon of Place' in Nesbitt, K., ed. *Theorizing a New Agenda for Architecture – An Anthology of Architectural Theory 1965–1995* (New York: Princeton Architectural Press, 1996) p.418.

[33] Weston, R. *Materials, Form and Architecture* (London: Laurence King, 2003) p.112.

[34] Norberg-Schulz, op. cit., p.420

[35] Sime, J. 'Creating Places or Designing Spaces', *Journal of Environmental Psychology*, 1986, 6, p.50.

[36] Grassby, R. 'Material Culture & Cultural History', *The Journal of Interdisciplinary History*, 35(4). See http://muse.jhu.edu/journals/journal_of_interdisciplinary_history/v035/35.4grassby.html (accessed on 9 September 2005).

[37] Hubbard, P., Kitchin, R. and Valentine, G., eds. *Key Thinkers on Space and Place* (London: Sage Publications, 2004) p.168.

[38] Heidegger, M. 'Art and Space' as cited by Norberg-Schulz, C., 'Heidegger's Thinking on Architecture' in Nesbitt, K., ed. *Theorizing a New Agenda for Architecture – An Anthology of Architectural Theory 1965–1995* (New York: Princeton Architectural Press, 1996) p.435.

[39] Manzini, op. cit., p.48

John BROWN

University of Calgary

THE TAILORED HOME – CREATING AN ALTERNATIVE TO THE NORTH AMERICAN COOKIE CUTTER HOUSE

Introduction

Residential construction accounts for 67 per cent of all building construction expenditure in North America. Over half of this is spent on the construction of new single family homes. Low-density suburban development is the single largest land use in our cities. Owning a free-standing house on a little plot of land is not only part of the North American Dream, it is the largest and most important purchase most people will ever make. In spite of this however, architects and interior designers continue to play only a very small role in the residential industry.

Lamenting the design profession's abdication of responsibility for this very significant segment of the built environment is nothing new. Edward Ford suggests that in the early twentieth century designers largely abandoned the single family housing industry and abdicated responsibility to planners, builders, and developers. Ford argues that the many attempts to reverse this trend did not succeed because they focused too narrowly on issues primarily of interest to designers, such as new materials and technological innovations, without accounting for the entrenched production processes that actually define the industry [1].

This chapter explores the roots of this dilemma in the North American culture of mass commoditization and introduces the tailored home as a case study example of one Canadian design firm's attempt to provide affordable, sensitively designed, modern residences within the normative housing market.

Fast food – fast houses

In 1949, Charles Levitt started a revolution in North American city building with the introduction of Levittown, the first comprehensively planned and mass-constructed suburban neighbourhood. By 1960 Levitt and other production builders would use modern mass production and financing methods to draw 20 million people to their housing developments on the rapidly expanding outskirts of America's cities.

At approximately the same time in Southern California, Carl Karcher, Richard McDonald and Glen Bell were getting ready to change the face of twentieth-century food with the creation of the first fast food restaurants – Carl's Jr., McDonald's, and Taco Bell. The flush baby boom economy of post-war America needed goods and services that were cheap and readily available and both industries responded with uniform standardized products, emphasizing quantity over quality, and a tightly integrated system of production, marketing, distribution and sales. The success of these industries has been staggering. According to Eric Schlosser:

> McDonald's annually hires more people than any other North American organization, public or private... During a relatively brief period of time, the fast food industry has helped to transform not only [our] diet, but also our landscape, economy, workforce, and popular culture. Fast food and its consequences have become inescapable, regardless of whether you eat it twice a day, try to avoid it, or have never taken a single bite [2].

In the housing industry, huge development and construction companies dominate the North American market. Since World War II, the housing stock in North America has increased from 34.9 million units to 105.5 million. The continent has the largest amount of private housing space per person in the history of civilization, with the size of the average home more than doubling since 1945 and one quarter of households having seven or more rooms. Housing in North America, Dolores Hayden states, 'is a big, big business [and the] banking, real estate, manufacturing, and transportation interests are intimately involved.' [3]

Most of this development has resulted in environmentally unsustainable, culturally homogeneous neighbourhoods of single family detached houses and strip retail malls. 70 per cent of the population resides in this seemingly endless landscape of suburban sprawl largely 'unaware of the subtle and not-so-subtle ramifications of its presence in their lives.' [4]

Like fast food, these so called fast houses eschew issues of quality, appropriateness, and good sense. They are nothing more than mass-produced products created to satisfy, however temporarily, a mass-media-induced hunger for over indulgence. The home in suburban America has become nothing more than a commodity, like Big Macs, handbags, and television sets. One of the most significant places in a person's life and one of 'the premier instruments for satisfying the expectation of selfhood,' [5] has been rendered instantaneous, ubiquitous, cheap and easy by a system that promises everything but delivers very little beyond the fleeting sense of satisfaction at the point of sale.

Like fat-free instant chocolate cake, abs without exercising, learning a second language in your sleep, or becoming the next pop star without really knowing how to sing, the fast suburban home exhibits 'the traits of a commerce with reality where the rootedness in the depth of things, i.e. in the irreplaceable context of time and place, has been dissolved.' [6] In many cases these post-industrial commodities are popular for the very fact that they can be enjoyed as a mere end, unencumbered by means, making little demand on our skill, strength, or attention.

The processed food industry fosters a society that cooks but does not know how to cook. The preparation of food has become 'almost exclusively the terrain of professionals as our own competence (and the confidence it engenders) ebbs away.' [7] Until the middle of the twentieth century, most households had a knowledge and control of the craft of cooking. Since that time, according to Waxman, we have become increasingly cut off from the roots of kitchen practice and the reasons for the cooking operations we are performing. 'We rely more and more on detailed written recipes with exhaustive step-by-step instructions that encourage obedience and conformity at the expense of knowledge and understanding.' [8]

Albert Borgmann characterizes this as a shift from a worldview conditioned by deep relationships with things to a worldview dominated by shallow commodities that are consumed individually without invoking, or becoming involved with, their context. In the same way that fast food unravels the deeper cultural context of cooking and dining, the fast housing industry has transformed us from a nation of home-makers into one of home-buyers, all too ready to blindly consume the latest marketing image of a super-sized idyllic dream home as a vision of individualization. In such a world of strictly limited choices 'notions of self and happiness are thus prone to disappear into categories of consumer products.' [9]

But the home is too important to be consumed by its own image.

This is a familiar, and probably welcome, observation for most designers. Architects and interior designers have been ready critics of standardized suburban development from its inception and the professionally designed houses that we create stand in stark contrast to their mass-produced cousins. These houses are unique, sophisticated responses to site, climate, materials and inhabitants. They engage the context of place, and the history of form. They respect the tradition of craft and rise to the promise of the new. Unfortunately however, and despite our good intentions, these professionally designed homes do little to alleviate the problems of a fast home world.

The design professions are involved in less than three per cent of all single family house construction in North America. The vast majority of these are patron commissions at the very top end of the economic scale. The simple reality is that almost no-one except for the fraction of people in the upper economic classes, who are not only interested but can afford what is perceived as a luxury, is actually able to live in a professionally designed home. This exclusivity means that these projects, and the architects and interior designers who create them, only reach the average homeowner through the pages of the so-called 'house porn' industry of lifestyle magazines. These images of unattainable perfection intensify the average homeowner's desire to consume. By not offering any reasonably achievable alternative however, these projects only serve to reinforce the hegemony of the fast home industry.

In many ways, the situation parallels our experience with food. Taken at face value, independent chef-operated restaurants would seem to be the perfect antidote to the processed food industry. The high-quality ingredients, careful preparation, and thoughtful presentation in a context that promotes the social culture of the table stand in sharp contrast to the numbing homogeneity, poor nutrition and shattered customs of our experiences with the processed food industry. However, like the architecturally designed house, these restaurants offer a one-off idealized experience rather than an everyday option. For most people, their relationship to this kind of food is confined to media images, many in the recipe section of the same lifestyle magazines that run profiles of architecturally designed houses. Again, these images really only serve to intensify the desire to consume the idealized imagery on the packaging of commoditized food.

Slow food – slow homes

Fortunately, in food, there is an option that sits between the perfect and the packaged. The slow food movement, as the name suggests, 'stands for everything that McDonald's does not; fresh local, seasonal produce, recipes handed down through generations; sustainable farming; artisan production; and leisurely dining with family and friends.' [10] Founded in Italy by Carlo Petrini in 1986, slow food is an international movement with a membership of over 100,000. Its mandate 'opposes the standardization of taste and protects cultural identities tied to food and gastronomic traditions.' [11]

Slow food is an attempt to reverse the commoditization of experience that occurs with fast food. It promotes a re-engagement with the culture of the table through individual everyday involvement with the selection, preparation and enjoyment of food. Slow food is the discipline of creating and enjoying our daily meals, however humble, as an act of individual engagement. Replacing the superficial consumption of a commodity with a practice promotes a more intentional, directed way of being in the world and begins to counteract some of our overdependence on market-driven consumption. Alongside other, perhaps more familiar slow practices like martial arts, playing a musical instrument, fly fishing, and canoeing, this engagement is based on the acquisition of skills and the adherence to a daily practice of activity. Activities of this kind tend to reduce consumption as the time and care required to be engaged in a practice reduces 'the spectre of boredom... which requires new and ever more consumption.' [12]

According to Carl Honoree:

> Fast and slow do more than just describe a rate of change. They are shorthand for ways of being. Fast is 'busy, controlling, aggressive, hurried, analytical, stressed, superficial, impatient, active, quantity over quality. Slow is the opposite, calm,

careful, receptive, still, intuitive, unhurried, patient, reflective, quality over quantity. It is about making real and meaningful connections – with people, culture, work, food, everything [13].

Does slow food offer a meaningful precedent for the residential construction industry?

Drawing on the precedent of the slow food movement, a so-called 'slow home' philosophy could be a potential antidote to the fast houses and communities churned out by the development industry. It would foster a re-engagement with the culture of the house by directing attention to the house as the focus of a practice to be lived rather than as a product to be consumed. This process would create a more mature role for the homeowner as they assume more responsibility for both the way in which the house is acquired and the manner in which it is lived in.

This does not mean, however, that we must all take a year off from work, buy a set of tools and physically construct our own house. The realities of twenty-first century society make withdrawal from the present commodity economy inconceivable if not impossible. According to Archer, 'Individually we do not have the opportunity to negotiate the categorical terms in which our dreams are realized. Rather, we choose from an array of options that our culture affords us.' [14]

A slow home philosophy would expand that array beyond the choice between one complete package of commodities or another and towards a more distributed and complex set of real decisions. At the same time, it would transfer control and responsibility for these choices away from big business and back to the individual. It would create a system in which decisions can be made by individual homeowners based on a mature understanding of the real cost of home ownership to the environment, our cities and ourselves. It also carves out a potential role for the design professional as a guide and enabler of this process of engagement.

The slow home philosophy is a political statement and an ideological position. It promotes a shift in the underlying structure of one of the largest components of the American economy. It transforms the myth of the dream house from a product to be purchased into an ongoing process of realization. It engages the idea of the home as:

> a social terrain in continuous process of production, a material artefact in which and by which people negotiate the resources and skills that they can marshal, the opportunities that their lives present and the various dreams and aspirations that they may choose to pursue… like everything in life it is a messy artefact, always incomplete and full of inconsistencies [15].

The tailored home

The tailored home is an example of how this slow home philosophy can be put into practice. It was developed by Housebrand, a Canadian architectural firm, as a way to empower individuals within a broad spectrum of the housing market to take responsibility for the creation of their homes. It explores and exploits the idea of the home as an incomplete and inconsistent 'messy artefact' by employing a bricolage method of design in which individuals work with a designer to assemble their domestic world as a combination of property, spatial interventions, custom-manufactured pieces and ready-made objects. By focusing design intent on the creation of a process rather than on a discrete product, the tailored home resists the commoditization of the house as a product and provides an affordable way for the average homeowner to engage in a design process and live in a professionally designed space.

The tailored home borrows heavily from precedents in clothing manufacturing. It replaces the one-off 'bespoke' made approach of a typical design practice with a mass-customization strategy. In clothing, high design is made affordable to a larger number of consumers with factory-produced garments that are individually customized through alterations at the point of sale. In the same way, the tailored home begins with the selection of an existing property that is the right size, price, and location which is then tailored to fit its owner and its site with a series of custom interventions completed under the watchful eye of a design professional.

The tailored home is based on the sensitive revitalization of the aging housing stock in the countless existing residential communities in Canada's major cities. These neighbourhoods are close to work, school and shopping. They have mature vegetation and good public infrastructure. Unfortunately, the housing stock in these communities was not designed to last more than 30 years. Most of it is wearing out and no longer fits the realities of twenty-first century life. The current political and economic reality of Canadian cities usually precludes the redevelopment of these neighbourhoods into higher-density housing in the immediate future. The tailored home is a strategy to extend the viability of this housing stock another twenty years. At that time, it is anticipated that a more whole-scale redevelopment of these neighbourhoods will be feasible.

The tailored home is both a product and a delivery system. As product it capitalizes on the rapidly expanding renovation industry and, on the surface at least, is simply a used home in an older community that has been modernized. As delivery system, it is a vertically integrated set of services that combines real estate brokerage, architectural and interior design, construction management and retail furniture sales. This structured approach to finding, designing, re-building and furnishing a used home overcomes the many problems encountered with traditional renovations while avoiding the limitations, and economic premium, of new construction and speculative development. It is an economically viable process for empowering the individual homeowner to take control of their domestic environment and maximize its potential by working with a professional designer from the very beginning of the process to the very end.

The tailored home process begins with the identification of a client's needs, abilities and priorities. A target pro-forma is developed that allocates the project budget, according to these needs, between the base house purchase, the constructed improvements and any required furnishings. Based on this information a short list of candidate sites is assembled and ranked for suitability. When the right property is found the purchase contract is negotiated with initial occupancy timed for the construction start. Financing is arranged to include the purchase price of the house, the firm's professional fees, the cost of all anticipated improvements, and the carrying costs required to allow the client to remain in their current home until the completion of construction. The design of the project is completed between the time that the property is purchased and the date of occupancy. Furniture is ordered at the outset in order for delivery to coincide with the completion of the project. Construction is normally completed within four to five months. The client lists their existing home for sale just prior to the end of construction and moves directly into their new tailored home.

From a design point of view, the tailored home incorporates a loft strategy that opens up the closed-room interior living spaces of the older homes. This increases flexibility and functionality, dramatically improves the quality of light, and creates a sense of spaciousness that compensates for the small footprint of these older houses. An open-plan kitchen is typically re-located to the front of the house in order to re-orient the primary living spaces towards the rear yard gardens. The rear façade is opened up to create a more seamless connection between the inside and the out. Other functional changes typically include an enlarged bathroom and additional closet space. For economic reasons, changes to the exterior are typically limited to new windows, doors and cladding.

Operations

Housebrand created the tailored home as a strategy to introduce the inherently slow nature of the design professional's expertise into the fast world of production home building. Like other mass production industries, residential construction is more focused on optimizing the process of production rather than the product being created. With the tailored home, Housebrand infiltrates this process and inserts a transparent yet powerful design presence into the core structure of the existing industry. Its operational strategy emerges from a design-build framework adapted to the specific constraints and opportunities of the residential industry.

From a client's perspective the firm offers a one-stop, simple and cost-effective process for building in an established community. It combines a strong architectural philosophy with an integrated model of production to make the option of a professionally designed residence as readily available as the status quo alternatives. From the industry perspective the firm assumes, as required, the normative roles within the process (realtor, builder, retailer, and developer). It translates its architectural agenda into the language of the everyday industry to minimize friction and maximize the opportunity for the client. Its innovation is neither technological nor aesthetic but lies in the conceptual design of a process. Its goal is to create an architectural presence within the everyday, subversively manipulating the status quo to offer a critical alternative within the too-fast world of the normative residential construction industry.

Housebrand's innovative form of practice combines the roles of real estate broker, designer, contractor, product retailer and developer into a vertically oriented system. Real estate agents are the undisputed first point of contact for people looking for a new place to live. Their exclusive access to the Multiple Listing Service database gives them the ability not only to identify quickly properties for sale but to appraise their value in terms of neighbouring properties.

Housebrand expanded its professional practice to include real estate brokerage and all of the primary designers are licensed estate agents. Having a designer assist in the search and selection of property transforms the purchase of the property from a one-off commodity transaction to an integrated component of an overall design process. The real estate commission provides up-front cash flow and allows the firm to defer the collection of their design fee to the end of the project when it can be incorporated into the client's mortgage financing. Coincidentally, this transformation of the professional design fee from a cash cost to an expenditure that is incorporated into the mortgage financing eliminates one of the primary barriers to the involvement of design professionals in residential projects.

Residential builders, like their commercial counterparts, are primarily managers and almost all general contractors, regardless of their size, draw from the same limited pool of sub-contractors. Unlike commercial work, however, the historical absence of detailed contract documents and the very tight margins in residential construction have resulted in a heavy reliance on the repetitive use of typical details and procedures by sub-trades. Construction drawings are typically understood to be general descriptions rather than precise instructions and the builder, balancing cost and time with client preferences, makes the majority of decisions immediately on site in consultation with the sub-trades. It is this working relationship with sub-trades that most conflicts with the traditional role of designers and their typical instruments of service.

Housebrand expanded their practice to include construction management. Each design team is responsible for managing costs and the trades and takes their projects from design through to the completion of construction. Having design staff on site in this way reduces the need for extensive contract documents. It increases the fluidity and consistency of the design process and puts the design professional in an undisputed leadership role without having to insert a separate, and foreign, consulting role into the normative residential process. Combining the role of designer and construction manager makes it affordable for almost any project to have extensive and complete design supervision throughout construction. The consistent use of the same sub-trades, led by an onsite design team, changes the culture of the construction site and shifts the focus from a Fordist model of assembly line production to a more artisan approach of crafted making.

Retailers play a significant role in the residential building industry that is not typically understood by the general public. In the absence of detailed contract documents, and in an attempt by builders to market their product at the lowest price point, dollar allowances are provided for a variety of items including floor coverings, cabinets and counters, appliances, and plumbing and electrical fixtures. During construction, clients are typically directed to a series of retail outlets that offer the basic allowance package and attempt to up-sell a variety of more expensive options. This creates an almost institutionalized process of cost over-runs, with money often being spent in inappropriate ways and resulting in an unevenly finished end product.

Housebrand expanded their practice to include a retail environment. This demonstration centre is the place where clients work with design staff to select all of their finishes, fixtures, and furniture. Consolidating all of the product-selection process 'in house' reduces costs and creates an assured market for the specialty finishes imported exclusively by the firm as well as the limited production design pieces it manufactures annually. The integration of product and furniture selection with property selection and concept design gives clients the knowledge and power to make responsible decisions based on a realistic and comprehensive understanding of the project as a whole.

Finally, the developer is responsible for assembling the property, design and construction and facilitating the creation of the final product. The developer is an established player in large projects and in speculative situations involving a great deal of risk and high potential returns. Within single family residential construction, however, it is usually not a specific and separate entity but a role that one member of the process assumes. The developer has the expertise to put all of the elements of a project together and the established financial relationships to provide financing for the project.

Housebrand's integrated set of services provides the individual homeowner with the complete range of consulting expertise necessary for them to act as their own developer. The firm's established track record assists the individual homeowner to obtain project financing and save the 15–20 per cent mark-up that a typical residential developer will charge for bringing land, design, and construction together into a realized end product.

Conclusion

The tailored home process incorporates the duties of realtor, builder, retailer and developer into an expanded new role for the design professional. It integrates core architectural values into the normative residential process to create a critical alternative to the mass production new home industry. This process enacts the slow home philosophy by increasing the potential level of engagement that the average person has with the creation of their home. It transfers control and responsibility for the home away from land developers, production home builders, real estate conglomerates and big box retailers and back to the individual. It promotes an active culture of home making rather than the passivity of simply buying a home. The design professional plays a crucial role as the enabler of this process.

The tailored home case study is an economically viable method for the profession to reach beyond its traditional clientele while pursuing the high-quality design of small-scale projects. It demonstrates the capacity of the profession to expand its definition of itself and discover new ways to be relevant and successful within our rapidly changing society.

References

[1]   Ford, E. *The Details of Modern Architecture* (Cambridge, MA: MIT Press, 1990) p.4.

[2]   Schlosser, E. *Fast Food Nation: The Dark Side of the All-American Meal* (Boston, MA: Houghton Mifflin Co., 2001) p.7.

[3]   Hayden, D. *Redesigning the American Dream* (New York: WW Norton, 2000) p.54.

[4]   Leach, W. *Country of Exiles: The Destruction of Place in American Life* (New York: Vintage Books, 1999) p.13.

[5]   Archer, J. *Architecture and Suburbia: From English Villa to American Dream House 1690–2000* (Minneapolis, MN: University of Minneapolis, 2005) p.292.

[6]   Borgmann, A. *Technology and the Character of Contemporary Life: A Philosophical Inquiry* (Chicago, IL: University of Chicago Press, 1984) p.51.

[7]   Washburn, K. and Thornton, J., eds. *Dumbing Down: Essays on the Strip Mining of American Culture* (New York: W.W. Norton & Co., 1996) p.15.

[8]   Waxman, N. 'Cooking Dumb, Eating Dumb' in Washburn and Thornton eds., op. cit., p.302.

[9]   Archer, op. cit., p.336

[10] Honoree, C. *In Praise of Slow* (Toronto: Random House, 2004) p.59.

[11] Petrini, C., http://www.slowfood.com (accessed on 1 September 2006).

[12] Borgmann, op. cit., p.271

[13] Honoree, op. cit., p.14

[14] Archer, op. cit., p.318

[15] Ibid., p.350

Saltuk ÖZEMİR

Istanbul Technical University

THE MASK OUTSIDE THE MACHINE, THE PERSONA INSIDE THE SPACE

The mask outside the machine

Just as Paul Valery wrote that 'The instrument is tending to disappear from consciousness', so, thanks to turbulence, people become aware of the fact that they are on an airplane. Otherwise, they tend to forget that they are travelling in a 'machine' [1]. Similarly, the material world, surrounding us can be likened to the blue sky where it is taken as a shelter (interface/mask) hiding what lies beyond, namely, the dark and pitch black outer-space, as in Paul Bowles' novel *The Sheltering Sky*.

Once the perceived *phenomenal* world is seen as a veil covering the *noumena* (a Jungian term for the psychic world of man) the term *persona* and its complementary term *shadow* directly imply the form (mask/interface) and substance (identity/mechanism) duality when applied to the material world. For 'design' according to designer Roberto Feo is 'the interface between our daily activities and us' and 'to design', for designer Ron Arad, is 'one's imposing his own will onto material'. The link between the *persona* and design seems to be a major issue in the context of *aestheticization* of the *shadow* of the *materia* that surrounds us.

As the balance between *persona* and what lies beneath, namely *shadow*, is what makes a person find peace in himself in Jungian terms, the same could also be true for the objects and places making up our surroundings. And, in return, the *aestheticization* to *persona* and the *shadow*, which is like what the *Holy Spirit/graphic card* is to the *Father/codes* and to the *Son/image*, seems to be the other crucial term, when one is to examine what lies beneath the glossy surface of the contemporary design world, represented in the pages of interior design magazines. Because, as Marshall McLuhan puts it 'medium is the message'.

Thus, if the technology and economic structure of an age are to be taken as the *shadow* or like 'the machine' of that age, then the *aestheticized* representation of that *shadow*, namely the culture, can be taken into hand as the *persona*, or the 'mask outside the machine'. Thanks to the Industrial Revolution and to the loss of an aesthetic authority like the Church or the palace in the nineteenth century, the balance between the 'emotional zeitgeist' (Romanticism, Historicism, etc.) and 'the intellectual zeitgeist' (Capitalism, Positivism, Scientism) of society was demolished. This imbalance was giving rise to an aesthetically chaotic atmosphere while the burgeoning bourgeois was becoming the new ruler class [2]. In this very hazy atmosphere, despite being historicist, the Ecole des Beaux-Arts was actually acting against the very foundation of itself, since the designers trained in this school were selecting historical 'forms', devoid of their 'substances' [3] from the 'designer's IKEA catalogues' – just like the consumer does in today's *nobrow* [4] culture, where there is no stable class infrastructure.

The uniqueness of that age must be the reason that made Walter Benjamin ambulate through the arcades of Paris of the nineteenth century. Rather than the train station or the factory, Benjamin thought the arcade was the most important building type of that century, signalling the modern society: for it served mass-consumption rather than mass-production. For Benjamin, with its theatrical and surrealistic prosceniums for visual intoxication – namely, the shop windows – in the *phantasmagorical* atmosphere of which, the interior and the exterior were merging thanks to the iron–glass skin, covering it, the arrival of the arcade at the same time with the new spectator experience promised by the proto-cinematic devices would not have been a coincidence. The cinema, in alliance with mass-production techniques, artificial light, railroads, telegram, journals and newspapers, would not only 'compress space and time' [5] so as to open the way to fashion, and to the ephemeral-ness of styles, but would also strengthen the separation of the subject from the object. Yet, before the advent of the flatness and reductionism of photography, film, etc., of mass-representation technologies, there was still a subject–object unity in the existential aesthetic distance experienced in the museum, thanks to the 'unique' object's 'aura' [6].

There were some efforts to resolve the conflicts, peculiar to that age, between the high and low arts and the between the bourgeois interior and the alienating exterior world. Jugendstil, where interiors welcomed the industrially processed materials like iron and glass, was an attempt to find a common ground between the industrial world outside, and the escapist interiors of the bourgeois. As Benjamin would point out, this was the private person's entrance onto the stage of history, gathering the distant and the past into his internal *phantasmagoria*, namely the living space, which was in direct contrast to the working space at that time. In this individual's environment, the diversity of things would impede the apperception of things which had no longer been objects, despite their material presence [7]. Consequently, in the age of the first crime novels, photography and Edgar Allen Poe, physiognomy would start taking command, for the flâneur, as the only way to react against this apperception of things in the interiors would be both to leave traces and to enclose with the velvet cases – to such an extent that in the Makart Style, the whole interior would turn into a velvet case [8].

As if acting as reminders of the early churches, built in the caves, or formed like caves, acting as wombs, protecting early believers from anxiety, posed by the outside world, the introvert 'proto-Modernist' interiors of Adolf Loos (who saw ornament and consequently the Jugendstil as a crime) would also reflect the conflicts of the individual and the burgeoning mass-society. 'Loos locates architecture at the mirror stage, at the threshold between the pre-castration comfort of the womb and the subsequent tension of split-subjectivity...' [9].

It would take some more time for the 'extrovert Gothic church' of the domestic interior to appear. Le Corbusier's very Modernist ribbon windows, making the habitant both the object and the subject by giving the totally 'integrated' subject the gaze of the camera – which, according to Benjamin, promised the analytical exploration of the material world. At the same time, along with capitalist pragmatism and scientism, Freudian psychopathological analysis of language would be one of the causes of the demise of the descriptive hermeneutical approaches, where – in contrast to structuralism – horizons of different ages meet in history, which is not 'flattened'.

On the other hand, with its utopias (on a larger scale), Modernism to Manfredo Tafuri is the tabula rasa 'which actually served the ends of both "social planning" and "capitalist development". And, Robert Venturi has demonstrated how such (utopist) projects were reduced to autonomous monuments.' [10] Modernism, wiping out history, can also be seen as the 'tabula rasa', or the next step, following the catalogue-based design understanding of Beaux-Arts in the gradual shift towards the 'formal lexicon' of the postmodern world, which is free of substances and, as being depthless, anachronistic by nature.

In contrast to the phantasmagoria/physiognomy of the flâneur's (not like Baudelaire, much more like Proust) interior mentioned above, with the utmost flatness and rational forms along with its brutalist aspects, De Stijl interiors (illusive, dematerializing mitred glass corners from ground to ceiling, meeting the water, the utmost interior–exterior unity, caused by the Richard Neutra's hygienic 'Prozac' interiors) seem to have made the interior, and subsequently the habitant, much closer to the corporate and the industrial world outside.

After Modernism and before Postmodernism, there would be two different styles, between which an analogy of the light and the dark sides of the design world can be drawn: Pop and Brutalism. Andy Warhol, the paper, silver foil and PVC surfaces of mini-skirts, depicting almost anything from comic strips to Op Art and Art Nouveau patterns, and inflatable plastic furniture, were the representations of a completely different world view from that of the *David* of Michelangelo, where *materia* were 'in-formed' [11]. Pop was the light side of design in a consumerist society. On the other hand, with its brutality, resembling World War II bunkers, a reflection of the anxiety of post-war generation, stemming both from the World War II and the anticipation of a nuclear war, Brutalism was the dark side of design.

Seeing that, in contrast to the Modernist utopia which aimed at unifying people in the consumer society, in the *heterotopic, post-optimal* [12] world, for Nigel Whiteley, in order not to fail, a product should pander to a particular group of consumers, it becomes clear why the light side of design dominated the world. Also becoming clear is why Nigel Whiteley points out that Pop, a style consisting of democratising and individualising plastic surfaces, almost devoid of substances, is the indicator of Postmodernism [13].

Besides, the success of the contemporary 'arcade', the postmodern shopping-mall, seems to be epitomizing the validity of Pop-Art, even today [15]. One of the most profitable examples is City Walk, Los Angeles, by John Jerde, a multi-cultural 'hetero-architecture' where Pop and the 'historicist, neo-conservative, pastiche-based' [14] side of Postmodernism come together so as to fit multi-cultural LA.

Compared to the existing *materia*, like wood, or marble, what the artificial glass and iron were to the 'arcade', plastic seems to be to Pop; and accordingly, to today's depthless surface architecture, and hyperspace where, to Fredric Jameson, there is 'not merely a liberation from anxiety, but a liberation from every other kind of feeling, as well, since there is no longer a self present to do the feeling.' [16]

Again, for Jameson, the flattening of human emotional range joins other postmodern collapses like the previous depth oppositions between essence and appearance, latent and manifest, authenticity and inauthenticity, and signifier and signified – as in *Alice in Wonderland* and *Through the Looking Glass*, both of which were celebrated by Deleuze as grand achievements where events are sought at the surface, rather than in the depths [17].

And, the surface revolution of plastic, a material like the signifier imperial maps replacing the signified territory in Borges' *The Garden of Forking Paths*, seems to have flattened our surroundings to such an extent that these desensitised plastic 'Roy Lichtenstein' interior spaces became the very embodiment of 'Prozac Culture'. Because, plastic creates objects, devoid of substances, as in the case of wood laminates, not sounding like wood, or the wood rosary beads, not giving the warmth of wood in winter. Therefore, if the individual's alienation in the corporate environments since the nineteenth century is to be recalled, even before the *aestheticisation* tendency, domesticating the public interiors of post-industrial society, as in the cases of boutique hotels, replacing the hangar-like, very corporate atmospheres of the hotels of the mass-society and the *aestheticised* version of McDonalds, namely, Starbucks, bringing the warmth of the domestic environment to its branches, it seems that in the age of 'plastic persona' the individual has already been moulded, or in other words, become docile.

Besides, seeing that bronze swords were made by pouring molten bronze into a stone mould, archaeologist Francis Pryor doesn't accept that the sword in the stone in the King Arthur legend is a complete fantasy. Once the molten bronze had cooled, the sword was withdrawn from the centre of the mould, making it look as though it was being drawn from stone, as was Excalibur [18]. Plastic products are also withdrawn from the moulds with an alienating, blink-of-the-eye speed, taking the aesthetic experience of production away. Further, plastic is a material simulating other materials in such a way that all their 'onomatopoeia-like' experienced qualities – the coldness of marble and steel – are removed. And like concrete*, lacking a natural form, plastic and its 'form lexicon', stripped of existential properties such as the sound and colour of wood, remind one of the abstractness of words (which, in Saussureian linguistics, have no rational relation with concepts).

For art historian Martin Wackernagel, the rise of collector occurred in Renaissance Florence. In contrast to the older generation of patrons, a collector orders 'art' not for a particular place, but simply for the sake of its artistic qualities. To E.H. Gombrich, this was the beginning of the gradual separation of a real 'art' from 'craft' [19]. With the arrival of the nineteenth-century modern collector (saving objects only by fetishising and turning them into 'art' within the *phantasmagoria* of his interior, in contrast to the harsh reality faced in the ambivalent social space) the whole interior would be almost filled with 'collectibles'. Finally, due to plastic's ability to simulate and its low manufacturing costs, the 'democraticisation' of taste in the world of plastic, where forms, free of substances, take command, seems to be another big step taken in the process of the evolution of 'users' into 'collectors'. Moreover, it can be claimed that for Nietzsche – for whom historical culture is not real culture, but only 'a kind of knowledge of culture' – the act of collecting is as pathological as cultural tourism. Along with the architecture and interior design magazines that *aestheticise* interiors in their glossy pages, both collecting and cultural tourism took part in the course of the *commodification* of space.

Recalling Jameson's flattened human emotional range, when questioning why lyric poetry does not attract the modern man, Benjamin is almost pointing at the recessed shadow behind the persona of the modern individual, since lyric poetry is of a more personal nature, addressing the reader directly while portraying his or her own feelings. And, in a reminder of Nietzsche's criticism of Hegelian historicism, classifications such

---

*   'By the 1890s, concrete was being used extensively for engineering projects, such as docks, riverbanks, and bridges, but not for "proper" architecture. It was the material's intrinsic qualities that were causing something of a moral dilemma. Concrete was considered pagan (given its Roman heritage) and so unsuitable as a construction material for Gothic Revival Christian buildings. As it had no natural form of its own, concrete was viewed as a material lacking in moral fibre, without character, and, if used at all, it should be faced with a more "moral" material, such as stone. According to Peter Collins in his book *Concrete: The Vision of a New Architecture*, when "Victorians first learnt of concrete they were not so much intrigued by the limitless possibilities offered by its plastic potential, as intimidated by the unprincipled character of its fabrication, since such methods found no place in the annals of Christian architecture and had no precedents except in pagan buildings and text."'
Gaventa, S. *Concrete Design* (London: Mitchell Beazley, 2001) p.16.

as Modernism, Art-Nouveau and so on cause the archetypal forms to be pastiches both in the interiors of domestic environments and in corporate spaces – together with the ones on the turntables of DJs. The turntable emits synthesized, genderless, hygienic and flat music under the glossy surface of the mirror-ball, a moon, illuminating shiny dresses, partly wrapping the plastic surgery skins in an escapist's paradise.

Besides, the man who lost his memory in Umberto Eco's *The Mysterious Flame of Queen Loana* says 'I was not sure which taste was the tea and which the sugar; one must have been bitter and the other sweet, but which was the sweet and which the bitter? In any case, I liked the combination.' Also, 'I don't remember images, or smells, or flavours. I only remember words.' In conversations between him and his doctor, he says 'Almost two hundred years ago Maine de Brian identified three types of memory: ideas, feelings, and habits. You remember ideas and habits but not feelings, which are of course the most personal.' [20]

As if to remind us both of the rise of 'the collector' with his illusions in the *phantasmagoria* of his interior space, and plastic surfaces, those forms almost without substances, Alice was sent through the two-dimensional surface of a mirror onto a giant flat chessboard in *Through the Looking Glass*. This also seems to be a reminder of the Lacanian mirror-stage where, by entering into the symbolic universe of the language, the child starts constructing his imaginative, *imago*-like *other*, whom he emulates. Thus, acting as a Lacanian *Other* (which can be likened to *maniera* in the mirrored interiors of Versailles) both the postmodern *phantasmagorical* interiors and postmodern lifestyle magazines, with their romanticized, surreal, pop imagery and glossy surfaces, surround *the other* in today's world. Today, every day is like those of the Venice Carnival and, as in *Alice in Wonderland*, not only the persona of the individual, but also the persona of the age is stripped of its shadow, due to the neck-breaking speed of constant change. This phenomenon is a gradual shift, which began in the nineteenth century, as mentioned at the beginning.

Just as quantum and Newtonian physics explain the same universe on different levels and, for Freud, the idea of human self was divided between two realms of consciousness (ego) and unconsciousness (id) – and also as in the arbitrary relationship between words and concepts – for the post-structuralist Lacanian psychoanalyst, 'I' was only an illusion in the symbolic universe, freeing the persona from humanistic understanding of a fixed notion of the *shadow*. And, while for Benjamin the arcade was a product of the infrastructure of the production techniques, the idea of a non-fixed *shadow* and a 'mask', without a face behind, seem to have found embodiment in today's '3D Xerox' like Philippe Starck's 'Louis Ghost Chair' for Kartell, and tomorrow's plastic surfaces where, thanks to SLS/SLA technologies, the *persona* and the *shadow* are one and the same – as in Rene Magritte's *Attempting the Impossible* (1928). Here, the *materia* are formed, yet any ideal form can be materialised, as in the idealist Greek Universe.

The persona inside the space

Today, the individual also materialises his ideal 'I' through already-materialised ideals like Harley Davidson. With its deterrent sound and form, this chrome monster claims the ownership of a 'universal' – namely, 'masculinity' – in a way that reminds of the primordial language, given directly by God, a transparent duplication of the universe, where the names of things were lodged in the things they represented, just as strength is written in the body of the lion [21].

The techniques of materialization grow ever more similar to those of filmmaking, in proportion with those of the day-by-day transformation of interior spaces into skins and the two-dimensional silver screen – the proto examples of which first appeared in the phantasmagorical atmosphere of the 'arcade'.

Benjamin interpreted the 'arcade' as a dream state (a bad one) that was not a direct reflection, but an expression of the infrastructure (full-stomach). Yet in the post-industrial world where the depth between the infrastructure and the dreams of society, which yields itself in the 'gold-ness' of a plastic credit card, has lessened to such an extent that there is only a pure simulacrum of signs (no more signifier and signified) left. Therefore, seeing the pragmatic necessity to apply the best-fit 'reading' techniques to those of the *auteur*'s writing, a post-structuralist Baudrillardian 'analysis' can be more helpful in order to reveal the dynamics of the contemporary over-designed world.

First of all, in this very world, an Aston Martin is 'Aston Martin' thanks to the cheap feminine Japanese mid-class cars; and Disneyland, a '3D TV world architecture documentary' for middle-class Americans, is there to prove the 'realness' of the rest of the continent – just as grey, when put next to black, seems whitish. Further, in this world, while in filmmaking the 'sound of a car crash' is that of a 'lorry' and it is always questioned: 'When the hero bites into an apple, is it "macho" enough? When [the heroine takes a] shower, does the water sound "wet" and "sexy" enough? And, does the silk negligee "whisper"?' [22], a plastic, quartz Swatch sounds as if it is a 'clock'! Lastly, in this *post-optimal* world of design, not only the designer, but also, as being a collector, the individual is adding value to his idealised *persona* by selecting from Ikea catalogues or from '3D catalogues' (namely, showrooms) – catalogues where a piece of furniture is *aestheticised* in a theatre-scene, made of cheap materials and pretending to be a room, as if the whole scene is there just to show us that Starbucks, or even our very rooms at home are 'real'. And this *aestheticisation* was even hidden in the very essence of Modernism, where form never followed function as Walter Gropius explicates: 'A thing that is technically excellent in all respects must be impregnated with an intellectual idea – with form – in order to secure preference among the large quantity of products of the same kind. As a result of greater knowledge one now attempts to guarantee the artistic quality of machine products from the outset and to seek the advice of the artist at the moment the form which is to be mass-produced is invented...' [23].

Consequently – in the time between the encyclopaedia, the Crystal Palace, the Great Exhibitions, the World Fairs (which were bringing fine art, technology and industry together in *phantasmagorical* stages) and today's Design Museum, Koolhaas's Prada shops, and the Milano International Furniture Fair ('the Temples' where use and exchange values are replaced with the sign value, as with Roman currency, which was exchanged with its sacred counterpart in the original Temple) – *commodified* and mass-produced Modernist products stole the 'aura' of the piece of art and became prostitutes, selling (advertising) their own bodies [24]. Today's sign system is reminiscent of Albrecht Durer's allegorical *Melancolia I* engraving (1514). In contrast to more connotative symbolism, the kind of a value to which a commodity directly refers is decipherable – metonymy (what makes the word 'crown' stand for 'the king') seems to be a section in the 'user-guide' of the user-consumer, who is an *objectified* person, both for the advertising person and for the designer. Today, an object in a shop window can easily be a 'crown' for an idealised 'I'. Consequently, *fetishisized* and *personified* commodities like Aston Martin, Rolex, and Turnbull & Asser make James Bond, the 'James Bond', who is in fact a stereotype. Like a brand or a product, the *protagonist user* also has to define his/her position well, since 'the ugly' was the only figure in Sergio Leone's *The Good, the Bad, and the Ugly* who was neither the stereotypical protagonist nor the antagonist. Therefore, just as the 'Gothic Church of the individual' was representing the industry's penetration into the domestic space, as flat as the magazines representing them, our interiors, made of plastic laminated surfaces are declaring the new 'imperial maps', namely, the post-industry.

Besides, if to many scholars, the depth in Edvard Munch's *Scream* was the perfect expression of anxiety, peculiar to the modern individual, then the ultimate flatness of the mass-reproduced Marilyn Monroe images of Andy Warhol makes the perfect representation of the postmodern society's dilemma. This dilemma is portrayed best in the Monty Python film *Life of Brian*, where the individual says 'No, I am not an individual', while the crowd shouts in unison 'We are all individuals' [25]. Therefore, in a world, where time and space are compressed and where the 'mass consumers' are all 'individuals', trying to differentiate themselves from the rest so as to avoid existential anxiety (which for many thinkers like Immanuel Kant, is related to the experience of time) the 'new' should be constantly reinvented. And that proves Reyner Banham's prediction that 'the two IDs (Interior and Industrial Design) were better equipped to actualize the modern as the perpetually new' [26], where even houses made of paper outlast the 'new'.

As to the escapist individual of that time, just before the *detournament* of the club experience to the 'experience economy', in his/her shiny dress, glittering under the flashes of disco light that was fragmenting time in sync with the neck-breaking speed of disco rhythm, just like a snake, biting its own tail, he/she was a protagonist in the middle of the dance-floor, dancing alone with Donna Summer, who was sounding 'oversexed but not the dirty blues mama or sensuous soul sista of old' [27], for the song 'I Feel Love' was too sterile, too robotic, too unnatural, to be dirty enough. So, if for Benjamin, the ideals of a given age are the dream of the next, and only by dreaming it can one awaken [28], then with his novels like *Crash* [29] – where the psychopathological effects of car accidents in our 'Prozac culture' are depicted, imprisoning our 'anxious' true selves that are behind our personas/masks – can J.G. Ballard, who created a new genre in science fiction for dreaming of the future in today's world, give some clues about the awakening state of our society in the context of interior design? The answer may be found in the 'flatness' of the film version of the novel by David Cronenberg, where the only depth can be found in the crashed cars and wounded bodies of the protagonists [30]. Or, after falling down a deep hole, Alice may find the Wonderland, where a new understanding of interior design encompasses real human needs, deep-down – instead of pandering either to the abstract 'socio-manikin' of the mass-society of 'modern times', or to the 'protagonist' individual's persona of postmodern times.

The protagonist in this very deep-down world is like that of a J.G. Ballard novel, who could easily be the antagonist in a conventional one. Consequently, in this world, the designer is not the *auteur,* who imposes his/her own ideologies onto the 'individual'. Because, in his/her mind there is no longer a stereotypical character to design for, like the ones personified in *The Good, the Bad, and the Ugly.* In a paradigm-shift like this (as with the necessity of using the body in order to transcend in psychosomatic rituals), instead of pandering to the *persona,* satisfying the *shadow,* even the 'surface' may lead to the freedom of the 'real' individual. Keeping in mind that, for Reyner Banham, interior design is better equipped to actualize the modern as the perpetually new, this new paradigm may also add to the autonomy of interior design as a discipline by emphasising its basic methodological difference from architecture, a discipline, intrinsically 'prêt-a-porter' for 'socio-manikins' and stereotypical protagonists.

References

[1] Virilio, P. *Unknown Quantity* (London: Thames & Hudson, 2003).

[2] Özer, B. '19.Yüzyılın Genel Nitelikleri ve Batı Mimarisinde Seçmecilik', *Mimari Tasarım,* 1961, 3, 107–12.

[3] Rykwert, J. 'The Ecole des Beaux-Arts and The Classical Tradition', in Middleton, R., ed. *The Beaux Arts and the Nineteenth Century French Architecture* (London: Thames and Hudson, 1984) p.17.

[4] Foster, H. *Tasarım ve Suç* (İstanbul: İletişim Yayınları, 2004) pp.51–4.

[5] Harvey, D. *The Condition of Postmodernity* (Oxford: Blackwell Publishers, 1990) pp.260–83.

[6] Benjamin, W. *Pasajlar* (İstanbul: YKY, 1993) p.55.

[7] Maldonado, T. and Cullars, J. 'The Idea of Comfort', *Design Issues,* 1991, 8(1), 35–43.

[8] Benjamin, W. *Pasajlar* (İstanbul: YKY, 1993) pp.140–1.

[9] Ho, J. 'The Mask of Architecture, Reviewed Work: Privacy and Publicity: Architecture and Mass Media by Beatriz Colomina', *Performing Arts Journal,* 1997, 19(3), 107–10.

[10] Foster, H. '(Post)Modern Polemics', *Perspecta,* 1984, 21, 148.

[11] Flusser, V. *The Shape of Things: A Philosophy of Design* (London: Reaktion Books, 1999) pp.17–21.

[12]   Dunne, A. *Hertzian Tales, Electronic Products, Aesthetic Experience and Critical Design* (London: RCA CRD Research Publications, 1999) p.28.

[13]   Whiteley, N. 'Pop, Consumerism, and the Design Shift', *Design Issues*, 1985, 2(2), 31–45.

[14]   Foster, H. '(Post)Modern Polemics', *Perspecta*, 1984, 21, 148.

[15]   Özer, F. Bir Pop-Mimari Örneği, Yapı, 2002, 245, 66–73.

[16]   Jameson, F. *Postmodernism or the Cultural Logic of Late Capitalism* (Durham: Duke University Press, 1991).

[17]   Springer, C. 'The Seduction of the Surface: From Alice to Crash', *Feminist Media Studies*, 2001, 1(2), 197–213.

[18]   Pryor, F. *Britain AD, A Quest for Arthur, England and the Anglo-Saxons* (Element Books, 2005).

[19]   Ackbar, A. 'Walter Benjamin's Collector: The Fate of Modern Experience', *New Literary History*, 1988, 20(1), 217–37.

[20]   Eco, U. *The Mysterious Flame of Queen Loana* (London: Vintage, 2006).

[21]   Foucault, M. *This is not a Pipe* (Los Angeles: University of California Press, 1983) p.6.

[22]   Mott, R.L. *Radio, TV and Film*, Focal Press, 1990. See http://www.filmsound.org (accessed on 27 April 2003).

[23]   Paper sent by Walter Gropius to Grand Ducal Saxon State Ministry in Weimar in January 1916, in response to its request to 'supplement his statement concerning architectural education in the art academy by an explanation of the kind of influence the crafts would receive from the artistic side and from the giving of instruction in handicrafts'. Bode, W. von, *Die Woche* (Berlin Newspaper), 1 April 1916; quoted in Hans M. Wingler, *The Bauhaus* (Cambridge, MA: MIT, 1980); quoted in Periton, D. 'The Bauhaus as Cultural Paradigm', *The Journal of Architecture*, 1996, 1, 189–205.

[24]   Benjamin, W. *Pasajlar* (İstanbul: YKY, 1993) pp.99–100.

[25]   Svendsen, L.Fr.H. *A Philosophy of Boredom* (London: Reaktion Books, 2005) p.101.

[26]   Mitchell, E. 'Lust for Lifestyle', *Assemblage*, 1999, 40, 80–8.

[27]   Shapiro, P. *Turn the Beat Around, The Secret History of Disco* (London: Faber and Faber, 2005).

[28]   Benjamin, W. *Pasajlar* (İstanbul: YKY, 1993) p.26.

[29]   Ballard, J.G. *Crash* (London: Vintage, 1995).

[30]   Springer, C. 'The Seduction of the Surface: From Alice to Crash', *Feminist Media Studies*, 2001, 1(2), 197–213.

Andrew STONE

London Metropolitan University

THE UNDERESTIMATION OF THE INTERIOR

Introduction

There is an underestimation of the interior that is rooted in the empirical development of the profession. Despite the complexity of its programme, the interior and its design have failed to be adequately investigated or represented. The creative and inhabited potential of the interior is rarely questioned or exposed theoretically and the contexts of the interior, as a stimulus or a social or cultural commentary, are rarely invoked. This reflects the subject's monocular professional evolution.

As an emerging, youthful discipline, interior design has yet to accommodate sufficient breadth of identity to recognise, support or represent the diversity of investigation and practice that will, or should, enable the potential of the subject to emerge.

Interior designers maintain a near-paranoiac need to define 'this is what we do'; it is part of our public and private ritual introduction, rehearsed and emphatic to the point of being proselytising. The source of this is reflected in the impact of architectural and artefactual heredity on the interior's emergence as a discrete area of design. The identification of, and with, the interior as a specific design discipline remains fluid and loose, and tensions prompted by perceived vagueness of definition lead regularly to a search for a level of prescription.

The risk of prescription is that the process can be necessarily reductive, limiting activities to those proffered by a dominant interest. Contrarily a lack of definition can lead those who assume representative validity or responsibility to assert it.

A significant benefit is that it allows distance and inflection. The edge of the subject is active, offering catalytic opportunities and coalitions, allowing non-specialists to provoke through their practice. It allows the interior designer to appropriate other design languages in order to tease other ideas, moulding values from one discipline with the practice of another – design is, as with all aspects of inhabitation, parasitic.

To consider how these contexts might be understood we need to identify certain prevailing interests. The possibilities in the design of the inhabited interior are typically identified with the early nineteenth century's emergent middle-class distinction between the place of work and the home:

> For the private person, living space becomes for the first time antithetical to the place of work. The former is constituted by the interior; the office is its complement [1].

The dialectical opposition Benjamin describes has evolved into a far more complex series of spatial, social and economic relations. The identification of the discrete value of the interior, however, provides the underlying context for our subject.

> For the private individual the private environment represents the universe. In it he gathers remote places and the past. His drawing room is a box in the world theatre [2].

The opportunity of the interior is set out as a place of collection and dispersal. The breadth and nature of the interior as point of exchange endures as the primary motivator for its design.

Occupying modernity

The illustrated plates of Tony Garnier's Une Cité Industrielle cascade from the balloonic overview down through the different quartiers until they step over the threshold of a worker's house resting finally on the vase of flowers; the aestheticised civility of domestic life in the modern industrial city. There is a familiar, picturesque, sense of home and the private, complimentary components that signify their economic and psychological value.

Contrarily, Le Corbusier in La Ville Radieuse symbolises the interior as a seeing eye, framing the city and framing the interior. A reciprocity that meant the interior was no longer visually discrete from the exterior; an inhabitation quite different to Benjamin's separation of the 'world theatre'; in the modern metropolis the interior is framed and absorbed. 'From our offices we will get the feeling of being look-outs dominating the world in order' [3].

As such, the integration of the interior into many of modern architecture's visions for the twentieth-century city is significant; here was the active appropriation of the interior environment as a designed component of urban and architectural imagination.

Le Corbusier's belief that 'the interior is always an exterior', Beatriz Colomina suggests, destabilises the constancy of the interior domain, stimulating a transience and movement from which it was previously protected. 'Inhabitation' implies a stability drawn from the relationship between space and inhabitant. 'Occupant' suggests the spatial relationship is temporary, that the occupier is in less control either of the space or the activities that take place there.

In a further evolution from Benjamin's dialectic, the architectural or designed control of the interior intertwines the domestic and the social; and in so doing, the terminology of spatial experience shifts. The occupant and the user, passive and active, are aligned to the nature of modernity's search for efficiency and function.

[T]he choice of 'user' in place of 'occupants', 'inhabitants' or 'clients' has held strong connotations of the disadvantaged or disenfranchised. It particularly implied those who could not normally be expected to contribute to the architect's brief [4].

There are two significant issues for the interior and its design here. One is that the economic or exchange value of the interior becomes more complex. If the interior is no longer inhabited but instead momentarily occupied then the condition, the thesis proposes, is that the interior is clearly representing or attempting to anticipate a shift in social experience. The second is that of disenfranchisement: interior design's attentiveness to the client established the professional ground, but the relationship between client and user is not always as successfully unpicked.

At the end of the nineteenth century, the distancing of individual spatial experience had been critiqued as being representative of the modern human condition. Benjamin's private connoisseur's interior was a place of desire, taste and status. With the advent of shopping and the arcades, the two issues combined: 'the arcades are a centre of trade in luxury goods. In their fittings art is brought into the service of commerce.' [5]

Shops, and the design of interiors for consumption or for consuming in, have been the most immediately visible commercial interior design work for much of the last 100 years. At the beginning of the twentieth century, the coincidence of artefact, efficiency and desire evolved from a 'leisured' activity to a necessary one linked to the modern expectation and intervention of function, and to studies such as those by Frederick Taylor [6]. This perception of need, or a use/value, in products and in the corresponding spaces of production, sale or use required efficiency and presented an overt economic value to interior design.

The abstraction of urban, metropolitan living in comparison with previous habitual and ritualised social relations had also been exposed in Georg Simmel's socio-economic critique, 'The Metropolis and Mental Life'.

Simmel's observations identified the city as a point of exchange, physically and economically, but his spatiality was non-specific. His pupil, Siegfried Kracauer, however, used particular public interior types to contextualise his critique of the modern human condition, the hotel lobby, employment exchanges; 'spaces of unrelatedness' [7] that actively contributed to the dislocation of individual spatial participation.

The silence and anonymity of Kracauer's places are ambiguous; they are representative of emergent social conditions and of the changes in the accompanying activity, which perhaps can be read as a new interior typology. For other commentators this invisibility is a potent tool in interrogating the city; it is the ability to be distant from the substance of the city whilst observing it. The observer is codified by Simmel as 'the Stranger'; for Walter Benjamin and Baudelaire, 'the Flaneur'; or for Hannah Arendt, 'the Exile'; individual representations of collective experience protected by a mask of anonymity and an apparently universal subject.

Tension in the abstraction of spatial experience was mirrored in the wider description of the places of architectural inhabitation – the room, the interior, the street. This was a conscious development. The intellectual construct of 'space' as the prevailing etymological term for architectural, or urban, environments was generated as part of the overt shift to the modern.

The typology of the interior, of 'rooms' as defined or implied by an activity, was denied. Instead, a more fluid and less prescriptive notion of the interior was conjured, whether in the Loosian 'Raumplan', 'Le Corbusier's Plan Libre', or the work of Rietveld or Kiesler: 'space' articulated the modern. 'Space offered a non-metaphorical, non-referential category for talking about architecture.' [8]

What is interesting at this time is that the interior, and the modern-ness of the environment that people inhabited, were seen to be of such intellectual and physical significance. 'Space' in these terms avoids the assumed physical or material qualities of architecture and parallels the psycho-sociological observations of Simmel and the spatial types of Kracauer.

Although the intellectual trajectory of this type of thinking has been used to support and critique Modernism, the majority of design practice was more general in its development. The inhabiting of an abstract place, domestic or public, provided divergent considerations for the designer. The relationship with the client is key. Although the dressing of the interior and of the aesthetic assemblage of artefact was maintained, the concern with the modernity of function, and of the emergent goods to achieve this was changing the designer's activity.

These products represented an alliance of design with commercial expectation of high levels of production, greater sales and a more efficient environment in which to work. In the middle-class home, the loss of domestic labour following the First World War and the subsequent flu pandemic would affect and inform an ideological shift in the perception of home. A demand for 'labour saving devices' would identify commercial notions of efficiency with the effectiveness of household management. The devices were promoted as machines for the home and 'industrial' designers merged craft 'types' with new products, modern technology and aesthetics. As well as informing changes to the operation and organisation of the domestic interior, the mobility of the workforce and resultant changes to housing patterns reflected back into the workplace.

The designed office, shop or showroom reflected the modernity of the client. As a commodity, the 'product' needed to be reflected in the environment in which it was designed, produced and sold. The commercial or corporate value of design was developed as a language through which a company and its product were recognized and through which their stock grew.

In achieving commercial success through the stylising of products and interiors, the designer could convince the client of the value of design and of the designer. The abstraction of Modernist thinking was distanced as the visual language was appropriated to assist in providing the image of modernity without the philosophical and political radicalism.

This commodification of a service and its output, and the focus on the client, had far more in common with the interior decorator than with the International style. It was without polemic or manifesto; it appropriated and adapted; it was about 'doing', articulated as a professional efficiency.

Educating a profession

But what constituted this new modern profession? Much of the resistance of interior designers to being defined as decorators is certainly about distinguishing their corporate and commercial credentials as opposed to a domestic repertoire. But this is less about a resistance to involvement with curtains and cushions than the nineteenth-century image of decoration, with its implication that therefore they are either suppliers or makers (and therefore 'trade') or specifiers, people of taste or aesthetes – as one hundred years earlier with the 'gentleman architect' – to a typically wealthy client, and therefore 'amateur'. Both imply a diminishment of a nascent professionalism.

Beyond a developing commercial presence, subject recognition and association evolved slowly. The two professional membership organisations of disciplines from whose shadow interior design emerged, the Royal Institute of British Architects (RIBA) and Chartered Society of Designers (CSD) – formerly the Society of Industrial Artists and Designers – are those to which interior designers are or seek to be attached.

The RIBA, although gradually acknowledging interior design as something that can operate independently of architecture, does not yet offer formal recognition. But it does have a layered structure that informs all aspects of its own professional identity. The CSD is more commercially focused – the business aspect of 'trade' was less problematic – with an explicit professional practice remit but without the facility to prescribe or protect.

Both therefore are that most English of devices used to assist the achievement of public recognition and status: a club, through which the presence of a discipline can be collectively and socially presented in an appropriate setting. This includes the registered validation of professional status, typically through education, examination, a fee and, ideally, the legal facility to restrict ('protect') participation unless these are fulfilled.

Once such devices are in place, the 'profession' can assure its clients of its proper practice.

As was suggested earlier, there is rightly debate about whether any of these are necessary, or desirable, for interior designers; and whether the fact that none of these exist in the UK (or at least none in a comprehensive or coherent way) has had any detrimental affect on professional activity.

The interior design profession is rooted in production. Over the last 50 years, the profession has successfully established a commercial understanding of its role in the design and production of interiors, distinct from that of the connoisseur and decorator. Education has developed to serve this.

This focus has been reflected in the structure and trajectory of interior design education. Emergent from either art or technical colleges, a vocational bias has always been at the fore. When in the early 1970s the facility was granted to award honours degrees, most of the former diploma courses simply incorporated existing History of Art or other 'contextual' studies to provide an 'academic' component in their award.

As an example, Middlesex Polytechnic's degree in interior design was validated in 1973–4, following the incorporation of Hornsey College of Art and its Diploma in Art and Design. By 1977 the intent to 'train' its students had been removed, but the focus remained on 'providing the necessary theory and practice in design and technology to understand, analyse and solve the problems of the professional designer' [9] – sentiments that remain common to the majority of design courses thirty years later.

In the prospectus at this time, there is no mention of academic or intellectual roots or of a greater ambition to further the subject. The History of Art provision is not mentioned, nor is the type of work that the student might have to undertake in this area. There are many reasons for this, not least the public, professional and even educational view that design courses are 'not academic' – a view that continues to be offered.

Such a precept effectively contains the development of the subject. By limiting this aspect of study, interior design education has largely prevented itself from entering into a canon of intellectual and creative activity independent from 'work'. If academic and creative energy is predominantly focused on students achieving what is necessary to be employed, then the opportunity that education provides to explore areas of investigation and study that would less typically be part of commercial output is severely limited.

Other areas of design – fashion and architecture most obviously – specifically look to develop within their students a consciousness of the difference they can, or will make to their field. Certainly some, perhaps a lot of this is driven by ego; but it is also about striving for excellence through a culture driven by academic, professional, practical and intellectual expectation, and the idea that, without such intent, they can't really contribute.

Architecture students are encouraged to aspire to 'a position' toward their subject that demands intellectual assessment and distance. There is an expectation that they will look to make a difference and that their work therefore has a specific value – without this your creative ability will not be fully realised. Without that framework, it is far harder for interior design students to embed themselves in the subject and they graduate without demonstrating such a level of aggressive ambition for their field.

It is therefore unsurprising that there is a significant lack of young interior designers who look to establish their own practice early in their career, or to test and experiment with their ideas through an economic and intellectual alliance with education. Similarly, parallel to attempts to define our practice, there have been re-designations of academic courses as interior architecture (despite restrictions on title) as a means of achieving an intellectual and creative freedom and to invest the interior with a rigour that interior design has yet to demonstrate.

The limited integration of the profession and academia, despite the mutually expected progression, has essentially nullified the intellectual growth of the subject. In so doing, the culture of practice becomes more and more explicit in identifying education's failings in the expectations of what will be provided by graduates. This insecurity is reflected in the demands on education to skill (train) rather than to extend, develop, or even establish a wider knowledge.

Recent policies and campaigns from organisations such as the Design Council and the CSD perpetuate and strengthen both the expectation that this is design education's sole purpose and that should the student, or their educational providers, choose to question or adversely critique this model, the learning would be deemed to be unacceptable or failing. In a culture of benchmarking and frequently misconceived notions of standards and 'employability', such leverage is powerful. But just as design education is criticised for failing to provide students with sufficient business or technical knowledge, so the polemic exposes a fundamental lack of knowledge of both structures of design education and the means through which it is monitored and regulated.

Hence interiors education in the UK could, in addition to institutional standards, national academic benchmarks, potentially be 'approved' by a variety of professional organisations vying for the right to claim professional legitimacy. The Design Council and the Creative and Cultural Skills Council have mooted a 'kitemark' for approved courses and the CSD has launched the 'CSD Course Recognition programme'. The British Interior Design Association (BIDA) currently has no plans to accredit courses.

The underlying rationale of the schemes is based upon the economic benefits of professional practice, whether to the organisation, its members, or to the state. In the report of the first meeting of the Design Skills Advisory Panel, a joint group of two Government-funded organisations, the Design Council and the Creative and Cultural Skills Council, it states that there are 'some fundamental problems. For example, too many people are being trained [sic] – there simply aren't enough design jobs for graduates' [10]. Later in the document, Tom Bewick, the Creative and Cultural Skills Council chairman, says a 'kitemark' would 'make sure education and training work better for employers' and that 'we need decent apprenticeships… Again this would benefit employers.' [11]

The consultation regarding this particular future of design education was undertaken by a panel of twenty-eight, of which two were from education. The findings contributed to the Leitch Review of Skills, published in December 2006 with the recommendation that '[b]y 2020, all publicly funded design courses will need to be endorsed by industry.' [12]

This is not in itself a threat, of course – except that it explicitly and solely identifies the educational process with commercial value. The commodity here is the student and specifically the facility of their skills to reinforce market values. But interior design, academically and professionally, must be able to distinguish between a provision which is endorsed and that which is subservient.

Provocation and responsibility

At which point does the designer, or educator, make a judgement on the ethics of our efficacy? Interior design, like many design areas, has offered very limited engagement with areas of work outside the immediate, commercially lead, remit of practice. The demise of the social agenda of Modernism regrettably coincided with the growth of the interior design profession and the emergence of specialist study.

The 1961 'Parker Morris' report shifted the recommendations for housing development to assess unit size rather than room size. In so doing it provided the opportunity to reassess the relevance of the domestic interior as a focused investigation of the interior as a social condition, as a place in which the designer's social responsibility rather than their business acumen was the creative prompt.

The profession, representative bodies and education have all failed significantly to address essentially unfashionable, or unprofitable, aspects of design work. The political context for Parker Morris has disappeared and the privatisation of responsibility places a greater onus on designers to be critical in their interrogation of project value.

We must not shy away from this. There has been very little testing of the interior in the social or economic contexts of poverty, ageing or even education. Access, mobility and disability are more evident because of recent legislation. Energy, climate and waste because of their threat to the economic stability and viability of our clients are now part of a general discourse but remain largely client led. Without these other contexts to respond to, the output of practice – and students – is remarkably repetitive and rather compliant.

> The approach to the problem of design starts with a clear recognition of these various activities and their relative importance in social, family and individual lives and goes on to assess the conditions necessary for their pursuit in terms of space, atmosphere, efficiency, comfort, furniture and equipment [13].

I studied interior design at Middlesex Polytechnic between 1981 and 1985. The prospectus had told me that as an interior designer I would be integral to the building process; part of a team responsible for creating the built environment; that there would be two periods of industrial release – an interesting term – that together with studio practice would combine my 'creative abilities, technical knowledge and practical experience' to enable me to be involved in the 'shaping and giving of appropriate form and meaning to the elements of the environment.' [14]

I graduated in 1985, into the heady days of Thatcher's society-less Britain. Never had the ascetic critique of design and society seemed so distant as a booming, salivating architecture and design profession paraded to clients their conspicuous eagerness to represent such aspirational times:

> On the ground floor was the glinting open plan Ogee office and on the two upper floors a flat that was full of eclectic features, lime-wood pediments, coloured glass, surprising apertures... The high tech of the office was less the logic of the future than another style in their postmodern repertoire... A system of minimized stress, of guaranteed flattery [15].

Such exhibited consumption has been one of constants of interior design since it has, in any way, been a defined discipline. Seventy years previously, it was described more subtly by Benjamin: 'The collector is a true inmate of the interior. He makes the transfiguration of things his business.' [16] And later, 'To live means to leave traces. In the interior these are emphasized... The traces of the occupant also leave their impression on the interior.' [17]

The act of transfiguring the design and experience of interior space is what we aspire toward. But to achieve this we need to be in a position to acknowledge and engage with a diversity of circumstance that informs what we do. To achieve that there has to be room to breathe, to invent and to fail.

The interior is a physical and intellectual incubator; a place where a coincidence of diverse elements is activated by circumstance; matrices of contexts and provocations facilitating a dialogue between activities and experience. Seeking to achieve an intellectual distance and difference from practice should not threaten a mature profession. The confluence of design and intellectual activity stimulated by modernity and Modernism enabled architecture to distinguish its practice beyond production:

> ['Space'] allowed architects to rub shoulders with the socially superior discourses of physics and philosophy. Insofar as architecture had always suffered the slur, of being no more than a trade, or a business, the claim to deal with the most immaterial of properties, 'space' allowed architects decisively to present their labour as mental rather than manual [18].

Unlike 'space', the interior defines a place; it is relative to what is containing or enclosing it, and so to present it as something other than this is problematic. 'Interiority' is perhaps an attempt at removing the intellectual confinement of place; identifying with qualities – physical, psychological, metaphysical – of the interior without the need to define the where or the what. This is significant in being able to give some distance from a definite article but problematic in that it does not offer sufficient terminological breadth or ambiguity to distinguish it.

Interior qualities; physical and material components, artefacts, furniture, equipment; memories and inhabitants, services and their relationship to the visual and physical limits of their environment, inform interior(ity).

As these are acknowledged, the interior is activated as the point where these components, their 'users' and the actions and influences upon them coincide, and the designer's responsibility and skill is the curatorial employment of an articulate and critical compositional control.

So the interior is a network of threads, links, lines of circumstance, interest and enquiry. These different prompts and contexts are discrete and entwined. They are like circulation spaces – always the best bits to design – places of activity, dialogue and inhabitation and a route to other places and ideas.

However, if as Frederic Jameson suggests, 'what remains of inner space' will be marked by individual visions and conceptions of how to 'congregat[e] your screens and furniture in one part of the warehouse and pil[e] up your boxes in the other,' [19] then we have failed.

The underestimation of the interior's intellectual and economic value is projected through a prevalence of superficial representation and commentary. If design education is to enable students to reflect seriously and confidently on their subject they must have the facility to distance themselves from industry demands in order to invest in the subject critically and creatively.

To demonstrate the relevance and value of diverse and speculative practice, of social responsibility, of technological innovation, of independent spatial experimentation, is to begin to articulate the matrices of contexts that inform the interior. The quality of the interior, however, is in its use. It is as mobile and as fluid, as complex and contradictory, as the attempts to define its practice.

So it is through the inhabitation of those matrices and the resultant design programme that the opportunity for transfiguration, as the interior designer's rather than the collector's realm, is provided.

References

[1]   Benjamin, W. 'Paris, Capital of the Nineteenth Century' in Leach, N. *Rethinking Architecture* (London: Routledge, 1997) p.36.
[2]   Ibid.
[3]   Le Corbusier, C. 'Urbanisme' (1925) in Colomina, B. *Sexuality and Space* (Princeton: Princeton Architectural Press, 1992).
[4]   Forty, A. 'Users', *Words and Buildings* (London: Thames & Hudson, 2000) p.312.
[5]   Benjamin, op. cit., p.34
[6]   Taylor, F.W. *Scientific Management: Comprising 'Shop Management' (1903), 'The Principles of Scientific Management' (1911) and 'Testimony Before the Special House Committee' (1912)* (London: Routledge, 2003).

[7] Kracauer, S. 'The Hotel Lobby' in Leach, N. *Rethinking Architecture* (London: Routledge, 1997) p.55.

[8] Forty, A. 'Space' *Words and Buildings* (London: Thames & Hudson, 2000) p.265.

[9] Middlesex Polytechnic, Art and Design prospectus 1977–8

[10] 'Designing the Future', notes from Design Skills Advisory Panel meeting 20 April 2005, p.2.

[11] Ibid., p.6

[12] 'Design Week', p.4 volume 22/1, 4 January 2007.

[13] 'Homes for today and tomorrow' (Parker Morris report) 1961, quoted in Forty, A. *Words and Buildings* (London: Thames & Hudson, 2000) p.313.

[14] Middlesex Polytechnic Art and Design prospectus 1980–81.

[15] Hollinghurst, A. *The Line of Beauty* (2004) p.197.

[16] Walter Benjamin, 'Paris, Capital of the Nineteenth Century' in Leach, N. *Rethinking Architecture* (London: Routledge, 1997) p.36

[17] Ibid.

[18] Forty, A. 'Space', op. cit., p.265

[19] Jameson, F. 'Demographies of the Anonymous' in *Anyone* (New York: A.N.Y., 1993) p.56.

Bibliography

Books

Arendt, H. *The Human Condition* (Chicago: University of Chicago press, 1956).

Baudrillard, J. *The System of Objects* (London: Verso, 1968/1996).

Benjamin, W. *Reflections: Essays, Aphorisms, Autobiographical Writings* (New York: Schocken Books, 1978).

Colomina, B. *Privacy and Publicity: Modern Architecture and Mass Media* (Cambridge, MA: MIT Press, 1994).

Garnier, T. *Une Cite Industrielle* (New York: Princeton Architectural Press, 1917/1989).

Le Corbusier *The City of Tomorrow and its Planning* (London: Butterworth, 1921/1971).

Le Corbusier *The Decorative Art of Today* (London: Butterworth, 1925/1987).

Le Corbusier *Towards a New Architecture* (London: Butterworth, 1923/1989).

Forty, A. *Words and Buildings* (London: Thames and Hudson 2000).

Hollinghurst, A. *The Line of Beauty* (London: Picador, 1994).

Leach, N. *Rethinking Architecture* (London: Routledge, 1997).

Lechte, J. *50 Key Contemporary Thinkers; from Structuralism to Postmodernism* (London: Routledge, 1994).

Middlesex Polytechnic, Art & Design Prospectus 1977–78 (London: Middlesex Polytechnic, 1977).

Middlesex Polytechnic, Art & Design Prospectus 1980–81 (London: Middlesex Polytechnic, 1980).

Pile, J. *A History of Interior Design* (London: Laurence King, 2000).

Zittel, A. *Critical Space* (New York: Prestel, 2005).

Book Selection/Chapter

Colomina, B. 'The Split Wall: Domestic Voyeurism' in Colomina, B., ed. *Sexuality and Space* (New York: Princton Architectural Press, 1988).

Jameson, F. 'Demographies of the Anonymous' in *Anyone* (New York: A.N.Y., 1993).

Kracauer, S. 'The Hotel Lobby' in Levin, T., ed. *The Mass Ornament* (Cambridge, MA: Harvard University press, 1995).

Simmel, G, 'Bridge and Door' in *Theory, Culture and Society*, vol.11, 1994, pp.5–10.

Simmel, G. 'Metropolis and Mental Life' in Hatt, P. and Reiss, A. *Cities and Society; the revised reader in urban sociology* (New York: The Free Press of Glencoe, 1951/1961).

Report

Taylor, F.W. 'Scientific Management; comprising shop management, the principles of scientific management; Testimony before the Special House Committee' (New York: Harper & Row, re-issued by W. W. Norton & Co., 1911/1967).

Website

Designing the Future', notes from Design Skills Advisory Panel meeting 20 April 2005: http://www.ccskills.org.uk/media/cms/documents/pdf/DSAP%20meeting,%2020%20April%2005.pdf

Magazine

Design Week, vol.22, Issue 1, 4 January 2007, p.4.

How do we teach interior design?

Ro SPANKIE

Oxford Brookes University

THINKING THROUGH DRAWING

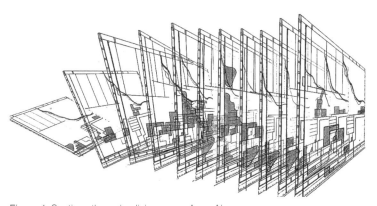

Figure 1: Sections through a living room, Anna Algne

Introduction

Perhaps because of its 'slippery… ephemeral and hard to define' [1] nature, interiors has been seen as belonging to the discipline of architecture. As such, it has historically operated under architecture's umbrella, borrowing its means of practice, ways of thinking and methods of representation. Increasingly however, interiors as a discipline is showing signs of separating, as it becomes a professional and educational route in itself, embraced by the media and seemingly practised by all. At this moment of juncture, the differences between 'interiors' and 'architecture' become more apparent, as does the need for new tools or a more tailored approach.

What are an architect's design tools?

An architect designs buildings rather than builds them. Unlike, say, a sculptor chipping at a stone, an 'architect never works directly on the object of their thought, always working at it through some intervening medium, almost always the drawing.' [2] Architectural form is therefore conceived in the abstract, static space of the drawing, defined through measurement and scale. The architectural drawing is propositional, rather than observational; a means of communication rather than an end-in-itself. The process of architectural production, due to the professional need to quantify the parts, to predict the end result, adheres to representational conventions defined in law. Although many other forms of drawing are used, the standard form of drawing is a two-dimensional scaled description of the proposed object, cut into a series of orthographic planes known as plan, section and elevation. This is a highly conventionalised non-pictorial method, which is more suited to describing form rather than the space it contains.

Things that are left out of the drawing

The conventions to which architectural drawings conform make it possible to see certain things more clearly by suppressing others. However, paradoxically, the very qualities that define the identity of the interior seem to fall into this suppressed category by the nature of being unquantifiable, immaterial and fluid. This has consequences not just for issues of representation but also intent, because the method in which we choose to draw influences the way we think, and therefore what we design.

This chapter proposes to examine what these 'suppressed' qualities might be and to look at ways in which we might attempt to put them back in the picture. However, this chapter does not intend to set architecture in opposition to interiors, nor is it concerned with definitions of 'architect', 'interior architect' or 'interior designer', recognising that these may be one and the same person. My interest lies in the relationship of the space we occupy to the form that contains it.

I have grouped interior qualities into four areas: use, movement, effect and the occupant. However, each is interlinked to the other and, by their nature, parasitical to the very thing I am claiming difference from: namely, the exterior.

Use, movement, effect and the occupant

There's the outside of the outside form, the inside of the outside form, and then a space in perpetual tension. Then there's the outside of the inside form and finally, the inside of the inside form... Inside and outside are both coincidental and discontinuous. Fit and misfit [3].

- While the exterior is described as a 'whole' (for instance, 'house'), the interior is described as a series of fragments that are defined by use: 'kitchen', 'bedroom' and so on. However, use is constructed by social/cultural customs as much as actual physical or formal necessity so, compared to the idea of the house, use provides at best an ambiguous brief.

If one uses the word 'house', the most immediate image that comes to mind is the exterior – the whole – an architecture that is solid and material with walls, windows and a roof. Besides the front elevation, the drawing most commonly used to describe the house is the plan. The fundamental principle of this descriptive technique is division of the internal space through the device of walls. The brief for the house is as good as given, as are the names applied to the spaces.

If, however, one accepts the word 'home' for the interior of one's house, the brief is less well written. The difficulty lies in the ambiguous nature of the interior. Form doesn't follow function in the same way. Even things that we might take as functional necessities such as the chair, for example, have less importance when one looks to India, China and Japan [4].

Home is a sequence of spaces – the hall, stairs, living room and so on. But we also understand it as more than this. It is particular 'moments on our way', objects to which we attach meaning; familiar colours and smells; things without obvious function or reason. It can involve different things for each occupant. These series of fragments are too complex to describe in plan. Home seems to be an idea that transcends the actuality of the built object. This is of course true for architecture but it touches something, which is the very essence of the interior.

One way to make sense of complex systems is to use another model as a metaphor and transfer understanding from one object to the other. One possible such model for the interior is the city, as it has a similar ability to act as a backdrop to life. It is also understood as a sequence of spaces and its streets and buildings act as walls, punctuated by a moments of significance particular to each individual.

Sir Denys Lasdun understood interior space as urban landscape, calling it 'pieces of city'. The Royal College of Physicians (1964) is a building designed from the inside out. Lasdun understood he was designing a living institution rather than a building and spent weeks observing the official functions of the College. He then divided the spaces into two groups by use: those that were formal, fixed and contained all 'the clobber of the ancestral memories' [5] and those that he called 'transient elements', such as offices and laboratories, which he placed in structurally independent zones, so as to be altered, adapted, and extended through a century of occupation.

The 'clobber' that Lasdun mentions is not so much actual 'stuff' but an understanding of the tradition and ceremony that is the Royal College. He therefore made the Censors' Room (where the students take their *viva voce* before being admitted to the college) 'the unchallenged focal point of the building' [6] and the climax of the ceremonial route. This importance is articulated by placing it in a glass wall, suspended between inside and outside, its exterior defined by its interior – the carved Spanish oak panelling designed by Robert Hooke. This panelling, along with the College, has moved home several times since 1678. Like a favourite armchair given pride of place, the institution defines its home by a more complicated arrangement of space and use than the building itself.

The question is: how can we draw this? At this point architectural representation, so adept at drawing a house, lets us down. It has been pointed out that 'architects do not draw space. They concern themselves with the surface of static objects, and assume that the manipulation of space can be achieved through this analogous activity.' [7] The space itself has no graphical presence yet the space is far from empty.

- Interiors include highly mobile elements: furniture and fittings. These form a (re)movable architecture that, through the actions of users and time, repositions and changes much faster than traditional architecture. As such, the interior has a fluid/short life expectancy compared to the architectural object.

So, if drawing only the architectural elements is insufficient, is it possible to describe a space through the more mobile elements, i.e. the furniture? By implication this becomes a question of spatial *arrangement* rather than spatial *division*. This is an important shift because division implies a measurable quantity while arrangement is more to do with the relationship of parts and their intrinsic properties. Time has to enter the picture, not as a continuous measured span but as a process relative to events that may speed up or slow down. The interior thus can be understood as shifting internal landscape. In compositional terms it can be described as 'field' rather than an 'object', somewhere individual elements cannot be seen in isolation but rather exist in the context of each other and the surrounding space. This relationship is, by nature, symbiotic.

This begs a new kind of graphic, one that is not predominantly visual or form based. One can look to other disciplines, particularly those that describe fluid or predictive conditions such as a weather map, a choreography or an analysis of play of a football game. It may not result in a scaled drawing but rather a diagram, storyboard, algorithm or even a set of simple rules. This offers the possibility of emergent results predicting unforeseen possibilities.

A more architectural example might be Cedric Price's unrealised Generator Project, Florida 1976. The brief for the project gave no name, no predefined use, only a desired end-effect: to provoke interaction between the building and user and in so doing 'generate ideas'. Price's response was a series of elements, defined by use (feed, route etc.), on a grid connected to a computer and a crane. In response to changing user needs, the computer suggests new arrangements of the site and the crane rearranges the elements accordingly, thus generating a new possibility or event. As an added twist, Price added the concept of boredom: if the site was not reorganised for a period of time, the computer would begin generating unsolicited plans and improvements [8].

The Generator Project makes no sense described in plan or section. Price has relinquished *control of form* in exchange for *embedded potential*. Whether or not that potential is used, is up to the user. In doing so, he has redefined the role of the designer. In an interview, Price, playing on the word 'menu' and the 'user as consumer', tells how 'all the designs we did for Generator were written as menus and then we would draw the menu... in the order the consumer would eat them. And that is related to the consumption or usefulness of architecture, not to the dispenser of it.' [9] It is not a huge leap of imagination to see the relevance of this project to the mobile nature of the interior – as a way of thinking, as a method of description – and, most importantly, the potential of change.

- The perceived or understood space of the interior, the 'effect', is predominantly surface, and a proposal may be just paper thin – literally. It is acceptable to 'lie'. The Modernist dictum of 'truth to materials' is pushed aside in a world of veneers, hybrid function and concealed services.

If we assume for the moment that the exterior is a given, it does not necessarily follow that the interior *inside* it is predetermined by it. The 'inside of the outside' and the 'outside of the inside' do not have to fit. There can be secrets, gaps and hidden spaces. The interior designer, because of the parasitical nature of his/her practice, accepts illusion, lighting effects, colour, screens, shadow gaps and the borrowed space of the mirror, as all part of his/her everyday pallette for the creation of what I have called 'the effect'.

What is the effect? The effect is the experience or reading that a space induces in the user. It can be overwhelming or gradual, striking or subtle, but it is this quality that allows us to use words such as 'masculine' or 'warm' in describing an interior. When described in the cinematic technique of montage, it is 'A + B = C' not 'AB'. The effect 'C' is something the user creates in their head. Whether designed by intent or accidental, it will exist. The effect 'touches something human which forms you without it being possible to define the nature or reason for the experience' [10].

An example of 'effect' is the false perspective in Borromini's Galleria at the Palazzo Spada in Rome. The shock of somebody appearing next to the scaled-down statue at the rear of the colonnade is at the realisation that you have been tricked. Architecture is not supposed to lie. The effect can also be constructed of more ephemeral stuff, leaving you unsure if it was intended or just a natural occurrence. For example, Mies van der Rohe (one of the masters of the interior) uses reflection to create ambiguity between inside and outside, solid and void in the Barcelona Pavilion.

Whichever it is, the effect takes careful construction; it is all in the detail. Like acoustics, the process is easy to record but the result more difficult to predict. What is important to note here is that the drawing does not contain the effect. It is something that has to be experienced. The drawing acts more like a set of instructions. Samples of actual material may be used, often tested in various combinations in maquette. Due to the level of control and precision needed to construct these effects, experiments and scribblings are key.

Designing the Galleria Spada, Borromini used the geometrical illusion of single-point perspective to translate three-dimensional space onto the two-dimensional page in order to construct his three-dimensional illusion. This is an example of a graphic construction inspiring space, rather than the other way around. One imagines a one-to-one drawing traced on the ground.

Mies constructs his magic through an understanding of the qualitative characteristics of material and their detail, controlling what the eye sees; hiding one thing to reveal another. The reflective chrome and cruciform form of the columns in the Barcelona Pavilion make the structure seem to float while reflections in the glass appear solid. The red velvet curtain has equivalent weight to the onyx marble. That this is conscious on Mies' part can be seen in his use of interior perspectives. In 'Interior Perspective of Living Room (view through north glass wall)' of the Resor House, Wyoming, 1937, the drawing, which consists only of a photograph of a view of mountains, is broken by gaps where the photograph has been literally cut and a strip removed. The interior is present only in its absence, its sole purpose being to frame the effect – the view. The drawing is so abstract it is virtually a sample akin to paint sample tests on a wall.

- In an age of economic wealth and consumer choice, the communicative capacity of space/objects is increasingly understood and refined by the occupant. The interior is seen as a means of self-representation/social differentiation, functioning in much the same way as clothes or personal appearance.

This final point picks up on all the previous points. There is a growing symbiosis in the relationship between the body, dress, furniture and architecture. The occupant is gaining an increasing confidence, fuelled by the media, to choose their interior in the same way they would choose a dress or a hairstyle. In this fast-paced world, architecture is slower to absorb change than the society that creates it. Interiors are better suited to reacting to style and taste, style being identified as historically specific, taste being more individual and idiosyncratic, their boundaries forever shifting with the changing landscape of identity construction [11].

According to architects FAT, taste plays a crucial role in the construction of space and is far more radical than the spatial gymnastics favoured by the mainstream architectural avant-garde, far more engaging to a wider culture beyond the architectural academy [12]. Seen like this, the interior is political in the sense that the 'personal is political'. It engages in a wider debate beyond its own references.

This viewpoint challenges the whole notion of the discipline of architecture and particularly the professional protection offered by an expertise in it. In a culture of DIY, new types of representation are emerging such as 'Ikea planning' where cut-out elements of their products are pushed around a piece of gridded paper and 'I'll have one-like-that' or 'Get the Look' images harvested from glossy magazines. Rather than be threatened by these developments, the interior architect or designer should look to these emergent and easily accessible methods.

Conclusion

The qualities outlined above imply that, in contrast to the static nature of architecture, interiors cannot be treated as a series of still lives; rather, they gain meaning and significance through their occupation. If perception and understanding of space are revealed through physical inhabitation and movement through space, they are also read through one's wider cultural/social position. This shifts the focus from the 'object' (architecture) to the 'subject' (the occupant) and places emphasis on use, position, time, view and the reaction or effect on the occupant.

As was pointed out at the beginning of this chapter, design is propositional as opposed to observational. As such, the drawing can be more than a communication tool: it can also become a design method in itself. The act of drawing, be it with pencil, keyboard or any other medium, is a combination of the eye, the mind, the imagination and the hand. It is an intellectual activity that links sensing, feeling, thinking and doing. When ideas are at the embryonic stage there can be a '"reflexive oscillation" between impulse, ideas and mark, the brain receiving feedback from marks appearing on the page.' [13] Drawing becomes a mode of thinking.

This leads to a dilemma, however: if thinking and drawing are one and the same thing, by *not* drawing these more ephemeral qualities are we editing them not only from the page but from our thoughts and the design itself? In doing so, the designer risks leaving themselves outside the wider debate as, in effect, a glorified draftsman.

Perhaps the point should be put the other way: now that we have identified them, what marks should these qualities make? We will have to look beyond the standard architectural canon to other disciplines. The possibilities are many, and there are no guidelines. It is an exciting moment for interiors. The very qualities that in the past have led to associations of superficiality and transience, especially in comparison to the gravitas of architecture, have placed the interior centre stage. The 'user/time/mobility/cultural readings' of form are all catch-words of today. The speed and relative inexpensiveness of the construction of interiors, compared to the value of the buildings they inhabit, make them a fertile ground for experiment. It seems interiors is the medium of the moment. If it keeps it head and doesn't get lost in an orgy of excess, it may find that architecture is borrowing from it.

Appendix: examples of practice

While setting up the course in interior architecture at Oxford Brookes, questions such as 'what is interiors?' and 'how should we teach it?' come up repeatedly. At university, one is taught to design through acquired knowledge (via lectures, reading and so on) and through praxis (practicing the skills of drawing and making). The aim is to feed the first into the second. The methods described below are ways we have attempted to embed some of the ideas discussed in this chapter into the design programme. All the examples are from second- and third-year degree students.

1 The drawing

We resurrected an eighteenth-century technique borrowed from descriptive geometry where the adjacent surfaces of a 3-D body are folded out so that all its faces can be shown on a sheet of paper. It becomes a way of turning architecture inside out, so that internal rather than external elevations are shown. It shows no wall thickness, just surface. Robin Evans describes the technique as the 'developed surface' [14]. It is an interesting method of working as it is quick to comprehend and it operates as both drawing and maquette at once. It is a fast route to proposition.

If the brief requires a new interior in an existing building, the 'developed surface' provides a method of building the models separately, clarifying the relationship of the 'inside of the outside' and the 'outside of the inside', reminding students there can be a space in-between. A 'developed surface' may be constructed almost like a dressmaker's pattern and, if skillfully used, can model complex spatial arrangements.

The 'developed surface', however, has its limitations: it is static and places the focus on surface, notably the walls. This in turn can result in a predominance of built-in furniture.

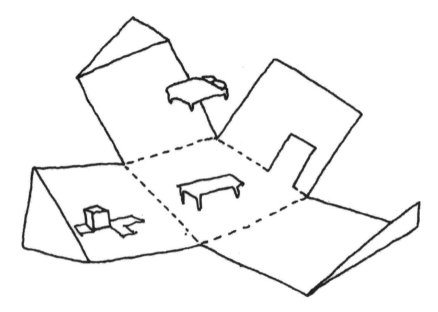

Figure 2: Diagram of a 'developed surface'

Another possibility is to discuss the idea of constructing the 'drawing as analogue', as opposed to the drawing as representation. The idea suggests that, in order to draw the more immaterial qualities of a space or building, you should build the drawing [15]. This suggests that, rather than the relationship to the proposed object being one of scale, it might be achieved through technique, material or process. Just like the built object, the drawing can be cut, built, erased or demolished. Drawing as analogue can describe qualities other than dimension and scale, such as effect. Drawing as analogue can engage senses other than the visual.

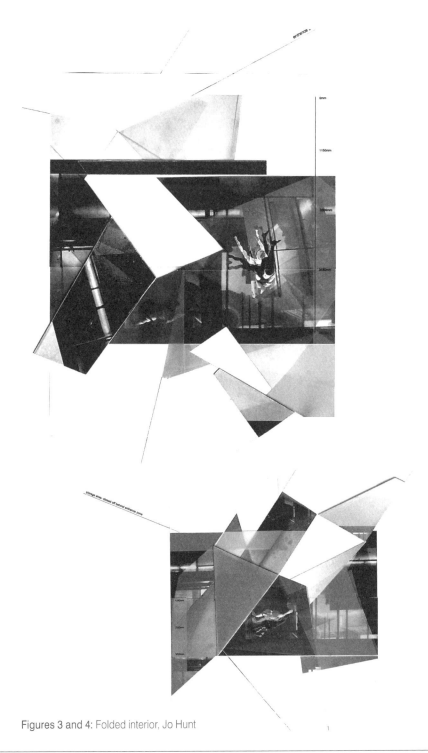

Figures 3 and 4: Folded interior, Jo Hunt

2 The model

One of the problems with three-dimensional modelling of the interior is scale. The 1:20/1:10 ratios resist abstraction; models gain an uncanny resemblance to a dolls' house, with all the unwanted connotations. We have therefore looked at exhibition design and 1:1 installation, particularly to explore the idea of 'effect'. This engages a level of detail and knowledge of construction that students enjoy.

This work also deals in a very direct way with the relationship of an object to a space and vice versa. What seems key is having a space with enough narrative to respond to. We have recently constructed an installation in Oxford Castle Prison called 'Furnishing the Debtors' Tower' which was photographed and exhibited at the Said Business School.

Figure 5: Casino table, Debtors' Tower, Oxford Castle, Katherine Ayres and Tom Parker

Figure 6: Depth of field studio installation, Rory MacLeod

3 Borrowed medium

We have also looked at the idea of transference from other mediums. One project was structured round film and the cinematic techniques of montage and storyboarding. Students were asked to choose a sequence of film where a piece of furniture was the main protagonist, record it and then use the same technique of recording to design a piece of hybrid mobile furniture.

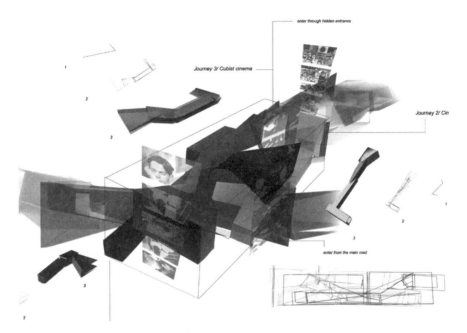

Figure 7: Three genre/screen cinema, Sarah Kahn

References

[1]   http://www.interiorsforumscotland.com
[2]   Evans, R. *Translations from Drawing to Building and Other Essays*, AA Documents No.2 (London: Architectural Association, 1997) p.156.
[3]   Owen Moss, E. *Gnostic Architecture* (New York: Monacelli Press, 1999).
[4]   Lucie-Smith, E. *Furniture: a Concise History* (London: Thames and Hudson, 1979) p.7.
[5]   Curtis, W.J.R. *Denys Lasdun: Architecture City & Landscape* (London: Phaidon, 1994) pp.64, 68.
[6]   Ibid.
[7]   Rhowbotham, K. *Form to Programme* (London: Black Dog Publishing, 1995) p.25.
[8]   Price, C. *The Square Book* (London: Wiley Academy, 2003) p.92–7.
[9]   Obrist, H.U., ed. *Re:CP* (Basel: Birkhauser2003) p.58.

[10] Wagstaff, S. *Jeff Wall Photographs 1978–2004* (London: Tate Publishing, 2005) p.8.

[11] Auslander, L. *Taste & Power: Furnishing Modern France* (Berkeley: University of California Press, 1996) p.2.

[12] Smith, C. and Ferrara, A., *Xtreme Interiors* (Munich: Prestel, 2003).

[13] *Professional Practices: Drawing Power*, The Campaign for Drawing, 2006, p.2.

[14] Evans, R. 'The Developed Surface. An Enquiry into the Brief Life of an Eighteenth-Century Drawing Technique' in *Translations from Drawing to Building*, AA Documents No.2 (London: Architectural Association, 1997) pp.195–231.

[15] Hill, J. 'Building the Drawing', Design through Making, *Architectural Design*, Vol.75, Wiley-Academy, 2005, p.13.

Acknowledgements

The author gratefully acknowledges the participation of Andrea Placidi, Allan Sylvester, Abi Abdolwahabi and all the students who study and have studied interior architecture at Oxford Brookes University.

José BERNARDI

Arizona State University

Beth HARMON-VAUGHAN

Gensler, USA

TEACHING INTERIOR DESIGN STUDIO – BASED ON A COLLABORATIVE PROCESS, SOCIAL EMBEDDEDNESS AND SUSTAINABLE DESIGN

Introduction

This chapter will discuss the ideas that provide a framework for the learning experience in a design studio at junior level in the College of Design at Arizona State University. The College of Design is located in Phoenix, a large metropolitan area that has experienced rapid growth in the last decades, becoming the fifth largest city in the US. The city is situated in one of the most beautiful yet extreme environments in the world, the Sonora desert. This is the place that inspired figures such as Frank Lloyd Wright, who – in response to the desert – constructed Taliesin West as a winter retreat, and Paolo Soleri, who is still experiencing his approach towards the desert at Cosanti and Arcosanti. While these two cases are based on an idealized vision of a community in harmonic relationship with the desert, the problem that characterizes Phoenix today is sprawl, and the continuous deterioration and destruction of the desert with all its attendant negative environmental consequences.

As part of its mission, in recent years the University has actively responded to this situation by encouraging its members to get involved in programs that are embedded in the community and which advance sustainable design, and contribute to the revitalization of historic districts, including downtown Phoenix.

This third-year studio is a response to these objectives and is structured around a learning experience based on three crucial aspects: the relationship between poetics and materiality; sustainable, green design; and interdisciplinary dialogue both inside and outside the University. This is a holistic experience involving practitioners from the Phoenix metro area, speakers who provide a deep and expert knowledge of the topics discussed in the studio as well as traditional interaction with students and professors.

The projects developed in the studio consist of designing the renovation of existing structures in downtown Phoenix and historic areas of the metropolitan area. Goals for the course are discussed as a group. Students discuss the issues and concerns related to the whole process, the professor serving as facilitator and guide. The course is structured around three learning components:

First, the basic learning experience offers the students the opportunity to be responsible information seekers, conduct research and share their efforts with the class.

Second, guest critics present relevant topics pertaining to different aspects of the project. These include experts on renovation, concept development, sustainable design, furniture system, LEED (US Green Building standards for sustainable building) standards adapted to the desert and, finally, project development, details and material. They bring their own perspectives to the whole class and spend time discussing specific aspects of each group. They are also members of the jury for mid-term and final reviews.

Third, the course also provides a lecture series that focuses on topics specifically relevant to the studio, but is also available to the entire college. Speakers bring deep knowledge and their own perspective to the design topic. Gensler, a global design firm specializing in the design of commercial environments, supports some of the lectures. Herman Miller offers scholarships to defray the cost of furniture systems and study models related to the project; the company also sponsors lectures. For the last three years, Cox James Architects, an architectural firm from the Valley, has offered scholarships awarded to projects that show excellence in detailing and craftsmanship. This academic year a new award has been added by Adolfson & Peterson Construction to advance sustainability in design and construction, as well as the application of the LEED standards in the projects.

Poetics, sustainability and collaboration

As human beings spend more than 85 per cent of their lives inside buildings, interior designers – more than members of any other design discipline – understand how people use interior space, interact within space and create spaces that house an enterprise or activity. While it is essential to accommodate the client's needs, successful interior space is more than meeting the functional requirements of the client's program.

During the review process students are encouraged to reflect about creating places, not just spaces, since this is fundamental to the success of an interior design. Remarkable spaces inspire and tell a story – they create memories. Spaces that tell a compelling story provide the basis for vivid, rich memories and are tightly linked to the concepts that formed the basis of their design.

In this context, the time to reveal the potentials of interior design education has arrived. From being considered an auxiliary activity where a preferred style of the client is added at the end of the process, it is now seen as an effective discipline capable of reshaping the environment. The unique character of interior design is now supported by a greater appreciation for the quality of life and the safely built environment, new product development and artefacts, and a better understanding of the uniqueness of place.

This studio develops a methodology that allows the students to acquire an understanding of interior design as a conceptual body of knowledge closely aligned to other disciplines and professions, but devoted to the resolution of particularized design problems. Relevant aspects of interior design knowledge relate human factors and behavioral psychology to spatial composition, the tectonic quality of materials, and the history and theory of objects and interior space. The overarching concept is the understanding of interior design as a profession devoted to the generation of livable and memorable places, always committed to the safety and wellbeing of those who inhabit the place, while generating better environments for a variety of people.

The basic questions raised in studio are:

First, is the design experiential – does it inspire, add value to the place that was created, enhance the inhabitant's experience; does the design add value to the enterprise through the experience of the user?

Through the exploration of the poetic capacity of materials and of processes involved in their assemblage, this course connects two important facets: environmental issues and a reflective process of making. As Giuseppe Zambonini has stated in his 'Notes for a theory of making': 'any activity of production is done with *a purpose*, and with *an intention*. This production is not isolated, but as a conscious activity enriches our quality of life. In this process, the nature of forms is inlaid in the process of making' [1].

The importance of materials extends beyond appearance and performance; they are part of the complex relationship between technology and social change. According to Paul Hawken, designers can add knowledge to a product and contribute to create environments that reflect the aspirations of people concerned with the quality of their everyday activities and lifestyles.

By poetics, this studio understands the study of environments and products as they are conceived and put together. The poetics in materials and design implies how we join materials, how we position them, how they interact, their assemblage and performance (from *Poietikos*: capable of making/to make/to create/to do). It is also related to tectonics (*tekton*: carpenter or builder) or the capacity to relate form, structural configuration, and the materials and processes of construction.

Second, is the design thoughtful – does it enhance the client's enterprise, it is economically sustainable, does it encourage collaboration; is the design responsive to users and the environment, is it appropriate to the site, indigenous and respectful of its context, does it consider the values of the users?

In an interdependent world characterized by rapid changes brought by globalization, this studio focuses on the implications of design and culture for a particular context. The process emphasises the understanding of how modes of inquiry, such as design disciplines and art, have interacted and are impacted by changes in society and contribute to innovate contemporary culture.

Third, does the design meet criteria for technical excellence – is it documented through quality practices, have opportunities for innovation been considered, have quality processes been planned and executed throughout?

The primary goal has been to develop the students' capacity to understand design strategies and to translate abstract data into distinct and poetic architectural interior spaces and forms at all levels: from the details and furniture to the building, and from the building to the environment. The emphasis on craft requires the students to explore the possibilities offered by three-dimensional design investigations and their environmental impact in order to question the fundamental nature of the discipline and provoke a broader definition of interior design.

Fourth, is the design ethical – is the project environmentally sustainable, does the design consider social responsibility, has the work been considered from a fair and unbiased point of view?

This studio evolves around principles of sustainable design, examining how it can reshape the environment and its potential contribution to a greater appreciation for the quality of life, uniqueness of place, and safely built architectural interiors.

Interior design is a mature, evolving discipline consisting of a unique core of techniques and skills, supported by an ever-increasing extensive body of knowledge. The discipline's coming of age is remarkably evident in its diverse discourse, its fresh insightful concepts, and its emerging research of historical, methodological and theoretical issues. This maturity is particularly advanced by the practice of many firms that have successfully put forward a new understanding of the profession of interior design.

To contribute to this new understanding, the premise of this design studio is that interior design is not isolated from the cultural context of the city or from place, but rather is imprinted within the architectural framework of conception and is thus integral to the design process. In this approach, city, landscape, architecture, materials, and interior space are engaged in a necessary and constant dialogue. It is that dialogue and multidisciplinary awareness that discloses new ways of exploration for the students. This approach strongly suggests that research is a source of new knowledge, which empowers students to formulate a theoretical background that strengthens and grounds their projects and ideas. Given the desert location, an important component of this research is the application of sustainable design principles, examining how they can reshape the environment, its contribution to the uniqueness of place, and the wellbeing of its occupants.

Since the fundamental characteristics of our time are globalization, diversity and pluralism, exposing the students to this learning experience enriches their lives and broadens their future professional opportunities. Through this interaction, the students learn about the diverse cultural frameworks from which different aspects of society operate and thus they are better prepared for dealing with the tensions and opportunities of a 'flat world'.

Conclusions

Interior design: potentials and possibilities

The changing nature of interior design

Historically, there has been the perception of the designer as an isolated individual who, arriving late in the design process, is unaware of the design intentions of those who generated the architectural framework. This experience advances a design education able to empower and prepare students to be team members who participate and contribute in the project from the beginning and who are capable of contributing a new understanding of the complex system that is part of an interior experience.

The term interior design connotes two approaches: the first originates from the decorative tradition; the second is presently characterized as a rich process centered around the discipline's redefined scope, value, and core of activities. The rich tension between these approaches characterizes interior design as a mature, evolving discipline consisting of a unique core of techniques and skills, supported by an ever-increasing extensive body of knowledge. The discipline's coming of age is remarkably evident in its diversity of discourse, its fresh insightful concepts and its emerging research of historical, methodological and theoretical issues. This maturity is particularly advanced by the practice of a few firms that have successfully put forward a new understanding of the profession of interior design.

Diversity informed by a philosophy of collaboration

Ours is a culture in transformation, characterized by multidisciplinary collaboration and by the rapid expansion of knowledge. Designing is a single enterprise with different scales, roles, and responsibilities.

The role of the interior designer is to become a professional team member and facilitator. Designers need an array of new skills and knowledge to become leaders in their area of expertise. The implication of a philosophy of collaboration for the interior design program implies encouraging students to actively participate in the intellectual life of their communities and schools, benefiting from the array of talented and passionate teachers in different specialties, while empowering the students with the necessary specific knowledge and skills, preparing them to critically engage and participate in the profession.

This approach advances a design education able to empower and prepare students to be team members who participate in and contribute to the project from the beginning and who are capable of contributing to a new understanding of the complex systems that create an interior environment.

Interior design is a profession with a multidisciplinary vocation. Since its origins have been related to other more established professions and disciplines, its roots are connected to the applied arts, architecture, psychology, the behavioural sciences and business management, among others. All of these disciplines have different methodologies and procedures. This multidisciplinary vocation has to be balanced with its capacity to see people who inhabit interiors more as *participants* than mere consumers of products or users of spaces.

The transformative role of research in interior design education and practice

Research can define interior design's specific role amongst the other disciplines of design. The implications of research in interior design mean to identify the critical issues that will shape the future of interior design. Research is a source of new knowledge and empowers the students to formulate a theoretical background that strengthens and grounds their projects and ideas.

Because design occurs within the realm of a particular culture and context, it is a cultural activity that contributes to shaping societal values. Design is an activity that mediates the relationship between the individual and her/his context. The cultural implications of design affect everyone in a direct way. Consequently, the research and creative work in this studio emphasize the relationship of human components (perceptual, functional, and emotional) within the environment and the tectonic capacity of materials.

Parallel to a strong emphasis on providing the students with all the necessary skills and knowledge to become leaders in design practice, an interior design program can also become a forum on the changing role of interior design by organizing a series of symposia, bringing together groups of recognized practitioners and scholars who can present their ideas and share their insights with local professionals, interior design faculties from schools around the country and, most importantly, the students.

The value of research in an interior design program is the continued successful collaboration with the community and corporate partnerships. Mature, developed disciplines are distinguished by a rich foundation in both theory and practice. Successful disciplines are those that can systematically generate a discourse and body of applicable knowledge, and contribute to other disciplines, ultimately being capable of improving and positively enriching people's quality of life.

References

[1]   Zambonini, G. 'Notes for a theory of making', *Perspecta 16* (Cambridge: The M.I.T. Press/The Yale Architectural Journal Press/Yale Architectural Press, 1980).

Julia DWYER

University of Brighton

ACROSS/BETWEEN: ART INTO DESIGN

Introduction

Art practice is an essential reference for interior architecture and design (IAD) education and practice. This year, to initiate an investigation into the characteristics of temporality, Studio 2 [1], from the interior architecture course at the University of

Figure 1: *Times Square*, Kei Ohara (Studio 2)

Brighton, referred its students to the works of Heather Ackroyd and Dan Harvey, Anya Gallaccio, Stephen Pippin, Jem Finer and public works, amongst others. Last year we turned to Tom Phillips, Anselm Kiefer, Richard Wentworth, Jake Tilson and others to demonstrate approaches to decon/recon-structing 'ready-made' books [2]. The studio discussed the artists' inventiveness, conceptual acuity, narrative skills and intellectual and professional discipline, alongside aspects of their technique and the aesthetic qualities of their work. Conceptually based, portable pieces were made for installation in live sites and exhibitions at the School.

The terms of the use of these references were influenced by my experience teaching designers [3] and artists studying public art [4]. Students and teaching staff engaged in continued debate, chat and banter aimed at unearthing that which the other was and they were not (while carrying out the same projects). The characterisations being used were revealing (the artists indignantly refuting any description of their work as 'design'), but more interesting was how ways of working within the 'other' discipline had been influenced by training. We found designers 'designing' sculpture using a familiar pattern of sketching followed by (iterative) orthogonal drawing, and artists applying orthogonal drawings as intriguing patterns within their work to infer connection with site. Despite the differences in these approaches, all the students undertook project-based work, generally connected with a live site, and evolved a clear position about the relationship of their work to a defined audience. The courses [5] merged teaching methods found across art and design, reflecting the hybrid nature of the activity of 'public art'.

Aspirations to adopt a kind of hybridity are evident in the interior architecture/spatial design courses I teach on; but consideration of the issues involved in moving, for example, closer towards art from design, and a corresponding re-evaluation of the qualities and characteristics of design, is still rare. As a contribution to this discussion, this chapter discusses some art practices which critically define site and audience, and parallel discourses within architectural practice. It questions how they are relevant to interior architecture and design education and practice.

Design and art: the issue of appropriation

> The artist places contemporary problems at the heart of his activity, whereas the architect tends to find these embarrassing, inconvenient, undesirable, even.
>
> Herzog and de Meuron [6]

In *Two Minds*, her review of artist–architect collaborations, Jes Fernie notes that 'Society's tendency to romanticise the role of the artist as an outsider with a hotline to authenticity is curiously adopted by many architects in this book.' [7] Artists are seen as explorers, as conceptual innovators, as experimenters, working with space, materials, objects and audiences differently. Designers refer to art, metaphorically collect it (gather images of it), experience and appreciate it not only as disinterested art lovers but also, strategically, to widen influences on their design work. The paradigms that designers operate within support the appropriation of art 'products' into design, but do not easily admit the issues with which this art, so appropriated, engages nor the processes by which it was produced.

Contemporary art practice and education [8] is substantially inflected by critical theory, with work developing out of critical approaches to normative social and ethical positions. Art, caught in the necessity of communication, and conscious of the nature of its 'viewer', is often didactic. Critical theory is not present in IAD education to the same extent as in art education, and is only exceptionally invoked in mainstream discourses about IAD practice. Even when a part of its purpose is to communicate certain values, directions or atmospheres, IAD rarely sets out to communicate a critical social/ethical position: it is primarily concerned with setting up conditions for inhabitation. Where such a critical position exists, it is often submerged in consultative or construction processes that do not exhibit themselves without accompanying interpretation.

In searching for innovative responses to design situations, design students can appropriate found 'work' and reconfigure it so that it sheds its original meaning and gains a new meaning subject to the designer's own intentions. A debate then arises about the validity of applying aspects of art to design processes or designed environments without transferring or referring to its critical content.

Public art?

'Public art', 'site specific art', 'activist art', 'new genre public art' and (less controversially) 'the new situationism' [9] group artwork associated with discourses about site, audience and practice. Beginning in the late 1960s and growing as postmodern critical theory evolved, these discourses followed artists out of the gallery to 'site' [10], out of the studio into schools, hospitals and streets, from individual practice to interdisciplinary practices, and from individual making to working in multidisciplinary production teams. They track the evolution of (public) art practice and its often difficult relationship to public space, urban processes, design contingencies and public desires. In the two decades that followed Robert Smithson's 'site' and 'non site' dialectic, site became recognised as socially and institutionally determined, and practice, correspondingly, became 'situated'. Rosalyn Deutsche described the consequences for public art discourse in her writings on homelessness, public space and public art in New York:

> Over the years, in what is now a familiar history, site-specificity underwent many permutations. Most fruitfully, context was extended to encompass the individual site's symbolic, social, and political meanings as well as the discursive and historical circumstances within which artwork, spectator, and site are situated [11].

Collections of theory and documentation emerge from time to time which capture a zeitgeist (that may have just passed), influence new art practices and enable the transfer of ideas across fields. Two collections came out of the United States in the mid-90s which drew out threads in public art over the preceding three decades and theorised them as, respectively, new genre public art [12] and activist art [13]. *Mapping the Terrain,* edited by Suzanne Lacey, an artist based in California, emerged from a series of lectures delivered by artists in 'non traditional sites'. It assembled the work of artists who have in common a way of working which:

> resembles political and social activity but is distinguished by its aesthetic sensibility... Unlike much of what has heretofore been called public art, new genre public art – visual art that uses both traditional and non-traditional media to communicate and interact with a broad and diversified audience about issues directly relevant to their lives – is based on engagement [14].

The heavily publicised removal in 1987 of Richard Serra's *Tilted Arc* from Federal Square New York was a postmodernist milestone, as significant to the debate about public art as the demolition of the Pruitt Igoe housing blocks in 1972 [15] was to architecture. An aspect of the ensuing debate was a questioning of the Modernist tradition of autonomous artistic practice. In *Connective Aesthetics: Art After Individualism*, Suzi Gablik comments:

> What the *Tilted Arc* controversy forces us to consider is whether art that is centred on notions of pure freedom and radical autonomy, and subsequently inserted in the public sphere without regard for the relationship it has to other people, to the community, or any consideration except the pursuit of art, can contribute to the common good. Merely to pose the question, however, indicates that what has most distinguished aesthetic philosophy in the modern paradigm is a desire for art that is absolutely free of the pretensions of doing the world any good [16].

But is it Art?, a collection of writings edited by Nina Felshin, focused on the subject matter of what she called 'activist art', with 'one foot in the art world and another in the world of political activism and community organizing' [17]. Felshin characterises activist art as process oriented, performance based, public sited, of short duration, with conscious use of mainstream media, and often collaborative.

Maintenance

One artist powerfully epitomises the positions outlined in both collections. Mierle Laderman Ukeles embarked on work to reconcile her personal status as a young mother and home maintenance worker with her status as an artist. In an extract from her *Manifesto for Maintenance Art* (1969), she says:

> I do a hell of a lot of washing, cleaning, cooking, renewing, supporting, preserving etc. Also, (up to now separately) I 'do' Art. Now I will simply do these maintenance everyday things, and flush them up to consciousness, exhibit them as art [18].

In *Touch Sanitation: Handshake Ritual* (1978–9), Ukeles shook the hand of over 8,000 New York City sanitation workers as a 'gesture of recognition' and a counter to their poor image and low self-esteem. Involving the creation of mapped routes that took her on 'sweeps' from one depot and shift to another, *Handshake Ritual* 'required the articulation of an entire metropolitan area's random conditions, with innumerable variables.' [19] This prefaced a long period as unpaid artist-in-residence to New York's sanitation department, and a series of works ending in a park design for the immense Freshkills landfill site.

In 1993, *RE-SPECT*, performed in the Rhone valley town of Givors, culminated in a choreographed display by public service vehicles, boats and barges on the quai and on the river, following a parade to the river's edge. Its outcomes were both ephemeral and tangible: the mayor was persuaded to release 80 per cent of the town's service vehicles and most of the sanitation staff for the event: children who lived in outlying housing estates and had rarely visited the town centre formed the core of the parade. The piece was evolved by means of persuasion, 'civic dialogue' and the continuous presence of the artist. Gablik describes the 'aesthetics of connectivity' in the work of artists such as Ukeles, and foresees a 'listener-centred paradigm' where 'the old specialization of artist and audience, creative and uncreative, professional and unprofessional – distinctions between who is and who is not an artist – begin to blur.' [20]

Architecture and participation

This observation is reminiscent of Giancarlo de Carlo's prescient and formidable text, *Architecture's Public* [21] published in 1969/1970, where he wrote that:

> architecture is… too important to be left to the architects… the intrinsic aggressiveness of architecture and the forced passivity of the user must dissolve in a condition of creative and decisional equivalence where each – with a different specific impact – is the architect, and every architectural event, regardless of who conceives it and carries it out – is considered architecture.

De Carlo's criticism of architecture which acts for 'financiers, politicians and bureaucrats' who, under the guise of neutrality, 'deal… with the problems of "how" when the problems of "why" are forgotten', was an expression of disappointment at the squandered ideals of Modernism and a response to a degraded urban environment. It placed the locus of critical action in 'collective participation' in the architectural process, a process which continued until 'the point of physical or technical obsolescence'. In 'The Negotiation of Hope' [22], Jeremy Till reclaims the pleasure inherent in (architectural) design, but suggests its anticipative, visionary and imaginative qualities be opened up in a participatory process of conversation and storytelling: 'conversations can actually describe what architecture may be, namely the temporal, contingent, social occupation of space.'

ECObox

In the *ECObox* project (2003–) in La Chapelle, an area isolated by railway lines serving two Parisian mainline stations, a vacant warehouse and yard was appropriated by aaa [23], its partners and local people, and transformed into a self-managed space for gatherings, performance, art exhibitions and teaching languages, with an allotment and an urban planning studio. Flexible devices – a mobile urban kitchen and a mobile cinema – were deployed as catalysts for events in and around the appropriated space. *ECObox* is reminiscent of dozens of urban actions carried out in European cities during the 1970s, but its realisation is remarkable in the context of the subsequent extension of state control over urban space. Doina Petrescu, a founding member of aaa, recognises that the temporary nature of the space and its preservation as a 'space of uncertainty' allows multiple collective and individual uses by 'others than the usual actors of the urban planning process, visible and less visible users' [24]. She describes the spatial nature of conversation at *ECObox*:

> Rigid discussion spaces produce rigid conclusions, and liberated speech can liberate space as well. What would this space be like that does not freeze speech and does not solidify the space produced by it? *ECObox* defines itself as a discussion space in which participation is organized along with 'vacuoles' [25]. Urban decisions can be taken during informal meetings, whilst cooking and laughing together.

Interdisciplinary works

Some recent interdisciplinary works I have undertaken involved collaborations with artists, architects, writers and craftspeople and, in some cases, the 'audience'. Beginning with research through writing, photography and conversation, they use film, furniture, architecture, writing and performance to make permanent and ephemeral work sited in suburban streets, domestic spaces, the lecture hall, the gallery, and municipal spaces.

Some of the work is associated with Taking Place, 'a shifting network of artists, architects, writers, geographers and theorists', which has carried out a series of interventions in sites including schools of architecture [26] and cultural spaces. Taking Place is:

> an unfolding process that engages with current concerns regarding gender and sexuality in architecture and spatial practice... an ongoing poetic and political space of discussion, investigation and exchange... Our practice has focused on events that have involved the appropriation of institutional space, and the foregrounding of preparatory and domestic activities usually hidden or marginalized in public events. We are interested in practices that critically test existing structures and regulations, subvert the ways in which the space is usually practiced and provide a variety of discursive situations [27].

Plantation

When my local council held a competition for a 'landmark' at a major road junction, Sue Ridge, Andreas Petrou and I entered, seeing the potential that working locally, in public, had for reconnecting us as artists/designers to our neighbourhood. We were intrigued by the oddness of the Council's proposal for a 'landmark' at the edge of a suburb whose character is defined by its indefiniteness, and a site that, because of its banality and the distracted way in which people pass through it, is almost invisible.

We started by exploring the naming of this place. If the site is an 'urban filament', something that Augé refers to as 'indescribable, unqualifiable, and uncontrolled

Figure 2: Plantation, Ridge and Dwyer

intellectually' [28], is it because it is undefined that it is uncontrolled? Can we control its definition in any case? I invited the TP group to walk around the competition site and tell me what they saw. As three of the group were unable to do the walk, I sent them a map drawn over the A–Z and they described what they saw over the phone. This collective exercise in describing the nondescript was called *Walking around the Block* [29]. These vivid and poetic contributions, inherently prejudiced, revealed multiple ways of 'seeing' place. They provoked questions about the relationships between place and personal histories, the ways in which media-disseminated opinions become collective 'fact', and the interpretative power of the codified drawing (the map).

The palimpsest revealed by overlaying three maps provided our layout: *Plantation* proposes eleven plantations where the 'prefabs' once stood, a bench in each living room. There is one plantation for every park and open space in Streatham. They would be planted over twenty years with input from local parks groups and Trees for London. A desire line is paved, and the site is edged with concave bus mirrors to reflect the incessant movement at the junction. A lightbox triptych on the main road holds a changing exhibition of photographic work.

Plantation meshes our desires for transformation with the desires of others (the indefinite public), setting up a framework for change but not controlling its details.

Photography is a way of creating a window into local fascinations and preoccupations. In *Plantation*, time runs on different clocks (seasonal and thematic) and our themes overlap with suburban dispositions.

Walking around the Schloss

On the weekend the park-like countryside surrounding London is dotted with groups of walkers ambling along its paths and rights of way. This is not the public space of the boulevard but of the field and lane, not a hike but a rolling conversation stimulated by exercise and space. A group walk is a free choreography which allows each individual to position herself within the group. The TP group's response to an invitation to contribute to a symposium in Stuttgart was to propose a walk through the spaces of the Schloss, interrupted by talks and exhibitions, ending in the woods. The walk was to follow a map prepared in *Walking around the Schloss* [30].

Whereas the London enquiry began with photography, *Walking around the Schloss* began with speculative sketches of the site, responses to my conversations with Helen Stratford, then a fellow at the Akademie. Next a base map was assembled from screenshots of the official city map. A 30-minute walk was drawn onto the base map and emailed to the Taking Place group and Akademie workers, who were invited to write a description of what they 'saw' when following the lines drawn over its bland iconography. Most of the respondents were based in London, and speculated about a walk: those in Stuttgart actually walked it. The 'speculated' responses expose positions in relation to landscape, Germany, language, architecture and map iconography: they also demonstrate each participant's storytelling abilities. The 'walked walk' views have a different quality: their style is economical; the observations are very specific and immediate, and there is a narrative of fragments. These multiple views became annotations on the walk map.

Michael Warner [31] refers to the 'circulating public' that, through 'temporal circulations' stimulated by news media and digital communication, develops judgements about contemporary moralities and issues 'not in the same place, or in the same idioms, and seldom structured by the same logic or reason'. The map, an instrument for state and individual agency, posits a fixed, rational point against Warner's 'discourse in flux'; but if the map is subject to interpretation, then should we look to the experience of the walk itself for the short moment when the group can arrive at shared judgements based on embodied experience?

Digitate

The act of cultural mapping is interested in analysing and then re-presenting patterns – the intersecting relationships of human life, space, form and objects. In *Digitate* the artists 'do this quite literally'.

Jos Boys [32]

Digitate, a collaboration with artist Sue Ridge, was six works for three sites and the journey which links them. The Council invited us to work with their museum at Forty Hall, and to remake its connections with Enfield Lock and the railhead at Enfield Town Station. Site was engaged through conversation, interview, photography, writing and library research.

As with *Plantation*, the site is suburban and inscrutable: nature is introduced in controllable measures into gardens and interiors as pattern, theme and decoration. Forty Hall itself is partially engulfed on its southern elevation by an ancient magnolia tree: to the east, a 350-year-old cedar of Lebanon tree challenges the domination of the house over its park. The trees appear again in Forty Hall's rooms, reflected in its mirrors and pushing up against the window glass. Architectural decoration and pattern carved on fireplaces, cast in stucco, formed in plaster ceilings and printed on wallpapers work over and over again with plant-based themes. A counter-patterning has been made over the years by the traces of people who lived and worked at Forty Hall. Hundreds of height measurements, initials and signatures are written on the back of an old privy door in soft lead pencil: a carved dated brick is built into the façade: workmen leave their graffiti under wallpaper: the house shows its age and usage in the marks and stains left in its fabric.

Figure 3: *Door Ghost,* Ridge and Dwyer

Door Ghost [33] sits in a shuttered, darkened space, a reminder of the lives lived there. Like a fresco lift, or a monoprint, it is a full-sized altered image of the back of the privy door, reproducing the traces of height marks and signatures which have accumulated on the door since 1800.

In *Cleaner's Cupboard Wallpaper* [34] an unadorned cleaner's cupboard is transformed with wallpaper whose patterning derives from the leaves of the ancient magnolia which presses against Forty Hall's windows: a rubber-gloved hand interrupts the pattern, recalling the servants who have passed through the house and the cleaners who maintain it today.

Ceiling Rose [35] has been developed from the patterns made by the silhouette of the great Forty Hall cedar against the sky, looking up. At Forty Hall, the eye is also drawn upwards by the elaborate patterning of the decorative plaster ceilings. Made for the ceiling of Enfield Town Station booking hall, placed where a plaster ceiling rose might have been in a different, earlier, building, it was later installed at Enfield Civic Centre.

Figure 4: *Walking to Work*, Ridge and Dwyer

In *Signs* [36], 12 temporary signs marked the journey between Enfield Town, Forty Hall and Enfield Lock. The cryptic forms 'name' everyday sights, histories and objects. The sign sequence is placed in reverse order, a game for car passengers taking rat runs through the back streets of Enfield.

Digitate describes in some pieces, and disorientates in others. The permanent works remain installed in Enfield. 'The unexpected lurks in and out of – and beyond – the shadows of the grand' [37].

aka

aka [38] is a collaborative project with Sue Ridge which expresses and enables the overlaps between social space and creative space. The piece opens up a dialogue between an active furniture-device and a video projecting from it and onto it. Here, the site is domestic and personal: research into personal rituals of display and collection, into meaningful objects and material characteristics is photographed (the site survey). The dual work (two makers, two media, two sites – but three translations) emerged from a story written at an early stage by one as an interpretation of the other.

Although there is much that separates them, the projects presented here can be connected through overlapping threads of performance, a conscious engagement with 'audience', risk taking, a remaking of the creative role, the overturning of normative spatial relations, and a temporary transformation of social relations. Jane Rendell calls 'critical spatial practice' that which 'transgresses the limits of art and architecture and engages with both the social and the aesthetic, the public and the private. This term,' she says, 'draws attention not only to the importance of the critical, but also to the spatial, indicating the interest in exploring the specifically spatial aspects of interdisciplinary processes or practices that operate between art and architecture.' [39] Adopting an intermediate position which allows us to operate across and between disciplines – not 'multi' but 'inter' disciplinary – offers the liberation of moving beyond categories which no longer fit with what is required to be done. Kristeva said 'Interdisciplinarity is always a site where expressions of resistance are latent', [40] noting the potentials inherent in this practice but reminding us of the necessity to negotiate that 'place between' with the outside world as much as with our collaborators, familiar territory to those studying, teaching and practising interior architecture.

Figure 5: *aka*, Ridge and Dwyer

Conclusion

Art practices, especially those that are spatially inventive and contextually aware, are a core part of the cultural references in an IAD course. The language of art practice: 'installation', 'juxtaposition', 'maquette', 'ready-made', 'found', 'site specific' and so on, infiltrates IAD alongside the language of architecture. With this comes the opportunity to study the practices that generate these positions, and their critical intent. An inherently interdisciplinary IAD discourse is weakened if it is unable to benefit either from the body of knowledge and well-rehearsed practices available to each discipline, or from interdisciplinarity's questioning and unstable dynamic. If IAD is engaged in investigating and shaping inhabitation and constructing space, then we, alongside artists and architects, are implicated in the critical theories and practices that this work implies.

Notes/References

[1]   Studio 2, BA Interior Architecture programme, the University of Brighton.

[2]   The ready-made books were usually paperbacks, and were selected from a shortlist of contemporary American writers, or from texts students had discovered when researching their dissertations.

[3]   The word 'designer' will be used to include 'architect' in this chapter, unless the source (as does Fernie) only refers to architects.

[4]   MA Theory and Practice of Public Art, then MA Design for the Environment, Chelsea College of Art and Design.

[5]   Includes the BA Design and Public Art programme at Chelsea, which I taught on before it closed in 2003.

[6]   Fernie, J., ed. *Two Minds: Artists and Architects in Collaboration* (London: Black Dog, 2006) p.110.

[7]   Ibid.

[8]   'Engagement with critical and theoretical issues is an integral part of practice for staff and students in Critical Fine Art Practice... Historical and contemporary developments in the practical and critical aspects of art are studied in the wider contexts of culture and society.' Programme specification 2005, BA Critical Fine Art Practice, University of Brighton.

[9]   'Artists who work beyond the confines of the gallery or studio and who use context as an impetus or research tool to make art.' Clare Doherty in Fernie, op. cit., p.11.

[10] 'I developed a method or a dialectic that involved what I call site and non-site... (it's a back and forth rhythm that moves between indoors and outdoors).' Robert Smithson in Rendell, J. *Art and Architecture: A Place Between* (London: I.B. Taurus, 2006) p.23.

[11] Deutsche, R. 'Uneven Development: Public Art in New York City' in Ghirardo, D., ed. *Out of Site: a Social Criticism of Architecture* (Seattle: Bay Press, 1991).

[12] Lacey, S., ed. *Mapping the Terrain: New Genre Public Art* (Seattle: Bay Press, 1995).

[13] Felshin, N., ed. *But is it Art?: The Spirit of Art as Activism* (Seattle: Bay Press, 1995).

[14] Lacey, op. cit., p.19

[15] Jencks, C. *The Language of Post-Modern Architecture* (London: Academy, 1977) p.9.

[16] Gablik, S. 'Connective Aesthetics: Art After Individualism' in Lacey, op. cit.

[17] Felshin, op. cit., p.9

[18] 'Avant-garde art, which claims utter development, is infected by strains of maintenance ideas, maintenance activities, and maintenance materials... I am an artist. I am a woman. I am a wife. I am a mother. (Random order.) I do a hell of a lot of washing, cleaning, cooking, renewing, supporting, preserving etc. Also, (up to now separately) I "do" Art. Now I will simply do these maintenance everyday things, and flush them up to consciousness, exhibit them as art.' Mierle L. Ukeles quoted in Phillips, P.C. 'Maintenance Activity: Creating a Climate for Change' in Felshin, op. cit.

[19] Phillips, P.C. in Felshin, op. cit., p.165

[20] Gablik, op. cit., p.86

[21] Zucchi, B. *Giancarlo de Carlo* (London: Butterworths, 1992) pp.204–15.

[22] Till, J. 'The Negotiation of Hope' in Blundell-Jones, P., Petrescu, D. and Till, J., eds. *Architecture and Participation* (Abingdon: Spon Press, 2005) pp.23–41.

[23] atelier d'architecture autogerée (studio of self-managed architecture).

[24] Petrescu, D. 'Losing Control, Keeping Desire' in Blundell-Jones, Petrescu and Till, op. cit., pp 43–63.

[25] '"[V]acuoles", to use Guattari's term, which are meetings where "nothing special is expected other than that things just happen and that what is important is said"', ibid., p.50.

[26] London Metropolitan University *(TP2)* and Sheffield University *(TP3)*.

[27] Stratford, H. 'Taking Place', *Scroope 14, Cambridge Architecture Journal*, July 2002, pp.44–8.

[28] Augé, M. 'Non Places' in Read, A., ed. *Architecturally Speaking* (London: Routledge, 2000).

[29] Performed at Taking Place 2, School of Architecture, London Metropolitan University, November 2001.

[30] Performed at Taking Place 5 as part of 'Technologies of Place' interdisciplinary symposium, February 2005.

[31] Michael Warner is author of *Publics and Counterpublics* (2002). Quotations from Warner's talk at the Tate Modern, 25 February 2005.

[32] Boys, J. 'Defining Patterns' in Ridge, S. and Dwyer, J. *Digitate Catalogue* (London: Chelsea College of Art and Design, 2004).

[33] Light box with full-scale image, 1930 x 780mm, Forty Hall Enfield, 2003–.

[34] Temporary installation: Printed paper, foamcore, 1900 x 2100mm, Forty Hall Enfield, 2004.

[35] Tondo light box, 1000mm diameter, Enfield Civic Centre, 2004.

[36] 12 temporary signs: 400 x 400mm, printed plastic, 2004.

[37] Greene, L. 'All about a Place' in Ridge and Dwyer, op. cit.

[38] Exhibited at *Performance Furniture*, Chelsea College of Art and Design, September 2005.

[39] Rendell, J. *Art and Architecture: A Place Between* (London: I.B. Taurus, 2006) p.6.

[40] Julia Kristeva in Rendell, op. cit., p.11

Lorraine FARRELLY

University of Portsmouth School of Architecture

TRANSLATION AND REPRESENTATION OF INTERIOR SPACE

Mapping space

There are various ways to map or describe space which have their origins in different cultural areas. These references and influences will initially be described, along with how they can be applied to the idea of representation in interior space and how they affect the perception and development of an understanding of the interior.

Movement in space

Understanding the body and how it relates to its environment provides an important sense of scale.

In his painting *Nude descending a staircase No.2*, 1912, Duchamp described the relationship between the body and space and how its movement created and described a visual image. A series of abstracted and superimposed images of an abstract figure moving down a staircase conveyed the impression of movement. Time and space are connected together in a two-dimensional image.

Oscar Schlemmer explored the body in space and devised three elements of theatre: man in space, light in motion and architecture. He was concerned with an abstract idea of theatre. Many of his studies were concerned with the human form and its relationship to the space around it and also connected to the idea of costume and how it exaggerated aspects of the body in physical space.

Schlemmer's *Figure in Space with Plane Geometry and Spatial Delineations*, 1920, describes space through a series of linear abstractions. His *Means of Transforming the Human Body by the Use of Costume*, 1920, is a series of illustrations concerned with the transformation of the human body by means of the disguise known as costume. The function of costume is to emphasize the identity of the body or to change it. It expresses the form of a body or it purposely misleads us regarding it. The consideration of a body in space connects to the idea of movement in space and dance.

Dance

Choreography describes movement in a particular way. It can be seen as a map of a room and potential movement around a room. Choreographic annotation is a way to describe space and time. It records the movement of a body. It can be understood as a spatial measurement of the room.

Figure 1: Movement through space, student sketch, 2005

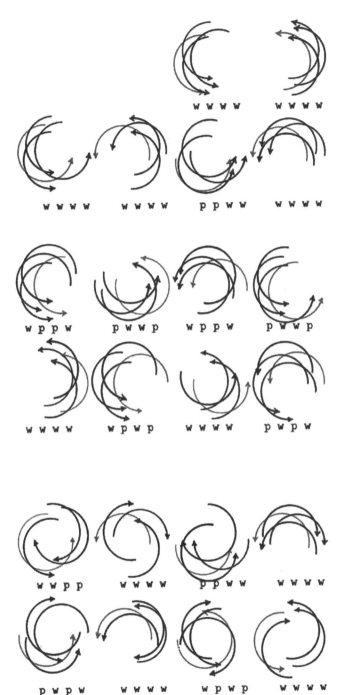

Figure ground

Figure ground is the relationship between built form and space and is a useful technique to map a city and describe the contrast of building density and space.

This is an idea that Giambattista Nolli explored when he recorded a physical map of Rome in the eighteenth century, He was an architect and surveyor who lived in Rome and devoted his life to documenting the architectural and urban foundations of the city. He produced *La Pianta Grande di Roma* (*The Great Plan of Rome*) in 1748 which is one of the most revealing urban plans of all time. The Nolli map is a plan map of the city, as opposed to a bird's-eye perspective, which was the dominant cartographic representation style before he started his investigations and measurements.

Figure 3: An interpretation of Nolli's plan from 1748

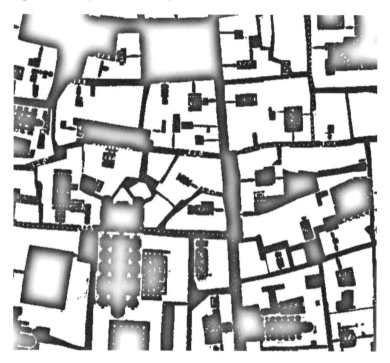

The map depicts the city in a great amount of detail. This was achieved by using scientific surveying techniques and carefully investigating, surveying and recording spaces. This was the first accurate map of Rome since antiquity and captures the city at the height of its cultural and artistic achievements. As the historic centre of Rome has changed little over the last 250 years, this map remains one of the best sources for understanding the contemporary city. The important aspect of this map is that it not only records the streets, squares and public urban spaces of Rome, but Nolli carefully renders hundreds of building interiors with detailed plans. The spaces that are recorded are the 'rooms' of the city. The map can also be easily read as it records figure (form) distinct from ground (space). The figure is the built form which is solid and heavy. The ground is the space between, left blank or white open space. This technique uniquely allows a city to be understood in terms of built density. This gives an impression of positive–negative space. It has similarities to a photographic negative, suggesting opposites of solid–light, building–space, public–private.

In the book *The Enclosed Garden*, Saskia de Wit refers to the idea that the 'landscape has become interior, its dimensions tamed with architectural means' [6].

In essence we can consider the urban square now as the urban room, an extension of our architectural experiences. Urban space can exist at the scale of the body like interior space, not just an urban scale, the scale of the skyscraper. We can consider urban spaces and squares as relating to interior scale, as rooms with no ceiling, 'the urban room'.

Chiaroscuro

Chiaroscuro (Italian, meaning literally *light–dark*) is defined as a bold contrast between light and dark. The term originated through Renaissance drawings on coloured paper, where the artist worked from a base tone towards light.

Chiaroscuro is also used in cinematography to indicate extreme low-key lighting to create distinct areas of light and darkness in scenes, especially in black and white films. This idea connects to interior space and a perception of light and dark, solid and heavy, referring to the modelling of volume by boldly depicting and contrasting light and shade.

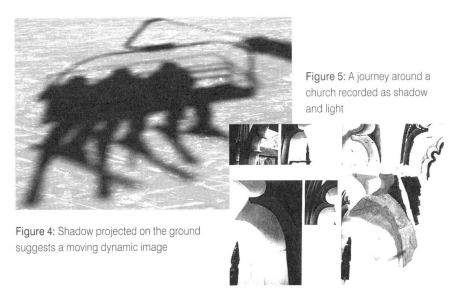

Figure 5: A journey around a church recorded as shadow and light

Figure 4: Shadow projected on the ground suggests a moving dynamic image

Artist Cornelia Parker, in *Cold Dark Matter: an Exploded View*, creates a three-dimensional experience of light and shadow. She took a shed and exploded it from within, to freeze that moment and allow it to be experienced in a room, a container of space, with a light source in the middle of it, projecting shadows, creating a three-dimensional space.

Caroline Broadhead, a textile artist, is interested in the idea of describing space through line and also the effect of shadow in space. *Still Light*, 1999, is a work which describes the shadow falling within a room. Elastic has been used to define the extent of the shadow in the space. It represents a frozen moment; light has become three-dimensional and static.

Figure 6: Caroline Broadhead, *Still Light*, 1999, elastic and talc.
A frozen moment of shadow.

Ways of seeing space

Sculpitecture

The sculptor Anthony Caro describes the interrelationship between the disciplines of architecture and culture as 'sculpitecture'.

> There is a relationship between sculptural thinking and architecture. At one time I was trying to formulate what sculpture is and what it could be. It is a thing – a thing you are outside of. Then I started worrying about why it was necessary to be outside it. Could not an internal space also be sculpture? Could it sometimes be a thing you were inside of as well – something I jokingly called 'sculpitecture'.

Figure 7: Serial views describe a journey or route around a city

This idea of inhabited sculpture holds an exciting potential for interior space. A sculpted, moulded interior that is formally rather than functionally driven. This needs to be explored through physical or CAD modelling rather than drawing; it has a potential for dynamic interior space.

Serial views

In his book *Concise Townscape*, Gordon Cullen developed an approach to representing urban space. The idea of serial vision is a map, imagined or real, of a journey through a city. This is then explained as a route and spatial sequence to describe that journey. It is an individual representation of a particular experience. This technique connects time with space and experience. It can be used to record experiences and observations or to describe imagined ideas for places or spaces.

Figure 8: Serial views, a journey around a building

Storyboard

The storyboard is used as a mechanism to explore creative ideas, particularly in the design of films. The framework of a storyboard provides potential to record a narrative, a sequence of ideas and events. Annotation can be used to further elaborate the story. Movement, time and space can be represented in the framework of the storyboard. This technique explores the story or experiences in the space and describes the characters that inhabit the story.

Figure 9: A flick book takes a series of images and suggests movement

Figure 10: A storyboard can describe a journey through a series of spaces

CONGESTION   SPEED   MOVEMENT

Event city

Bernard Tschumi uses the idea of the storyboard to describe the city as a series of 'events'. Mapping events rather than the materiality of the spaces is an alternative design technique. The events which occur within interiors are triggers for the design of the spaces.

Interpretation in design ideas

The sketchbook is an important means of recording ideas and can be used to describe a journey through a spatial design and chronicle its development. All the techniques described can be explored within a sketchbook to connect a range of techniques and explorations.

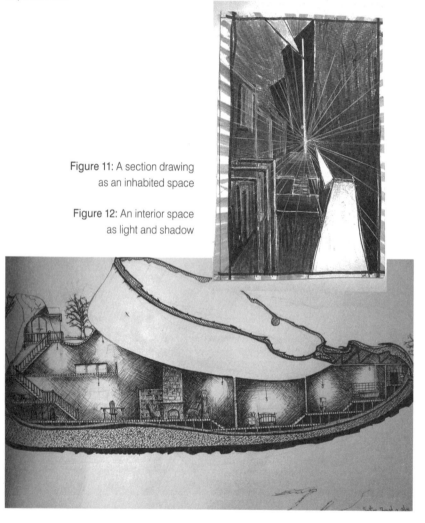

Figure 11: A section drawing as an inhabited space

Figure 12: An interior space as light and shadow

All of these techniques of mapping are varied and exciting. To consider a range of ways to explore, represent and define space allows a new understanding of design: an understanding of varying scale; the body in relationship to space; its movement and definition of space around it; the static space; the moving body.

In contrast, the idea of moving through a space and an individual's perceptions of the space can be described sequentially, the space through perspective images appearing to move around the body or observer. Space can introduce contrasts: heavy–light, solid–transparent. These ideas need to be experienced to allow them to inform and affect an idea of spatial design. Initially these techniques can be used to describe existing spaces and then imagined ideas.

This encourages a range of new possibilities to represent and consider interior and architectural space, that move beyond the conventional 'interior perspective' to a new paradigm of interior representation, involving scale, movement, light, shadow, driven by narrative and event, characters and movement. The interior space is not confined to perspective, but can connect to perception, emotion, movement and journey.

These considerations can be the basis for interpreting and designing interiors.

References

[1]   Cullen, R. *Concise Townscape* (Architectural Press, 1995).
[2]   Crowe, N. and Laseau, P. *Visual Notes for Artists and Designers* (Von Nostrand Rheinhold, 1984).
[3]   Tschumi, B. *Event City* (Cambridge, MA: MIT, 2001).
[4]   de Wit, S. *The Enclosed Garden* (Rotterdam: 010 publishers, 2001).
[5]   Goldberg, R. *Oscar Schlemmer's notes* (London: Thames and Hudson, 1988).
[6]   de Wit, op. cit., p.5

Acknowledgments

Caroline Broadhead for use of her images of *Still Light*, 1999.

Gerry and Her Pacemakers

Living with Congenital Heart Disease—Practical Advice and
Emotional Support for Families Facing Heart Disease

Gerry Shepherd

To my wonderful husband, Sam,
Thank you for always believing in me. x
I hope we can grow old together and I hope I don't give you too
many more scares along the way.
I just love you and our silliness together, long may it continue.

Dr. Seuss said it well …

*'You know you're in love when you can't fall asleep because
reality is finally better than your dreams.'*

Contents

Thank you to my readers!

As a way of saying thank you for purchasing my book and supporting me, I wanted to give you a free gift.

Hospital Preparation List

I have created the Five-minute Hospital Preparation checklist for the things I do in preparation for an upcoming operation or hospital visit: essential tips to plan and simplify hospital trips. This list has been developed by me over three decades of hospital visits and experience.

You will discover:
- My to-do list and reminders before an op
- My packing list before an op
- The BIG Book of Heart-Happy Fun
- And more!

To receive all of this, please visit the link below:

http://gerryandherpacemakers.com

If you have any difficulties downloading the checklist, please contact me at www.GerryShepherd.com and I will send you a copy as soon as possible.

As a small independent writer, I would love to hear what you think of Gerry and Her Pacemakers. If you have the time I would so appreciate a review and even to hear from you on our Facebook Group (see contact page). Thank you once again.

'Love all, trust a few, do wrong to none.'
William Shakespeare, *All's Well That Ends Well*

Dear kids with CHD,
Be fierce, be kind, be someone you would be proud of: be you!
Everyone spends their life trying to fit in – whoever you are! New school, new job, new home … there is always something. Stop trying and just live!
You are so much more than you think you are, and your scars are so much less noticeable than you feel. Never be scared to put yourself out there; do your best to always stay in your BMI (body mass index). Be pleased and grateful for your body – it is the only one you will have. Optimism and your sense of humour will get you anywhere. Get over what you can, live the way you can and know how to, and enjoy yourself. You only get one chance, so try your best to live it well!
If you need a friend to talk to, join the Facebook group and say hi; there are people just like you waiting, to say hi back! Like me!
Gerry x

HOLDING HANDS.

Introduction
Dinner and a Show

'Do you want to see?' I asked the sweet couple sat opposite me at their kitchen dinner table. The candle had barely enough time to flicker. They didn't need to look at one another.

My cheeks went scarlet in the short wait. I asked myself, Why did I offer to show them, knowing humans are inherently curious? Of course …

'Yes!' they replied enthusiastically.

Why did I choose that blue dress, knowing it would be too snug to easily show them? Why did I pull my tights up so high when getting dressed for this evening, and most damning of all, why did I wear such terrible underwear?

And then it hit me: it's not about me, this is about them. It's all about them and their little one. My moment of self-imposed Bridget Jones-esque embarrassment may give them some relief, calm or answers in a time of crisis. So, after a very mature and enjoyable dinner with them, where only sensible things were discussed, I got to my feet and lifted the dining chair over the tiled floor so as not to wake the sleeping child in the room next door. The night air was so still and fresh, they had calming symphonies playing in the background, and on the table there was a lit candle and jovial pink and white hydrangeas in a glass vase too small for the blooms. I tried – in the most ladylike way – to show them … but alas, it was not easy; having had unnecessary second helpings of the main meal (just to be polite! OK, OK, because it was delicious!) did not help matters! What was I thinking? So, I did what any Brit does in a moment of adversity, and just got on with it. In one fell swoop, I lifted my dress, almost taking out the vase, flowers and a jug of water. The hem of the dress was fully over my head, terrible underwear on display, tights stretched up higher than I'd like to admit, to finally show them.

You may be wondering what sort of book you have bought. You would be right to ask. Well, to explain, I will have to start from the beginning.

My parents experienced intense emotions when they learned that their new baby had heart problems. My mother, an amazing and loving Belgian lady, described the pain she went through as like being mauled in the heart by a lion. My amazing and kind British dad described it as agonising and impossible to put into words.

After meeting a few remarkable families who asked me many questions, I thought it was time to share my knowledge. I wrote this book to help families like mine feel an element of control in this moment and know you are not alone. I may not know your exact stories and voyages, but I understand how hard the journey can be.

Please don't be fooled by my optimism; this book has been unbelievably emotionally expensive and, at times, just horrendous to write. But even if I help just one family, with one of my tips, pieces of advice or stories, it will all have been worth it.

I wish you all the strength to keep going, no matter how hard; the tools to find humour where there is none; and the ability

to enjoy all the good moments together, for as long as you can –
whenever and wherever they may be found. x

Chapter 1
The Start

'My mother groaned, my father wept,
into the dangerous world I leapt.'
William Blake

There was excitement in the air. My three older sisters were getting a new baby sister. I was born on 5 May 1987 at St Thomas' Hospital in London. Everything appeared normal. My mother was tired from giving birth, my father was nervous and worried about another mouth to feed, but both were still full of joy. I was an 8.02lb bundle of anticipation and delight.

When I was brought home, my Belgian grandmother looked at me and said, 'Gerry does not breathe like other babies; she breathes through her chest, not through her tummy. Also, her lips are darker.' The family – happy to be reunited, with a lot going on, and all rather tired – did not think too much about this until the next day, when they received a routine check-up from a health visitor. She told my parents, 'Geraldine needs to go back to hospital, immediately, and I will take no responsibility for her if she does not.' Something wasn't right with my health.

My mum followed her instructions and took me straight back to the hospital, where they wanted to monitor me overnight. Mum was horrified to leave without me.[1] Nevertheless, she went home. The next day started like any other. Dad went to work, and Mum looked after my sisters, but there was an air of trepidation and suspense about what would happen next. Late in the day, Mum finally received a phone call from St Thomas'. 'I am very sorry to say, Geraldine has a heart problem. Do you give us permission to send Geraldine with a doctor in an ambulance to Great Ormond Street Hospital?' She was shocked, but replied, 'Of course.'

My mother arranged for her mother to watch my siblings. She raced over to Great Ormond Street Hospital. In the days before mobile phones, getting hold of people was not always easy, and in their haste to get to hospital, nobody thought to contact Dad. He got home after a long day's work, put down his bag, took off his coat and heard the cheers for his triumphant return from his other offspring all the way from upstairs. He went to join the commotion and counted one grandmother, one Charlotte, one Vanessa, one Samantha … but where was his wife? Why wasn't Gerry home?

Dad asked my grandmother in French, 'Where is Guillmette and where is Gerry?' After such a day of concern, he was anxious for news but assumed and hoped – not having heard anything since calling at lunchtime – they would both be home, safe and sound, that evening.[2]

---

[1] Mainly due to anxiety about the theft of children from hospitals, which was in the news at the time; she was also worried that I might be mixed up with another baby if she wasn't there (you can see where I get my excitable mind from).

[2] Mum and Dad remember this differently. Mum is sure she left a message with Dad's office explaining what was going on, and Dad is sure he got home to find out.

My grandmother replied, empathetically, in French, 'She went to Great Ormond Street Hospital. Gerry went via ambulance; she has a heart problem.'

Dad, taken aback, quickly went to the downstairs phone. As soon as he'd got the hospital number from directory enquires, he rang and got through to the switchboard. 'Can I speak to someone who can give me some information? My child has been admitted with heart problems today in an ambulance. Geraldine Nicholson.' He waited, the rising concern and adrenaline coursing through his veins.

The receptionist put him on hold for what felt like a lifetime.

'Hello, I'm the doctor monitoring Geraldine, who am I speaking to?' an assertive voice answered at last.

'Yes, hello, doctor, I'm Michael, Geraldine's father. Could you tell me what's going on?'

'Hello, Michael, yes, so, your daughter has pulmonary atresia. The valve that controls blood flow from your daughter's heart to her lungs has not formed correctly in the womb. In turn, this affects the oxygen distributed to the rest of the body,' the doctor replied.

Dad took a moment to allow this to sink in. 'How rare is this?' he asked. He thought this was a good way to gauge how serious pulmonary atresia was.

'Oh, it is quite frequent,' came the reply. 'In this hospital, we see two cases a year,' he answered confident of his statistic.

Dad – a man of facts – reflected that that was not a lot, and that he hadn't learned what he needed to. 'How serious is it?'

The doctor paused before calmly responding, 'Well, if you are thinking of getting her baptised, I would do it soon.'

Dad felt like he had been hit by an anvil falling from the sky as he promised the doctor he would be at the hospital immediately.[3]

Dad arrived at Great Ormond Street Hospital and was directed to a room filled with doctors in white coats. In the middle of it all was Mum, a Professor Marc de Laval, and me.

Professor de Lavel was the sort of man you wouldn't ordinarily give a second glance; he was small, with round librarian's reading glasses and a serious look on his face – a child would be certain he was a descendant of wise owls. However, he had the eye and ear of every single student in that room. When he smiled, a wash of reassurance would fall over you.

This was the start of a medical file that would grow to be heavier and wider than the Lord of the Rings trilogy stacked one on top of the other, and depending on whether you work in the medical profession, a better read too.

---

[3] I don't want to rock the boat on this subject, but I find it impossible to accept the idea that whether someone is baptised or not would decide the place we end up. There are a lot of people I hope and expect to continue to have fun with in the afterlife who perhaps don't share the same views or religion as me.

Who am I?

I was one of around 4,600 babies born with congenital heart disease in the UK in 1987.[4] Everyone's start in the world is different. One in around every 180 births in the country is born with a heart defect. What I have – pulmonary atresia with an intact ventricular septum – 'is one of the rare forms of congenital heart disease (CHD), accounting for less than 1% of total heart defects'.[5] Some would say I was lucky, others would say quite the opposite.[6]

Due to the development of surgeries, and medical intervention, survival rates of patients are better than ever. Now 95 per cent of CHD patients survive to adulthood.[7] Around '3,100 operations and 725 interventional cardiac catheterisations are performed each year on babies and children with congenital heart disease'.[8] I beat the odds!

---

[4] I don't love that the word genital is in the name of the thing I have, but it simply comes from the Latin congenit(us), meaning 'inborn, innate'. According to the *Oxford English Dictionary*, congenital refers to traits or conditions existing or dating from one's birth.

[5] Sudheer R. et al., 2021.

[6] It was explained to my parents that my heart was probably initially normal but then a blockage in an artery stopped one half of the heart developing properly. I was born with 'half a heart' functioning. Not ideal!

[7] Shepherd, M. 2022.

[8] Paterson, S. et al., 2003.

A brief history of my medical notes

- o Pulmonary atresia, intact ventricular septum
- o Brock procedure and bilateral modified BT (Blalock-Taussig) shunts
- o RPA (Right Pulmonary Artery) stenosis requiring balloon dilatation
- o Classic Glenn shunt, closure of ASD
- o Severe RV (right ventricle) and LPA hypertension
- o Takedown of classic Glenn, and anastomosis of SVC to RA with Gore-Tex tube, re-establishment of continuity between Pas using 16mm Gore-Tex graft, insertion of 22mm pulmonary homograft in RVOT (right ventricular outflow Tract)
- o SVC reconnected to RA using 14mm Gore-Tex graft
- o Dual chamber permanent pacemaker implant
- o Atrial flutter at time of pacemaker box change
- o Atrial flutter, after thirty-seven hours electrically cardioversion

The list continues, but I suspect you get the picture: I do not have a phantom heart problem. It is very much present and accounted for.

Put simply:

First open-heart surgery	At three days old
Second and third open-heart surgery	Two years old
Fourth and fifth open-heart surgery	Four years old
Sixth open-heart surgery with the addition of a pacemaker	Twelve years old

With smaller procedures dotted in among the big ones. My sister asked if there was a way of understanding the risk in each operation to rank them in some way, but each full open-heart surgery was as dangerous as each other, with equally uncertain outcomes.

We are all different. I have taken the stance of not wanting to know everything about what I have. I know what I need to know, I ask questions when I need to and look up what I want, but I don't feel the need to have a comprehensive knowledge of my condition. This control over how much knowledge I have protects me in a way nothing else will. I feel that too much knowledge of the severity and the ins and outs would make me worried, anxious and start feeling pains that were potentially not there. I very much understand those who need to know every detail, but that's not me.

Who I *really* am (more than just medical notes)[9]

My favourite thing is being at home with my family and husband, Sam. I am happy to be alive and I live life, as much as possible, to the fullest, as my savings account and pension will vouch for! I am a bit disorganised and lacking in concentration, but I have a heart of gold.

I think of myself as an old car – a bit of an old banger that looks OK from the outside but has had a lot of work done under the bonnet. Mum and Dad have said that the thing that made me different from my sisters from a young age was that I always believed that anything is possible, and I was fearless. Mum also says I *tu petes le feu*, which is rather rude – it literally means I start the fire! The true meaning is that I am bursting with energy (full of beans), all action, with no time to waste.

I am people- and travel-driven. I am not rude, I never lie; I just call things as I see them, and perhaps I am a little too direct at times. However, your time and energy are valuable commodities when you are not 100 per cent well, so why waste time and energy holding things in?

I have remained childlike (not childish), ever playful, ever hopeful and ever joyful. I believe in karma, in the sense of 'what goes around comes around': give good out and good will come back. I laugh at my own jokes, especially when they are terrible. I love watching murder mysteries and writing (mysteries, thrillers, TV scripts, poetry, all sorts). Both are great forms of escapism for me. My family and I play board games together. Perhaps this started because they were a static activity that we could all do altogether, but I still love them!

I am always looking for beautiful things, mainly patterned material, and due to this I am a slight hoarder (my husband, Sam, has permission – in his mind – to edit the word 'slight'). I am just too

---

[9] Fun fact: I am related to Florence Nightingale!

sentimental to chuck things out. I am never going to win *University Challenge* or any amazing brainiac competition, but I feel like the luckiest person in the world at times; I still buy lottery tickets, but I know I have already won, on more than one occasion, every sort of lottery that's out there.

I dedicate this book to all those within its pages (and many more outside them) who have made and make my life not only a possibility, but also a healthy and happy existence. Especially to my family, forever in my thoughts, forever loved; I thank them so much for all they had to go through and still do, and I'm sorry, too.

I also need to be very clear: we are all different. So, what happened to me and my family will be different from your own experiences. This is my story.

Finally, I can't tell you if my personality is from nature or nurture, but I can tell you I'm happy far more often then not, optimistic in each cell of my body, and I know I would not be who I am today without everything I have been through with my heart.

I must warn you that I cannot take your pain away and I cannot tell you that all will be well. We all have our own paths to follow. I will share my own family and life experiences, how my heart problem affected our family in different ways, tips and things my family and I have learned, and mistakes we made along the way. If you are a new parent to a cardio-vascularly challenged child, you may only be able to live for the here and now at this precise time, but I must tell you that things change. It may be bad now, but that doesn't necessarily mean that it always will be. Whether it be meeting a kindred spirit in the hospital or seeing your little one smile for the first time, there is often some good in bad times.

Chapter 2
Hospitals, Blood tests, Doctors and Nurses

'Hope' is the thing with feathers –
That perches in the soul –
And sings the tune without the words –
And never stops – at all –'
Emily Dickinson, 'Hope is the Thing with Feathers'

Holding each other, with a beeper between them, Mum and Dad were waiting to hear news of their little girl during her arduously long first operation. There was only pain and worry whirling around in their heads.

A nurse came to find them. 'The Nicholsons?'

They both jumped up to attention, exclaiming quickly, 'Yes!'

'Come with me,' the nurse said without looking at them. She turned and walked.

They were led along hospital corridors which twisted and turned; a turquoise-coloured labyrinth. Pungent cleaning-chemical smells greeted them each time they passed a new ward. They tried to get the attention of the ever-hastening nurse, but realised it was futile.

The nurse stopped at a set of closed double doors. 'Infant ICU' (intensive care unit), the sign above read. The nurse turned to look at them. Shaking off a momentary glint of sadness and swallowing down a croak in her voice, she explained, 'This is what Geraldine will look like when she comes out of surgery.'

She gave them both surgical masks to put on and led them in.

What Mum and Dad saw was a room full of small little bodies, covered in more tubes and wires than flesh. This was harrowing, this was unbearable. Mum was in shock and Dad found it excruciating. They said nothing and didn't look at each other. They knew what the other was thinking all too well.

It is hard to imagine – unless you have been through what my Mum and Dad have – how upsetting it must have been. I interviewed them for this book as I wanted to get different perspectives. It is all well and good for me to tell you about my experience, but Mum, Dad and my sisters' perspectives are just as important. Interestingly my parents remember certain details slightly differently from one another, and from me.

I want to paint a picture for you, of our family life. My parents had just had their fourth child and they had three at home, so it was a lively house, to say the least. Dad had recently started a company, which meant he had a demanding role with pressures from shareholders and stakeholders, lovely employees he wanted to keep employed, and of course his family to support financially. They were unimaginably tired, so to be told their child was not well and would look like a mini bionic being at the end of a long operation. Even the best of us would struggle.

Dad says that after this nurse's tour, 'You have a lot of serious conversations, about the chances of death, and the answers never seem to be what you want to hear. You see a world, which unless you are part of the medical profession you never really see.'

They both cried, prayed and hoped for the best. This was a fraught situation where they could only live in the moment and take everything one step at a time. Mum describes the whole process of hospital treatments and the start of a very long road as 'being whisked into it all'. In one breath their lives changed for ever. They didn't quite know how or by how much yet, but there was no doubt that life had changed. Dad says, 'the extraordinary thing is, I think that mothers, and to a lesser extent fathers, find the strength to deal with it.' They have no choice.

Hospitals

Someone once said to me, if you are leaving the hospital via the front door you are doing better than those leaving from the back door. I would tend to agree. I feel I have been incredibly privileged with all the hospitals I have had the honour of being treated or seen in. My family and I have learned the hard way to always be grateful and happy about small mercies like when blood tests work the first time around.

I know that NHS staff work so hard, so I hate to comment negatively on anything they do, but I must question the choice of chairs in waiting rooms and next to beds for patients' loved ones to sit on: why do they always have to be so upright, hard, itchy, slippery or a combination of all four? I have sat for hours at a time in some very depressing waiting rooms. In one hospital, where I used to get annual check-ups, the waiting rooms were so terrible that no matter how healthy I was when I arrived, I felt very unwell by the end of the day.

Another aspect of hospitals that can make me feel sick is the smell. It's such a strong, distinctively clinical, sweet aroma, and you never encounter it anywhere else. You even end up taking it home with you after an overnight stay, and then sweat the same smell for a couple of days afterwards. The bizarre thing is that I find it reassuring when I am in hospital, but unpleasant when I can smell it at home.

I have always preferred patterned or colourful bedding so there was a distinct divide between sterile, clinical hospital white sheets and super cosy, individually styled, homely feel.[10]

Another thing I have noticed is I really enjoy watching medical series like *House*, *New Amsterdam* and *The Good Doctor*,

---

[10] On occasion Sam and I have a tug of war when we remake our bed with fresh sheets as – working in hospitality – he loves crisp white sheets.

although I struggle to watch *24 Hours in A&E*. It is so beautifully filmed, but the memory of the beeps from the machines catches me off guard. I am not uncomfortable with the thought of hospitals, but I don't need to be reminded of them unless I need a check-up or a visit myself. Clearly the hospital sitcoms are less realistic, then perhaps they would want us to think they are.

Great Ormond Street Hospital

Of all the hospitals that I could have ended up at, I was 'lucky' enough (and I do feel very fortunate) to be looked after by Great Ormond Street Hospital (GOSH) and their <u>AMAZING</u> team.

What a place! I could tell you about what a great job it does and how it is the country's leading centre for treating sick children, how it is the largest centre for child heart surgery in the UK and one of the largest centres for heart transplantation in the world, that it has the widest range of specialists under one roof in the UK, that it has helped countless children and families ... All of which is true, but instead, I am going to tell you my own experiences and memories.

For me, it is a little bittersweet. It was, to a child, a house of horrors and pain at times. And yet it was also a place of such happiness and *real miracles* (I really mean that). Amazingly, Mum and Dad said the same thing to me during their interview!

There were so many reasons why GOSH was so magic, but here are just a few:

Mum sometimes tells me stories of amazing things she saw there, such as a Jewish and a Palestinian mother who used to share their pain, food and support with each other as their children were in neighbouring beds. Certain things bring people together, and nothing more so than sharing the pain of gravely ill children.

GOSH knows the importance of the role parents play in the recovery of a child and always maintain this as a guiding principle. The staff made sure my parents knew as much as the doctors knew, as much of the time as possible.

Aside from doctors, nurses and parents, days at GOSH are enlivened by visitors and volunteers. In my time at GOSH, they had play therapists, who were like happy angels delivering glue, glitter and pompoms (the sacred trinity of arts and crafts), to all the kids to play with in bed. They were very memorable and very good at what they did. As an unwell child, I'd play for about ten minutes (at a push) and then be so exhausted, I'd pass out for the rest of the day. Nevertheless, I'd remember having the best day!

There was the most incredible man, Peter Gurney, who we kids called 'The Guinea Pig Man' – and he really was! Peter would visit with these gigantic guinea pigs. I'd stroke them in my hospital bed, and I can't tell you how soothing it was, especially because I had guinea pigs at home too. It was like a slice of home and a great distraction. Even later in the day, if I found a guinea pig's hair left behind I'd be so happily reminded of what a lovely time I'd had. The Guinea Pig Man and I ended up getting to know each other quite well and he kindly gave me a book of remedies for guinea pig ailments. I have it to this day on my sitting-room bookcase. He also gave me an array of pictures of his house, which was a guinea pig heaven. Sadly, he died of cancer in 2006. I so wish I had written to him to tell him just how much his visits meant to me and all of us in hospital. His guinea pigs were a real highlight of my time there.

It's rare to have strong feelings towards a lift (an elevator), but the one at GOSH, which I only ever noticed as a child on the way to theatre to have an operation – in a bed, looking up – had a beautifully dreamy starry lit ceiling, which helped me to daydream, instead of worrying about the op I was about to have.

As an outpatient, I remember the *Peter Pan* themed canteen and how exquisitely all the hospital wing walls were painted with my favourite cartoon characters; in such foreign territory, they kept me company and gave me support. The waiting rooms were full of toys and quite comfy for the mums and dads waiting too.

While I was an inpatient, the tea company PG Tips gave away many cuddly toy monkeys (their brand advertising characters) to children in GOSH. I received a female monkey called Samantha and a male one called Kevin, and to me they were wonderful. Samantha made me feel like Sammy (my sister and again a part of home) was with me in a tiny way, and all would be OK. Samantha (the toy) went everywhere with me for a while. She and Kevin still live at my parents' house.

GOSH has an extra building nearby, called the 'Italian hospital', for parents to spend the night if you are coming from very far, if you need to be in very early for your child's operation, or if you need to stay through the night. I never saw their accommodation, but I heard it was perfect for what it was or for what was needed. It helped my family and I'm sure hundreds if not thousands of others. However my mum kindly told me recently whenever he could my dad would sleep in a camp bed next to me in hospital, or, when I was really tiny, in a chair next to me.[11]

I love home-cooked meals, but they are very different from hospital food. I loved hospital food because it was like party food every meal: mini jelly pots, curly fries, fish fingers, spaghetti letters and potato smiles.

The attention to detail that went into things was extraordinary. For example, a <u>HUGE</u> thank you to whoever was assigned to stick cartoon character stickers on the plasters for blood tests. I am ever so grateful – it made an unpleasant experience suddenly wonderful, especially if it was the third time 'lucky' to find a vein. I think of this every time I have a blood test as an adult and really wished it continued into adult hospitals, but I understand budgets need to be used wisely and cartoon stickers are probably not top of the list for adults. One can dream though.

---

[11] The things we do for love. Straight from a really intense job to go get a terrible night's sleep in hospital.

I was with GOSH as an outpatient from being born in St Thomas' until I was about seventeen years old. They let me stay on a little longer than normal, as I was 'such a regular'! It was a sad day when I had to move on to The Heart Hospital (UCL).[12] They ended up being great too. I was sad to say goodbye to both Professor Deanfield (cardiologist) and Professor de Leval (heart surgeon). On occasion, I would see Professor Deanfield in the corridors of UCL. We used to acknowledge each other with a silent smile and a wave from afar as he is always 'in the zone', talking technically to worried families or a patient on their way to theatre, and it's never quite the moment to tell him how wonderful I think he and Professor de Leval are. To me, Professors Deanfield and de Leval were and are total superstars: bigger than Prince, Madonna, Beyoncé and Coldplay all rolled into one.

As well as The Heart Hospital, I was a patient at St Bartholemew's Hospital, I had a few trips to A & E in Chelsea and Westminster[13], a Cambodian hospital or two, and then a Singaporean one, and now I am with Southampton. I have moved around quite a bit and each hospital has had wonderful teams.

---

[12] Now named University College Hospital at Westmoreland Street since 2015, for adolescents and adults.
[13] Where receptionists came to know me by name, for the wrong accident-prone reasons!

Doctors

When I was little, it was always explained that the cardiologist is the plumber and the pacing doctor is the electrician, I've always liked that analogy.

I feel very biased on this subject, but Professor Deanfield and Professor de Leval always seemed to have the time of day for both patient and parent, even when they were in a rush. They have a very difficult, full-on job. They are total miracle workers, with both exceptionally kind smiles and fantastic bedside manners.

Bedside manners are the most underrated things. I feel passionate about them; if you are in a service industry, you should be good with people and it is, of course, the National Health Service. Researchers from Cedars-Sinai Medical Center in Los Angeles and Johns Hopkins University compared surgeons' behaviour outside the operating room with their patients' outcomes. The study showed that poor bedside manner can negatively affect patients' health.

Manners cost nothing, but could mean everything in terms of outcome! It's an art form to make it seem like you have all the time in the world for someone and wholeheartedly listen to them when you are a very busy individual. These two men always had this skill and showed courtesy towards me and my family. On the flipside, their amazing warmth and thoroughness meant at times those in outpatients would spend a little while longer in the waiting room. They wanted both the parents and (if they were old enough) the child to understand the situation and 'the plan'. It is always hard waiting around, but if you know it's for a good reason and realise that one day it may be you who needs to be treated a little longer than others (and if you bring enough things to do) it isn't much of a hardship.

Mum and Dad remember following Professor Deanfield on multiple occasions, through corridors at a brisk pace and up and down lifts while being told what was going on. Mum and Dad were pleased that these conversations did not take place in a more formal setting, like an office or boardroom. To be told on the go must have been a little distracting, in a good way, as it didn't demand an immediate response and gave you more time to process the new information.

Even at the hardest of times, Mum noticed that Professor Deanfield was what you might call 'a fitty'! Perhaps not on first meeting him, but maybe when her kid got a little better, she realised. I know this is an inappropriate comment. Your child is unwell, and you are checking out the doctor – but how wonderful to be distracted by this at a terrible time. Eye candy never hurt anyone at terribly low points of life. And Dad knew about this – don't worry! Communication is the key to all good relationships.

Mum and Dad tell me what a relief it was that Marc de Leval was from Belgium, the same country as Mum, as it meant they could slip into French should they need to, which was especially helpful when explaining technical things. It is also easier to trust what you know or feel close to, and Dad subscribed to the philosophy of happy wife, happy life. Mum explained to me that her relief was so great that she sighed, 'God is Belgian!' Of course, God is from your own country! Why wouldn't He (or She) be? But also, the idea of 'God' being a saviour or surgeon who would save and help her child. That was more the crux of it.

However, Mum was sure and very worried that the hospital was doing experiments on me. So worried in fact, at the time of my first operation, she asked a friend of the family, who was a doctor, to go and see me in hospital to check. He did and found everything to be as it should. She spoke to her eldest sister about it, who is very matter of fact and said that in all likelihood they *were* experimenting to some extent. How else would science develop and improve?

All were correct, at one stage my doctors combined two operations into one to try something new which had never been done before at the time, because they had 'hope' this could help me, and it did.

Professor de Leval was a man of facts and not so much tactile warmth, but I remember so well how kind he was as he explained to me what he was going to do, asking if I'd understood or had any questions. We as a family went through some questions and then he reassuringly clutched my ankle, smiled and left the hospital room – that was a big sign of affection for this man, you could really tell.

As a cardiologist, Professor Deanfield was more comfortable expressing human emotion, and when he smiled the whole room lit up and you knew you would be OK. I thought both men were quite handsome and charismatic in their own way. and I always felt completely safe and trusted both them and their teams.

Since moving to Southampton Hospital's outpatient department, I have fallen just as deeply in love with the team there.

I have huge respect for doctors, as well as awe.[14] They do a very tough job which they can never switch off from, they are under pressure all the time and they must always be brave and bold. They have to be caring at times when they are incredibly tired. They give the most devastating news and perform the most life-changing, amazing procedures, all on the same day. When I was around nine years old, I wanted to become one, but I found it hard to absorb information, especially the sciences. I blame a lack of oxygen at birth!

I always try my best to have a good relationship with my doctors and everyone I encounter at hospital (and I would advise others to do the same). I have always had complete unfailing faith in their ability to help and look after me. To be honest, if you're going to flash people – internally or externally – it's best to like who you are flashing!

'The purpose of a doctor or any human in general should not be to simply delay the death of a patient but to increase the person's quality of life.'
Patch Adams in *Patch Adams*

… and they did and still do for me!

The older I get, the more I enjoy making very serious doctors smile or even giggle. It is always my goal by the end of the consultation, meeting or encounter. On occasion, this stops me from

---

[14] My eyes are fine, but I just don't know how doctors can operate on a new-born so small, even with magnifying glasses on or with machines.

listening to what they are saying, which is not so good, but I still do it. You have to find joy in the little things, wherever you can.

Blood tests

Blood tests have never been a phobia for me. As a kid, they can be a stressful scenario, especially when the vein gets tired after multiple hospital check-ups and changing of cannulas.[15] I have experienced nurses and doctors going into the skin and then fishing for a vein, which is not OK and (in my opinion) worse than just starting again. From my experience, nurses are best at blood tests (sorry doctors). Nurses just tend to have so much more experience and patience.

After my big operations around the age of nine, I went through a phase where I was on warfarin, a medication that thins the blood. This helps to prevent your blood clotting, but means you need to be tested regularly to make sure you are on the right dosage. Mum never complained but I felt bad as it was so annoying for her to have to drive me twenty minutes to a surgery in Andover every week for one blood test. But the nurses there were always lovely and made the whole experience fun, rather than a chore or a scary needle experience.

I have a strange ritual; I'm not sure how it started, but for anything needle related (blood tests, vaccinations, cannulas) I like to do a count (One, two, three, it is going in). I have always imagined myself jumping

---

[15] A small hollow flexible plastic tube inserted into a vein, to pass liquids in or out of veins. Normally attached to your back of the hand or lower arm.

if I didn't count, so I always ask. I recently had a Covid-19 jab and I forgot to ask for the One, two, three … and I didn't feel a thing. Clearly, I need to change my routine.

Tips

I have always found it surprising how people treat hospital curtains as solid soundproofed walls. The things you hear are often incredible and at times comical. It's like when people pick their nose in a car and feel that as it's a private space, the glass is somehow an opaque wall. Please remember that curtains and windows are not walls!

A tip I have learned along the way is always to eat and drink lots of water before a blood test. If you have an empty stomach, you may faint; if you are well hydrated you will be able to give blood more easily. I have also been advised by a nurse that if you breathe deeply and calmly this helps with blood flow for a blood test.[16]

When you are on anticoagulants (blood thinners) you bruise more easily. But during a recent blood test, a nurse told me that if you press and hold hard for as long as you can on the vein the blood was removed from with a cotton wool ball, you are less likely to bruise.

I feel like nurses and doctors must have had one module in training that teaches them to stick the plaster or the cotton ball with tape onto the hairiest part of your arm. They always seem to! Maybe I just have very hairy arms (nice!). However, if you are ready but struggling to remove the plaster (or super extra strength sticky tape), get a hard bar of soap (the cheaper the better, as this will have fewer chemicals, which avoids

---

[16] There are a lot of reasons why taking blood may be more difficult from one day to the next, but the main reasons are having small or deep veins, rolling veins, collapsing veins, constricted vessels, being dehydrated, and having an inexperienced drawing technician.

stinging or irritating your skin), gently wet your arm and lather the soap onto the tape; this will make it easier and less painful to remove.

There is such a thing called 'magic numbing cream' or lidocaine skin cream. This was only offered to me as a child. Mum and Dad were always amazing at letting me have it, even though it meant we had to wait an extra forty-five mins for it to take effect for a blood test. Let your child have it even if it makes the appointment that much longer; it will help their state of mind and, in the long run, yours.

After a blood test, I normally bruise, especially if they were unable to find the vein the first time. I have always found arnica (in cream or pill form) fantastic for relieving bruising after blood tests, and it can even be taken before operations to minimise bruising. Please check with your doctor beforehand to ensure that you or your child can take it safely.

A little bit of blood-test humour to end the chapter: I remember my second eldest sister, Nessie, who is made of beautiful, bright, witty, funny bones and is, in my opinion, the best storyteller of all time. She runs her own pre-nursery and pre-school bespoke children's books company, Honeycomb Books, and I'm exceptionally proud of her. She came with me on one occasion to hospital. It was just a routine check-up and she said to the nurse, who was taking more and more vials of blood from me. 'Leave her enough to get home!' It made us all laugh so hard, which is exactly what you need to do at a hospital appointment; it didn't need to be a good joke, but a joke just needed to be told and heard at that moment in time.

Chapter 3
Operations

The exquisitely fragrant, dusty African air was still. A few birds chirped in trees, sleepily waking up, stretching their feathers and vocal cords and preparing to greet a rainbow-filled sunrise on the horizon. In the distance, rumblings of noises could be heard getting louder and more pronounced. A small crowd could be heard.

Around the corner came an open-topped Land Rover with two guides in the front, one driving the vehicle and the other with a 'noise maker' (shotgun). In the rear were seven British teenagers. All wrapped up in layers of rugs, scarfs and coats, having a whale of a time. Singing at the top of their lungs and scaring away any possibility of seeing any picturesque wildlife from far and wide. Most of the songs being sung were from a lion-related children's film, which for legal reasons I can't name.

This was our once-in-a-lifetime trip to Zambia, with our family and family friends. Our parents were in one jeep and would go on their own adventure and the kids went in another. Even though the guides told us to keep quiet, we sang our hearts out from the moment we set out to the moment we returned to camp in the evening, and we definitely saw more of the totally magical big five than our parents. I think my parents wish they had been in the kids' truck simply to have seen more of the larger creatures. Sadly, they seemed to have gone on a rather different twitchers' holiday. Nevertheless, we and they all had an incredible time – and I think the animals were attracted to our ruckus.

I doubt that they hear much cheesy off-pitch group singing in the savannah! We fell in love with our guides, the country, and just about everything else. We slept in tents and had the most wonderful time listening to the hippos' deep calls at night and sliding their heavy bodies towards the water's edge. We saw lions feeding on carcasses, hyenas giggling, stunning impala, graceful antelope and beautiful African elephants: my favourite creatures. We went looking for the red-hearty-beast, which then became a family 'in' joke – 'have you found the Red-Hearty-Beast?'[17]

We even had an adventure getting stuck in a tiny canoe-like boat in a very shallow muddy river which was full of crocs and hippos, where one of the nervous-looking local team members had to get out and push – not cool. The whole thing was remarkable and so memorable.

Why did we find ourselves in Zambia? Well … about eighteen months earlier I had been about to go in for my sixth open-heart surgery. We were all set. I was nil by mouth. I was lying in a bed, in the GOSH star-ceiling lift with Mum and Dad.

Dad bent down to be closer to me and asked in a calm, low voice, stroking my hair comfortingly, which he knew I loved, 'Gerry, when you come out of surgery, what would you like to do?'

I thought to myself for a moment and then said, 'to see elephants'.

---

[17] Clearly you had to be there!

'Great idea, yes!' he said. 'Let's go to London Zoo.'

I turned to him quite shocked and responded, 'Real elephants!'

Dad, slightly taken aback, replied, 'Oh, right.'

I looked up to the stars and dreamed of Africa.

Poor dad is still paying this holiday off, but with such fragility of life and uncertainty within our family for all of us for so long, the experience of seeing 'real' African creatures was worth it and a moment in time none of us will ever forget. The moral of this story is to be careful what you ask your child just before an operation: it may be a very expensive adventure!

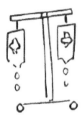

How was I told I needed an op?

When I was twelve, my poor parents had to tell me that I needed another operation. They had bid on a stunning doll's house at a GOSH charity gala and won it. So I always felt a little funny, like it was a consolation prize: *you have won a doll's house but to get it you need a painful and risky operation.* I never played with it that much and also, to be fair, I was twelve and trying to move away from doll's houses on to Avril Lavigne, Linkin Park and super baggy trousers which absorbed a foot of water when it rained (which it seemed to a lot that fashion cycle). I still feel guilty that I wasn't more grateful for the doll's house and that I didn't appreciate and play with it more at the time. I must say my nephews and nieces have adopted it wholeheartedly, which I love to see, and I do play with them and it now.

In the lead-up to any operation or procedure I know I don't want to talk about the impending op non-stop before it happens but I know this is not necessarily healthy. Even now, I like the no-fuss attitude of going in and getting it done. But this is not necessarily healthy; it is important to talk about what's going to happen with your kids and as a family. See how they are feeling and if they have any questions. Run through everything, step by step, so that the whole family can process it and to avoid any surprises at the hospital; no aspect of the procedure should be seen as taboo. But everyone is different. Overall, my mum and dad were good at accepting that I did *not* want to do this preparation. It is impossible to be exceptional at telling your child they will need an operation. I didn't really want to hear about it, and just wanted to get it out the way and carry on with life. It's like going to the dentist to have a tooth out; thinking about the pain before is not great or helpful, but afterwards there is a sense of relief.

My family all love each other, but we were and are not a lovey-dovey family. We weren't very good at speaking about feelings, and nobody pushed us to, so our family's dynamic worked. Looking back, we should have all been a bit more open about the whole thing to one another and perhaps had family meetings where we discussed it and had a bit of a Q and A where nothing was off-limits. But at the same time, it is such a hard thing to cope well with, and you just try to do the best you can with the tools, energy and resources at your disposal. We did what we could to get through a difficult situation, but looking back it could have been handled better by all of us.

I feared that if I started talking about my feelings, I might never be able to stop. I also thought this was how my family all felt too, but none of us vocalised it. I can see now that holding in our emotions was a protection mechanism for all of us. It felt like a new very tight stitch holding a wound together. Taut, painful, and we thought we needed to treat it delicately so as not to break or reopen it. We felt we had to be strong for each other and not show any cracks in our armour, or who knows what might happen! My sisters may also have felt that if anyone could fall apart it was me, but they weren't allowed to (for whatever reason).

I can't bear the 'and how does this make you feel' approach, but talking as a family is soooooo important, both one on one with each of your kids and as a group. It doesn't need to be formal, and can be easier on the child if it's a calm conversation over ice-cream on a park bench. Every child is an individual, and we are all very differently emotionally hardwired. Regardless of whether they are more emotional, quiet or chatty, it is important to check in.

There are many reasons why communication is so important, but a big one is due to miscommunication. The doctors were always open about the fact that my operations were risky. Much of the time it didn't look good for me and perhaps the doctors didn't tell us the extent of danger. I don't fully understand why or how, but at the age of around thirteen I had assumed – perhaps because I hadn't asked or had misunderstood something I'd been told – that I was not going to make it past the age of twenty-one. This then led me to be careless and a bit of a wild child at times, as I thought I had to cram so much life into so few years.

During my annual check-ups as an outpatient when I was very young, when doctors saw I was going downhill and realised that I needed another procedure, they would tell me and my parents,

'We think this is probably going to be the evolution of Gerry's therapy and you should be thinking of another operation in due course.'

As soon as the doctors decided that I could understand what was going on, they told me as much as they possibly could. Mum and Dad felt this was 'sometimes more than we thought you should be bearing ... but you bore it.'

They say this is also why I was very comfortable and confident around adults as my interactions with them were candid from a young age. They always tried to make sure I understood everything, and they always asked if I – or my family – had questions.

It's like an interview: *always* have questions prepared for the end of the consultation, even if you are just an outpatient or if you are about to have an operation, have questions prepared, because the moment you or the doctor leaves suddenly a question will pop into your head, and question time will be over.

Friends occasionally try to ask questions about upcoming procedures but I normally shoot them down, in fact I'm very good at that. Now they have learned my tricks and push me harder than before. In the past it made me feel like Chandler from *Friends*: no one knows what his job is and it's become too late to ask. I think friends felt this with me and my heart. They also sweetly see an operation as 'done'. But it doesn't quite work like that! It is lovely when people take an interest, though, and I am sorry I always shoot you down, I just want to hear about the fun things you are up to. Like in Stephen King's novella *Rita Hayworth and Shawshank Redemption*, my attitude was always 'Get busy living or get busy dying'.

My sister Sammy used to lend me a mini troll with pink hair to take with me for stressful things like exams and operations, but this was the only consistent talisman I had. I used to bring a few Polly Pockets to hospital as they were so small and easy to pack, and they were perfect for playing in bed as there were not too many loose bits. Growing up it felt important not to step on the pavement cracks in the lead-up to an operation. When I was older I brought to hospital perhaps a cuddly toy, and now I bring my husband.[18]

Tip

A coping mechanism I have for the days and weeks before a dreaded op is trying to think of something to look forward to afterwards or when I've recovered. You accept that the next two or three days will

---

[18] If I need extra luck for whatever reason – and this is very odd, but I have always done it and still do now – I lift my feet just a little off the ground if I am sitting down or make sure they are up if I'm in bed. If I am standing this isn't possible, so in these moments I ask for luck.

be terrible, you will be in pain, uncomfortable, not in your own home and miserable, but in a week or so's time you will be able to see friends or play in the park or go home to see your guinea pigs! As a kid, the 'goals' are quite different from adult ones, but it's the same idea.

The point is if you have a goal or something to look forward to, there is always the feeling of *I can do this*: there is light at the end of the tunnel and you have something to work towards. It's like an equation – speed = distance/time. You must do X to get to Y. This has helped me in the past and still does now.

Going through operations as an adult, I would advise against online clothes shopping when you are recovering. You are bound to spend more than you should on things that you don't need, then when you receive the deliveries while you are recuperating you are too tired to try the items on, and by the time you *do* try them on you may have changed body shape from not being so mobile.

There is so much information out there to learn from. GOSH has a lot of resources that can help not only in the lead-up to an operation, managing worry but also family support so please have a look at their website.

What were the signs I needed an op?

Not everyone will have the same signs – don't panic! But also, don't ignore them.

I didn't know what 'normal' was supposed to feel like; so my normal was normal to me, and I just lived as I did. I didn't know anything different. I didn't know or notice when I was not doing as well as before and needed an op, as the change was gradual. As a child, time doesn't pass the same way as it does for adults. I would experience a mixture of turning a Smurf-like blue, getting out of breath more easily, wheezing, becoming (very) lethargic and I would gradually get slower – especially climbing hills or stairs: my adversaries!

When it was really time for an operation I would on occasion faint. Perhaps most memorably, when I was four and we were all piling out of an aeroplane having just landed in Greece. When you have a family of six it's a bit like *Home Alone*: you never travel light, and you are always late so there is always an air of rushing around. Thankfully we have never actually left anyone behind (so far). We got to the exit door of the plane and the dry Cephalonian heat hit me: it was stifling. I walked carefully down the stairs, concentrating on holding the rail (as a clumsy kid always learns the hard way) all the while getting hotter and hotter. I made it to the tarmac, which felt more like being in a fan oven and walked straight into the entrance of the terminal with my family and then everything started to go similar to the snow static on an old TV screen. I could see the faint outline of a huge pillar in front of me and I thought to myself, gosh, I must not hit that! Obviously, I headed straight for it. Luckily, as ever, my aim was terrible, and I just crumpled to the ground. Apparently, I came to, apologised, and then Dad scooped me up and carried me through the terminal and both Mum and Dad said we didn't think too much of it: 'We just took you to passport control and had a lovely holiday.'

To be honest, of all the attitudes to have, I'm glad that's what happened: I would have hated to ruin what was a fantastic trip.

Then again, when I was twelve, I went home with a friend after school. We were dropped at the end of her street to get a few sweets and a fizzy drink from a small village shop. To get to her house there was a large hill; it was not a long distance, but the hill was steep. I remember trying to keep up with my friend, which I did, for the most part, reaching her house, getting to her kitchen, and then, again, the TV static switched on. I crumpled to the floor. Luckily her mum was a nurse, so was not fazed in the slightest. She put me on a sofa, my head between my knees, fed me a bit of sugar, and that was that.

Mum said that we would wait to be 'on our knees' before conceding that a new op was necessary. She would ask the doctor, 'Are you sure? Do we have to do it now, can we wait?'
Doctors know that the family needs to be ready to give their child to them as well as the child being ready. But there is a difficult balance to be struck: doctors will often try to postpone invasive surgery for as long as possible without risking the child's recovery.

Dad said, 'The other thing which is tough, is that, you know the last thing you want is for your child to be operated on with something massive like a heart operation, the absolutely last thing, but actually there comes a point where the child will just get weaker and less able to withstand the operation, and so even though the risks are very high, you know that your child may not survive (by waiting). The likelihood of them surviving is going to start to diminish. So, although you want to keep your child and the last thing you want to do is put your child through pain, there comes a time where you have to actually make a decision.'

The doctors and my parents would wait until I was blue or fainting and then mum said that she would beg for me to be well looked after. Each op carried an enormous risk of death, but it's better to take that risk than to not take the risk, in which case the child will definitely die. So when it came to the crunch, and Mum and Dad knew I was struggling for oxygen, it really was do or die. Anyone could see I was too blue and was struggling at times. I have memories of falling asleep as a child where I was playing, (predominantly on my bedroom carpet) and then waking up a little while later to continue playing. I was often tired.

Mum reminded me how the consultant wouldn't always know what the operation would entail until closer to the time and even sometimes at the time of opening me up to assess. Even with all the x-rays, ECGs (electrocardiograms) and echoes (echocardiograms) to plan well, they couldn't always tell what they were going to find that they hadn't accounted for or expected.

What are operations really like?

When I was a tot I couldn't answer this question, but at four I remember the anticipation in the air before an operation. Remember, everything is heightened when young, but this is how I experienced it. I felt very small in the oversized beds. The temperature in the hospital is always very fresh and the hospital gowns seem big and soft. There is a sense of people rushing around getting ready. I was cranky, hungry and thirsty. I'd been poked and prodded earlier in the day to get a cannula into my hand or arm. I felt tired of waiting for something ominous.

A lovely friendly face appears in scrubs to say, 'It's time.' My tummy does a mini sideways jolt, in a way it never normally does. If I'm well enough to walk, I'll do a final bathroom pit stop.[19] I'm starting to get nervous. This is something new and unknown, and it can feel nerve-wracking. It's explained that my parents are not going with me. The penny drops, and I understand I will soon be alone with strangers.

Next, everyone (Mum, Dad, bed-drivers, extra nurses and me) goes into a lift, and that's when I realise that there is no going back: I'm locked in. I hear the lift *bings* of each floor being reached, the movement of the lift taking us down until we reach the right floor, all the while my tummy is copying the lift's movement with a more pronounced sinking feeling. We come out and I feel every push of the drivers at the helm magnified like a car chase, with every corner or push amplified.

All stop. I am introduced to a smiling person as the anaesthetist. Mum and Dad then need to leave me, I say goodbye to my teddy

---

[19] I call this 'a nervous wee', when you don't really need to go but you go anyway.

and parents, and I am left with blue- and green-coated humans, all wearing masks. I am taken into the operating room where I notice I am surrounded by all things foreign to me. I am alone and yet surrounded by people. Everyone is being so kind to me, but I know none of them. I also know they are going to do their best for me and my family. I try to relax, but in such white spaceship interiors it's hard to do so, and all the while the fresh air is still beating down on me from who knows where. It feels chilly even with a crocheted rug on; this is not the sort of rug we have at home. My feet don't reach the end of the bed; I wiggle my toes. I'm interrupted by being introduced to almost everyone in the room. Due to nerves, I instantly forget their names, but their smiles, crinkled eyes and waves from those further in the room remain with me. I am told, 'you will see me when you wake up', although even if I did, I have no recollection of it. They check my cannula, they help to get me comfortable in the bed and then they explain, 'I am going to make you very sleepy; please can you count to ten, Gerry?' I feel a different cold sensation from normal in my arm, a foreign taste in my mouth and with every moment it spreads. I oblige and start to count 'One, two, three …' The counting is getting too hard, I lose focus, and my body somehow feels heavy, and weightless at the same time. I can hear voices in the background, which get muffled. Then quieter until I hear nothing: all is still. I am asleep. I'm in such a deep sleep it is hard to imagine ever stirring. I wonder if this is the spell the fairy-tale princesses were under.[20]

It's very important to mention the emotions a parent feels when their little one is taken away or put to sleep in front of them for an

---

[20] On a random note: I do feel we should change the anaesthetists' term 'put to sleep' regarding operations. Something friendlier. Please let me know if you come up with a better term.

operation. Mum described it as being *déchirée* (ripped) from your child, and just so upsetting. She explained, 'To say goodbye is terrible. You are very tight. The (hospital) beeper helped, so you have a link to the hospital and the hospital team wanted parents to go out. Your thoughts are never reality for example the idea of: I have betrayed my child for going out for a walk, instead of being closer to them in the hospital pacing the corridors.'

I asked Mum if I ever grumbled about having an operation, assuming she would say no, not at all, but I was wrong! Mum said that at the age of four, I'd get upset at the idea of having an operation. The nurses in the ward would ask my parents to show me a book explaining operations. They told Mum and Dad that the reason I was upset was because I understood that something unpleasant was going to happen. But I had to read the book to understand what was going to happen, step by step, and when, where and how I would wake up – e.g. what tubes and other things would be attached to me, and how I would feel. I don't remember this book.

It's hard to explain, but at that age I believed all children experienced heart problems and to grow up you needed operations, which in my case was true. I sometimes think I must not have been the brightest of kids to think this. As none of my sisters, parents, classmates or teachers ever had scars or time off for an operation. I don't understand where this belief came from either and I never asked. Perhaps it was a coping mechanism or a subconscious desire not to be different for the other children?

I was occasionally taken into a small room beside the operating theatre to be put to sleep, which was less intense as it meant being surrounded by a tenth of the equipment of the main space. I always have a nervous wee before an operation, even now. I am 5'1", so I still feel small in hospital beds and the only thing missing in adult hospitals is starry ceilings in the lifts – which I feel all hospitals should have.

As a child (and as an adult) I could (and can) find the waiting before an operation particularly hard; and I know my parents felt the same way, and now Sam does too. It's amazing if I am one of the first in the day to be operated on, so there is less waiting around, and time to think. I have always found comfort in music or the radio at this time, to transport me somewhere else.

What is it like waking up in ICU (intensive care unit) after open heart surgery as a child?

After a hazy half-snooze of the mind and half-rest of the body, I wake up to a multitude of beeps, and open my eyes in slow motion. Bright white lights fuzzily come into focus around me. With each near impossible blink, my eyelids held down with the weight of the Sandman's whole inventory of stock, I notice monitors surrounding me. Without moving my head, I look around at the other beds and white curtains opposite and to my left. There are nurses wearing gloves and white plastic aprons. All the things surrounding me are light blue or white. I blink my heavy eyelids but it's almost impossible to re-lift them. The enormity of the task at hand is immeasurable. I have no choice but to accept it and surrender to sleep.

Time passes, although I have no idea how much, but I re-wake. Again, with the same senses in-turn reactivating, like a wind-up generator. First the ears, which twitch from the beeps of the monitors, then my throat as I realise I have never been so desperate for liquids. I try to swallow and realise, like a machine, my throat has no lubrication to function properly. I then try to open my still heavy eyes, one always more at ease to stay within the easy land of slumber than the other. Finally, one chooses to open and join the living world again. The light is blinding, shining, and I wonder just for a moment where I am. For a fleeting moment, it's unclear. My mind wanders. Every thought and physical process is exhausting. The second eye suddenly has freedom of will, to help the other focus on the unfamiliar surroundings. I see foreign spaghetti attached all over me.

Like the final crash of the cymbals in an orchestra, the next sense comes into play: touch. I am never ready for this one and it will always greet me with open arms which turn into a too-tight embrace. Suddenly my nerves come to the party like I have never experienced and I find out where every part of me starts and ends, like electricity finding the tips of my nerves. There is a heat, I notice, as the air around me is so fresh. I slightly move but regret it instantly. Certain parts of my body I have never noticed before, like my central ribcage, suddenly come to the front of the conga line; the surging pain finds me and then a face comes up close to see how I am. I'm side-tracked for a moment from the pain while I readjust my thoughts and perspectives and try to answer with a smile but end up only blinking. I gently nod but regret it so try to force my body to stop moving, but in doing so my head ends in a neck-tweaking position. They offer me water through a straw on my lower lip. I try not to move again, realising more pain will follow if I do. I take a sip to aid my thirsty throat, and in doing this I notice how the bottom of my neck is attached to the top of my ribs so when I swallow it tugs the skin all around the newly stitched wound and plaster sticker surrounding it. In a flash, I am given morphine and a surge of fatigue falls over me faster than you could ever anticipate; I succumb. Happy for the relief and too tired to argue.

I am then woken up at intervals to be checked on, but it feels constant; I never quite get the rest I need, and my body so craves. I am stiff and unable to move because when I do the searing pain returns and no position quite feels the same as the first. I find myself on a revolving conveyor belt, waking up to loved ones and then not. Like an Advent calendar, you never know who or what test will be waiting behind each blink. My teddy has suddenly joined me, and with every blink I notice a little more, like the strong smell of iodine (antiseptic) used on the newly created scar, the sticky wound covering, the entrance of the ICU, the nurse's occasional familiar faces.

Mum spoke to me about when I was a new-born having just had an operation how worried she was that I would catch my stiches and open my new operation site if I was wiggling around too much. I feel every parent must have this worry, but at least if I had reopened the site, I was in the right place to be patched back up.

One time in ICU I remember being visited by Nessie. We were giggling so much, I had to ask her to stop being so funny as it hurt to laugh with my new central scar, but I am still glad we did as it felt good for the soul. It is the first and only time I have ever asked anyone to stop making me laugh. At the same time, I wanted to continue for days.

When I was in ICU for a long time, I was bathed there, which is so strange. As I was sleepily being sponged in bed and then dried it is weirdly relaxing and slightly awkward at the same time – but when you're that tired you go with it, and it ends up being a lovely fresh snoozy massage when done well. When done poorly I was left in a cold wet bed and too tired to say anything, but this was rare.

When I woke up after my operation at twelve years old, my throat was so dry, and I couldn't open my mouth properly to speak. It can feel like your skin is on fire and has a life of its own, and is pulling your fresh scar open from every angle.

Mum was by my side and she came in close and stroked my head lovingly to say, in French, 'Hello, are you all right darling?'

I quietly croaked some words which I thought made sense. 'I'm … ngry ', surprised that so little came out.

Mum panicked, raising her voice: 'You are angry?'

I swallowed in haste so she wouldn't get the wrong impression, but even this hurt when done too quickly 'I'm 'ungry', I struggled to say, my voice still husky.

'You're angry, why are you angry?'

I started to get worried that she was getting very concerned. 'No, I am hungry.'

'Oh, you're hungry!' She paused, absolutely elated. 'Phew!'

The moment dissipated, the panic was over, Mum knew I was doing OK if I was hungry. I was always OK if I was hungry.

We both smiled and Mum had a tiny chuckle, did a second exaggerated sigh of relief and put her hand flat against her chest, before stepping into action like all mums do to become the provider once again.

Growing up, there really was a worry that I wouldn't make it, and I am not sure that feeling, once planted, ever truly goes away in a family. The intermittent operations in my life – and my family's – meant we were regularly reminded of the frailty of one of us and how life could change considerably at any moment. So much so that when Nessie visited me in ICU with bronchitis the nurse had said it was fine: the benefit of a sister's visit outweighed the risk of infection. I hadn't understood how unwell I was.

Recovery

I was in a recovery bed after having had an ablation in my early thirties. An ablation is where they burn or freeze away the scars in your heart. Tiny scars and electrical connections that have been formed over time, they are like roundabouts your blood can't exit off, so you have a very raised heartbeat which won't go back to normal, normally, without an intervention. An ablation helps break up these electrical signals that are causing irregular heartbeats, atrial fibrillation. An ablation helps the heart maintain a regular heartbeat. It is not a huge procedure but it's a procedure all the same.

The wooziness from the drugs and fatigue camouflaged well what time of day it was. The hospital ward was dark, the only light the glow coming from the nurses' station outside the room, the reassuring warm orange outline of the call button nearby, and the moon's calm white borrowed sunlight. These highlights danced on the paler items in the room: the separation curtains, the white sheets rising and falling ever so slightly holding their overnight guests' breaths and letting them go again.

Visiting hours were over, but the full-grown wildebeests in the corners were making quite a racket snoring away to the evening's silence, though their melody more like white noise then disturbance. I couldn't help thinking how different this was from the kids' wards at GOSH. Tired, trying to find my slumber again, I moved my head ever so slightly in the crisp pillow to get cosy once again. This made me too aware of the doctors' first and second stab at their procedure. My neck was tight and I instantly regretted moving. I tried to stop myself stirring more but my neck was now in an awkward position, and I had to move it more to get to the sweet spot of comfort, while also lightly freaking out that moving too much would open the wounds and blood would spurt from my neck; evidently I had watched too many disaster movies.

Far away, in my semi-conscious state, I heard the noise that must have woken me. A very small croaky voice was coming from the bed opposite me. It was too far away to see detail of the culprit in the dark, but close enough to hear again 'help me … help me.'

Had I imagined it? Were the drugs I had been given a lot stronger than I'd initially thought? 'Help me … help me,' the croak came again, so rasping and haunting, as if it were being projected from a desert-dry voice box. But no! It was there. As tired and sore as I was, I squinted my eyes, trying not to move the rest of me, in that direction so as to hear better or at least see more detail. Neither happened. Swaddled in blankets, this individual rivalled Tutankhamun for layers, had the same raspy voice and was possibly in the same state.

I looked for the call button to get help for her, trying not to wake others in the room by doing so. Like a strange floppy doll lacking in joints, I moved my whole body to the left towards the button before grabbing it with my arm. 'Help me … help me,' I heard once again. Poor thing, I thought. They must be in real trouble not too be able to push or find their own button; I must help them! I pressed the button – luckily there was no ailment in my fingers to stop me doing so. A shallow beeeeep beeeeep in the distance could be heard and I thought, thank goodness, help is on the way!

A short, plump nurse with very kempt auburn hair bounded in enthusiastically, 'You rang the bell, are you OK?' she said in a loud whisper, ignoring those around her sleeping. I didn't recognise her face. It must be a different shift, I thought.

'Hi, thank you for coming. The person opposite me needs help!' I said in a quiet whisper back, still trying not to move, but my European roots couldn't resist expressing how grateful I was by crossing my hands on my chest. Again, instant regret.

'Oh, thank you for letting me know,' she said, calm and controlled, as, in my fevered imagination, I imagined a spider would speak to its self-made web before grabbing and devouring its prey. A shudder went down my spine. She went over to the voice to help.

They discussed a little in hushed tones too hard to hear. Did I see her shadow grow and change into monstrous shapes? She slid out of the ward with haste before I could verify this. Moments later she came back to the room with a commode and drew the curtains. After a little while, she left the room and once all the commotion was over, the ward fell silent again, except for the distant grants from the corner snorers.

Too soon after I had found an incomplete and sorely needed forty winks, I heard 'help me … help me' again. My heart sank. Poor thing, their voice sounded so anxious. I thought to myself, *Gosh, what now?* After the operation I'd been told to stay in bed, so I hoped someone would come to help her or check on us. I waited and waited. I also didn't want to annoy the nurse as I thought I may need her for myself in the future! Time passed slowly – very slowly. Nothing. Once again, 'help me … help me', this time with a noticeably drier throat, missing half the letters when vocalised. Hearing their tongue desperately searching for saliva on their palate with no avail, making a 'Ta' noise with every attempt, I knew I had to do something. I looked at the call button. She had moved it! The nurse had moved it. Had she meant to? By just moving my arm and as little of the rest of me as possible, I found it on the bedside table after a serious fumble. In my blind haste I knocked over my lip balm, which rolled under my bed, my good luck mini troll with florescent pink standing hair, and a plastic cup of water. I pressed with all my might and again the reassuring shallow beeeeeep beeeep could be heard in the distance. What a relief: all would be well now, our saviour was coming!

But then relief turned to panic. I waited, but no one came. I kept my ears pricked – nothing. Just the beeps. So, slower than a sloth I huffed and I puffed, getting to my feet. I very carefully got out of bed, trying not to break any stitches or open any fresh wounds. It felt like an escape room where every clue leads you closer to a truth. Moving my head the smallest amount created a domino effect: my shoulders, knees and toes couldn't help themselves. This combination made me find out quickly where they had been able to find the right area for their incision: the groin. Great! As luck would have it, their first groin attempt hadn't worked. However, fourth time had been the charm.

The voice had cried out another five times by this point. I kept my ears very alert in case footsteps could be heard to save the day, but none could be heard! I carefully got up and walked out of the room towards the nurse's desk. Struggling to lift my head with a curved back to keep my veins, and muscles in my groin and neck slack. I thought to myself, I should be the new bell ringer of Notre Dame! When I got out of the ward, no one was there! I turned towards a noise, of a squeaky metal wheel heading my way from a corner which met this corridor. I carefully looked up and saw a night janitor. I was pleased to see they took cleanliness seriously, but I was disappointed to see this gentleman rather than a nurse.

Suddenly, heavy footsteps with purpose came around the corner. I turned to see that the once-nice nurse had morphed into a tiger. And she was unamused by my recurring presence, spitting through her teeth, 'You shouldn't be out of bed!' Did I see sharp teeth? Flashes of misbehaving at senior school came to the forefront of my mind. I shook them off.

'The lady in my room is calling for help,' I tried to lift my head as I spoke to her, but it was too much of an effort.

Getting cross, she ushered me to my bed muttering, 'Enough now, go to bed; I'll see to her, she just needs a catheter.' I hastened to bed and collapsed with the weight of post-operation lethargy. This time, my forty winks were uninterrupted.

This hospital trip opened my eyes to a lot of things. Firstly, you are never expected to help others in hospital unless you work there, but it's important to be willing to as one day you may be the person calling for help. Secondly, you can't blame doctors if their first, second or sometimes third attempt does not work, especially when encroaching on sensitive parts of your body. It will always be the luck of the draw on the day, and each body is slightly different – remember, it's your body! Thirdly, you can't choose your roommates or blame hospitals for assigning them. You can't be cross or judge them for being scared or worried. Some people will have their first experience of hospitals at an older age, and with golden oldies taking over, the likelihood is you will be around elderly patients if you have a heart problem and you're out of your teens. Lastly, drugs will play tricks on you when you are tired and in pain; if you have a very creative imagination, be warned!

Be kind and patient, and remember that you will have plenty of time to rest when you are home if it hasn't quite gone to plan in hospital.

You may make a quick and easy recovery, so you may not need any of this, but just in case, here it is. I have noticed the older I get, the longer I am fragile after an operation, and the longer I take to recover. I think it's because I'm now less supple and more brittle. I never worked with a physio, nevertheless I have learned that the more normally you behave and move after an op, the easier it is for your body to heal. If you hold yourself awkwardly because you are stiff on one side, the other side will suffer and become uncomfortable quite quickly and overcompensate over time. I know this is hard, but try to use balanced and equal movement on both sides – your body will thank you for it in the long run.

Tip

When recovering as an adult, something I found really useful for post operative care was first of all stocking up on pain relief before the op so you are ready should you need it. Secondly, ready for your return, have a small bag or basket to carry your paracetamol, ibuprofen, activities to keep you busy if you have the energy, a pen and paper, drinks and snacks. Plug in a phone charger where you plan on being most of the time, so you don't need to crouch down and plug it in when you are in pain. The paper and pen is to make notes of which drugs you've taken and when you took them. Another tactic for the more forgetful of us is to take a screenshot on your phone of what time you took the painkiller – it's quick, easy and clear when you look back. This way, if you're exhausted or in pain, you can keep track of your medication and avoid taking too many.

Always double check with your doctors what you are allowed to take; I can't have ibuprofen, for example.

I found that day three (depending on the op) was usually the worst, when all the pain relief from the op had worn off, so be warned! The hospital normally (depending on the op) wants you to recover 'naturally'. You may feel 100 per cent fantastic, you may not. It's always the luck of the draw.

As a child, I knew operations were not great, but what I really didn't like at the time was when I was starting to get a little better but I was still in hospital. Sometimes a pair of specialist hospital physios would come into my hospital room, ask me to go on my side and then proceed to firmly hit my back in such a strong way I would have to spit out phlegm. The process happened often to move liquid from the lungs, and seemed to go on for ever. I hated it, but it was always such charming people doing this to me, which made it worse; you couldn't bring yourself to dislike them. Of all the procedures and ordeals I went through in hospital, I particularly loathed this one because it seemed so unnecessary. It is like someone else putting a finger up your nose: it's very invasive. Looking back, it probably was necessary, especially if you are spending a lot of time in bed not moving, but it's hard to be so rational when you're a child and a nurse is thumping you from all sides.

One last thing I mentally struggle with during recovery is bedpans. I physically hate using them. Obviously, when you are bed-bound or straight after an op (and you don't have a catheter) you sort of need to use them or the doctors and nurses get worried, about wobbly legs, stitches breaking and pain management, and they need to see your (I want to say this politely) 'output'. I will do almost anything to not use them unless I am really unwell or fresh out of recovery, when I give in. Don't get me started on the commode!

Linked to this is making sure you are hydrated after an operation. This will help your recovery and flush out your body from the drugs used in surgery. Water is really important however you will get fed up with drinking it! So I'd advise you to by big bottles of squash and juice for recovery at home and small bottles of squash or cartons of juice for in the hospital. Something with a (paper) straw makes life easier, to reach for if you are immobile from an operation.

I have always loved getting my hospital tags off; it's a very exciting moment. I never kept mine. I don't quite understand why you would. The moment I got home, a member of my family or I would get the scissors out. if I was allowed to, I would have a shower or a wash to get the hospital smell off and that was it. I was home.

The Nicholson Operation

I refer to what I have as 'heart problems' mainly due to the name pulmonary atresia being such a mouthful. Rather embarrassingly, I also don't think I can spell it without the help of spell check, and I think even spell check gets a little nervous with it! When I was little, I was the first patient to have the remedial operation they had planned and so inevitably it was called the 'Nicholson Operation' (my maiden name). I was a very little guinea pig (yes, I'm still talking about guinea pigs! ☺

Tips

(For family and friends of patients undergoing an operation)

While an operation is going on, as parents I would advise you to get out of the hospital, do anything to distract yourself. I know some will be crippled with sadness, fear and worry. But just try to normalise things. My parents said they went out to breakfast, they went shopping or they visited nearby galleries. They mentioned how important it was to get out and get air and 'just breathe'. So as hard as this may sound to do, try.

Mum and Dad were given a beeper by GOSH, so if there was any news they could easily and quickly come back. The one time they went out to breakfast they went to a place in jeans, which had a strict dress code. The head waiter took pity on them and found them a small table right at the back of the restaurant. It's funny what you remember in moments like these. They also told me it is OK to laugh, even at the most frightening moments. While you are out together during your child's operation; you may not laugh outrageously, but it's cathartic and healthy to find humour even in the most anxious times.

Tips

(For the patient being operated on)

- When coming home from an operation, think about where your seatbelt will fall on you (or your child). If your new scar is the full length of your chest, hold the seatbelt ever so slightly away from the scar otherwise it can rub or catch and hurt. No one thinks they use the brakes too strongly, but it will be the one time your driver will and you will regret not holding the seatbelt just slightly away. Obviously still wear a seatbelt and be safe, but just be aware of the situation, and if you are really worried or having real problems, check with the DVLA or your hospital about what is possible.

- Anaesthetising gas makes me feel very sick. I always pack sea-sickness bands just in case it is used. They are small and you will not regret bringing them. They work on just pressure points on your wrists and have worked for me in the past after procedures.

- I always bring snacks. I used to love rice cakes or Doritos (tangy cheesy flavour). Fresh food is slightly harder to transport and keep if in hospital for a while with no fridge. Otherwise, a lovely memory I have from GOSH is of when they used to make me apricot jam on toast with butter and cut it into four squares – dreamy. I didn't have it again at home until I was an adult, but I just loved them. Thank you to whoever cut them into four for me, as it made all the difference.

- Getting throat tubes out is a bit of an art form. My trick is to gently and slowly swallow as they remove the tubes, so that the motion of the throat goes with the direction of the tube. This is easier said than done, but worth a try, otherwise it can feel like three layers of skin have been removed from your throat at the same time as the tube being removed.

- Catheters (a small tube that goes from your bladder into a receptacle normally by your bed, in times of need like when you are not awake or static after an operation) are not my favourite subject, but important all the same to talk about. I learned from experience that when catheters are being removed, if you don't clench, you sort of do the pre-wee sensation without weeing (a very important detail) then it is slightly less harsh on that body part post extraction.

- For families with girls this is a tip for the future: if you have had open-heart surgery your sternum does not always heal in the best way and can sometimes be a bit bobbly or lightly lumpy. So, I have found some bra shapes do not work as well as others. For me, wired ones that went high in the middle/front of your chest were no good and painful. I only seemed to find out after taking off the tags and wearing them for a few hours. Frustratingly, I had to buy and try them to know.

- As spoken about earlier, I am all up for giggling, but not *directly* after an op if I can help it: I never wanted to break my stitches. Laughing is scientifically proven to be good for you. Don't stop!

- Luckily in hospitals nowadays, they offer you two hospital gowns – I recommend wearing both, so you don't moon strangers by mistake.

- As you get a bit older, or if you don't have your parents with you, you should always bring a very trusted plus one who has your best intentions totally at the forefront of their mind. At times you will need someone to fight your corner in the hospital because you have no energy; or you are being operated on and someone needs to suddenly make decisions on your behalf, to ask and to think of further things to ask doctors about procedures and post-op care. Two heads are always better than one – sometimes you are not compos mentis. If you are feeling woozy or exhausted after an op, your plus one can write down or remember for you the instructions the doctors or nurses give you for post-op care. On a basic level, you will need help getting home. And last but not least, never underestimate the value of the moral support of having a loved one with you: sometimes it can be utterly boring, and you'll just want someone to chat to.
- I have learned a good thing to do while bored or in pain recovering or preparing for an op, is to make a list of all the fun things you want to do once you are better. This motivates you to get better and gets you excited to plan for the future. Then when you are able to actually do the activities, it will feel amazing.

As hectic and stressful as an operation can be, it must be done. It is not a question of 'Do I have to?' It is just a question of 'When?'

My dad remembers driving me back from the hospital after my last major operation. We arrived home and I jumped out of the car – having only had my operation a week or so ago – and ran to the swings in our garden. It hit him at that moment that it was the first time he had seen me run in over three years.

Chapter 4
Pacemakers

'A sense of humour is a good thing to arm yourself with because sometimes you don't have anything other than that.'
Jordan Peterson

At the age of twelve, a few days after having open heart surgery, I was lying in bed in the hospital. Mum and I were waiting very optimistically for the doctor's rounds to see whether we would be going home. We were both excited as we had been told things were looking good earlier in the day.

Professor Deanfield walked into the room, took the chart from the end of the bed and had a read. He looked at me and smiled. Both Mum and I were trying to buy our freedom with a smile back. He broke the silence, 'Geraldine, you are doing really well. We hear you want to go home?'

I nodded frantically, ready to pack my things and scoot on out of there!

'We want you to go home,' the doctor explained.

Hope, wow! I thought

'However …'

Oh no!

He paused. The pause was worrying. The pause was too long by anyone's standard. The pause made Mum and me realise this was not going to be easy.

'However, the only way I would feel comfortable and confident for you to go home is to fit a pacemaker. It will be more of a precaution than anything else.'

What! I thought to myself, a pacemaker? A pacemaker! This was never a discussion we had had before. A sudden flash of an open coffin with a rotting human corpse, primarily bones and dust with a little flesh still holding on to sparse bits of dirty rags on the bones, blowing in the night air and then this disgusting round plastic disk with metal wires which had fallen through the rotting body in pristine condition. Forever to outlive me, forever artificial and forever ugly. This was my view on pacemakers. This was my view on an AI (artificial intelligence) alien item being placed in my body. I stirred from this vision; I looked halfway down my abdomen. A set of two external pacemakers were attached to an upside-down lid of an egg carton with wires feeding into the central part of my torso under my gown into my heart. Neither the imaginary pacemaker nor the pacemakers attached to me in that moment offered a tempting image of my future.

I am not one to question doctors; I respect their decisions fully. He said that to go home, I would need a pacemaker. All I wanted to do was go home. Home to me is just heaven: it was Inky the black Labrador retriever, my three older sisters, Mum and Dad at dinner together in our very draughty colonial style bungalow with a sunset in the distance over the valley discussing our days and playing the country and capital game I was always terrible at. Home is somewhere I can be completely myself (which most of the time is resting or over-excited: there is no middle ground), safety, a place with open spaces full of the best people that I love, no beeping machines, food that is still the best I've ever tasted, noise, French, English cosy mayhem, more craziness than calm even when you are resting, playing shoe shops or post office with my sisters. It's my friends at school, it's the chickens we find eggs under each morning, it's the squeaking guinea pigs, it's Mum's chocolate cake, it's my bedroom, and it's my bed.

Mum and I looked at each other; she knew how I felt about pacemakers, having had to bathe her twelve-year-old child the night before holding the external pacemaker electronic equipment on the side of the bath to keep it from getting wet. Neither of us knew which of us felt more uncomfortable in that moment: me being an awkward adolescent or Mum not wanting to invade my privacy or hurt me by accidentally pulling on the wires attached to me. Luckily, as almost always, we found our sense of humour got us through. Mum took my hand and nodded to see if I understood, I nodded back, with a tight blink and a hand squeeze; she knew I understood the situation.

I said, 'No, thank you.'

He said, 'OK, but I'm not comfortable letting you leave without a pacemaker.'

With each day that passed I got a little stronger, and each day I was asked if I was ready to go home with a pacemaker fitted. Each day I said no, I didn't want a pacemaker. I was so against it I stayed in hospital not making the decision. After three days, I had reached a point where I was tired of being poked and prodded. The veins in my hands, wrists and inner elbows were sore from drips, the skin on my tummy hurt from the external pacemaker wires tugging on it and continually giving me painful wake-ups to reality, and the wires meant I could never find a comfortable position to get to sleep. I was exhausted and I just wanted to go home. That morning, I decided enough was enough. I folded; I agreed to the pacemaker and the next day I had one fitted all the while thinking of the ugly coffin vision.

The next morning the doctor who had fitted my pacemaker returned to tell Mum alone, 'The position of the wires is not in the correct placement for the pacemaker to the heart to communicate with one another, please can you tell your child we will need to fix this.'

Mum asked, 'The pacemaker is incorrectly fitted?'

He replied, 'Yes.'

She said, 'You will tell my daughter and I will pick up the pieces.'

The doctor was surprised, but he came into the hospital room, swishing his white coat authoritatively. A gaggle of fresh-faced students pursued him, watching and listening intently. The room went silent. The doctor dramatically picked up my notes and had a quick flick through. He passed it to a student and, in turn, the chart went around the room. He explained the situation to me and that it would need to be rectified.

I remember feeling quite miffed. This thing (the pacemaker) that I didn't even want in the first place, which had been in me for less than twenty-four hours, was already causing me issues. It might have been because I was tired, but I was annoyed with the doctor too; he was one of the only doctors we didn't already have a relationship with that had treated me. It felt to me like he was a little arrogant, and that he wasn't fully invested in my care – the opposite of Professor Deanfield and Professor de Leval, who were all in from the start. This doctor was more interested in looking great in front of his students.

I listened to his proposal. Growing up, I had played a lot of *Monopoly* with my sisters, and if it taught me anything it was that negotiation was key. I had already given away Mayfair with a hotel to go home, I was not about to do the same with Park Lane for nothing! I thought a little longer. I bit the side of my mouth, a little too nervous to ask. I looked away from Mum, thinking she may disapprove of what was about to happen.

The doctor, assuming this was nearing the end of the discussion, asked, 'Do you have any questions?'

I knew I couldn't sound sheepish; this was a now-or-never moment. I said firmly, 'If I have to have another procedure, I want you to take out all of the remaining tubes that need to be removed, remove the two pacemakers that are attached to me by my tummy, take all the blood tests you need, as well as any other painful tests needed, remove any catheters and throat tubes and change or put in any other necessary cannulas ALL while I am under general anaesthetic – and I want to go home in the next two days!' This was not a negotiation; I'd had it, and had nothing to lose. Alan Sugar may have employed me as his next and youngest apprentice at that moment.

I knew I had to hold my ground, so I tried desperately not to look at Mum, who was on my left side, but I could see her beautiful big brown eyes widen as she processed my demands, then turning to see the doctor's reaction. He looked shocked. Clearly no twelve-year-old paediatric patient had ever bargained with him before. The student doctors all looked at him, unsure what would transpire next. A nurse had her back to him, and had been checking my vitals for an exceedingly long time. I could see from the corner of my eye that she had pursed her lips tightly together in a smile, and was sneaking a glance to see what the doctor's reaction would be.

I waited, hoping for a positive outcome, tightly holding the hairy monkey hand of Samantha on one side and Mum's soft hand on the other, hoping for luck from both.

He paused, assessed the situation, and said calmly, slowly, and in a very measured voice, 'I can't promise anything, but we will do our best.'

I replied, 'Thank you, when is the operation?'

He replied slowly, still taken aback, 'tomorrow', possibly worried I would ask for more.

'OK,' I said.

He nodded, turned and left, trying to dodge the students blocking his exit. He seemed visibly shaken by what had just happened.

Later, I found out that Mum and Dad were very impressed with what had transpired that day.[21]

You may be wondering what happened. Well, the doctor was true to his word. He did all the tests and removed and replaced everything while I was asleep. I thank him deeply for this. I would advise all parents to ask their child's doctor politely and respectfully to do the same. Any required procedure that can be done while a patient is under can help

---

[21] Side note: always be kind and respectful to everyone who looks after you or your family! You don't know when you may need their life-saving help, and they have a very tough job – don't make it any harder!

lessen their suffering. Even a cannula change is immeasurably helpful in that moment of your child's life. I know it is not always possible and I know doctors are focusing on the big picture, but just ask what could be done.

I am clearly not a sales rep for pacemakers or any pacemaker-related item! I have a love–hate relationship with mine. I finally went home after having the operation to fix the one which was fitted.

As a small twelve-year-old, I was totally flat-chested – no boobs, nada – and the pacemaker was very pronounced. This didn't bother me. I was happy, I was home. As the pacemaker was more of a precaution than an essential for day-to-day life, I thought it was a bit pointless. The doctors had told me I would rarely use it. I went back to school soon after and with the help of my best friend, Gem, we named my first pacemaker Homer after Homer Simpson, as I thought it was lazy, fat and a bit of a joke.

As a twelve-year-old I wasn't thinking, *Gosh, this isn't sexy*, but I knew it was ugly and, quite frankly, pants! I was also quite disgusted by it and ignored it as much as I could. But I knew I had the least attractive version of a single chest implant.

When you first have a pacemaker fitted it annoys you often. It feels like it's in the way, all the time. I loved sleeping on my tummy, and this was off the cards for the foreseeable future. Things got a bit easier when I grew boobs, as the pacemaker became less noticeable and ended up looking a bit more like a wrong-way-round breast implant scar than anything else. The moment this happens to your daughter, it is SO important to get her a sports bra or good bra straight away: because of the way the scar is joined, the weight of the breast sometimes makes the scar feel like it is pulling open or apart and it can hurt. Also, without a good bra you may stretch or thicken your scar. Small details like this make your child's life that little bit easier or better. Scars pulling hurts, whoever you are or wherever the scars are on your body!

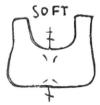

What is a pacemaker?

It does what it says on the tin. Basically, a pacemaker has settings set for its specific wearer that can sense when a heart is beating normally and will not interfere, but if it senses that a heart is beating too few times a minute it will send out a small pulse to lightly shock the heart and create a beat.

After a pacemaker operation, they tell you not to lift your arm over your shoulder and not to lift more than the weight of a full kettle, which is so hard to remember!

Later, at senior school (after I was thirteen years old) my friends lovingly gave me the nickname Gerry-atric due to my pacemaker. I know what you're thinking – *oh no, she doesn't realise she was bullied* – but I know it was a kind and well-meaning name and we had about ten names each. Another was Cherub (for my chubby cheeks) and a third was Duracell Bunny (as I had waves of boundless energy).

Another thing that happened was that for almost a year I didn't grow hair under my left armpit, the side my pacemaker is on. I think it was the body's way of saying it had had a shock. Also my nails had what are called 'stress ripples', where the body focuses on other things rather than growing nail, which produces ridges on your nails.

My pacemaker battery lasts about seven to ten years. They say I rarely use it. It really is there just as a precaution, which is slightly annoying, but as someone who lives life to the full it is better to have it and not use it than not have it and desperately need it, like an umbrella in England.

Once I had healed from my operation and it had stopped feeling sore, if people were questioning or if I knew the person was squeamish, I would sort of show them on the outside. I wouldn't quite pop it out, but I could show them the edge closest to my arm where it sat. My dad used to always do a fake faint, which as a kid I loved. I knew it was quite gross, so I made the most of it!

My check-ups were yearly for my pacemaker which, exasperatingly, were not always on the same day as my heart check-ups as in some hospitals they are overseen by different departments.

The pacing check-ups consist of a quite chunky disk being placed over the pacemaker, which then connects to it. Technicians speed up the heart and then check each wire and function is working as it should. In recent years, the technology has moved forward; now they only need to place a thin disc over the pacemaker for a moment and it automatically connects. It feels unbelievably modern and like a real change. I also sleep next to a reader which sends my pacemaker's output to the hospital every night so they can see if any intervention is needed before the next check-up. When I first set up the reader by my bed, the lights on it kept us up, so I recommend keeping it in a drawer or in its original box, or perhaps covering the box in nice paper so don't have an ugly reminder in your bedroom. Remember to make a note of the helpline and reader's ID number before!

Limitations to a pacemaker

Having a pacemaker is not as easy as just getting one fitted, as we found out in the first twenty-four hours. For the first six months you can't sit on the right-hand side of the car as the seatbelt rubs on your new pacemaker and scar, or you have to hold the seatbelt just a little away from you. Occasionally you either do too vigorous exercise or you stretch your left arm across your body to the right too quickly and feel the pacemaker, which is a bit gross, and can bruise the area for a while. I was advised not to speak on the phone with my left ear as it was too close to my pacemaker. I shouldn't get too close to microwaves when they're switched on. And I am not able to have an induction hob, which doesn't matter to me now and mattered even less when I was twelve. I always had to tell my boyfriends that if I am ever about to be Tasered, they need to jump in and take the

Taser or I am finished – kaput! Luckily their love never had to be tested.

Bumper cars are off the table due to magnets, as are MRI machines. To be fair, the bumper cars are not a great loss to me; they just bruise you. I can't go through traditional security scanners, as I now have metal in me. I have a pacemaker card which I show, but I still consistently get stopped at airports. I explain that I have a pacemaker and they always think it is the little old lady in the wheelchair in front of me! Every time! I do see the funny side in this.

On one occasion, on the way back from France, I was patted down in a separate room. It was a small airport, so they didn't have the modern full body scanners they have now. The lady who searched me grabbed my pacemaker – really grabbed it – with each finger creating the outline of my pacemaker like a dot-to-dot children's drawing.

I got very cross with her, which she was not expecting. I told her in French that it was unacceptable to grab pacemakers like that. You can do a flat hand movement, but you can't just grab it unless someone gives their express consent, which I hadn't. I explained that if I had only recently had it done, it would be very painful to have done what she just did. In that moment I thought to myself that someone must stand up for people with pacemakers. *Vive la résistance!*

One final airport story. My heart problem and pacemaker mean I can use the 'special assistance' bag check, which is the same one that families may use. I always feel awkward using it, but when you are late for a flight it really does save you. I once had a comedy moment when I was looking for the families and special assistance bag check area in a London airport. I asked a lovely worker bee at the airport, 'Hi there, please can I ask where to go for families and special assistance?'

The individual looked me up and down, took a moment and nosily said 'Wha' you got?'

I paused, a bit shocked, but it was a fair question. I seem fine if I wear a round-neck T-shirt. I walk and talk like anyone else, and it made me realise that of course I look fine, so from an outside point of view why would I be in that queue?

My frustrations with pacemakers continue. As with all medical interventions, things can go wrong. As I have had the pacemaker in since I was twelve, clearly I have grown internally (OK, OK, not so much vertically!), my cells have changed and like any organism, things grow around foreign bodies and move them slightly, that's normal. So clearly what they fitted when I was twelve is not in its original position. Due to this, they have advised me that the two wires they initially put in are not positioned as effectively as they should be. I have now had one of the wires replaced, and they continue to monitor the other, and it's no drama, but still not optimal when you think about things inside your body not working as they should.

Changing the pacemaker battery is a relatively straightforward procedure which takes about an hour – most people go home the same day. However, for my first change at the age of nineteen, in 2007, I had a local anaesthetic, and it did not go well. I honestly felt that I could feel the procedure, which was excruciatingly painful, and I then got into a very fast heart rhythm. When I am in pain, I instinctively hold my breath. Which is very unhelpful, but it distracts me from the painful area. The doctors got very cross with me for not telling them about the pain sooner. They quickly took me out of surgery and monitored me. They told me I had to get out of the heart rhythm I was in, or I could have a stroke, or a blood clot could go to the brain, and I could die. All things you really want to avoid, if you can. I was so woozy; it was terrible. They came in with papers for me to sign, to say that I understood the risks of the next procedure, which was to stop my heart and start it again – but that it may not start again, and I may not survive. I could hardly hold the pen. My sister Sammy, who was with me, gently said, 'Gerry, do you understand what you are signing?' and I just bobbed my head in no particular direction. 'Are you sure? Gerry, do you understand what is going on?'

I had no idea what was going on. I signed the paper with a nondescript scribble, wanting all this drama and pain to conclude and for life to get back to normal.

Sammy looked at me just as the doctor was coming in to take me to theatre 'Gerry, you have turned green! How are you feeling?'

I turned to Sammy and said, 'I'm going to be sick!'

Sammy grabbed one of the ever-useful hospital paper card bowls from the side of the bed.

I vomited very violently, and my heart returned to a normal rhythm. I now have general anaesthetic for everything except dental work.

This procedure going wrong, which scared me so much, entrenched my feelings of having an expiry date of twenty-one years old. I always knew I was lucky to be here, and that I had skirted death more than once. I never spoke to anyone about this 'death date', but I knew I had to live each day to the fullest, I had no time to waste.

To this day I don't think I was meant to have that procedure to stop my heart. I am relieved I didn't have to undergo it and I am so pleased Sammy was there with me. I am also sorry she was. I am devastated to think that it has scarred her for life.

'There is no friend like a sister in calm or stormy weather; To cheer one on the tedious way, to fetch one if one goes astray, to lift one if one totters down, to strengthen whilst one stands.'
Christina Rossetti

Tip

Cry, vomit and poop, at the same time if you want to! All these lower your heart rate and blood pressure.[22]

My most recent pacemaker blooper happened when I was having a new pacing wire and battery fitted in 2018. Whoever opened and sewed me up clearly took inspiration from Sylvester Stallone's mouth! I can giggle about it now, but it was so shocking at the time. They doubled the size of the scar and didn't even follow the shape of the original one. Thankfully the scar ageing process has lessened the look over time, but it still makes me think my new nickname should be Hot Lips!

I have a slightly larger left boob due to the pacemaker. For any young'un who has noticed that they have this too, don't worry – it's normal, and nobody else can tell; I don't feel weird about it, and nor should you.

Final pacing thoughts

What really gets my goat is endless talk about amazing scientific breakthroughs with technology. Making a pacemaker a tenth of the

---

[22] I don't think Christina Rossetti ever expected to be quoted before such a statement!

size of an original pacemaker. The size of a 'multivitamin' it is described as, not just a vitamin but a *multivitamin*. It's too funny.

Anyway, I digress – I have never been offered one, and have never heard of anyone who has. I would almost prefer not to know what is out there and then be pleasantly excited to find out I'm getting one of the smaller ones than know they exist and that I am not getting one.

My first pacemaker still makes me chuckle due to how old fashioned it was. Any travel into another time zone, the device had to be manually programmed in hospital, for the correct time zones. For most holidays my family were very good at getting this set and set back. Although on one holiday, I think we must have been in a rush and couldn't get an appointment with the pacing clinic in time, so I stayed a little more awake during the nights and a little sleepier by day.

Although I am not the biggest fan of pacemakers, I know mine has saved my bacon more than once, and I will have one for ever. If anything, I am ahead of the trend of my generation in an ever-ageing population. Some could say I am fashion forward!

But don't let me put you off. I have had an ambivalent relationship with my past and present pacemakers, but I could never have done so much if it wasn't for the pacemaker. It was the right decision to have one and it has enabled me to discover the world, make friends, and live! When you are little, everything seems so dramatic, and you can only see one thing – an ugly pacemaker which has given me a very visible scar and on occasion has really annoyed me, especially while sleeping. Nevertheless, you learn to live with things, and now I see it as a lifeline. Without that ugly pacemaker I would not have been able to go home from the hospital, and I wouldn't be able to lead the life I live – of joy, discovery and happiness. And if all else fails, at least I would be easy to identify if I was murdered. You have to focus on the perks!

My artificial intelligence (AI) and I live a nice life together – he used to be a parasite and now I am too used to him being there as a silent parachute. In case you were wondering, Homer is now retired; Dumb and Dumber took his place. Name suggestions for my next one on a postcard please.

Chapter 5

Scars

When I was nineteen, I visited our village summer fete. The population is just over six hundred people. It was a very low-key event, the sun was shining, one of the truly beautiful five days of the year for England! Happy, smiling people were going around, taking part in the tombola, buying cakes at the cake stall and guessing the number of jelly beans in a giant glass jar, and occasional squeals of excitement from children winning prizes could be heard in the distance. As a natural hoarder, I was drawn to a bric-a-brac table. I looked at all the fun and interesting pieces, feeling a rush of excitement for a possible purchase!

I looked up, not expecting to see the stallholder: an aged, rather plump, short, bearded man, like a Father Christmas figure but a little shorter. He was looking at my chest!

I thought to myself, gosh that's pretty pervy! In fact, that's not pretty pervy, that's *very* pervy!

He noticed me looking and looked down.

I must have made a displeased face. I thought again to myself. How embarrassing, should I leave? I can't buy anything, then I am condoning his inappropriate behaviour, but all the money goes to charity, and it is all for a good cause. This has now got really weird!

He then started undoing the top button of his short-sleeved blue country-check shirt. Then a second, and slowly a third …

My panicked thoughts escalated: *Oh my goodness! What is going on? I have never had this effect on a man in public ... as of yet! If I leave, I will offend him if I stay, I am saying ... I approve?*

Then, like after monsoon rain, it all became clear ... Low and behold, he had the same chalky-crimson outline on his sternum: from his manubrium to his xiphoid process. We made eye contact, we blinked, stayed still for just a second and then small very warm smiles came across both our faces: we knew exactly what the other was thinking. *Arrr! You're in The Club too!*

Michael was a totally charming man. He loved donkeys and lived close to our family's home. I went for tea with him and his wife on occasion. I was proud to be in the same club as him and it was cool to meet someone with matching battle scars. It was the first and last time someone has ever taken their clothes off in front of me in broad daylight at a village fete. I know young people have confidence, but *really*! What a wally and a half I was/am!

'The Club'

I like thinking of what I have as being in a members' club. A members' club no one wants to be in.

Admission fee

Your life and the lives of your loved ones will be permanently changed. A few scars (you can see and some you can't) for you and your family and even possibly a top of the range AI (artificial intelligence) for free!

Facilities

Check-ups in badly lit white rooms, being poked and prodded, and meeting some of the best doctors in the world. Making amazing friends along the way and seeing a world you never knew existed.

Membership card perks

Fast track entry to many exciting locations, including Disney World and the Eiffel Tower. Skipping the queues on aeroplanes on occasion, first-row seats to Covid lockdown, to stay indoors!

Terms and conditions

Differ per person but for me it was no: bumper cars, running[23] and steep hills,[24] certain medication, extreme altitude, growing to six feet. Plus frequent fatigue, a rubbish white blood cell count, a left boob bigger than the other and getting frisked at the airport every time. Car seatbelts on the right of the car are more comfortable, chatting on mobile phones only on the right, best not to stand near microwaves and no induction hobs.

For full Ts & Cs, call your hospital!

I was taught to avoid the topics of politics, religion, money and sex, but thought on the whole I was a very open person. But I was surprised when my best friend, Gem, told me that she thought I was

---

My family made me highlight both [23] and [24]: I can do both but I choose not to. I find it uncomfortable and never found that euphoric runner high people speak of yet.

really private about my heart-related stuff. Perhaps its due to not wanting to be depressing or self-centred, or just wanting to talk about topics that are fun! I honestly thought if anyone ever asked me about, well ... almost anything, I would be ready to talk. I feel it is the best way to be when you are what people call 'different'.[25]

This is one of the reasons why I don't hide my scars. I am not loud and proud and I don't 'wear them proudly', but nor do I try to conceal them ... I just get on with things and live! I'm not overthinking what I'm going to wear or how my chest looks (for different reasons than Pamela Anderson). To me it's like having ears: they're there and they've always been there.

I have one scar down my front, which has six circular scars dotted around it at the base, about 10 cm up from my naval, from the temporary fitting of external pacemaker wires and drainage tubes. I sometimes think it looks like a bird's-eye view of Stonehenge (a circular prehistoric stone monument). I have one for the pacemaker on my upper left, a couple of random groin and neck scars which just look like skin blemishes really, and two on my back which sort of look like mini shark bites (if the shark was a hockey player wearing a gum shield, so my front was not affected). I think with modern technology, the likelihood is that any child undergoing heart surgery today would have smaller and more discreet scars, and may even have had keyhole surgery, depending on the operations they require. We can hope, but you will rarely find me in a one-piece swimsuit. Life has given me lemons, so I wear them like lemons should be worn.

---

[25] Please don't get politically correct about the terms I use – it is what it is. Most people don't have a heart problem therefore we are the minority and are therefore a little bit different.

The funny thing is, most of the time I forget that I have really quite obvious, un-neat scars due to multiple procedures, or that I am not just like everyone else. I don't see them anymore. So, my initial thought when I notice someone looking, is, gosh I must have great bangers, they're always getting checked out! Then I remember and feel a bit sheepish for the moment of overconfidence. What an idiot!

Because I was born like this, I think I have come to terms with most things, to make do with what I have. I don't know my chest (visually), any other way than with a scar down the middle, and I don't know my health any other way either.

Now that I'm older, I see the comedy in what I have more than the serious truth. For example, in developing countries you will receive the most obvious and extreme stares you can ever receive when you are slightly 'different' from whatever the 'norm' is. The awkward thing about human nature is that if you notice something different about another human, you want to look … and again … and then three more times. The more you look, the more obvious you become; humans are just inquisitive.

Sam and I lived in Cambodia for two totally magical years in 2016 and 2017. We were co-managers of a four-star beachside hotel. It was adventurous, beautiful, unbelievable, surprising at every turn and just plain bonkers. Every day brought new challenges, but overall it was a beautiful time of our lives. I paint it as a beautiful picture and looking back, it was, but at the time it was seriously hard work.

In Cambodia we used to walk around the local food market, weaving into shops with hand-painted ceramics, smelly durian fruit, all sorts. Although I'd be wearing sensible outfits, lovely locals walking in the opposite direction would stare at my scars. They could not help but gawp – and I mean mouth open, head-turning. People were so transfixed, they would trip over, head first. Once this happened and a gentleman face-planted into an oversized bucket of fish heads, and the fishmonger got very cross with the man in question. It was rather comical.

Obviously, conversations don't normally start with, 'so, I have scars', and yet bizarrely, scars are sometimes the biggest conversation starters and even relationship starters.

Growing up with scars

Due to 1001 things, I got to the point of not seeing my scars. But being young is hard, growing up is hard and there is that really awkward stage, before you feel comfortable in your skin, where you feel like everyone is looking at you all the time and your skin is simultaneously hot and cold and doesn't fit you correctly. Your cheeks turn red constantly and you feel like a dork in whatever you are wearing.

It was the first day of prep school, and I was nine. I was in the playground at break time with a few of the classmates I had met that morning. I heard a voice from a boy in my class who was with us saying, 'What's that?' He pointed at my chest, where my scar was.

'It's from an operation,' I told him in a nonchalant manner.

He shrugged and went about his business in a different direction. Another child in my class came up to me ten minutes later and asked me, 'What's your name again and what is that?' All the kids nearby stopped what they were doing and looked up to see my reaction. It felt like the playground fell silent.

I replied, feeling my first response was a bit boring, 'I'm Gerry. Oh, this? It's a shark bite.'

SHARK BITE

His eyes widened; his mouth dropped. Everyone nearby said in a calm low voice, 'Wooooooooooooow.'

Later in the break, I was with (we didn't know it at this point but) my new BFF, Gem. A girl who was a couple years older than us came over to where we were, who I thought looked like a 'coolie-coolie'[26] she chewed pink bubble gum and asked what my scar was.

I told her, 'It's a boob job gone wrong.' She stopped chewing and her mouth stayed open, her bubble gum, teetering on the edge of her lower teeth, almost falling out her mouth. I did this for my own entertainment. The reaction I got from a shark bite was the most extreme, and it was fun to see all their reactions. Gem and

---

[26] Someone who hung out with cool people and who was a cool kid.

I chuckled and walked off. If you can't have fun with something like this, what *can* you have fun with? I never really minded what people thought of it all. Adults will look but not ask, whereas kids will always ask very blunt questions. To be honest, I prefer the kids' method.

In recent years, those who need open heart surgery have such thin scars. I am now the one staring at their chests in wonder and awe and falling into buckets of fish heads!

There is a lot of pressure growing up, especially now with social media, to look a certain way … I've never looked that way, and I've never cared too much! However, I did have a small moment in 2018, when I had to decide if I wanted to show my scars in my wedding dress. I thought maybe I could wear lace over my shoulders and chest. But then I went shopping in the first shop and tried on the first dress and knew I'd fallen in love; I didn't want to take the dress off and didn't care two hoots about showing the scars – but I did ask for thin straps to be added to the dress to support my pacemaker scar.

Nonetheless, it is so important to do what you feel makes you happy. Plastic surgery has never appealed to me personally. Firstly, why would I have more unnecessary operations? Secondly, I know in the future I may need more work done, so why would I pay a lot of money for something that doesn't really bother me anyway and would need to be done again in the future? And three, I know it wouldn't make me happy; only you can make yourself happy! You are the solution to your problems. Nevertheless, I would get more joy from getting a boob job over hiding my scars … it's best to be honest about these things!

When I was thirteen I was excited before my prep school leavers' ball, and my mum had kindly organised through GOSH for me to go to a make-up class for camouflaging scars. It was a ninety-minute lesson with such a patient, kind, lovely young lady. She showed us so much and then I had a go. The number of layers it took for the scar to be almost unnoticeable was astonishing, but together we made them disappear. It was an amazing skill to have but it took so much time and effort that there and then, I decided that I would much rather spend time and have fun getting ready for the ball with my girlfriends. I did not disguise my scar and nor did I ever feel the need to do so again. I really, really, would recommend that parents of any child with scars (especially girls) try make-up and this sort of course. In my case, it made me measure my priorities, realise what was important to me at the time and provide me with another option if the scars really bothered me. I am so grateful to Mum for searching for the course in the first place and to GOSH and the lovely lady that taught it, without whom I would never have known. In my opinion this should be offered to anyone who wants it.

In your teenage years you are self-conscious. It's just what happens. The make-up course gave me confidence and highlighted the fact that none of my friends gave two hoots about my scars; if anything it made me a bit hardcore, which kids at the time thought was cool, or at least a good thing.

When I was twelve, I got really into fashion – not because I wanted to hide my scars, but because it made me happy to choose and have control over how I dressed for my body shape and my skin colouring. If Mum had her way, I would still be in frilly pastel or maroon floral dresses now, but I was never allowed to dress from Tammy – that was an absolute no-no: far too risqué for our family's values.

I found Gok Wan's body-positive TV programme *How to Look Good Naked* so inspiring. It was caring, genuine and it gave people confidence, which I feel is always important – most of us need a bit of a boost from time to time. He showed the importance of 'look good, feel good' and gave tips like if you have big boobs, a round high neck is not the way forward, and that it's flattering to have pockets on the rear of jeans. Most of all, he taught us that if you believe in yourself, confidence will flow, and confidence is attractive. He also showed us that imperfection is beautiful, which I believe to this day. If we all looked, acted and sounded the same, the world would be a very boring place.

I never dressed for my scars, but I knew what suited me from a young age. Saying this, I preferred having long hair and by writing this book and examining myself, I realised I wear and have worn my hair down on my left side and my parting has always fallen on the left side. I wasn't intentionally trying to hide my pacemaker scar, but perhaps I was subconsciously.

I remember also a comically large device that on a scrawny nine-year-old would have stuck out so much. It was a twenty-four-hour or forty-eight-hour heart-recording device. I would wear it for the allotted time, live a normal life and the machine would record my heart rhythm. Half the time the sticky electrodes would fall off, and it took so much space in my bed; it was hilarious. One of the cool things about growing older is seeing technology change and become more compact. I wish this device could have been a bit smaller – it was immense on someone my size at the time, whereas now it is so compact nobody could tell you were wearing it at all under your clothes.

Having a scar has got me out of trouble a few times and I occasionally refer to it as my 'get out of jail' free card. While Sam and I were working at the hotel in Cambodia we would occasionally get complaints about things that were out of our control. Such as in May one year somebody moaned that 'the sea is too hot'. Sam and I were proud hoteliers, and we would go above and beyond for our guests, team and owners, but controlling ocean currents and nature was a little over our pay grade. So Sam and I would play rock, paper, scissors (terribly professional) to see who would deal with the complaint. We would listen to the guest and show we understood their frustrations – but if it was me dealing with the complaint, on the whole, if they saw my scar, they realised life is actually pretty rosy.

Jealousy

I have only ever really had one pang of jealously in my life, and it happens, every so often, when I look at a lovely scar-free chest.

105

Normally it's a lady in a stunning dress, all beautifully made up, normally on TV or at a red-carpet event and I will admire how nice and clear their chest looks. I'm not looking at breasts, just top chest, and thinking, *oh, that would be nice*, but never craving it more than that. I'd love a centimetre or two more height, and sensible-sized feet would be helpful too.

But I am a little strange. I found out recently, talking to a friend about jealousy, that I don't really experience it the way I thought others did. My friend said, 'I am so jealous of how big their (a different friend's) house is.'

I said to her, 'Yeah, but then you would have needed to work all hours of the day, have no life, be mortgaged to the hilt, have married that terrible man and have that smelly little yappy dog!' My friend laughed and then explained to me in great detail that that's not how jealousy works – but I feel I still wouldn't want their life, even with a big house!

'Do not spoil what you have by desiring what you have not.'
Ann Brashares

Healing Tips

There was not a lot of advice at the time of my first few operations on the best way to help a scar to heal. As children, we would all be covered from head to toe in sun cream if we went to the playground when it was sunny – but there was no special treatment for my scars. As an adult I am also not very careful when it comes to my skin.

Nowadays they do advise moisturising. Obviously not when the scar is totally new. I have found Sudocrem really soothing at times of discomfort (please check with your doctor before using it). However, I never really find the time to moisturise my scars, let alone any other part of my body.

If you have ever had an operation where you need to get a long operation protection plaster off, you'll know that this is sometimes as traumatic as having the operation itself, because you are so sore from the procedure and added accoutrements of blood tests and IVs. The plasters and bandages are just so sticky! The glue has warmed up with your body temperature over time and upgraded itself to superglue. It is a moment when being a mammal covered in hair is really highlighted.

If you are ready and struggling to remove a plaster, the best technique I have learned is the same trick as taking off a sticky plaster from a blood test, but on a bigger scale. Get warm (not hot) water and a <u>BAR</u> of soap and slowly lather over the plaster's corners first, one end at a time. You must be slow and patient, as this will make it easier and much less painful. I put the soap directly on the plaster and make small circular motions. Sometimes a flannel can help to dampen rather than totally soak an area a little at a time.

I have found scars formed against the grain of the muscle and those that are cut along the muscle heal very differently. Scars running in the same direction as the muscle will always heal better. My pacemaker scar is not as well healed as my central chest scar for this reason.

This is gross, so if you're squeamish, please brace yourself. Do not pick at your scars. From an outside point of view, this may seem like an obvious and easy task: that's disgusting, who would do that?! But when you are the person with the fresh scar, it is harder than slaying a dragon! Dissolvable stitches either get absorbed by the body or they fall off. After one operation, my stitches were ready to drop. At this time, you are healing and wow-wee is it itchy, especially at the highest and lowest point of the scar! It is chicken-pox itchy, maybe worse. The last few stitches attached (normally the top and base) just get so scratchy all you want to do is pick them off. But my family were so good at making sure I never did this. Even when I insisted, 'I'm just rolling, I'm just rolling!' This was my way of itching without scratching, which basically consisted of me rolling my knuckles gently and slowly against the scar and the skin nearby a little just so the itching would halt momentarily. Or from above my top, I would gently touch the skin on the scar. I didn't like touching the scar directly. It sent a shiver up my spine. Let your child lightly itch but stop them from picking anything off – they will want to! My scar is not a thing of beauty, but I believe that if it wasn't for my family (constantly) telling me to not to itch or pick at it, it would look worse.

Some people form keloid scars. This is a type of scar which develops in a way which is very pronounced. They can be 3D, shiny and red. Keloid scars run in families, and you either heal this way or you don't. I don't, but I know for many this is a topic of great anxiety, as it means that scars are far more noticeable – even when they're as small as an acne scar.

I may have physical scars, but all my family have scars too. Emotional and psychological scars. This pains me as, because of what I have, they have developed emotional scars. Everyone was affected.

I believe people who don't have any scars haven't lived … I don't mean they have to have one a foot long one to have existed, I just mean that we all have scars. For most, it starts on the school playground with you scraping your knee, and then you grow up. Everyone has something, whether they are visual and physical like my scars, or more subtle like anxiety, addiction or mental illness. It is a person as a whole. They tell a story, they tell us where we have journeyed, and if you open yourself up to them and accept them, they won't control where we go, or who we become. Only you can choose that. As Oscar Wild said,

'Be yourself; everyone else is already taken.'

Chapter 6
Pain

'If you're going through hell, keep going.'
Winston Churchill

A lovely nurse I had never met before bounded into my hospital room joyfully, 'Good morning, Geraldine, we are going to take your tubes out today.' She was tall and slim with short brown hair in the style of Gwyneth Paltrow in *Sliding Doors*.

I was nine. It was a couple of days after one of my biggest operations. I looked at her and assumed we would be going somewhere like an operating room and there would be a team. The tubes she spoke about had been attached during an operation: a pair of drains about 2 cm in diameter in the middle of my stomach, about 10 cm apart which led down to a plastic receptacle by the side of my bed, like a catheter for internal gunk after an op. They were see-through so at times they were revolting. Even as a child I knew this. In a child's mind and body they seemed huge. They had been in me for quite a while, so like any well-behaved organic being, my body was starting to grow around the plastic intruders. She started to set up by putting absorbent paper down under me, the type that puppies wee on for potty training, which smells like a new plastic bag. She

111

continued prepping and laying out instruments. 'How are you feeling today?'

I enthusiastically replied, 'Good, thank you. You can call me Gerry.' As ever, I was unfailingly polite, even when nervous. I also preferred to be called by my nickname when having procedures done, as it was more familiar. Geraldine was only for when I was being told off at home, and always gave me a visual of a tired, stubborn, old donkey carrying a lot of weight being pulled up a hill – *come on, Geraldine!* – with a tug of its frayed rope bridle.

She said, 'Very good. So, Gerry, we are going to snip the stitches and make small incisions around the tubes, and then I am going to pull them out. Do you have any questions?'

I was still a little confused as to why I was having what sounded like quite a big procedure in bed. 'Here?'

The nurse sweetly smiled, looked to the ground and nodded, looking like she was in a bit of a hurry. 'Yes, here, now.' Later I found out that it was not that she was in a hurry but that she hated doing this procedure.

I obliged, thinking she must know what she was doing: 'Oh, OK.'

Mum, who was in the room with us, asked, 'Should I stay?'

She replied, 'Yes, that's fine, best to look at Gerry and hold her hand.'

If that wasn't a warning sign, I don't know what is.

'Right, all set, I want you to close your eyes or look at your mum.'

Another red flag.

I pursed my lip with nerves, and she began. She chose the right side first. It was painful to start with as she snipped the already imbedded stitches that had grown too comfortable in a short space of time. She pulled lightly. All my nerves were too awake.

Everything is magnified when you are sore from fresh wounds and openings are being reopened. She pulled at them harder and then began to cut around the drains which had taken root. Again, this was painful. She cut a bit deeper into the wound. She then stopped, looked up, and said 'OK, are you ready?'

I looked up at her, assuming she had completed one side fully and this that was the end, not the beginning. Not the start! Surely not the start?

'OK, I'm going to pull now,' she said in a loud, clear voice. She was sweating. 'Three, two, one.'

The feeling is hard to describe, but I finally understood the expression 'blinding pain'. I looked up at her with the tube in her hand. She was sweating heavily and looked like she had aged a decade in two minutes. She was short of breath. 'OK, right. How are you doing?' I couldn't answer. 'Let's take just a moment. Do you want a drink of water or juice?'

I took a sip, still unable to talk. I was in shock at what had just transpired. She had looked like such a nice lady! I caught my breath. I was sure I had turned red. I held my breath to distract myself, which was very unwise to as it made me dizzy on top of everything else.

She said – too soon in my opinion, clearly desperate to complete the task – 'Are you ready for the next? One more to go and then we are done.'

I didn't answer, I got back into position and lightly nodded.

She began, and the same pains started again. Mirroring the right. The left was no easier. I looked at Mum, thinking, poor Mum; this was less than ideal for either of us.

'Ready again, Gerry …' You could hear and see in her face that she wanted it to be over, not just for me but for her; this was a form of torture for all involved. One watching, one doing and one receiving! It's a little like what I imagine hell to be like: you take turns being each character, and each character is as hard to be as the other. 'One, two three,' she said, panting. The end was such a relief. There are no words. I thought to myself how terrible it must have been to be Prometheus from Greek mythology having his liver ripped out, and how glad I was glad I had only gone through that once.

This was the most painful thing that I have ever experienced to date. When it was over, I found myself feeling sorry for the nurse that had to do this to people. Looking back, it gets even worse: she had to do this to *children*. The poor thing was drenched in sweat, and once I was patched up she left as quickly as she could to leave me to recover and rest from the ordeal! This experience was why I bargained with the doctors when getting a pacemaker fitted. I knew I didn't want to go through that again. No way, Jose! It also made me really re-assess films like James Bond: I don't know how he gets tortured and beaten up and then five minutes later he is saving the world again.

Not all of my painful experiences have been related to my heart. I've also had a second-degree burn on my calf; a collapsed lung (this was agony); I bit the curb by falling off someone's shoulders, subsequently needed a root canal; my general anaesthetic did not work properly for the pacemaker battery, as mentioned before; I've had pneumonia twice; and reoccurring shingles on my right hip. I never lived in cotton wool, although occasionally I think my parents wanted me to![27]

I have very few memories of what I would classify as 'bad times'. But the tube extraction is one of them. Having said this, I feel like there is a real difference between physical pain that is short-lived and physical pain that is prolonged. We cannot escape pain in our lives. In my opinion, pain – like art – is subjective. We all experience pain differently. Whether it be physical or emotional. I have felt lots of different types of pain: pain after an operation, pain of bruising after blood tests, pain of losing a loved one, pain of missing friends or family and pain of not being able to completely enjoy a wonderful moment *because of* pain. Pain is all around us. Your outlook on pain changes the way you live and experience your life.

Everyone has a different pain threshold. It's surprising how many footballers have hyperalgesia and scrunch into a ball at the slightest touch! Luckily, my pain threshold is high, and if anything, it grew with every operation.

I have always felt blessed that I never had consistent pain and I cannot imagine how tough that must be. Obviously when you are healing your body hurts, but the pain usually lessens with every

---

[27] Dad read my manuscript and crossed out the words 'a little more' from the end of this sentence – clearly they did!

On a random note, I have always loved having my head stroked. I find it reassuring and it instantly makes me sleepy. I believe this is not just because my parents did it as a child at the darkest of times to help me sleep but also it was one of the few places growing up that I never experienced pain on my tiny body as a child, and that it was safe to be touched and to touch without causing or experiencing pain. It was my way of receiving affection as a kid. That or I was a pet in a past life.

day and within a few weeks you are back to normal (or almost back to normal).

While post-op pain can be awful, being in constant pain would be worse. Pain changes a person. Pain makes you think and feel very differently about yourself, others, and life as a whole. Constant pain can be crippling and can affect all parts of your life. It makes you think and feel differently, everything becomes more of an effort, everything saps your energy, and being kind and in a good mood when you are in pain is hard. For a few years I had musculoskeletal pain which affected my chest and left top side and boob. It affected my mood, I didn't want to see people and I didn't want to do anything. I wanted to be alone, and I was popping paracetamol every four hours (though like the label says, never more than eight pills in a day). If you are in pain, it's OK not to be yourself. If someone you know is in pain, forgive them for not behaving like themselves, they know not what they do! I was such a grouch to my husband; I was mean and harsh and I am very sorry for this and grateful for his patience!

Managing pain and forms of protection

For all those in pain, it may be arduous but it's essential to find ways to manage it. It is essential to find an outlet. It is important to open your eyes and to try not to push loved ones away. There may come a point where they reach their limit and won't come back.

I have always found distraction to be good, even if you really don't feel like it. Whether it be going for a walk and getting some air, watching a film, taking part in a class, going to a museum or art gallery or calling a friend – just so for a moment you have relief, and you are not thinking of the pain. Music has always helped me out of pain, or a negative headspace. I like to put on a mad super-hyper, beautiful song like *The Greatest Showman's* 'This Is Me' or 'Trashin' the Camp' from *Tarzan* – or anything from Motown. Anything that makes me smile, tap my feet or jump up on stage – but whatever music you're into, it can be a great way of taking your mind off the pain.

When I was back at home after an op around the age of nine, when the pain was at its most extreme I would sometimes visualise it leaving all the cells of my body. It made me feel calm and in control of something I didn't have much control over at all. Sleep was also a challenge – sometimes the pain would knock me out and I'd sleep like a log, but there were also nights when it was impossible to nod off due to the pain.

When I was little and I first woke up from an operation, the pain was paralysing. I would be drenched in sweat, I couldn't talk and then the nurse or doctor gave me morphine which offers an immediate world of relaxation. But after a few days, the morphine is stopped and my body had to heal on its own. In hospitals I was woken up a lot by noisy machines or being checked on and I could struggle to sleep, especially if I was in pain. I had a good imagination from a young age and created a beautiful dream world in which I felt completely safe and comfortable. It was a mental place I could go to where there were no needles, no pain, no constant beeping machines and no bright lights. I took a lot of inspiration from Walt Disney's *Fantasia*, particularly the section with the really cute Pegasus family: it was like the Garden of Eden but with a touch of My Little Pony, rainbows, Care Bears, sometimes Barbie, a stunning lagoon, and just so much glitter. I loved going to this dream land and finding rest for a while. I can still see it vividly, and at times, if I can't sleep, I can go there even now. I'm feeling battier by the second, but I would recommend talking to your child about all their favourite things and helping them piece together a safe space they can go to for themselves if they want to.

As I got older, I came to enjoy Pre-Raphaelite art and poetry, and I found this a good outlet to use my brain and try and shut off or at least tune down my nerves if I needed to – I even wrote my own poetry. Then, I found a passion for more colourful, joyful, mad paintings from the Fauvist movement, especially André Derain and Henri Matisse. They were wonderfully distracting. From this love I ended up doing art GCSE, AS and A level and got good grades – really good grades. I ended up doing my final project on my back scars, inspired by Frida Kahlo, because she also references her scars, her pain and her health in her work.

There are two things that I always find funny on the subject of pain. Firstly, the way that doctors and nurses ask, 'How much pain are you in on a scale of one to ten?' Apparently it is the universal pain scale, but the really expressive facial signs they use to represent the numbers are so extreme, I hope never to encounter the poor guy it was based on! Secondly, people asking you how you are when you are recovering from an operation – what do they expect?! You are sore all over, but you're fine as you are in recovery and the right place to be treated. My reply is always, 'Sh*t, but fine.' It covers a multitude of sins.

I do feel talking to a professional can help, as the doctors told me in my thirties, my musculoskeletal pain was most likely psychosomatic, knowing this helped. Nevertheless, it felt like real, physical pain; it was so strong and crippling that I couldn't breathe at times and I felt like I needed to lie down for full days.

There is one thing which has not been touched upon yet which is that no one teaches you how to cope in terrible times; there is no handbook. There is no guide, and no one tells you what is right or wrong as there is just so much to deal with at the time and everyone's circumstances are different. You learn to cope however you can in the moment, and this can lead to some deep-seated habits: both good and bad. My sisters feel I have a very rosy view on everything which has happened, on the whole, which was one of my coping mechanisms. This is another reason why it's so important to talk to medical professionals: to help find some order in times of absolute disarray. They may not have the answer to everything, but sometimes saying things out loud makes you realise how loony your thoughts are. Another bad coping mechanism I have is finding humour in dark times, which may have given me a dark sense of humour; but again, this is something I have needed to get me to where I am today. I also appreciated that each of my family members have their own coping mechanisms, different to mine but still with the same objective of helping us continue.

Healthy or not, these little tricks and mental techniques are what get us through.

Tips

Try to look after yourself: you only have one body to live in. Try to find coping mechanisms otherwise pain will consume you, and remember that post-op pain is only temporary.

Pain is a way for our body to show us it is healing. It is a protection mechanism and reminds us we are human. Mum gets upset that I suffered so much as a baby, and endured the sadness of seeing something so small which she felt was hers suffer so much, but – while in no ways do I mean this in a cry-me-a-river or tiny violins way – it is the only life I knew. I knew I had to experience pain to be OK, to get to see my friends again, go home, be with family, see Inky and eat Mum's chocolate cake!

'There is an ancient tribal proverb I once heard in India. It says that before we can see properly we must first shed our tears to clear the way.'
Libba Bray

Chapter 7
Bravery

I don't feel I am qualified to tell you about bravery, but I can tell you about fear. There have been three times in my life I have experienced true fear. The first time was touched on previously: crossing the crocodile- and hippo-infested river when our boat ran aground in Africa. The second two were while I was living in Cambodia, desperately trying to get medical treatment.

It was 15 January 2016, a normal day in Cambodia; the sun was beating down and all seemed well. I had woken up with a bit of a light pain which swept round from under my left shoulder blade to my left arm pit. I felt a little dizzy, but nothing out of the ordinary; I shrugged it off as a pulled muscle and it being a very hot day. Just before 3 p.m., Sam and I were driving around the busy aroma-filled markets and shops in Sihanoukville picking up hotel supplies when I suddenly experienced an immobilising shooting, throbbing pain which went straight through me, in my left chest and back. The pain became unbearable and suffocating. I was struggling to breathe. It was like no pain I had ever experienced before. I started to wonder if this was it – I'd had so much borrowed time. I'm dying. I checked my arm, and I had no pain there. This was not a heart attack, I thought.[28] I turned to Sam and said, 'Something isn't right.'

'What?' he replied, surprised, trying to dodge oncoming small mopeds, bicycles and frighteningly driven cars.

'I have bad pain', I struggled to say due to the pain. I tried to breathe in a controlled way, but it was very difficult.

Sam almost caused an accident stopping the car. 'Where?' he said, turning to look at me. Tiny, angry moped horns could be heard, whizzing past at high speed.

I pointed to my left side. 'Can ... we go ... back ... home?' I breathlessly said.

'Of course,' said Sam in haste.

We got home and went upstairs to the master bedroom. I sat on the bed; I wanted to be still for a moment in a calm space, to assess the situation. No arm pain, no sweating: this was definitely not a heart attack. I felt reassured for a second time, but the pain was so strong. I tried to catch my breath. The pain didn't get better. We called our international health insurer, which told us to go to our nearest hospital for tests and we were given an authorisation number for the next steps.

'I think its best we follow the insurer's advice and go to hospital,' I said.

'OK, let's go,' Sam said, but he was clearly concerned. He started running around the house grabbing things he thought we may need, for who knows how long; passports and clothes, ready for whatever decision we would need to take. We were both silently anxious by this strange new unknown we now faced.

---

[28] Years later I was advised that not having pain in the arm does not rule out a heart attack. Great!

We had heard from expats managing neighbouring hotels which hospital was the best in the area. We headed to that hospital with a small bag of belongings for a few nights' stay.

Sam and I were surprised that the road to the hospital was a dirt track. But to keep one another calm, neither of us commented on it. The building we found at the end of this track differed drastically from its rustic surroundings: its slick modern dark reflective windows conflicted with the white outer shell of the building. A long set of neon lights shone white bright, equally day and night, giving the institution's name in both Khmer and English. This was meant to be 'the place' expats go to get medical treatment, but it was still like no hospital I had ever visited. Looking back, this was all a glossy mask, hiding the true, basic levels of medical training. Until we arrived, we also hadn't realised this was more of a clinic than a hospital, and this would have a big impact on our care. We parked up and still the pain was just as it had been: sharp and relentless. We walked into a large, tiled room where we met three nurses in a booth under yet more neon signage. There were so many locals speaking at the top of their lungs, the reverberating tiles made it hard to focus on checking in. The process was chaotic and haphazard. No one seemed to be in charge, hear what was happening or understand our English. However, the biggest problem came with diagnosing me. I was starting to get more anxious as not only did they not understand my medical history, but the hospital staff didn't know how to turn on certain machines – and the machines they *did* have looked like World War One rejects: ECG machines with attachments that reminded me of octopus tentacles. The team also couldn't read the data that they were receiving from these machines and had to send everything off to a larger hospital in the capital, four hours away. They seemed baffled by my ECG result but diagnosed me with Brugada syndrome (a rare but serious condition that affects the way electrical signals pass through the heart). This was not the case.

Once we realised the clinic couldn't read or understand my ECG results, we called my insurers once again to ask for help to be able to compare past scans, but my insurers had very limited notes on me, only really the history that I had given them when applying, and were therefore unable to help or advise.

Sam and I knew this was not a great situation to be in. We were completely at a loss as to what to do. They clearly didn't know how to look after me there but if we headed to the capital, something could go wrong or I could get worse on the way. Four hours is a long journey. Prior to this, while visiting the capital on a hotel shopping trip, Sam and I had seen an ambulance with a large book in its front window titled *Medicine: Part 2*. Neither one of us brought this up to the other at the time but we were both thinking, would the capital really have more of an idea then here?

We tried to contact my British hospital, St Bart's, to let them know what was going on; we wanted the doctors at the clinic to speak to my UK doctors to explain the situation, for the UK to give any advice and for them to be sent my present ECG to compare with past ones, but it was tricky to get hold of anyone as by this time it was lunchtime on a Friday. So we left a phone message with our contact details and an email with our results attached, hoping someone would reply quickly.

The hospital in Sihanoukville advised us to go via ambulance to the capital to their sister hospital, which they thought would have a better idea about the situation. Sam and I were bundled into an ambulance; I was lying down and Sam was sat next to me. It all felt mad; yesterday things had been fine, and the day before that, but now they most definitely were not.

The normally four-hour journey to Phnom Penh had never taken so little time! With deafening sirens blaring, we whizzed along the dirt tracks passing dark brown wooden shack-filled villages, then more sophisticated buildings of concrete and glass, finally hitting the smooth highways at high speed. Dodging graceful skinny cows crossing the roads, mopeds constantly in the way and cars behind us which thought they could take advantage of the ambulance's wake.

We arrived safely, although we knew our ears may never be the same again. We were shown into our own room where tests began again. The hospital was more modern and in many ways Sam and I felt more at home here, recognising the similarities to back home in the UK, but there was still an air of naivety. Again, the doctors were confused by my ECG results and as Sam and I had nothing to compare them to it was tricky for them to diagnose me. They decided I had angina and started to try to treat me for this with isosorbide dinitrate, which I stubbornly refused. I had a feeling it wasn't angina, and I felt they didn't really knew I had angina, so why treat me for this. I was transferred to the Intensive Care Unit as they were stumped!

It was now the next day in Cambodia. We kept trying St Bart's to no avail as it was the weekend, so there were fewer staff to field messages. I was still uncomfortable but also tired, as was Sam. I was prescribed Omeprazole,[29] Biocalm[30] and tolperisone.[31] I took one Omeprazole. Being offered so many drugs at once, made

---

[29] Which neutralises acid in the stomach.
[30] A muscle relaxant.
[31] Another type of muscle relaxant and not a drug offered to patients in the UK.

us feel like they were shooting in the dark during a very poorly performed drug trial. We did not feel confident in their ability to look after me and this highlighted how unreliable this establishment of care was and how far we were from any real care even though we were in the capital. It was a really scary moment. This was not a situation you want to be in in a developing country

They kept taking my SATS (blood oxygen saturation level) day and night; nothing abnormal was found, and in the afternoon of the 17th I was transferred to the general ward and then soon after doctors were happy for me to be discharged.

For me, there was still a worry about unanswered questions and what to do if this happens again. On the 19th, St Bart's told us all the tests that Sam had so diligently sent to them 'looked normal' for me, and that the most likely cause of the pain was muscular skeletal, that with a few painkillers this could have been avoided. This occasion was a huge wake up call for Sam and me for so many reasons, and brought us back down to earth with a bump. We realised we had to be far more organised with my hospital notes to always have them at hand if needed, and that we needed to know the location of the closest and safest hospital in any areas we were living in or visiting. It also made us realise Cambodia probably had an expiry date for us which we hadn't thought about before. I also stopped secretly and stupidly (since passing the age of twenty-one) thinking I was invincible, which none of us are, but which is a rather fun fantasy for someone fragile to have. I'll never be a nervous nelly, as that's no way to live, but Sam and I did end up staying in a hotel nearby (which we call the airport hotel) for a couple of nights after this experience, just in case it happened again!

The second occasion of fear in Cambodia was on 30 May 2017, and it started in bed. We had decided to stay in the hotel as Sam and I had worked late and a storm had arrived overhead. It was 9 p.m. and we were both tired and settling down for some light scrolling on our phones and background TV before passing out, when my heart started going incredibly quickly out of nowhere. I wasn't in pain, nothing felt different, it was just a fast pulse. I thought to myself that this was a bit random and hoped it would return to normal as suddenly as it had started, but disappointingly it persisted.

I had recently downloaded a free app to measure heart rate, due to what had happened the year before. They were known not to be completely accurate, but it brought me comfort knowing I had it and could occasionally check it. I tried to be subtle, to not worry Sam unnecessarily. I put my finger on my phone's torch, and – lo and behold – my heart was going 140 bpm. Sam could tell something was up as I kept reaching for my chest in the hope that it would feel normal on the outside, but it didn't! I knew this was not good. I once again turned to Sam and said, 'I am so so so sorry, but something isn't right again.'

Sam looked at me and his face said it all – *oh no, not again* – 'What is it?'

'My heart is going randomly really fast.' I pulled his hand to my chest so he could feel it, and showed him the app results. His eyes met mine with a concerned look. I realised at that moment that you could also see my heart beating through my clothes, due to the beats being so strong.

'What do you want to do?' he asked.

I paused, trying to think if I had ever had anything like this before. I hadn't. 'I don't know.'

We both waited for the other to speak first, neither did, not knowing what to do. I suddenly jumped out of bed and started to do jumping jacks.

'What are you doing?' Sam asked, raising his voice in disbelief.

I said in a definitely unsure tone of voice, puffing through the exertion, 'I thought maybe my heart could be shaken back into a new normal rhythm or back to "normal"' – stopping the arm movements for a moment to make air quotes with a cheerful smile.

I lay back down on the bed, annoyed at the lack of instant results, hoping the cool-down would jolt things back to how they had been minutes before, but nothing. Sam looked at me as if my reasoning sort of made some sense. Annoyingly, when retesting the heart rate, it seemed to have made the bpm faster – reaching 170–180 rather than fixing the problem as I'd optimistically thought it might.

'OK, that didn't work,' I said out loud, still panting.

'Now what? How are you feeling?' Sam asked.

'I'm not in pain – it's like running but totally static. I think we should try to chill and get some rest and hopefully it will go back to a normal rhythm, as quickly and as randomly as it came,' I steadfastly explained, while hearing the rain splatter on the large sliding doors and the shushing of the palm tree leaves dancing with one another high up.

Sam agreed, looking at me hesitantly.

This instance I was very wary about going to hospital. Mainly as they weren't that helpful last time, there was a bad storm outside, and I felt a bit silly from the previous hospital visit. I'd assumed I was dying and it all seemed rather dramatic, when really it wasn't that serious, and it made me feel at the time like the boy that cried wolf – that was something I wanted to avoid at all costs. We calmly watched a David Attenborough documentary and meditated, but neither helped. In the meantime, Sam had spoken to his father who was in the UK. He had advised him it was likely to be Afib (atrial fibrillation) and that two outcomes were possible. It would either go on its own, or intervention within forty-eight hours will be needed, with drugs or a cardioversion. Either way it is uncomfortable and would need to be dealt with soon. I realised at this moment that this was actually the second time I had had atrial fibrillation. The first time was with a pacemaker box change.

'Gerry, it's been a few hours. I think it may be worth letting St Bart's know what's going on?' Sam said tentatively, knowing I didn't want any fuss and that I just wanted to hibernate and for it to go back to normal. 'I can go home and grab the pacemaker reader, so we can send a transition to them, maybe it is your pacemaker malfunctioning, they may be able to reset it from here or at least just send a reading to them, so they can see.'

I very reluctantly agreed to him getting the machine, even though the storm was worse than before and I wanted to stick my head in the sand, so he left to get it and came back incredibly quickly. While away, he also added to a small go-bag we had made in case something happened, with a few more pieces of clothing. When he returned, we tried to do the reading but struggled to get any signal – it was a very remote beach area and the storm was still raging; we climbed to the top floor and stuck the machine as high as it would go while still being plugged in at the wall, and thought we had just about got a strong enough signal.

We emailed St Bart's, having not been able to get hold of them as it was so late in the day in UK. I was tired as it had been a long workday, so we both decided to rest and check our phones for messages in the morning. As an individual which can sleep through anything, I slept even with a very elevated heart rhythm; poor Sam on the other hand struggled, constantly checking on me, thinking perhaps I was downplaying how worried I was.

We woke early, remained calm and stayed at the hotel till we heard from St Bart's over email; they said they had not received (no doubt due to the storm) the pacemaker transition but to get to a hospital and send the image of my ECG results as soon as possible. We went to the same small village clinic as before. The idea of this was better the devil you know, rather than reexplaining everything to a new and possibly less equipped clinic. We drove down the familiar dirt track and once again they attached the octopus suckers onto me; it literally sucked! We knew they couldn't really help and the worry of how far we were from St Bart's, who could, was at the forefront of our minds.

I noticed this time, due to not being distracted by pain, the ECG results were printed on a slip of receipt-roll paper, which was the same printing paper my hospitals had used when I was younger. This made me think how far technology had come, but also provided a another mini knock to my confidence in the hospital, and made me reflect on how much I didn't want to go to Phnom Penh again. We took pictures of the results and emailed them over to St Bart's.

We received a surpisingly speedy email reply: 'Hi Geraldine, I have spoken with our doctors who report that you are in atrial flutter … she has advised that you should have a cardioversion within forty-eight hours of the onset of symptoms … are you able to get to Bangkok to see a cardiologist in this time frame?'

From the moment we received this email, we wanted to get out of the country. We had expatriate (evacuation) insurance. Due to our last hospital experience in the capital, we firmly wanted to go to Singapore or Bangkok to get any medical treatment there, rather than in Phnom Penh. We began looking into flights to go elsewhere for medical treatment, and even asked my dad to look into this for us to save time. We quickly asked my insurers for help in facilitating this. The insurers were not in agreement with St Bart's and said they wanted more information from local cardiologist before agreeing to anything.

In the meantime, we chatted with the owners of our hotel, who had kindly appeared at the hospital having been told by a member of our reception team where we had gone. They very generously were trying to organise a helicopter to take us to the capital to the larger hospital once again. Sam and I felt the ambulance was a terrifying experience and was sure a helicopter would be just as, if not more so, so opted for a taxi, which was booked in and met us at the hospital. We took the go-bag, knowing where we were in Sihanoukville we couldn't do anything and we therefore needed to get out. Our aim was to get to Singapore or Bangkok, but we didn't have authorisation from our insurers to do this, and they didn't appear to be in any hurry. We booked a room at the hotel we'd stayed in after the first scary experience, as we knew it was comfortable and near to the airport, and headed there. Our best-case scenario was to go straight to the airport, but if we couldn't do that, we'd go to the hotel and wait, still close enough to the hospital in case things got worse and we needed to – at least they were better then Sihanoukville.

As we neared the capital, over thirty hours had passed since my heart had begun this very inconvenient behaviour. We knew we were running out of time, so there was no point staying in the hotel, and our insurers were pushing for another ECG to assess the situation, so we made our way to the hospital in Phnom Penh. We arrived at the capital at 1.15 a.m. on 1 June, and I had another ECG, but still my bpm was 140. The time was ticking. The cardiologist was happy to send me to Singapore to have a cardioversion, but my travel healthcare provider would not let me fly. They believed it was not safe for me, they said I had to have a cardioversion at the hospital where I was in Cambodia and only then I could fly to Singapore to get everything checked and receive any further treatment if needed. Sam and I made it very clear to my insurers that we were concerned at the level of medical care we would receive and that we did not feel particularly safe or certain that the hospital would not know whether they have done it correctly. We had multiple phone calls with doctors and admin staff in different departments and countries within the organisation, begging them to reconsider, but none did. They said we could go to a different hospital, but we had to stay in Cambodia. There were very few to choose from! People of power in Cambodia never trust the

Cambodian healthcare and always go abroad. If I had known this at the time, I would have been more persistent to get out of the country.

We arrived at another new hospital, a swish-looking building which wore aviator sunglasses reflective windows and whitewashed walls. I was then taken to ICU. The cardiologist, who was Thai, offered to give medicine to treat the arterial flutter (Amadrione) or to have a cardioversion and beta blockers. Sam called the healthcare provider, in a final attempt to change their mind, and they said, 'I am not a cardiologist but in my opinion it is important to have the cardioversion as soon as possible and it is safe.'

Sam answered, 'Are you sure it is safe bearing in mind Gerry has a complex medical history and she has a pacemaker?'

'What! No one told me she had a pacemaker!' There was silence on the phone, an exhale and then, after what felt like a long time to Sam, 'I am not a cardiologist but it would be prudent to move forward with the cardioversion.'

The idea of time running out was a constant stressful reminder. Your heartbeat is a little too comparable to a clock ticking at that moment in time! Everything suddenly felt like a rush, we didn't now have time to fly elsewhere and we felt completely marooned by our insurer. Our fear of time running out was too strong and my energy levels were dwindling, so I agreed to begin the preparation to have a cardioversion. We asked the doctor who was lined up to perform it if he had done one before, and he said, 'many times before' – again giving us a little growing confidence. The doctor asked Sam to wait in the waiting room till after the procedure. They put sticky pads, the size of a man's hand, on my front and back to the side. Looking back, my inability to ask enough or any questions at each point of this process is extraordinary to me.

There was the doctor and a nurse in the room, I was lying in bed not fully aware what was about to happen. For a cardioversion, patients need some type of sedation to prevent mental trauma and potential PTSD. I had none.

The pain was unspeakable, paralysing and brought fear into every cell of my body. It was the most terrifying moment in my life. The only upside was that the cardioversion did work first time and my heart rate went back to normal.

I remained in ICU, being monitored, for the reminder of the day. I was prescribed a beta blocker: 2.5 mg of Concor (bisoprolol) to be taken each morning for two weeks after breakfast. A salesman (not doctor, not a medical practitioner, not technician ... one more time ... a salesman!) for the pacemaker in the country I had, came to take readings for over two hours. Sam and I were stunned at the madness and ridiculousness of it all. They printed off hundreds of reports. Sending the information back to their head office in Singapore to check the settings were as they should be.

I moved out of ICU into a ward for observation for my recovery. I had pain and discomfort in my chest which the doctor said was linked to the burns of the cardioversion. My heart rate was continuing to drop further so the cardiologist advised it would be better to take me off the beta blocker and suggested I do some light exercise to check my heart rate.

Four days later, on 5 June, the cardiologist was happy for me to be discharged and referred me to the National University Heart Hospital in Singapore to see Dr Pipin Kojodjojo for follow-up, to plan for the future and to check the pacemaker again. My insurer was very slow to agree for me to be discharged and to agree to pay for the past two days of care. Their subsidiary in Denmark also took a similar time – from 7 a.m. to 5 p.m. to organise and authorise the flights to be booked to go to Singapore. I liaised with the National University Hospital to organise an appointment with Dr Pipin, but as my insurer took so long to respond we could not fly to meet him that day (which was his normal clinic day) and had to arrange to meet him outside of his working time – 9 a.m. on 8 June.

Dr Pipin was completely charming; he had done his medical studies in the UK so we had lots to talk about, having spent time in some of the same haunts. If I was ever to have heart problems again in Asia I would want to go straight to him. He was unbelievably kind in a moment of real worry; he understood the stress and real fear.

I felt supported by St Bart's and Dr Pipin, but completely let down by my insurers. At a time of fright – a real exception to your everyday life – you expect better and you expect more.

Tip

Never feel silly for kicking up a fuss if something really is wrong like an elevated heart rate and always ask questions.

I hope I never again have to have a cardioversion without sedation. It is important to note that I would not change my time in Cambodia, but if I were to do it all again, I would be more organised, have my hospital notes really easily to hand, a brief A4 piece of paper with the main notes of contacts and health (pacemaker) settings and know where to go if anything were to happen – wherever I happened to be. I'd also look up the drugs I am offered, when offered and any procedures, as I could have highlighted at the time – if I had researched cardioversions – that I needed sedation of some kind.

I don't think Sam and I will ever truly recover from what happened that day, how at the final moment of the cardioversion I unleashed a spine-chilling scream and then shouted, 'I was awake, I was awake' and 'I felt everything, I felt everything' for minutes afterwards, and how Sam ran in, having heard my scream down the corridor in the waiting area. I like to joke that my hair was a little frizzier after being electrocuted and to say to Sam that 'it was the shock of it', but there was nothing funny about any of it at the time and we were both truly terrified.

Moments of absolute wussy-ness!

There was one occasion where my family were all shocked at what an absolute wuss I had been. We were at Sea World in Florida, all swimsuited up, I was about ten years old and ready to jump into a tank. The day had consisted of us screaming down log flumes and kicking away in inflatable doughnuts, but this ride was a little different. We put on face masks and snorkels and had been told we had to swim slowly to the other side of the tank without splashing or using our arms or legs. We had queued for our turn and now we were all getting into the water quietly. Before getting in, I turned and asked Dad, 'What's in the water?'

Arranging his snorkel and mask on his face, Dad calmly said 'sharks'.

'Sharks!'

'Yes, Gerry. Sharks.'

'Oh!' I hadn't realised I had signed up for a near-death experience. I also couldn't work out how to swim to the other side without moving my arms or legs. Sheepishly I decided to sit this one out, but I wasn't quite sure why my family had decided to put themselves in harm's way in no less than shark-infested waters while not being allowed to move! I watched my family one by one make the gentlest movements to get to the other side and then go around again; they loved it! They shouted, 'They are only little, Gerry!' I was a gullible kid at the best of times, but I wasn't going to fall for that!

Another very wussy moment of mine was when I was about seven, and Nessie was reading me a book. It was a stunning book about all the different sharks in the world and their characteristics. She is such a good storyteller, and my imagination runs so wild that I honestly felt I was in the water with her and them. I got so freaked out by how they hunt and the types of bites they give that I got very upset. I started crying and ran to Mum and Dad. Ness got in real trouble – I felt very guilty afterwards.

There is clearly a theme of being afraid of sharks – they bring out the wuss in me. I would like to publicly apologise to Nessie for crying to Mum and Dad and getting you into trouble – I'm so sorry Nessie, you are just so good at telling stories; they come alive!

'I learned that courage was not the absence of fear, but the triumph over it. The brave man is not he who does not feel afraid, but he who conquers that fear.'
Nelson Mandela

Getting on with it.

The *Oxford English Dictionary* defines 'brave' as 'Of persons and their attributes: Courageous, daring, intrepid, stout-hearted'. And 'bravery' as 'Daring, courage, valour, fortitude'. When I was little, I had friends, family, nurses and doctors say, 'Oh, Gerry you're so brave'. When they said this, I always felt like a fraud. When I think of me, my character, or my past, bravery doesn't pop into my head – ever!

Even at three years old I could understand: I wasn't 'brave'. I knew that wasn't me. Growing up, in no particular order, I felt people who are brave were people like: firefighters, Mulan from the Disney movie, the wives of Henry VIII, Jewish families during World War Two, Martin Luther King, Mother Teresa, military personnel, the police, doctors and nurses – and these are just a few examples. But I knew *I* was definitely not brave. I was just trying to live. The bravest I ever felt was holding a tarantula called Charlie at my seventh birthday party. I hate spiders, big or small, so it was a big deal!

It wasn't as if I could just walk out of the hospital, take the Yellow Brick Road to Oz and opt not to have any operations. It was what it was: I had one choice, so I had to pull up my socks and do it. I often speak about just 'getting on with it' and often to me it felt like that. I had to stop fannying around and just get on with my life.

I knew if I felt like a victim and acted like a victim, I would always *be* a victim. So I didn't let myself be a victim! I tried to be more. To be better than that. I knew if I sat on my bum all day every day with a tiny air violin playing sad music in my head nothing would change and this would be the rest of my life. A wasted existence. I knew the only thing you can control in life is your mindset, and I knew I always wanted to focus on positives not negatives. 'Today was a great day because ...' rather than 'I didn't achieve X, Y and Z'. If today wasn't good, I would try to do better tomorrow.

The natural human responses to an event perceived as stressful or frightening are fight, flight or freeze. The neanderthal in you sees the danger, even if you can't. For me there was only one option: to fight.

The funny thing is, I never thought I was different until I was about eight; I believed that all kids went through this to become a grown-up. It was just a super painful step in life you just had to go through, like a maths lesson or colouring with very dry felt-tip pens. Therefore, if I wanted to get to the next stage of life, 'adulthood', I had to go through it. Like levels in a PlayStation game, do or die?

As bad as maths lessons or operations were, I knew I didn't want to die. I liked my family and friends too much and I hadn't completed the level I was on in *Tomb Raider*.

Although your parents are very important to you when you are a child, at times you are braver or hardier alone than with them. For example, at GOSH on occasion they would ask Mum and Dad to wait outside while I had a small procedure or blood test, as they knew children were likely to kick up slightly more of a fuss with their parents there. I call it being a bit 'waah-waah'.

I have never felt immune to fear, and sometimes I know fear all too well. So, while growing up I used to be bold. Sometimes too bold. I found courage allows you to accept the presence of fear and move forward to face whatever challenge, although nothing is that easy! What also helped was that I had a complete, unfailing belief that I would go home after the operation and all would be well. It never crossed my mind that I wouldn't.

Pema Chödrön a very interesting American female Tibetan-Buddhist said, 'Usually we think that brave people have no fear. The truth is that they are intimate with fear.' Now that I can relate to.

I have recently found a real affinity for Brené Brown, PhD, MSW, a research professor at the University of Houston. She speaks about bravery within your life and owning your story: the feeling that if you don't put yourself out there, then you are a fool! I don't like being vulnerable; no one does. If you have not seen any of her work, it is worth watching her TED Talks. She really is a very human, honest, storyteller.

I think because I always felt love and I never felt alone or abandoned or not cared for, even at the worst of times I was happy and kept going. If anyone is brave it is my family for going through this. That might sound a bit topsy-turvy, but to me, to watch is in many ways worse than to experience. Mum has spoken to me about coming in to see me as a baby in hospital when I was recuperating from my first operation and in the room I was in she found a dead baby. This is terrible and harrowing. A nurse quickly ran in and said, 'that's not your baby', but you never forget that experience of thinking that was your child; Mum described the infant as 'like a doll made in wax'.

A long time ago the *Sunday Times* included an insert called the *Funday Times*. This was a kids' newspaper. We loved it. It was full of silly cartoons and fun things to do. One week there was a competition that asked, 'Who is your hero and why?' I wrote in, all guns blazing, saying how I felt my hero was my mum and I described why. She is and was totally amazing and yes, she is my hero. I am proud to say I won the competition, which was a CD player, a copy of the *Hercules* soundtrack and a lot of telephone cards. All of which were such fantastic prizes to win at the time. This prize really shows my age; it was the decade before everyone had mobile phones. My whole family are heroes in my eyes. They are so strong and have been through so much together and individually. Just to be clear, Dad is just as fantastic – but I could only choose one of them for the competition.

As a family we went to church most Sundays. This again reinforced the idea of never being alone: I could pray or chat away to the spirit in the sky, so even when I was in hospital, away from my parents and family, I was never really alone. I wear a St Christopher, and/or a St Marie. They were given to me by my Belgian granny, so I wear them out of love for my family rather than religious devotion. And it never hurts to hedge one's bets, so I wear both. When I wear them I feel like I have 'powered up' on a video game to more than full health, or I have eaten ten of my five a day for seven years and am reaping the benefits instantly! I may not be the most religious person, but religion has felt like a friend or a hand to hold in dark times.

J. R. R. Tolkien wrote, 'Courage is found in unlikely places.' I didn't feel I had courage or bravery at any point, but my desire to be home overtook any primal need and I knew I had to survive to go home, to be home at least one more time.

Whatever procedure I had, however big or small, I always just wanted to go HOME – that was the goal! When I got older and started seeing friends, I'd want to be well enough to go to a party, but my primary motivation was always the thought of home.

So, when people talk about bravery, I find it very difficult to relate to. When there was and is no choice or other options it becomes sink or swim. Now I realise that 'home' is not the place, it is the people. The thing that really kept me going was love, just love.

'Tied together in hardship and kept together by love'
Christine Duts, *A Right to Live*

Chapter 8
Starlight Children's Charity

Mum, Sammy and I were all in the lift together in London. I was nine at the time, and we didn't know what to expect: we were all excited and nervous. It was very rare to come up to London for anything other than a doctor's appointment, so this was a real treat. The building seemed to go on up for ever; the anticipation was too much! We got to the top. The lift doors opened and then the smiliest of faces and happy people greeted us. We stepped out. We were welcomed and handed white fluffy bunny ears, tails and bow ties. Which was most amusing. We put them straight on with no hesitation. Dick and Dom (yes, Dick and Dom – then known as Richard McCourt and Dominic Wood) bounded up to us to say 'hello and welcome'. They were no Ant and Dec but this day was just getting better and better. We had a little chat with them, had a picture taken and then they welcomed the next small group in.

I noticed lots of little bubbles of families looking as happy and excited as we did. We were advised to get a drink and have a little explore, so we did. The party was Alice in Wonderland themed with characters from the book dotted around. There was a terrace which was like nothing I had ever seen before, filled with flamingos, tropical birds and plants. It felt like a rainforest with a small river flowing through it. All this on a roof-garden in the centre of London. It felt like we had walked into another world. It was beautiful.

Some people may think that being in that room meant I was an unlucky person but, in that moment, I felt like the *luckiest* person! I always feel lucky! We had been invited by Starlight to their party to celebrate the kids they had helped. There was a mini ceremony where the kids went on stage and shook Dick and Dom's hands. I looked around at the other kids who were there and wondered, what is your story?

What is Starlight?

While ill in GOSH, I had been nominated for a Starlight 'Wish', and the event with Dick and Dom was a party for children who had been granted wishes. I believe I was nominated by one of the nurses who worked on my ward at the time. Disappointingly, I was so in and out of pain medication and consciousness I am not sure who it even was. I'd love to find them to thank them and tell them what a positive impact it had on me and my life to have been chosen!

Starlight is a children's charity founded in 1986 by Emma Samms and Peter Samuelson. It 'brightens the lives of seriously ill children'. From Boost Boxes and Distraction Boxes in hospital to

Starlight escapes, which are amazing days out for kids, they grant wishes and so much more. Starlight is amazing, and in 2019/20 they reached 1.5 million children in the UK. I feel helping that many people in a pandemic is incredible. They are lovely people, full of hope and happiness.

Starlight asked me to think of three wishes and they would grant me one. Mine were:

1. Have my room designed by Carol Smillie in an African theme
2. A laptop
3. Go to Disneyland

Starlight agreed to the room makeover!

Why Carol? Well, while recuperating I watched a lot of the BBC's *Changing Rooms*. Sadly, Carol Smillie was busy at the time and so was unable to help. She wrote a note to me, and to be honest at the time I was as happy as a monkey let loose in a banana farm that she'd even acknowledged me! I think I even brought it to school to show everyone. I still think she's great and that TV is a sadder place without her. Please come back, Carol!

I ended up having a lovely local interior designer and family friend design and fit out my room in a safari theme, and my goodness, she did a great job! My obsession with Africa, safari and African elephants continues to this day. My room ended up being plastered on all four walls with timeless (some would say) beige elephant wallpaper. I also had a beautiful rattan chest for a bedside table and a bamboo lamp – I could not have been happier.

Whether it be a tiny sculpture, a trinket box or art, I now have an elephant in every room of our own house. I don't think my husband knows – he does now!

The fantastic thing about Starlight is that they provide experiences for the whole family to enjoy. They allow families to create a lasting story to tell and memory to reflect on a really happy time during terrible moments. They bring so much joy to families' lives in so many ways and I know within my family, we have spoken so much about that day out, the flamingos, Dick and Dom and much more for years – and will do for years to come. Having my room decorated turned it into an amazing space to recuperate after every operation, big or small. It was a sanctuary for me, and one of my requests was that it was not a childish room and that I could grow with it; and I did.

My condition made me need to rest more than my friends. Whether that meant sleeping, doing a calm activity like drawing, writing or watching TV. This made me far more aware of being comfortable, my five senses (especially touch, due to pain) and the environment I was in at any given time.

What Starlight couldn't have known is that in granting me this wish, they undoubtedly changed the course of my future career. I became an interior designer. When I was younger, I saw first-hand what a profound impact a beautifully decorated, tranquil space could have on recuperation and your life, and I wanted to share that gift with others.

Chapter 9
Frustrations and Limitations

'You will fail at some point in your life. Accept it. You will lose. You will embarrass yourself. You will suck at something. There is no doubt about it. ... Never be discouraged. Never hold back. Give everything you've got. And when you fall throughout life ... fall forward.'
Denzel Washington

What a pin-up! I fail often. Especially at not getting frustrated by my body's limitations. I get annoyed about not having as much energy and go-go-go all day and every day as my friends and sisters. I am the tortoise not the hare: slowly, slowly wins the race. I'll get there, just at my own speed. Sam has noted that I have more energy than others however I live at 200 per cent energy when I have it but can't sustain it. Where others use less for longer.

My main goal in life growing up was to be like everyone else. I didn't want any fuss and I didn't want any special treatment. From the outside I looked pretty much like everyone else, but I definitely had more limitations. Even small things made me feel different, like my lips turning purple and my nails blue when I swam due to the cold or staying in water too long. I only realised recently that my condition gives me slightly swollen ankles due to poor circulation. I always wanted fantastically slinky ankles, but alas, they are not for me. I love to dance, and I love parties, but I am not the person you call if you have party balloons to blow up. Blowing up balloons was so hard for me, I'd almost black out at times when I was not 100 per cent. I found it so frustrating when I was unwell or tired and had to cancel things at the last minute or miss parties.

I had the opposite experience when my prep school organised a trip to Legoland. What a treat. We were all thrilled. The one thing I hadn't realised was that if I was to go with the school, I would have to be pushed around the park in a wheelchair. This was not OK. I agreed to come as I did not want to miss out, and for the whole year to be talking about it until the end of time and not be able to join in, but I was anxious about being confined to the chair. The whole day was fabulous; we all went on rides and had the most wonderful time. At the back of my mind, I did not like that I was not like everyone else on that day, but at least I was with everyone. My schoolfriends sweetly took it in turns to push me. I felt this was a way to show their friendship and that they accepted the wheelchair.

At our leavers' ball, the headmaster, a seriously kind man with a giant moustache compared to the size of the rest of him (it's funny what you remember as a kid) gave a speech. He mentioned me and all the hardship and adversities I had experienced in that final year and how I had come out of it all. He was incredibly flattering about me, but I was so embarrassed to get a special mention, I went red in the face. Gem and I stood watching and listening like everyone else, but she put out her hand to hold mine tight, knowing it was what I needed.

'If you are always trying to be normal you will never know how amazing you can be.'
Maya Angelou

I was so desperate to be like everyone else. A few years later the family all went to Disney World where my family asked me if I wanted to have a wheelchair. I hadn't enjoyed being in a wheelchair at Legoland, so I refused to use one at Disney World. This was a pity. I have subsequently found out the family would not have needed to queue for the rides if I had been in a wheelchair. Dear family, I am really sorry for my stubbornness and the hours we spent queuing.

Tip

Remember always to read the signs at funfairs and theme parks – sometimes cardiac patients should not go on certain rides. Definitely adhere to these signs, even if your peers are pressuring you to get on the ride, as you would hate to regret it halfway through!

The challenging thing for all the family was that even though I was home and 'well', other things would affect me, such as fatigue and sickness due to my low white blood cell count.

I asked my parents if they treated me differently from my sisters in any way, and they said no, for the most part, except that Mum would always make sure I had a coat on in winter because I used to catch every cold it (and sometimes summer) had to offer. It's still true: I pick up everything and I am out of action for at least a week if I do nothing but rest and a fortnight or more if not. I have had pneumonia twice, which has scarred my lungs badly. Subsequently, colds are even harder to shrug off.

When I was younger, I always felt like I was off school with a cold or waiting in a GP's office for antibiotics to help get over a cold. I also know, I am a bit of a hygiene nut these days in my efforts to try not to get colds.

Immunity Tip

I love watching Agatha Christie's Poirot with my dad. In one episode, Poirot says, 'Prevention is always better than a cure.' He was talking about murder, but it applies to your health and immunity too! Whenever I think I am getting a cold or worse, I take echinacea, a herbal remedy which helps fights early signs of colds. I don't take too many or for too long, as some pill coatings have been known to cause heart palpitations. But you would really need to take a lot for this to happen. I now also take multivitamins daily. Remember to speak to a doctor before starting any medication, even if it's herbal.

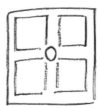

When we were travelling, my family would always have the details and telephone number of a doctor or my hospital. We also had a list of potential hospital support in the area or country we would be visiting, in case anything went wrong. Which is much easier now that we have all our numbers on our phones and the internet.

After my big operation at twelve I returned to school quite quickly. I loved my prep school; I loved the people, the building, the school food, the sugary, milky tea and Garibaldi biscuits we used to call squashed-fly biscuits at 11 o'clock, the boiler suits we played in, the forest for a playground: everything. So I was desperate to return, but the only problem was that I got tired very easily. So Mum and Dad thought it best I should do no sports classes and take half a day off on Wednesdays. In this time, I would go to extra maths in a nearby village for an hour and then Mum had tennis at her friend's house so I would snuggle up on her friend's sofa and watch *Murder, She Wrote* and then *Diagnosis: Murder* while doing homework or even having a snooze. This worked well as it was a great compromise: I was back at school with my friends, but I also had time to rest.

I could not always keep up; I remember on one occasion, when I was about eight, Dad suggested an autumnal walk after lunch. As kids we all resisted, wanting to stay in the cosy indoors. Mum and Dad were saying, 'It's good for you, let's get ready and go.' So, we drove to a lovely spot, jumped out with our wellies on and set off. The ground was difficult to walk on as it had been raining for weeks before. It felt like a foot of mud was holding our feet in position. It was very tiring. Wanting to keep up, I kept walking, but the heavy, sucking mud felt more like sinking sand and every step was a battle. Finally, I stopped to catch my breath as my family moved ahead of me slowly. I couldn't move any more, and I suddenly didn't feel well. I vomited so heavily that my lunch of boiled egg mayo sandwiches graced us with its presence once again. I refused to move, mainly due to being stuck in the mud and now vomit. Dad came racing over, gathering all the family on his way. They checked I was OK and he went back to the car, drove it up the muddy path and we all jumped in and went home. This was a moment where we were all reminded that I was not like the rest of them; I couldn't always keep up. There were few moments like this. I haven't eaten an egg mayo sandwich since.

I asked Mum and Dad if they ever needed to limit what we did as a family due to me and normally they didn't; they knew what I could handle, and never really overthought it. Sometimes Dad would go skiing with my sisters (I'm sounding pretty middle-class right now!) and Mum and I would do something else instead as I couldn't cope with altitude that well. It never bothered me, and it didn't bother Mum as she broke her thumb skiing once, and she was so frustrated she swore she would never ski again.

Our holidays tended to be local affairs, often Brittany in the north of France or in England, both for financial reasons and in case I became unwell. There was sometimes an emotional air of wondering, 'Will this be our last holiday as a family?' A lot of photos were always taken, as well as videos on enormous video recording devices; Dad enthusiastically embraced new camera technology.

I was quite a still and unenergetic child; I didn't know anything else. I loved making things for my doll's houses, plasticine cakes, arts and crafts and board games. I'm sure if all my buddies were playing extreme tag that I'd have felt gutted not to be more like them, but my friends and I enjoyed making dens or calm roller blading.

There is a running joke in the family that I am like a professional sleeper, I could just pass out anywhere, at any time. This in turn made me a little chubby, and to this day not much has changed. My sisters reminded me recently that I loved to lean on people. It was a sign of affection.

Due to not having the best immunity I would also get the heebie-jeebies easily. For example I don't like sharing lip balms, which got me into trouble on occasion in the girl world I was in at school.

Something I didn't like as a child was the touch of a rough towel. I think it's because I was sore in places, so to be scratched dry rather than dried softly was an added discomfort. I didn't know anything different, but the discomfort was always short-lived, and life went on. The towels didn't get replaced till I was much older and I didn't care enough to make a fuss; the family had bigger things on their minds and so did I. But to this day I really don't like touching dry towels with dry hands.

My immunology is damaged due to chronic disease, and this has made me more vulnerable than others. Having heart problems also affects other parts of my body and life. For example, I have needed special antibiotics before a dentist appointment due to the risk of bleeding and infection. I also have, in my opinion, a rather rounder rib cage than most due to being opened, closed and healing so many times, and that's OK!

I live in the moment as much as I can, I was always confident by nature, but I also have a nervous disposition. I used to bite my nails badly and occasionally got anxious about new experiences, like all kids. I have few bad memories, but certain tastes and smells catch me off guard and take me back to a hospital bed.

I got very good at forgetting memories of being in hospital. Although perhaps I got so good at deleting memories that I am now so forgetful I can't remember what I had for lunch. I know I don't want to relive all my hospital memories, but they do not haunt me. Memories of embarrassing moments growing up haunt me far more!

In 2019 I went to see the Spice Girls live at the O2 in London. I was with my friends from uni, Becky, Holly and Julia. We were having a great time dancing in the seated area we were in, but then they stared singing Viva Forever I just started crying. I'm not a crier; my friends were so confused. They were happy tears but it was still so embarrassing. It made me remember listening to them in hospital, where I had one cassette (yes, Zoomers, *cassette*) of the album *Spice*, which I played on repeat (rather intricate to do with a cassette). I never got to the end; I would always fall asleep halfway through. A second memory, which shocked me, coming out of nowhere, was when I was watching *Five Days at Memorial* (a harrowing drama about a New Orleans hospital during Hurricane Katrina). There was one scene where a lady who was dying was being given water on her lip with a small pink sponge on a stick as she was too frail to drink properly. I instantly recalled exactly what that sensation was like – and even the taste of the sponge.

Operations affect you in so many ways: not just through memories and emotions but also physiologically. When Sam and I came back from Cambodia and I again needed a cardioversion (this time I had an anaesthetic first). When I was recovering, I noticed that I was slower and more tired than normal. I found myself in a parking lot needing to do grocery shopping. I was surrounded by a sea of disabled parking spaces. I was discouraged to find that the only non-disabled parking was miles away. I struggled to the shop and then I struggled around the shop and back to the car with my heavy bags. I decided that I would apply for a blue disabled badge as I ended up completely exhausted having to walk so far to pick up some food in an already more fragile than normal body. I was denied the badge, as apparently, I could walk too far to be permitted and too capable for one. I never argued the point as I was back to my normal self soon afterwards. I did slightly wish there was a temporary blue badge you could have in times like these.

Nightmares

Infrequently I would have a nightmare, but it was always the same one. I would be in a big dark hall; I couldn't see the edges of the room, but I could see unclear figures dancing. Faceless men and women, all similar just in different coloured dresses and suits. The dancing would start slowly, the people gliding gracefully, their dresses moving with every twirl and then they would all get faster and faster until I had to look away as it was too much to look at. I normally slept well. I believe it was about the idea of losing control or not keeping up.

Guilt

'Guilt is to the spirit what pain is to the body.'
Elder David A. Bednar

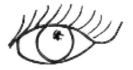

Another subject that came up while I was interviewing my parents was the guilt they felt that this had happened. Mum said she always questioned if she'd taken an aspirin for a headache when she shouldn't have or done something she wasn't supposed to while pregnant with me. I told them I felt immeasurably guilty too, for putting my family through this pain and anguish throughout their adult lives.

I sometimes felt that I could never complain about anything because I had survived something so big, I also felt like I could never be in a bad mood as it was unfair on the family who had looked after me so well and so carefully. I felt I could never be sad or unhappy as I had been so lucky in all that had happened. To be honest, I didn't feel particularly sad: I was like a puppy distracted by the next playful moment most of the time.

I felt like my family and friends felt like they couldn't complain in front of me about aches and pains or colds – which is so unhealthy! And I felt like I couldn't either, as I'd put my family through so much already. I would never cry wolf, I never wanted to be that person; I only kicked up a fuss when things were bad, when I was in pain. Dad said in his speech at my wedding, 'In all the years, Gerry has never complained' – so kind, but I think I probably did – I must have. I also wanted to be a fun character to hang out with, not the sickly kid, so I would push myself as much as possible – sometimes too much! Crying wolf sounds harsh but it is so important not to cry wolf so when something is wrong people know to take it and you seriously. Like in Cambodia: Sam knew straight away it was no joke.

Milking your illness to relax at home rather than go out into the world is easy, but I would advise against it: you risk becoming very insular and not appreciating what is out there. And no one wants to be known by their peers as the creepy pale indoor kid; a bit of vitamin D from the sun is always good. The more you stay inside, the harder it becomes to go out.

I also experience what I think is a form of survivor's guilt, but I hope I have brought more happiness into my family's lives than worry or pain.

My parents and I realised that if both parties felt perpetually guilty, we were not going to get anywhere in our lives and the best thing to do was put it to one side and live the best life possible without guilt. We have done our best, and we must now just live. Guilt is a waste of time and will anchor you to the spot, draining you rather than helping you live. We have to move forward and enjoy the ride.

But talking is critical. Again, I would advise anyone who has been through any sort of trauma to speak to a professional counsellor. I wish when I was younger there had been more resources to get in contact with like-bodied and -minded people. Not just so I could meet them, but also so that my sisters, mum and dad could have met their families, swapped war stories and not felt so alone. Not expressing myself clearly and feeling uncomfortable talking about my feelings has given me heart palpitations in the past, so it really is good and important to talk.

Feel free to start by saying hi to me! I'm not scary! If you have a heart condition, regardless of your age, gender, nationality, I would love to hear from you. ☺

I feel sad that I took so much of Mum and Dad's energy and time away from my sisters and the silly and fun life they expected with four little girls. They are making up for it now by being with my sisters and their children as much as possible. I wish I hadn't brought so much stress and worry into my family's life. I know I have unhealthy misplaced emotions towards this, and I am working on evolving beyond thinking I *imposed* a heart issue on my family, but it's not easy to change a self-inflicted ingrained mindset.

I often tell Sam that I am annoyed about X, Y and Z, and how I am limited by them, and he reminds me that most people are too! Growing up, the thing I found the hardest with having a heart problem was getting tired or getting ill more easily than others and the resulting knock-on effect of not giving my best to the people I love. That hurts me a lot as so many have done so much for me and I want to give back. I know I need to be kind and forgive myself – I'm not perfect, nobody is; we just have to do our best.

A while ago someone told me that hope is knowing all pain, and all discomfort is temporary. I have held onto this for a long time. The older I get, the more I realise that I must stop wasting energy on things I can't change or control. I wanted to be like everyone else, but I'm not. I get frustrated, but I know I must not. At the time, when I realised I wasn't like everyone else, there was a bit of anger and 'why me' feeling, but I have a temperament which is 'life isn't fair, sh*t happens, get over it, move on'. So, I did.

'Laughs are exactly as honourable as tears. Laughter and tears are both responses to frustration and exhaustion, to the futility of thinking and striving anymore. I myself prefer to laugh, since there is less cleaning up to do afterward.'
Kurt Vonnegut

Chapter 10
Advice

'I always pass on good advice. It is the only thing to do with it. It is never of any use to oneself.'
Oscar Wilde, An Ideal Husband

You will all have your own experiences. Like pain, advice is subjective. These are the things that my family and I learned along the way. What we wish we had known and done for both ourselves and others.

When I was born, Mum and Dad's hearts were so broken and saddened by the whole thing they couldn't express to their closest friends and family what they needed or what they were going through. Our family knows we did not deal with me being ill and how to cope at the time very well. They didn't and couldn't talk about it at first; it hurt too much. We were all living a different sort of life, as if they were waiting to know what was going to happen. My parents felt very isolated, not being able to talk about anything or explain anything as none of us understood what was going on.

In my late teens, during my A levels, we were tested a second time on how we dealt with disaster when Mum was diagnosed with breast cancer. It was terrible. But we had all learned a lot about how *not* to do things, and this time we handled it differently. Mum insists this changed everything for the better for her and the family. She is a rock star, and she pulled through.

I think it is important to mention that in 1987, when I was born, hospitals' sole focus was making the child well, so there was very little other support or advice for our family on what best to do or how to deal with the situation. Whereas now hospitals have a much more rounded duty of care to the family.

The differences in managing

When I was ill in 1987	Mum getting ill in the nineties
Mum and Dad were in too much pain, couldn't talk about it at the time and found it hard afterwards. So, no friends or family knew what was going on and no one dared ask. Even if they were not alone, they felt alone.	Mum told everyone from the start. She didn't want it to be a topic of gossip; she wanted it to be fact, her own narrative and she wanted support from everyone from the start.
They didn't ask for help. So, few people helped as they didn't know they needed to or didn't know how to help or were too nervous to ask. Even close friends and family.	She asked for help straight away and her friends <u>all</u> rallied around, made a rota of when they would each take her for chemo and who would take us to school , they kindly made dinner and lunches for Mum and our family.

| We had few visitors, as no one knew and those who did were too anxious to ask or visit. Consequently: they felt very alone, and it was a terrible, unbearable time. Which created a vicious cycle of not talking about it, feeling alone and it being unbearable. | Her friends and family visited her lots … almost too much. Occasionally we had to ask chatterboxes to leave after an hour so as not to exhaust Mum. Consequently: Mum felt supported as did the family and while it was a terrible time, other people helped to make it bearable. |

'Being vulnerable means being honest about what you're going through in work and life, and communicating that to your team.'
Brené Brown, *PhD, MSW.*

If you have just had a baby, you are possibly not going to have lots of phone calls anyway, as people don't necessarily want to disturb the mum resting or the baby. But having experienced two very different ways of dealing with cripplingly painful moments in our family's lives, we now know being as open about things as possible and really spelling out want you need and would love from your friends and family members works a lot better than holding it in, even if it makes whatever it is suddenly real. Like a breath, you cannot hold it in for ever.

I have found it is always hard to live with illness, whether it's been me that is unwell or a family member. It is not fun and it frustrates you at every turn. Nonetheless, it has made me who I am today. I have also realised I find it even harder when the tables turn and a loved one becomes a patient. All our relationships are better suited to me being the patient.

My mum spoke to me about a friend of hers who had lost her son. She was always happy. Mum asked her, 'How are you always so happy, I would be one the floor crying?'

She said, 'There is a time to cry and a time to smile. If you cry, you cry alone. If you laugh the world laughs with you'.

I feel like my family have been tested time and time again, but we have just kept getting back up … it may not have been the same day, but we get up and keep going. If we did, you can too.

Families

Communicate, communicate, communicate – if you don't speak about it, nobody knows about it and no one can support you. Speak to your kids and explain what is going on in terms they can understand, so they know that their brother or sister is unwell and how they can help.

Don't be scared to ask for help. People like helping and feeling useful. It gives them purpose. Don't be afraid to be honest about what you need and want from your friends and family. If you have older children, why not create a rota to help you with the housework? Every little helps, as your emotional energy will affect your physical energy.

There are 101 things which can go wrong at any time. Sam says to me, 'Worrying is like a rocking chair; it will give you something to do but won't get you anywhere.' He got this quote from a film (*Van Wilder*), but he is right. Live your life and try not to get worried about all the things which may go wrong. Baz Luhrmann's song 'Everybody's Free (To Wear Sunscreen)' covers so many points in life. Almost every sentence has a goldmine of advice within. If you haven't heard it, you must!

You can't control everything; it's just not possible. Despite the pressures of my dad's new business, he came to all of my procedures and appointments. On the one occasion that he didn't as he had an immovable appointment, things went wrong for me.[32] It is so important as a parent not to kick yourself. There is only so much you can do, there are only so many places you can be. Things go wrong, that's life. Maybe he was or is my lucky charm. But ultimately, things would have gone wrong whether he was there or not.

Mum said she wished she had done more at the time, like signed me up to a golf club. I'm not quite sure why she thought I'd be a keen golfer, and I have told her I wouldn't have wanted that. Again, it is so important not to beat yourself up about the past or what could have been. You can only do what you can do, with the knowledge, experience you have and with the resources you have in front of you. My parents always sent me to tennis club in the summer holidays, and I got quite good, but my favourite part was the packed lunch and chatting to new acquaintances in the queue to hit the ball.

---

[32] If anything were to ever go wrong – of course it would be this occasion!

What also really didn't help the situation and put everyone slightly on edge is that I don't have great co-ordination, I'm clumsy and I'm accident prone. It's a terrible trait to have when you are on aspirin to thin your blood. I believe it is genetics not heart -related – don't worry! It began when I was young, when I would break eggs while baking cakes. Mum would kindly tell me: 'He who does nothing, breaks nothing' (*celui qui ne fait rien, ne casse rien*). Poor Dad, he had to eat an inordinate amount of pink fairy cakes in his time. The accidents then graduated to things like a second-degree burn on my leg from a fluke popcorn-making accident, falling off a stage in Italy and scraping my back badly, breaking a finger while chasing a sister and a lot more. As the sickly kid in the family, the anxiety level around the idea of 'Gerry getting hurt' was always a little heightened – in part because it happened so often, but also because after so many operations, everyone became sure that it was going to be a random accident that finished me off, especially when I was on blood thinners. You can only control so much in life, and the rest you have to just let happen.

Celui fait ne
qui rien casse
ne ♡ rien

Advice to parents

Hospital appointments

There are four things to keep in mind:

1) Leave well in advance: I remember when I was very little always rushing around on the Underground and arriving stressed and soaking with sweat to our appointment, then catching a chill as the sweat would get cold with the hospital air conditioning. Giving yourself plenty of time takes the stress out of rushing around. Also, hospitals are notorious for having too few parking spots.

2) Bring things to do: you may be waiting a while so take lots of things to keep your child busy, to read or play with. Not all hospitals are as well-equipped as GOSH.

3) Be ready to wait: There is always an emergency that which will go ahead of you (rightly so); meaning you will be waiting even longer. There will also be times you need to change appointments to get your preferred doctor. There will be times appointments will be hard to match with other tests. Be patient – all will be well in the end and hospitals do their best.

4) If you think you have been waiting a really long time, check you haven't been forgotten (I'm not joking!): I was once waiting for a routine check-up, but we had been there well past our allotted slot. It was towards the end of the day, so we thought we would just double check on progress as occasionally the reception

tells you how many people there are ahead of you – it is completely fine to ask them. We asked and were surprised to learn the doctor was nowhere to be found. After a little while he was discovered getting into his car to go home. We giggled, but it is always good to check. He came back and his rickety NHS computer, crammed full of information and notes, took for ever to restart and get to the right log-in page. He obviously hadn't read my notes, and everything was rushed and a bit mad.

Tip (Dad gave me this tip!)

For any long scans, if you are being offered music in the background. Make sure you know what album and musician is being offered to you. Poor dad had a terrible experience where he was offered three or four albums of a mix of musicians and genres. He chose Coldplay thinking he liked a few of their songs and that it would be nice to discover more … but it was one of the more depressing albums. So he was stuck in a scan for almost an hour, unable to move or tell them to change it. He said it was terrible! He rarely complains so it must have been really bad. Honestly, that would be the last thing you would want in a long scan, especially if you are already anxious!

Behaviour

Try to treat your kids all the same. Mum and Dad tell me they believed they treated us all the same. After speaking with my sisters, it was quite clear that this wasn't the way they saw it. I got away with murder and the brainboxes of the family were pushed to be the best they could be. I had nothing to prove and others had low expectations of me, as I had already accomplished my biggest achievement just by surviving. It is hard to hear, but honest. Mum and Dad tried their hardest and thought they were doing the right thing for each sprog and each sprog's character. Only time will tell if you got things right for your family.[33]

Try to make sure you spend little pods of time with each of your kids and even make that a thing, so they all have some one-on-one time, and they each feel special.

Men and women handle things differently. It is so important to speak to one another. You are a team, and a team has to look after all its members to work well. I looked up the top qualities of a successful team online[34] and this popped up:

    1) they communicate well with one another,

    2) they focus on goals and results,

    3) everyone contributes their fair share,

    4) they offer each other support,

    5) team members are diverse,

    6) good leadership,

    7) they're organised,

---

[33] Sam read this book and noted that the youngest always gets away with a lot more than the first kid, as the first always breaks down barriers. Sam and I are both the youngest for four!

[34] By Sophie Deering from theundercoverrecruiter.com

8) they have fun.

So, a few of these don't apply but you see what I am getting at – to work well together you must lean on each other, and communication is key.

Learn

I would hate to force anyone into anything they don't want to do, but I believe anyone considering partnership, companionship or marriage (or even those who are already married) should go on is a pre-marriage or marriage course. It makes you open up about areas you possibly wouldn't have done unprompted. It makes you think about you and your partner's hopes and dreams. It needn't be a religion-based course – there are plenty of beneficial courses run by therapists – but taking the time to really consider what your partnership means, in a structured way, can help make you a stronger family unit straight from the get-go, and can improve your communication.

Self-worth and self-care

As parents you are important and integral to your children; they look up to you for guidance. Mum spoke to me about how powerless she felt at times as she wasn't a doctor and didn't always know all the ins and outs of what was going on. There were other times where she was more able to take charge.

When I was four in GOSH, she was woken at 2 a.m. by a call to say that I needed a blood test. She got up from the hospital accommodation for parents and rushed to meet me at the hospital. I was crying and the nurse was getting crosser and crosser with me for her own inability to find a vein to take blood (she was struggling either due to my blood being very viscous from lack of oxygen or from damaged veins from a lot of blood tests). She tried a third time, and again failed, at which point Mum said that that was it: three tries was enough. I remember Mum being a very powerful person in my eyes while the nurse – still very annoyed – said 'that's fine'. It is important as parents to know your worth. You know your child better than anyone. Don't be annoying and get in the way of doctor and nurses – they are only trying to help – but know that you *can* intervene or comment, and it will often be helpful input. Try not to embarrass the clinician; sometimes things just don't work the way they are meant to and it's not their fault.

I also remember my parents stepping in when I was four years old. I had gradually started to have (more) problems with my circulation, which meant I wasn't draining fluids as I should be so I had a really swollen head. The doctors said not to worry as I could have drugs for the rest of my life for it. Mum said that wouldn't do. Professor Deanfield had to work out what needed to be done to fix the problem, which was to do with my arteries, and then had to persuade Professor de Laval that it was the solution and to try what he was suggesting. He did and it worked!

There was also another moment in hospital when I was having my first set of operations. I had just been given warfarin to thin my blood. Mum and Dad were watching over me very late at night after this procedure and Mum, like any good new mum, checked her baby's nappy to discover it was wet. I was sitting in a pool of blood. Mum and Dad obviously raised the alarm straight away and I was quickly looked after. Dad said if Mum hadn't have checked at that moment, then I would have died of blood loss. They said they suspected a nurse lost their job that day due to not checking regularly enough on me.[35]

Don't sweat the small things. Don't blame yourself if you prioritise time with your family over having a perfectly pristine home. Things always get in the way; just try and asses what you are more likely to have regrets over. Spending too much time with family or too much time cleaning?

Self-care as a parent is so important. You are not helpful to anyone in your family if you do not look after yourself. You must try to be well rested, eat well and healthily. You must find a way to do this. It is so important for you to try and have a 'normal life', so don't feel guilty if you want to dress up and go on a date night (or date moment). Try to find the time. You must nourish your relationship to be strong for your little ones.

I am trying to get better at positive self-talk; you have to ask yourself what your best friend would say to you in any moment of self-doubt. It's important not to beat yourself up over what you should have done better, move on and learn from the past and try and do better next time. I find mindfulness helps with this too, to stay in the moment and appreciate the small things.

---

[35] On a little side note: I find it a scary thought that there has been more than one occasion in my life when I could have died, in several different ways.

I must also mention if you, as parents of a child with CHD, are a good example of being active and eating right, this will trickle down to the children. If they see you having fun being active in different ways, experimenting with cooking (healthier dishes) again this all shows that being healthy is easy, fun and part of everyday life, rather than a hassle and a slog! Kids watch parents and take their cues from you, so show them the way.

Environment

Your child with CHD will do a lot of calm relaxing, so give your child a nice room to relax in; it doesn't need to be the best in the house, but they will need a space which is their own that they can retreat to when they want to, whether that's to fall asleep or to play. I shared with Sammy until I was about eleven and I loved it. So it doesn't have to be snazzy, just a nice space for them to recoup.

When I was in GOSH, at the age of nine, Mum and Dad asked if there was anything they could get me. I thought long and hard. This was not a question that was posed often, but I knew I could not ask for a pony: it was more a 'do you want a Refresher bar?' sort of a question. I always loved hospital food, but the food I loved the most was Italian. I tentatively asked if they thought I could get a carbonara from Cagney's on Cosmo Place, sadly now closed. We had eaten once before for lunch when visiting GOSH as an outpatient previously and the carbonara was memorable. Another fantastic perk of GOSH in my eyes was having the best carbonara in London just next door. Takeaway from restaurants was not very common back then, but they came back with a little box of carbonara – it was amazing. Small things to boost morale are always welcome but should not happen every day or then they are not treats – and a carbonara a day would bring a doctor to your door!

I always found our dog, Inky, provided wonderful therapy. She was the seventh member of the family and always in a good, playful mood. She was rather disobedient because we didn't have time to train her well as a puppy but we adored her. She was always doing something naughty like chasing pheasants for miles or eating a whole bag of horse nuts (which made her tummy swell up to the point where the vet wasn't sure she would survive the night). I would recommend having a pet, but only if you can look after them properly. Otherwise, they can add stress to an already difficult situation. Sadly, Inky is no longer with us, but she is always in my thoughts. She was a great companion, and I shared many sleepy afternoons with her in her basket.

Remember, don't be scared to ask for help and try to have a 'normal family life'.

Advice to kids (or adults) going through this

Mental health

Growing up, I never wanted my CHD to be 'the only thing' my family spoke or thought about. That would be horrendously self-centred and boring. Nor did I want it to be the elephant in the room that people whispered in the background about. By talking more you don't exactly normalise it but you bring understanding. I also remember this feeling of not wanting my CHD to be all-encompassing but at times it really was. As I have said before, I am not good at talking about my feelings and expressing myself most of the time, but the best way to get better is to speak to a professional. You have nothing to lose and everything to gain. Make your relationship and family unit healthy and open.

Stress can affect people in their body, mind and soul. In my twenties I used to get so stressed that I would get very dizzy and experience a type of vertigo. I would also get armpit pain, very tight muscles on my left-hand side and feel like I was on a boat. It was terrible and all-consuming, and it stopped me in my tracks. It was all because I was not processing stress well.

Positive thinking helps boost your cardiovascular health, increase your lifespan and reduce depression, and there is scientific proof that this is the case. It's too late for those of us with CHD to have less heart disease, but it could lessen possible future cardiac problems, lower blood pressure and lead to healthier blood-sugar levels. Even with incurable illness, positive feelings and thoughts can greatly improve our quality of life. It is worth trying.

Otherwise (not straight after an operation) find a quiet secluded field or hilltop and scream as loud as you can. This is called 'primal scream therapy'. Experts suggest having a skilled specialist there to guide you in this form of therapy, but I feel you can handle this without one!

Physical health – If you don't use it, you lose it!

SELF
LOVE
ROCKS

Your body is a temple! Don't forget it, and do not give yourself any more problems by not looking after yourself! I am not saying you have to go vegan, but you already know too much sugar, salt and fat is bad for you. Keep yourself moving, fit and well. I know it's easier to eat Maltesers and watch a box set on TV or play PlayStation all day than it is to move. But if you stay static, you will create more problems for yourself and your future. Find a hobby you enjoy. It doesn't have to be hugely active, but at least something to get you outside and/or moving. You only have one body and one mind, and only you can look after it, so try to do so wisely. I read an article on the British Heart Foundation's blog, where my childhood cardiologist Professor Deanfield wrote, 'You wouldn't start saving for retirement when you're sixty-four'. This is the same with your health. You must look after yourself early on to make later easier!

I have seen first-hand how putting on weight changed things for my health negatively and brought other problems. I believe that due to my BMI (body mass index) changing, things started going wrong: it was my body's way of saying I needed to change my lifestyle. Maintaining a safe BMI and eating fruit and veg really does help to keep your body healthy and happy. If you don't know what your BMI is or should be, have a look on the NHS website, it's all there for free!

With free YouTube, so many free apps out there and free parks or open spaces to walk in, I know I really have no excuse. Personally, I have a £60 fold-away static bike which Sam bought just before the pandemic with amazing foresight. I also pay £30 per year for a nutrition app, and that's it. You don't need a pricey gym membership, but gyms and exercise classes do give you more variation. I set myself a target of cycling: at least three times a week for an hour, and if I have the time or energy, I go for walks in between.

I knew I needed to lose weight, and I felt I couldn't do it alone. But I love all three: the bike, app and walks have really helped me. As for the app, it is not like 'being on a diet', it is eating what I like, when I like, but in moderation. It has made me understand more about portion size, what I am actually eating and the importance of exercise for your body and mind. I lost 12kg between May 2020 and Feb 2021, and I did it at my own pace.

According to Julia Stroll, the average person in the UK spent 158 minutes a day watching TV in 2022. When you think about how often you sit and watch TV at the end of a day. What if you did this on a static bike ride? Even for half an hour? I did this during lockdown, and it changed things dramatically.

You are the solution to your own problems. Or at least you could help some of them or mitigate others for the future. Crisps, cheese, and any type of canapé or aperitif are my kryptonite. I have a cheese and noodle addiction (not together), so if I don't move, I become a human blob! If I could, I would not have them in the house, but my husband needs cheese and crisps in the house to survive his days. I recognise these foods as too tempting for me, so I try to not have them under my nose. They are always higher than I can reach and I would need to make a real effort to get to them.

Over the last century our dinner plates have increased in size by 22 per cent. This is a lot! Science suggests that reducing the size of the dinner plates themselves will help us with our portion control and health.

Technology now more than ever can help us achieve our goals. There is so much out there to help us we need to make sure we help ourselves – whether it be a Fitbit, a smart watch or just an app on our phones. I love having the goal of 10,000 steps a day, and I use my phone, which is on me most of the time, to track this. However, when I asked my hospital what they thought of me getting a watch that could do ECGs and monitor the heart, they said it was probably not the best idea for me. The likelihood was that it would get worried something bad was happening and actually it is just my weird set up that isn't 'normal' to it. Then I would get worried and book in with the hospital, and they would say all was well and not to worry. So I haven't bought one! My step counter is quite enough.

Other fantastic things that will happen if you keep yourself fit, filled with fruit and veg, and healthy:

☐ You are less likely to need future cardiac intervention as you are putting less pressure on your body

☐ You are less likely to have other problems with your body, like joint pain, back pain or diabetes

☐ People are going to find you ludicrously good looking as you will be shining with confidence and with the joy of what you have achieved.

☐ Your skin will glow with all the vitamins and outside air and your sweating will eject bad toxins.

☐ You will sleep better, be in a good mood and have more energy

☐ You are going to live longer as your body will be fed on wonderful vitamin-rich nutrients which will be stored for

---

times you need the health benefits
- ☐ Your immune system will be stronger
- ☐ You are less likely to have dark thoughts and you will see more clearly
- ☐ You will be helping the NHS, the economy and even your country by eating well and staying active.[36] To me it's a no brainer!
- ☐ A thirty minute walk a day could lift your spirits, get your joints going and will be good for your heart – and fresh air in the lungs always feels good

It is always hard at the beginning of a new exercise regimen. You will be stiff in muscles you have never used before, you will ache sometimes for three days straight and you may not have the nicest sports outfits, but keep the goal in mind and remember that it will get easier. I remember doing a YouTube exercise class once and the next day I was so stiff I was trying to run for a train, completely missed it but succeeded in looking like I had a debilitating health problem in the way I ran. If you don't succeed today, don't beat yourself up – but make sure tomorrow happens. Don't make excuses indefinitely or bad things will catch up with you sooner than you think! I gave it a week or so and tried the class again; this time the next day was easier and I made sure not to book a dinner for the next day!

---

[36] The UK Government website states that 'the UK-wide NHS costs attributable to overweight and obesity are projected to reach £9.7 billion by 2050, with wider costs to society estimated to reach £49.9 billion per year.' Can you imagine if we could halve this or even try to eliminate it?

Oral Hygiene

Endocarditis – inflammation of your heart's inner lining – is no laughing matter. Brush your teeth twice a day, every day, for at least two minutes. This can help keep it at bay. The mouth is linked to the heart in so many ways. Get regular dental check-ups too!

If you have been told by your doctor to do so, don't forget to take the drugs they advise before seeing the dentist. This will help fight infection and we CHD patients need as much help as we can get in this department to stay fit as a fiddle.

I also find that when I have the flu, I see rapid or faster improvements if I brush really well, floss and rinse with mouth wash. I feel better and stronger day after day when I take good care of my mouth through an illness. I would really advise trying this. Again, you have nothing to lose and everything to gain – and with flossing sticks it really is very easy now.

Advice to siblings

Just be yourself and treat your brother or sister with heart problems like you would any other brother and sister. Include them in games and playing if you can. Try not to be too rough. They are a tiny bit more delicate than you, but don't treat them like they are made of glass either. Be there for your big or little brother or sister. Don't put pressure on yourself to be the best brother or sister out there, just like in *Black Beauty*: 'Do your best and leave the rest'. Possibly the best quote of all time!

Advice to friends and family

My mum and dad had no expectations from their friends or family; they were living in a small bubble of pain. However, they remember every ounce of kindness they were shown, big and small. Every accompanied hospital visit by their friends or family members. This works both ways: they also remember everyone who didn't, who were and still are so close to them. This is something they would never bring up, but it is something to be aware of. You are so integral to the lives around you, and at a time of emergency even more so. You are the difference in how they cope and how well they fare.

You can make a huge difference in someone's life. Why would you not want to? Friendship lasts a lifetime for many of us, so how do you want to be remembered? As someone who went above and beyond and could be really counted on, or someone who stood on the sidelines watching their friends' home burn down? It is an extreme analogy, but a truthful one!

'A best friend is the only one that walks into your life when the world has walked out.'
Shannon I. Alder

Don't stop talking to your friends because they have an ill child! They need to chat, they need normality. They need distractions; save up your stories for hospital visits so you have lots to say to distract your friend. If you have no stories to tell, read up on the lighter side of the news and talk about that. Text them silly memes or gifs. They need to hear the latest celebrity gossip; it doesn't matter what you tell them – they just need to forget where they are for a moment.

Think of ways of helping your friends which you can do easily and will not put a strain on your own family or relationships. This needn't be huge acts, time-consuming or major sacrifices; small kindnesses make a difference. If you're cooking a meal for your family, make an extra portion so that one evening your friend doesn't have to think of something nutritious to make for themselves.

HoLDING HANDS.

Don't be scared to ask them what would be helpful, or how you can help. It feels so good to be asked. On occasion they will not know, so do not be nervous about taking the reins on decision-making if your friend and their family seem like rabbits in the headlights; it may be hard for them to see past the present moment.

Offer to babysit their kids, take them to the park, do a school run, sit down for homework time, have a sleepover. This way maybe your friends could have a date night (if you're struggling to have a date night, they *really* must be!) or both be in hospital watching over their little one without worrying about their other kids. When you visit, why not roll up your sleeves and do the washing up or hoovering, or pick up their dry cleaning – every little helps. Love is small acts of kindness. You love your friend; this is the moment to show it.

Remember that families going through this are likely to be exhausted. Do not overstay your welcome; feel the room and (please) know when it is time to leave or help. There was one family friend who would visit Mum when she was unwell all the time and would never leave, endlessly talking at her. Mum always looked so drained after their visit. They would never get the obvious hints we were dropping that it was time to leave.

Something that no family wants is to be pitied. This is unhelpful and doesn't get anyone anywhere. Speak to them, listen, enjoy a cup of tea together, be a good friend. Treat them like you would want to be treated in a time of crisis. I remember occasionally getting anxious glances from friends or extended family members, and even as a young child I thought that was very unconstructive. I call it 'the look'. Show you are worried, and you care but don't show panic or fear; it will only heighten the anxiety of the child and their family.

It is also important not to judge how others live. With great loss, hardship or sadness comes a need to fill the void with unnecessary stuff, so the pain is not obvious. With great worry, lack of time management or stress comes untidy, slightly chaotic homes. Of course, the opposite is also true; with no control in one's life, some people seek control by making their homes squeaky clean and ordered. Life holds its own difficulties and challenges, whether you are a prince or a pauper. Kindness is key.

'Life is short and we have never too much time for gladdening the hearts of those who are travelling the dark journey with us. Oh be swift to love, make haste to be kind.'
Henri-Frédéric Amiel

It's how you say things, not always what you say

Mum and Dad were obviously asked a lot, 'How is little Gerry?' They mentioned that it was so annoying being asked this when the person asking didn't really seem to care or want to know the answer. If you want to know, ask, of course – but be sincere.

Being asked all the time is further unhelpful as it constantly reminds you that your child is 'in the wars' (a great British expression).

One family acquaintance of ours always asks, 'And how are you?' in such a way that makes me feel unwell, weak and as if they know more about my health predicament than I do. It's become a bit of a family in-joke; now, when we ask each other how we are, we say it in that tone of voice.

Visiting friends in hospital

Mum, Dad and I can tell you exactly who came to the hospital with us for either a routine appointment or in-patient hospital visit. There are four visits that have stayed in our minds.

One was when I was nine, recovering from a big operation in hospital. Mum had reached her limit. She had found it all too much. There was a moment of agony when she couldn't manage any more, and she rang her best friend, Mimi, an explosively charismatic Belgian who had married Dad's best friend. What are the chances! Mimi picked up the phone.

Mum told her in French, 'It's too much, Mimi; it's like butchery. I can't handle it any more.'

Mimi – with no hesitation – replied, 'I'm coming. I'll be there soon.'

She walked into my hospital room, perspiring, rosy cheeked and exhausted. In that moment she looked as beautiful as ever to Mum and me. Full of life, joy and always wearing bright, colourful clothing. I was in bed with Mum sat next to me in a chair, relived to see her best friend. They hugged.

She said to me ,'I've just cycled here. Move over; I need this bed more than you!'

So I did. Mimi and I shared the bed that afternoon. She lifted both our spirits so much that day, especially Mum's, just when we needed it most.

Another person who visited was a family friend called Yannis, a man our family knew and loved but didn't see regularly. He came to visit Mum and me in hospital with a big smile and a gift. We were blown away by his kindness and generosity with his time. It was a perfectly chosen gift, but above all things we were not expecting a visit from him, which made it all the more wonderful. We have never forgotten it and still sometimes speak about it around the dinner table.

There was one family member who I know has also supported Mum so much, and that's my aunt and god-mum Tante Patricia. An effortlessly chic, yoga-loving Parisian, she is unfailingly kind and has been a pillar of strength to Mum and, without me realising it until I got older, to me too. She was always there with the family while we were growing up. I am very appreciative of all she did for us, including staying with Mum in hospital and so much more. We are not the easiest lot! I thanked her a little while ago for all she did through the years; she wasn't expecting it and I think was rather taken aback. She is just lovely.

Fourth, but by no means last, Tante Pousinette, my mum's other sister, who visited us during the eclipse in 1999 and brought us glasses so we wouldn't go blind from looking at the sun. She also bought me a small ceramic jewellery box with an elephant painted on.

Bring stories and a gift, even if it's small. Everyone always remembers, and who doesn't love a gift?

One especially memorable visitor arrived in my room when I was around nine and just burst into tears. I hate to criticise as a visit is so wonderful and that individual had come from afar, but it was so unhelpful for Mum and me to suddenly have to start consoling someone when we were struggling so much ourselves. So please, if you visit, do not start crying or ending up needing support from the patient or their family yourself. But at least she visited, which is a lot more than most.

It is so important to support your friends. If your friend's child is unwell, offer to join them for a hospital check-up. Wait outside for the main consultations for the family to have privacy, but the family will be grateful for the company. Sometimes people will want a normalising coffee afterwards, but sometimes they'll be desperate to get home.

Tip

Something I have learned by receiving flowers when back home recuperating is, when giving a bunch of flowers it is so important to offer to put them in a vase. Trim the stems, put the plant food in a vase with water and arrange them yourself, otherwise it is a gift that some would see as 'more to do' when they are already tired. Give them the VIP service so they can enjoy the flowers to the full.

A round up of advice to all

'Happiness can be found, even in the darkest of times, if one only remembers to turn on the light.'
J.K. Rowling, *Harry Potter and the Prisoner of Azkaban*

J.K. Rowling is right: find your light!

You must have a sense of humour; it will get you through anything! Don't lose it either. Laughter has been proven to help boost our immune systems, lower stress hormones, decrease pain, relax your muscles, and prevent heart disease. I know it's too late for us on the last point, but this may help us in things not getting worse or more complicated.

Mum read a book called *Your Life In Your Hands* by Professor Jane Plant, which explains that we must always leave space for the people who didn't feel the courage to come and see you when the pain was at the highest; some people just can't face seeing their friends in pain and other I think just don't know what to do. They may come back and be your friend. Mum gave me a name of friends who never visited or called when she was at her lowest, but she said that later they were good friends. We are all different and we all deal with things in different ways.

As a family unit, consider therapy. I know we are British and terrible at talking about our feelings, but you have been through trauma. Whether you are the parents, siblings or patient, it is important to talk. You will feel lighter for it. You may find out things about yourself you didn't know. Try to meet like-minded people; I wish I had. Once again communicate, communicate, communicate. Speak to your kids, speak to your family and friends. Don't stop talking. It's tiring at first if you are not used to it, but it will get easier. Your extended family and friends will never truly know the pain, but they can be pillars to help hold you up if you let them in.

Look after yourself. Eat well, and don't overdo it. Try to enjoy the small things in life and the bigger things will come on their own. Dream it, believe it, achieve it. A lot of people believe anything is possible and so do I – because I'm still here! You have got a wonderful chance; it may not be the life you were expecting, but try to live life the best way you can.

If you have any great advice – share it! Let me know what you have learned; it's always interesting to learn from others!

Chapter 11
Schools, Growing up, Jobs

I asked my parents if they planned much in advance when it came to schools, work and my future. They quite sweetly said they sort of never really thought of the next steps as they were living in the moment when I was little and so much was going on at the time they couldn't think too far ahead. Then I grew and my health started to improve.

I never went to 'special schools' or a school chosen for any other reasons than being sort of all-rounder schools – they were the same schools my sisters went to till the age of nine. Our schools were not too rigidly academic, not too extremely sporty and they didn't have enormous year groups. I found out recently that my schools always told the other pupils in my year to expect a girl with heart problems before I arrived. A senior-school friend told me that before I arrived at school, they'd had a meeting about me, but when she met me I was not what she was expecting: I was not a sickly creature, nor was I lacking in energy. I am glad I never knew about the schools telling everyone before I arrived until a lot later or I think I would have been quite embarrassed by the attention.

I always enjoyed my schools. I was never very academic and always blamed (without vocalising it) a lack of oxygen at birth for my cognitive abilities and my terrible retention for names when meeting new people.

When I was young, I always felt dyslexia held me back, I would get anxious about reading in class, so when the teacher said lets go round the class and read a paragraph, I would figure out which paragraph would be mine to read and practise that section before it came to my turn. Now as an adult I see it as a strength, and from writing this I recognised within myself, that I am an empath with dyslexia. Dyslexia and ADAH often overlap. This explains so much and I now feel a weird amount of new love towards myself compared to before where I felt cross and frustrated all the time at myself. I'm now weirdly excited about where my mind takes me. Also, with people like Richard Branson being dyslexic, you cannot use dyslexia as an excuse for failure. He may have struggled in school and dropped out at sixteen, but he is now worth an estimated $3 billion! Very impressive.

Tip

Concentrate at school – you never know when you will need that information. The joke's on me for thinking I wouldn't live past twenty-one.

'Live like you were to die tomorrow. Learn like you were to live forever'
Mahatma Gandhi

Early Years

My nursery in London was a lovely little school. Every day was wonderful, and the team was always cheerful and positive. I was the 'Guiding Star' (star of Bethlehem) in the nativity play one year and couldn't have been happier. The earliest memory I have of being different was one day when they had a heart day to raise money for GOSH. I remember getting a little bit more attention that day and the heart theme was everywhere. I was having a great time with glitter and my tiny buddies, and I assumed my other classmates would have a wonderful day dedicated to each of them in turn over time. This never happened, but I never really thought about it as life goes on and you get distracted by playing with Play-Doh, nap time and finger painting.

When I was four, I loved playing shoe-shops with Sammy. I asked for a PlayStation at the age of eight or nine, although I was only allowed to play for an hour a day. I wasn't tremendous at it, but I really enjoyed it, and it gave me some calm time to recharge my batteries.

I always suspected that my sisters found me very annoying, but they always looked out for me. I loved hanging out with them and they probably felt irritated that I was there sometimes, but they never showed it. Thank you for always giving me the time.

As coincidence would have it, we lived in a bungalow growing up, which I used to think was not very cool, but looking back it was probably quite a good way for me to save energy when I needed to. I remember going to friends' houses that had stairs and finding it a bit harder on the legs and lung-puff. I would never say never to a future bungalow but for now, I like to live in homes where I go upstairs to bed.

Quite an important rite-of-passage for a young child is learning how to swim – but not *just* how to swim. How to swim underwater and block your nose without using your hand. To be honest this didn't happen for me. I can swim, I can go underwater, but I never got to grips with the how to block your nose underwater without using your hand. I tried, but as a kid who struggled to oxygenate my blood on land, to have to learn how to stay oxidised under water is quite hard. Also, as a land mammal, I prioritised my time out of the water. As a family we used to giggle that in theory, with only one arm swimming, I'd swim in circles underwater, makes me chuckle still.

School

I never really saw the point of school (sorry Mum and Dad). I didn't love it, and I wasn't a natural at learning. I thought if I only have a certain number of years left, why should I waste them in the classroom, bored out of my mind, rather than playing outside, seeing as much of the world as possible and meeting as many new friends as I could? This gave me terrible concentration and not a huge sense of urgency to do homework.

School wasn't always easy with dyslexia; my reading age was younger than my age and I was also told my short-term memory was very poor. What I don't understand is – if that is the case – how did I make long-term memories? Missing some school due to being in hospital was not a great situation to be in either. I was put down a year at the age of nine when I entered my prep school, so I was always older than the other kids in my year. I never minded, as I had a great year group every time.

Mum and Dad always did what they could for me and signed me up to extra classes for maths and English. Sammy helped me with maths and science. I used to get the giggles and want to do anything other than do what she was asking me. But because of her devotion, I was always good and enjoyed maths and science. She helped me to achieve fantastic GCSEs and I even A-C-E-D my A levels. I am forever grateful for her dedication and unbelievable patience.

I went to a few schools over the years, but I loved my prep school the most. It was conveniently close to home so if I was ever unwell, I could easily be picked up which was helpful. On my first day, Mum's watch had stopped working and she was late picking me up. As a kid, you assume your mum has forgotten you when you are the last one at school; I can remember sitting in their grand hall and the head matron asking if I wanted her to call Mum and see if she was coming. But I'd had such a good day I didn't mind – I just wanted to tell Mum all about it. Poor Mum felt terrible! No matter how hard you try to be a good parent, things happen that you can't control.

My eldest sister, Charlie, would sometimes drop me off at prep school, and I loved riding in the car with her, singing, Britney Spears's 'Autumn Goodbye' at the top of our lungs. I felt so cool! Not just because I had a sister pick me up rather then a parent, but because I had a big sister just like Charlotte pick me up. She is now a life coach and motivational speaker with her own company.[37] I'm incredibly proud of her and everything she has achieved.

My prep school has closed now but there was a special something about it when I was there. It seemed to be filled with caring people. There was an extra English teacher for the special needs kids, Miss Jones.[38] She was like another family member to me. She was immeasurably kind-hearted, happy and genuine, and she made learning fun. We had weekly one-to-one classes in her small colourful room. What made it better was she had a sofa and two large Labradors who welcomed you every time you came for a lesson.

After lunch one afternoon, I knocked on her door and asked if I could come and stroke the dogs at break time. It was winter and occasionally I would ask to do this to have a quiet moment inside in the warm. She went about her business preparing for her afternoon

---

[37]Called Nicholson Coaching.
[38] 'Special needs' is such a bad term!

students while I lovingly stroked the dogs, Barney and Digger, who were fighting for my affection. When Miss Jones turned to look at me, I was very pale and shaking with chills, despite being sat by the heater. She quickly put a rug over me and called for the school nurse who said that I needed to go to a doctor straight away. I had pneumonia. Without Miss Jones, things would have been a lot worse. Everyone needs a Miss Jones at school – and in their lives. She was (and is) like a real-life Miss Honey from *Matilda*. I loved my family unconditionally, but I was ready for her to adopt me.

I was never good at the game British bulldog but very kindly my schoolmates didn't try to catch me first all the time, they would always give me a fighting chance as I was easy prey – or at least that's how I felt.

I am still unsure why, but at the age of ten, I decided I would learn the clarinet. I had mastered the simple art of the ocarina, an instrument seemingly made to annoy parents, and I must have thought clarinet was the next step. This was an unbelievably silly decision. My parents were not pushing me to learn and neither was school. I was terrible: every note sounded like a mouse squeaking, escaping the grasp of a cat and its impending doom. I had a stern but fair teacher who turned to me after almost a term of this and said, 'Gerry, I don't think you have enough puff for the clarinet.' She was right. Why-oh-why did I choose to play a wind instrument when I had terrible to average lungs to go with the heart problem? The clarinet and I parted ways, and there was no love lost.

My senior school was a Catholic all-girls school. I had asked Mum and Dad for a mixed boarding school, but I think I started to behave a bit badly and they got nervous. So girls and religion it was!

My senior school, like my prep school, has now closed (there is a terrible pattern emerging here which I promise has nothing to do with me). It was a lovely school which brought up lovely girls. At the start of my time there, they had nuns, but while I was there they were replaced by less-frightening teachers.

However, this sentiment only came after my first few weeks at the school due to a terrible mishap with a missing 'a'. Which for a moment in time, meant the school thought I had lesbian parents, as I had mistakenly written Michel instead of Michael on a form. My house mistress highlighting it very publicly in a house meeting with a quarter of the school present.

Senior school also taught me about the 'beep test'. It is a terrible way to see how fit individuals are. As an individual with heart problems, you can imagine this was not my favourite activity to do and I was not good at it at all. I especially dislike running or doing sport in the cold. I get a sensation of my saliva getting so sticky I can't breathe or swallow it down, I can't catch my breath properly and my lungs and the passages the air takes to them ache. This sensation takes a long time to dissipate and go back to normal; my lungs would still have a throbbing sensation the next day. When I was not terribly well, these feelings were magnified.

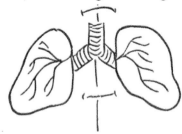

Bullying

I experienced one instance of bullying at prep school, when I was about eleven years old. A boy in my year called me 'Scar', from *The Lion King*. I was taken aback that he had said it as I had only ever been kind to him, but maybe he was trying to be the cool kid on the block. Who knows? But it went down like a lead balloon with the others in our class. He never did it again. At the time I was hurt, but I forgave him quickly as we were all close friends and staying cross with someone takes up more energy than not. And I didn't have much energy to spare.

Maybe I was lucky to have been bullied so little. Maybe because there were only six girls in a small year group of twenty-one kids, we were all able to be individual in our own way. Maybe because my BFF was the twelve-year-old version of the hottie of the year group. Maybe because I had my cool eldest sister drop me off at school, or maybe it's as simple as my classmates not wanting to be unkind to a sick kid.

I asked Mum and Dad if they were ever worried about bullying and they said no, that I was always different, but I was kind. You get back what you give out. I was only ever friendly and calm to others, so I think this came back around. I hated drama and conflict and I would do my utmost to avoid it at all costs, even now.

Mean girls

I have never understood mean girls. You must expel so much negative energy, and for what? It sounds tiring. I'm sure it's a caveman survival technique, but we are about 2.5 million years past this. Why can't we be kind to one another? Life is hard enough as it is.

I was lucky, I was never particularly cool, nor the opposite. I think as I just didn't care about that sort of thing, I was just as I am, 'Gerry', take it or leave it.

I never tried to be popular at school; I was never a competitive person, I never won awards for sport or academic subjects, but rather amazingly I won one prize, the Mary Ward prize, which was voted for by my year group and the teachers in my senior school. It was for integrity, felicity and verity. I won it almost every year, and I was completely flattered and thrilled each time.

All schools have 'mean girls', whether they're just catty people or proper bullies. I tried to rise above it and kill with kindness.

Periods

After going through all I had gone through, I then got really painful periods. It was like adding insult to injury! At birth, I was always told I wouldn't be able to have kids, so to still have periods seemed like the punchline of a bad joke. To be reminded of said punchline every month, painfully, was a separate joke in itself. Not cool!

University

University started with a bang at the Freshers' Fair of Oxford Brookes, where new students can learn about and sign up for all the clubs and sports which are on offer. I applied for the rowing team. I thought it was a great idea as I was small and the youngest of a family of six, so you have to be good at being loud to be heard. I imagined I could sit in the boat as their cox and boss all the rowers around.

At the time of signing up, I hadn't realised there was more than one way of spelling cox! So when signing up on the application form, I gave my preferred position as 'cocks'! Needless to say, I got the role. Rather embarrassingly, I learned the correct spelling a couple of hours later from my new friends.

I really enjoyed the camaraderie of being on the team. I sort of assumed, very incorrectly, that the cox would not need to work out, and just had to be small and a certain weight. In fact I found myself having to do forty-five minute a pop egos, forty-five-minute sessions on the rowing machine sessions that were really so tough, measuring work performed on the machine. I suspect I have never again been as fit as I was back then.

The team also had to do terrifying runs at night in winter around the poorly lit park. I would always be near the back alone or with my new cox friend Holly. This is what finished our rowing careers early. Holly and I realised we preferred getting dressed up and mingling together on the social scene to running for our lives in the dark. We stayed close, and after university we went travelling for a few weeks in Asia. We are both rather short, smallish girls – a real loss to the world of coxes! – so both sets of parents were very worried about us being kidnapped or worse!

Tip

When you first get to university, meet as many people as you can and be kind and friendly to all. You will soon find people you completely adore. Do not date straight away, just get settled into your surroundings and figure out who you want to spend time with and get to know better.

I studied retail and business management, which I continually referred to as retail therapy by mistake. Blooming dyslexia! But the course had a great buzz, and I loved it, apart from the accounting module.

Due to having rubbish immunity owing to my heart problems, the university allowed me to drive to classes and have a reserved parking space so that I wouldn't have to wait in the cold for the bus.

The thing with heart problems is unless you are *really* unwell, you sort of look fine. So I always felt terrible taking this parking space as it was next to a spot belonging to a young lad who used a wheelchair. Holly and I did some of the same courses so I would give her a lift, and I'm sure he thought, why do those two have a space?

Life wasn't always peachy at uni. I made the best friends and had the most wonderful time, but in my final year I had crippling depression. If you meet me now, depression would not come to mind. But I struggled with thoughts of not being good enough, not understanding why people would want to be friends with me and not being worthy for anything and anyone. I can only describe it as my head being in a storm cloud or thick fog that was impossible to see through and exhausting to fight through. I couldn't understand where it came from, as I always felt loved and secure by my friends, family and home. This was a sudden change in mood that felt like it had come out of nowhere, attached itself to me and wouldn't let go. I knew things had to change as I was numb to all the wonderful things around me, especially my friends. They tried so hard to make me happy by taking me out dancing, shopping, and on all sorts of fun excursions, but I just couldn't escape the clutches. I couldn't see past it.

I felt like a plonker but I sheepishly signed myself up to a free university service to see a counsellor. We began our sessions. I love to chat, but I wasn't good at speaking about my feelings, the past or, often, myself. The counsellor reminded me of my Parisian aunt a lot of the time. She was lovely, composed and patient. There was no patronising 'and how does this make you feel'. She never pushed me, she just gently guided me to come to my own conclusions. She unshackled and un-burdened me completely and I haven't looked back. It took a while, but I learned a lot about myself and developed some really helpful coping mechanisms.

RAINBOWS

The root of it was that I had to tell my inner b*tch to shut the f**k up! (Sorry to swear, Mum.) The b*tch was my inner voice, inner doubt, inner crack-wh*re, and I hated that discouraging presence! I had to take control of her and turn her negative energy into positive to make sure she worked *for* me not *against* me. This is easier said than done. I am a very confident individual, but I have a lot of self-doubt – which is unhelpful and unhealthy.

Every so often I must remind myself that the inner b*tch does not have control over me. To be honest, using the word b*tch felt very uncouth in her office, as she was such a sweet looking late-middle-aged lady, but she seemed to like the word being used in the context of healing. It was a sad day when she told me we no longer needed to see each other. It was time to free up her office for someone who needed her more than me.

As an adult, I experience forty-eight hours (in a row) each year of deep depression. I allow myself this and then I come out of it reborn and rejuvenated. I need the sadness to remember how wonderful life really is.

Like all young people at university, I needed money; I hadn't quite appreciated a credit card was not 'real money'. The bank really should make this clearer. So, in my first year of uni, I applied to be a TV extra at a company that took people who were different from the norm. It was not the only place I had approached, and luckily a job as a club promoter became available and hired me. My credit-card problems were solved, and I'd averted the possible dilemma of flashing my scars on TV. I completely loved the job as it was so sociable, and I was good at it, but each shift began by handing out flyers to students, trying to entice them into the club. This was my downfall: even layered up in a massive branded black bomber jacket given to me by the club, I was freezing. I looked more like a blackcurrant with legs than a club promoter. I got colds from being outside, so I had to go job-hunting again. Luckily a weekend job in retail at Jigsaw opened up. So I got a fashion fix, it helped with my studies, and my credit-card problems were solved once again.

Towards the end of my time at university, it transpired that either me or the uni (there really was confusion) had slightly messed up which modules I needed to take and I ended up needing to get a few more under my belt to complete my degree. I decided that as most of my friends had left already, I would have six months abroad studying to finish my degree. I chose to live in a small beach town in France called Juan-les-Pins near Antibes. It was heavenly, so much fun, and it gave me the bug to save up and travel again.

So after graduating, I ended up doing a master's in interior design in Florence. It was incredible – I swear the air smells different in Italy, of sweet tomatoes and basil. My dad said, 'If you don't pass the master's, don't worry, but try to come back with Italian.' I did the complete opposite. Not realising all my classmates would be very well versed, most with degrees in interior design or architecture already under their belts, I stayed up till sunrise trying to decipher the 2D and 3D programs we were being taught. After so much hard work, and many, many late nights and early mornings, I left with a first. But it also meant I didn't have time to learn Italian. Please don't be sad for me though; I ate my fair share of pizza and got to see some of the stunning surrounding areas. I'm so pleased I got to study abroad in both France and Italy; I really would recommend it to anyone who is able to. If you have even a slight adventurer gene in you – and even if you don't – it totally widens your eyes to so many beautiful experiences, people, places and, of course, food. I may not have found the time to learn Italian, but I did learn that Italian men are complete mummies' boys – not something I wanted to be part of!

Jobs

When I was about seven, my sisters and I had a serious meeting about my future and what would be possible in terms of work and my physical abilities. I was desperate to become a belly dancer. I was ready with a tangerine-filled bikini top and a jangly coin-layered sarong. My sisters thought long and hard about what more tranquil, sat-down roles might suit me. The conclusion was a job censoring movies. To rate them U, PG, 12, 15 or 18. The only problem was that I hated scary movies (and I still do).

As I mentioned before, there was no pressure to succeed from Mum and Dad. They felt I already had. I know my sisters felt differently about their upbringing. They were and are highly driven souls and they continue to impress me. They have all become high-flyers and I know they felt pressure to do their best and fulfil the potential Mum and Dad saw in them.

I didn't know, either at school or after uni, exactly what I wanted to be or do with my life. My self-predicted death at twenty-one hadn't happened, so I suddenly had to think of 'a plan'. When you're not exceptional or passionate about one thing, it's hard to identify your future path. But I was always creative. I enjoyed marketing and touched on this in my early career.

I have worked as a brand licensing assistant, a retail assistant, a junior interior designer, an art gallery assistant, a creative manager at a five-star hotel, a general manager of a four-star hotel, and more. I tried quite a few positions to know what I *didn't* want to do in order to narrow down what I *did*.

One career choice that didn't go well was when I was hired as a PA to a high-end interior designer, based in London and France. I was the worst PA in history! I was rightly and rather embarrassingly fired. I think everyone should be fired once. It puts a fire in your belly and can be very character building. However, this was not the first time I had been fired! When Sammy and I were around five and seven, we visited Dad's office. This happened rarely, so it was very exciting. We would take it in turns to pretend to be each other's boss. On one of these occasions, Sammy and I were chatting away on the uber fun internal phone systems, one room next to one another.

Sammy said over the phone system to me, absolutely self-assured sat behind Dad's desk, 'Gerry, you have lost your job!'

I replied, 'You've lost my job?'

'No! *You* have lost your job!'

The conversation went round and round, but Dad remembers it fondly as a sweet moment of miscommunication and amazing child crossover to the adult world. Sammy always knew how to keep me grounded!

'Just because you fail once, doesn't mean you're gonna fail at everything. Keep trying, hold on, and always, always, always believe in yourself, because if you don't, then who will, sweetie?'
Marilyn Monroe

When you are a poorly kid and you seem to be on the mend (a great English saying) and possibly even out of the woods (and another), you sort of assume it will be plain sailing in other areas of your life for the rest of your time on this mad planet. How wrong you would be!

I had an interview with Candy & Candy after I completed my interior design master's in Florence. Candy & Candy (now Candy London) is a high-end interior design company. It was all planned for my return back to the UK. This was a huge deal to me; I was so excited and nervous at the same time.

Two days before I was due to come home to London, I picked up my outfit, all dry cleaned and ready; I polished my shoes beautifully; I chose small, simple jewellery to show a polished (but not over-the-top) look; I practised my make-up for a light, neat appearance.

The night before I flew back to the UK, my left front tooth felt very loose. I carefully ate and drank that night, but the tooth decided, kamikaze style, to jump ship.

This was not the first time, nor would it be the last time, this tooth had defriended me. The flight for London came too soon and I had to get on it. It was too late to change the date and time of the interview, and there was no time to find a dentist to fix the problem. As hard as you can be prepared for all eventualities, sometimes things just happen, and you end up looking like a hillbilly in a very slick city firm.

Obviously, the interview did not go well. My whole demeanour was affected by this one thing. I couldn't remember any of my interview preparation as I was so put off. I downplay how annoyed, frustrated and beyond gutted I was, but I really wanted that job. It's important to remember that things don't always go your way, things don't always go to plan, and the smallest unplanned things can trip you up completely. To be honest, if I were the interviewer, I wouldn't have employed me either!

The irony of losing a front tooth before going for a meeting at a company called Candy & Candy did not escape me – but at the time it was not funny at all. This failure and others before it brought me to where I am today. I am the owner of an interior design studio called Bamboo Elephant (yes, I am still mad about elephants and all things tropical). I love my job. I get to bring colour and joy into people's lives through their interiors. To be frank, I think I may use a little too much colour for Candy & Candy, so maybe it was my (white-ish) teeth telling me it wasn't meant to be.

My friend Gem gave me some great advice: 'the grass is greener where you water it'. The more you put into something, the better the results. It took me a long time to find my calling, and it's an ongoing process, but for me creativity has always been the root of anything I have done and enjoyed. Interior design is a way I express myself. I love making a client's property the best it can be for the way they use the space, starting off with the items they already own and the property's architecture and incorporating pattern, colour and *joie de vivre* to creating a home for them to be proud of – but more than that, a home that they love living in. Your space should not just reflect who you are but uplift you. Each room in our home brings me joy. You also don't have to spend a fortune to make a real impact in your home. I could bang on about interior design all day long; I just love a great before and after!

Let your kids find their paths. Don't be anxious about your children finding work or their own path in the future; there is something out there for everyone. Never allow your kid to be lazy or to not understand the sense of satisfaction in earning their own money and carving a career that they can be proud of for themselves. Whether it is to belly dance with a tangerine-filled bikini top or to become a graphic designer, there really are so many options. Mum and Dad taught us that with hard work, anything is possible, and encouraged us to dream big.

I asked Mum and Dad if they were ever worried about me finding a job. They said no, that they just wanted me to leave the world a better place than I found it, and that's it.

Chapter 12
Sex, Drugs and Rock 'n' Roll

I put this chapter in not to make my family blush, but because surprisingly I get asked about these subjects by parents of children with heart conditions. The more friendly the parents and I get, the more of the three get asked.

Everyone who knows and loves me knows what I am like, so I am not worried about writing this! I am not condoning what I have done. I believed I was only living to twenty-one, so I had to pack a life into too few years. At the back of my mind, I also was thinking that you only live once, and you don't want to live or die with any regrets. But I never tried anything I did not feel was safe; I just lived!

I had a pretty normal teenage life. I was well behaved and so polite that I would feel guilty if I had been distracted and not said thank you to the dinner ladies when they served me at school – I would always go back. However, I was not a 100 per cent, gold-star, goody two-shoes. I was a normal teenager! I got piercings, although tattoos never tempted me as I felt I had enough body art already. When I was little, I felt like I always had to be good because I had brought so much bad our family's way. But as a teenager I exploded and did everything I shouldn't, but with exemplary table manners.

Mum and Dad mentioned that I would push the boundaries a bit more than my sisters as a teen and I would do different things from them at a younger age. I would agree. Perhaps they were more lenient on me than my sisters. Or perhaps as I was the youngest of four girls, the first three bore the brunt of the rules, but by number four Mum and Dad were more relaxed.

Teenage behaviour

I was not the best-behaved teenager because I believed in *carpe diem* (seize the day) wholeheartedly and I made lifestyle decisions I wouldn't make now. I loved socialising, having fun and drinking snakebites and purple wizards. Snakebite made traditionally is equal parts: lager (or stout) and cider with a dash of blackcurrant cordial. I have tried to find out what a purple wizard contained by calling both schoolfriends and the pub we drank at, but neither can tell me any of the ingredients except for a shot of sambuca; clearly both drinks were pretty lethal! I wouldn't want to drink either of them now. I loved meeting new people and going to new places. It helped in a way that I was a year older than the rest of my year group, so the moment they wanted to go to the pub I could join them, even being 5'1" with a fake ID. Country pubs couldn't tell the difference or just didn't really care. Then I turned eighteen before my peers, and getting into places the legal way was even easier.

Mum and Dad received a few late-night calls over the years thanks to my clumsiness, stupidity and sheer confidence. One evening, having drunk too much, I very foolishly lost my left front tooth: (the same one that would later desert me ahead of my Candy & Candy interview) a few girls from senior school and I were getting ready upstairs in a new friend's house for their house party in London. We were seventeen. If you are brought up in the countryside, London is so exciting when you are let out of your boarding school; it's a whole different level. Visits were very infrequent, so we would go all out. Great outfits, nice make-up, good hair – the works. The night started fantastically; we were all having fun. Suddenly, one of us spilled a glass of vodka on the carpet. By this point we had already accomplished quite a bit of pre-drinking, so we were a bit tipsy, and, being teens, we were complete lightweights. We had a brief conversation in which we decided that as there were no towels to mop it up, the best way to get rid of the stain was to iron it out so it would evaporate. This was a terrible idea which started a small fire, but we were quick enough to stop it from spreading. We instantly realised how stupid we had been; we had turned a spill that might not have stained at all into a large black patch of singed carpet. We placed a rug over it, and it felt like we were covering up a murder scene.

We tidied our things up then realised that the room smelled very strongly of burnt plastic. We tried to mask it with perfume and spray deodorant, which made it so much worse. Before leaving, we made sure the iron was off to make sure things didn't go from bad to worse, but they were destined to anyway!

We enjoyed the party; drinks were flowing, and I had consumed far too much for my small body to cope with. I reacted by passing out while we were walking around the streets of London. A friend of mine and one of the boys decided the only way to transport me was via piggyback. We started walking, but I soon started to slip down the boy's back. He bent lower to push me up his back, and I pushed against his shoulders with all my might to try and get myself higher. It all happened very fast. I flew off, landing on my face. The boy said he lived close by, so we popped into his house to see what the damage was. His mother woke up to find blood all over her bespoke hall flooring, seeping quickly into her porous parquet and marble washroom. My friends and the lad were trying to clean me up, but his mother was too cross and sent us out into the night, shouting 'get out, get out!' at the top of her voice.[39]

We flagged down a taxi and called my sister Charlie to explain what had happened. We went to A & E, where Charlie met up with us. I chatted-up everyone I met that night in hospital, which I was bashful about later. Nothing was damaged apart from the tooth, which was still holding on by a tiny painful thread, and my pride. We got home, got into bed and fell asleep. The next morning

---

[39] Side tip: if you ever find an injured child/young human in your house, be a better parent than that mum and actually help them!

was terrible; the hangover was atrocious and the pain hit me like a lorry. I woke up in a pool of blood with Charlie looking over me with her arms crossed – rightly so – saying, 'I'm not telling them [our parents], you are'. I never got that drunk again. I was not a good friend that night, I'm sorry. I wasn't put off alcohol altogether, but my consumption levels were never the same as that night. The tooth was looked over by a dentist soon after that; they removed most of it and performed a root canal – not fun at all!

Tip

Look after your teeth – you only have one adult set!

Drinking and Partying

I find festivals a different level of exhausting. I was always invited by buddies to weekend ones like the Isle of Wight Festival and Wilderness. I do better at smaller festivals as I can keep up a bit more easily. It is not the drinking, dancing and sleeping badly but the walking around that gets me. When the grounds are huge, just getting to the different stages is tiring for me. I used to buy Lucozade for the sugar/energy, but security take drinks off you, assuming that they're alcoholic. Whenever festivals are over, I sleep for twenty-four hours straight. If your child is thinking of going to a festival, start small and work up. That way they build their fitness and stamina alongside their love for the festivals. I am yet to go to Glastonbury, but maybe one day …

For a schoolfriend's twenty-first, a small group of us decided to travel to Paris, where she lived. It had all been organised months in advance and we were so excited. I had a very full-on job at the time, working all hours of the day and night in a hotel as a creative manager. Just before we set off, I wasn't feeling 100 per cent. Thinking it was a bit of a sniffle and nothing more, I still went on the trip. The sniffle got a bit worse, but still I didn't think it was too serious. We had a wonderful weekend in Paris, enjoying the sights and food and stopping at quite a few bars along the way. I decided whisky would shift what was turning into a cold. I drank my fair share, but this did not seem to work. It helped but did not sort me out completely. By the time we got home, I was feeling really rubbish, so I went to the doctor, who told me I had pneumonia. I couldn't believe it had happened again. Whisky doesn't fix pneumonia! Shame!

In my early teens there were balls (parties) where we could meet new people, get dressed up, have a little boogie and some would have their first snog. I found these parties so awkward; I loved the getting dressed up and the planning before, but never enjoyed the car ride there or the initial walk into the room. I don't know why. I still sometimes get that uneasy feeling walking into a pub now.

We all have to learn our limits as teenagers, and find that sweet spot where we can socialise with a drink without causing problems. I completely understand if a young'un with a heart condition that you might want to drink heavily, lamenting 'why me' and trying to forget you are different for a moment, but this wasn't me; I just partied to have fun, dance and socialise. And I clearly learned my limits with a bump.

Drugs

I often am asked by parents of lovely kids with heart problems. 'What about drugs and smoking?' The thing is, we all know they're bad for us. We get told from day one never to take them. Illegal drugs are dangerous, as you just don't know what's in them or where they come from. I was educated by my parents and school to 'say no to drugs and smoking', full stop. At school we had to watch a video that looked like it had been filmed in the very early eighties about a poor young girl who had died from an MDMA overdose. I truly felt for her family, and it certainly put me off.

I had also heard drugs had long-lasting psychological side-effects like paranoia. To be honest, I felt I had enough issues without adding paranoia to the mix! I also feared having a 'bad trip' and hated the thought of back in a hospital bed, having tubes removed yet again.

Due to my hyperactivity and overly smiley nature, people often mistook me for being on drugs.

'Are you on something?' they'd ask.

I would reply, 'I'm high on life.'

Frogs, toads and finding your prince

I have never been too shy, except at the awkward pre-pubescent stage, so boyfriends have never been too hard to come by for me.

Maybe because I always asked them out and never the other way around!

Dad describes me as 'very sociable', and says that I would chat up everyone. He's not wrong – I even charmed the ageing actor Leslie Phillips once, who gave me his telephone number at an event in London. We got on so well he asked me to tea. I said I would love to go, but sadly he passed away before this appointment materialised. For the first – and only – time, Dad said he was pleased to read someone's obituary, concerned about the nature of the rendezvous!

I've never really had 'a type', but I've always been drawn to fun-loving, funny guys with great smiles. I have dated the nicest of guys and for the most part they have been great, but I think that's like everyone's dating history. A few dodgy apples and the rest OK – till you find the one.

My scars never held me back when it came to dating and getting boyfriends, and boys never seemed to mind, as far as I know. My confidence probably made things easy, as my scars are a bit of a hard sell.

Because I thought I had an expiry date, I never wanted to get too deeply involved with boys, which looking back was very foolish. I often pushed them away, or told people I really cared about that I felt they should be with someone who would be around longer. I only ever dated someone if I really liked them, but even then I normally tried not to let relationships get too serious.

I tended to choose well, but the biggest test of any relationship came if I became unwell or had to have an operation. How well did the guy cope if I went home for a couple of weeks and hibernated at my parents; how well did they cope if I didn't want to go out as I was still recuperating, or had zero energy for anything other than sleep; and finally, how well did they cope with looking after me if I needed it? When choosing a partner, all these aspects are important. If your partner finds you boring because you are recuperating, not fun, unsociable, not giving them enough attention, or if they don't have compassion or understanding, they are not right for you.

With whoever I was going out with, I was always 100 per cent honest from the start about not being able to have children. There is no point in being with someone who wants something so much, that you cannot give them, and as mentioned before, honesty is the key to any successful relationship.

Matters of the heart and heartache really do feel similar to heart pain after an op. It is unlikely you will find 'the one' in the first person you date, and often, the moment you stop caring and stop looking he or she will appear and make your life that much better.

People who know and love me know what I am like and know I'm no angel, but I'm not stupid – even if I have made some stupid lifestyle decisions in the past! But I've learned from my mistakes. And if I could talk to the twenty-year-old me now, I'd tell her not to be so flippant with her life. Try to eat and live cleanly, I'd say, as the future you will thank you. But I was fearless and unstoppable. I wouldn't make the same decisions again. I love and respect the people that have looked after and supported me for many years too much to risk damaging myself, physically or emotionally, but in my early twenties I ended up doing exactly that, which I regret. I am now a two-sip Sally when it comes to drinking and nights out.

Parents, don't get worried about the future, just enjoy the present and make memories that will last. Just remember that kids will be kids, and as a parent think about what you were like when you were younger. What did you get up to? The tighter hold you have on a child, the more they will act up or go wild later.

Kids, care for those who love you and have looked after you so well. Be grateful for all they have done for you. Do not be thoughtless with your life; it is so important to so many. Live smart and well. Appreciate all you have, and give back as much as possible whenever you can. I am sorry for the pain I have put my family through over the years, but I know that they wouldn't have wanted to deny me the 'normal life of a youth', albeit with a few more disco naps in between.

I didn't want to die without experiencing what the world has to offer. I am not condoning everything I got up to, but I never put myself in (extreme) danger. Remember to try and make yourself proud and not to embarrass yourself too much, especially that now everything seems to be recorded and posted online for all to see for eternity. Life is long if you live past twenty-one, and you are only in a race with yourself.

Chapter 13
Relationships

I love the songs 'I'll Be There' and 'You'll Never Walk Alone' by Gerry and the Pacemakers. I never felt alone, not once; I felt 100 per cent supported, loved and cared for. But if you do feel alone, feel free to say hi to me! Relationships and connections are so important to me. Even if you aren't low or feeling alone, say hi! I would love it; let me know what you think of this book, tell me your story, send me a photo. (I'm a very visual person and I love a cheesy grin!) The world is not perfect, but with friends and/or family, anything is possible.

When Sam and I were planning our wedding in 2018, I decided I would do a speech in addition to the father of the bride, best man and groom. I made notes in my head on what I was going to talk about, and it was going to be a thank you to my family for everything they ever had to put up with. At the time I worked in central London, so I tried to write my speech while commuting on the Tube. But every time I put pen to paper, I would start crying. It was so embarrassing on so many levels. Fellow passengers would ask if I was all right, and I would get in to work all red and blotchy faced. I realised I found it impossible because I love my family so much – I just couldn't put it into words. My body and mind hit a wall every time I tried. Luckily, I hadn't told anyone I was considering speaking, so there was no awkward backtrack! But I am beyond grateful for everything, and I love my friends and family to the moon and back and more each day. At the end of the speech, I planned to raise a toast to love, family and friendship.

Friends and Family

I hold myriad memories of my sisters dear, like Charlie's Gina G music, Nessie's amazing birthday poetry and recording songs with Sammy on her karaoke machine and learning the words off by heart for hours. I loved being able to chill with them in their rooms if I was tired. These are small snippets of life, but they're all part of how I knew they all believed in me from a young age. How could I let them down and leave? I had far too much dancing in the kitchen with them to do!

Mum, Dad and I have seen into some of the brightest and darkest parts of each other's souls. Perhaps it has joined us in subtly different ways than my siblings: the whole family shares the external scars, but my parents and I have the same internal scar tissue. I love all my family equally, though Mum and I have probably spent the most amount of time together, and we share the same eyes and very naughty sense of humour. We all get on well and this helps when you go through troubled times together.

I studied psychology at school and loved it. We learned about a psychologist called Abraham Maslow who wrote a paper in 1943 that argues that we have needs, we are motivated to fulfil them, and we fill them in a certain way. From a young age I felt lucky that I had my physiological needs (food, water, warmth, rest), safety needs (a home, physical and financial security), and above all my love and belonging needs met (intimate relationships and friends). I was young, and these were all the needs I had – I was happy. I think that's why I have always felt grateful for everything and anything in my life.

Because so much of my life has been dealing with serious issues, I don't waste time with people who don't love me (and I them) or people who don't value kindness. I've never had a problem with coupling up, and anyone who didn't want to be my friend wasn't worth knowing anyway. I don't mean this arrogantly; I just don't want to waste time with people who don't care about me or don't enjoy spending time with me. I have never understood people not being kind to one another. It costs nothing and it can make people's day, month or even year. Why aren't we trying to make people's lives easier?

Since I was often alone with responsible adults (doctors and nurses) I developed an instinct for who I liked or didn't like. Bizarrely, when I was under the age of ten, I felt I had an antenna for sniffing out bad humans, who seemed to me to give-off a terrible smell. Perhaps it was really just their aftershave I did not like the smell of, but it happened quite a bit and sometimes these people were subsequently found to be pretty un-wholesome. For example, the police suddenly took my prep-school tutor away. He was later found to have inappropriate pictures of children in his home. I had immediately smelled that he was bad. It was like a strange sixth sense; I never spoke to anyone about it as I didn't want people thinking I was loopy. As I got older it changed to a feeling rather than a smell.

Thankfully I have been blessed with fantastic friends throughout the whole of my life. Deborah Griffin-Woodson said, 'A shared happiness is twice the happiness. A shared sadness is half the sadness.' And Helen Keller wrote, 'Walking with a friend in the dark is better than walking alone in the light.' They're both very accurate: every step with a buddy is that much more fun together and every terrible moment is also not as terrible.

'As soon as I saw you, I knew an adventure was going to happen.'
Winnie the Pooh

I was lucky enough to meet a girl who showed me, if not exactly life in the fast lane then a sort of eight-year-old version of it, which was so freeing! This was Gem, my BFF … it may be sad to still talk about BFFs in your thirties, but Gem is so special to me, I can't call her anything else. She was always there for me and understood me. We are both insane characters and if we met for the first time now, we probably wouldn't be friends, but because we have been through very awkward adolescences side-by-side, we are welded together and will probably never part (or at least I hope not). She was a cool kid who saw me as someone to have fun with. I think Gem taught me a lot. Especially about fashion. She encouraged me to be bold, wear big earrings, and she told me that flared trousers are (or at least were) cool, that Shania Twain was the 'bee's knees' and you couldn't sing loud enough to 'That Don't Impress Me Much'. I still remember her TGI Fridays birthday parties as being a hot ticket to attend, and have fond memories of jumping into the school pool together, fully clothed, and getting a real telling-off.

Gem and I grew up together, and there was nothing we wouldn't do as a pair. I hoped to go to the same school as her after prep school but, alas, Mum and Dad had different plans for me.

My close childhood friends had brilliant parents – they were so kind and loving, and they understood my situation, my energy levels and what to do if I was unwell. They weren't worried about having me over, were prepared to look after me after school and understood that if I didn't feel well or feel right, I would say so and I would get taken straight home. I think this only happened a couple of times, but I was glad of the security. I always loved going to friends' houses, especially when it ended up as a sleepover and there were movies with sweets or popcorn involved. I sound so greedy!

It's normal to be worried when your little one has a sleepover, but don't worry, they can always just come home if something's not right. For me, most of the time I was too distracted having fun to think of anything else. I remember mum staying for a coffee with the parent of my friend before leaving, so I could have a bit of time to get settled and she could explain if anything was wrong to just call her, or any other details.

Later, I found out that quite a few parents *were* nervous about having me to stay over and were not happy to look after me alone. But as they got to know me, they softened. So, they would start with a daytime play date and progress to sleepovers. I don't blame them – no one likes the unknown -- but it is hard for a child to understand being left out.

When I was around eleven, Jo and Jeremy, family friends with kids the same age as me, offered to look after me for a week while my parents visited my sister abroad. They were the only people to take me and look after me for a week. I had the best sticky toffee pudding of my life at Jo and Jeremy's house and was introduced to *The Bill*, the police TV show, so I really did have a great time.

What's so important is to forgive your friends if they don't offer to look after your child for more than a night, an afternoon or at all. Even my granny felt I was a 'liability'. My Belgian granny looked after me for a week at one point as a child and described me as a ticking bomb; she refused to have me for so long again. No one wanted to look after me! And that's OK. Shortly after staying with Jo and Jeremy I was diagnosed with pneumonia; Jo said to Mum she didn't know what she would have done if it had happened while they were looking after me!

My relationship with myself

I am not always kind to myself. I am not always fair to myself. I think this is normal human behaviour that never truly goes away. I want to give my best to the relationships I value the most. I am still learning to find the right balance between giving my best to my core relationships and allowing myself the space I need if I am not feeling great. I try not to beat myself up and just do what I can, how and when I can. Try and be kind to yourself – you will get further. Test and push yourself, but don't kill yourself. Try to love yourself.

Another reason to have private moments with each of your kids and even your partner is to work out what their inner dialogue is doing: are they too hard on themselves, are they putting up a front, are they thinking, *I'm having this terrible treatment, so my siblings don't need to*? To try and work out what reality they are living in and see if you can help with this. When I was nine, I believed that if I had ten ailments then nine kids would be saved from having any. This made me feel like the more things that went wrong, the better it was, because it meant fewer kids would have problems. The line was drawn when the internal tubes were taken out of me, and I started to regret my decision to shoulder everyone else's burdens (sorry, nine other kids).

♡ ♡ ♡
♡ ♡ ♡
♡ ♡ ♡

However, I also went through a stage of anger. This could have happened to anyone, but it happened to *me*. Why? I wouldn't wish it on anyone, but it still didn't seem fair. In a way, I won the statistical lottery by being born with this condition, but I'm not going to lie, I'd have preferred to win the actual lottery.

My inner b*tch sometimes rears its very ugly, Medusa-like head, even now. I try and keep her under control when possible. For me, counselling really helped, and I can't emphasise enough that if you find the right person and an environment that you feel comfortable with, it really can be the best thing you will ever do. These are people who are trained to equip you with tools for coping unhealthy belief systems, or to dismantle them altogether. The process takes time, and if the therapist isn't on the same page as you, do change them, but remember to always give the individual a try and the benefit of the doubt; the more open you are, the more positive change can happen.

Guardian angels

'Without faith a man can do nothing; with it all things are possible.'
Sir William Osler

At a time of crisis it is normal to turn to something, whether it be lady luck, faith or another vice. So much went wrong so early on that I felt like a cat with nine lives. I knew someone or something was watching over me. Due to this, at times I felt completely invincible, which was a dangerous way to live.

During the worst times in hospital I felt a lot of emotions: scared, tired and exasperated, but never alone. I knew I had a guardian angel watching over me, and what's more, my guardian angel and I definitely shared the same sense of humour – who would spend that much time together otherwise?

As I have mentioned before, I am immeasurably grateful to so many and without always realising I am doing it, I often 'give thanks' in my head, every day. Not just for my survival, but the small things: 'thank you for the good weather' (so British!), 'thank you for not waking up in pain', 'thank you for today', 'I'm grateful for always knowing who I was and am,', 'thank you for always having a support network' – the list goes on.

A second guardian angel I had, who was far more tangible, was Sister Mary of the Nativity, my nun pen pal. I loved writing to her. It comforted me. She was in a Carmelite order in London. It began because Mum liked the idea of nuns praying for me when I was a baby. The idea being that they would have a direct line to big G. I was flattered by the thought of people I had never met before thinking of me, let alone praying for me, and as a child they did feel extra holy. I pictured Sister Mary as *The Madonna of The Lilies* by William-Adolphe Bouguereau – the sort of figure who had rings around their head to show additional holiness. When I grew older, I visited her. She was lovely and far more 'normal' (forgive me) than I could have ever imagined. She had spent time in the army and had an amazingly full life before joining, and she loved her order.

I feel faith or a belief in something greater than us gives us purpose, meaning and sometimes a drive or understanding of why bad things happen such as death or sickness.

I believe there is a reason I am here and that I didn't die. Possibly to lessen others' pain, whether that be by spending time with other suffering families, or just giving a kind word to a shopkeeper. Søren Kierkegaard (who shares the same birthday as me! Fifth of the fifth – but not the year!), the Danish philosopher, theologian, poet, social critic and religious author wrote, 'Life can only be understood backwards; but it must be lived forwards.'

My Husband

My poor, sweet, kind husband has occasionally found me crying while writing this book (very embarrassing). The poor man has put up with a lot these ten years, but being locked in with a loony over lockdown really took the biscuit!

I told Sam I was writing this over dinner, and he asked whether he was featured. I replied saying yes of course. He then looked troubled, slowly made eye contact and said, 'The bad stuff?'

'Even the bad stuff,' I replied. We chuckled.

In 2007, when Sam was studying anthropology and hospitality at Oxford Brookes University, we met at a house party, although there was no formal introduction at this time. I had stuck in his mind for more than one reason. Our second encounter, we were at a wedding. I was placed on the children's table despite being in my twenties. I wasn't thrilled by this, and proceeded to drink all the wine at the table, since none of the youngsters could. Not quite realising the quantity of alcohol I had drunk when the dancing started, I sat down on a beanbag next to an indoor fire pit. Enjoying the music, my head lolled to the DJ's tracks. Someone came to sit down next to me, and I said 'sh*t shoes!' and told him that it was outrageous he was wearing brown shoes with a black suit. He assured me they were Paul Smith, but in my drunken judgement the damage was done. I wanted nothing more to do with him. It took all my might to get up and out of the beanbag, leaving him for the heaving dance floor. We didn't speak again that night.

Third time lucky. About a year after we had left university, we had both been invited to a rather pretentious cheese and wine night. We were both dreading it. Separately, we had both considered pulling a 'sickie' of some sort! To be clear, it wasn't just the cheese and the wine that made this evening shockingly fancy and affected, but – one of many examples – one individual, without being asked, had decided to bring their very own bagpipes, and played them throughout the evening. Neither Sam nor I have anything against bagpipes, but there is a time and a place for them (in Scotland when I'm not around). At the time it felt like a very bizarre thing to do in a central London flat when nobody had been asked to bring a musical instrument. Nevertheless, we finally met properly that night and laughed from start to finish – not just due to the bagpipes. You could say bagpipes brought us together.

I felt I hadn't finished laughing with him, so I asked if Sam was free that Wednesday to go for *moules-frites* in a little place I knew in Richmond near where he lived. Sam told me later his interest in me outweighed his hatred of moules. Curiosity got the better of him … he agreed, and the rest is history!

Life is hard enough as it is. I know that with my heart problems I can't have a cr*ppy partner, as it will make life and my heart problem worse! No scientific or technical knowledge is needed to know this. I need a good support system when I get ill or need help after an op. I have found a partner who is the best for me, someone who understands my wants and needs and I theirs (I hope). My partner had to understand my limitations and very kindly pick up the slack, if needed. Above all things, I looked for a really good sense of humour to help with dark times, kindness for all times, and someone who does not let himself fall down the rabbit hole of sorrow or feeling sorry for himself.

I was so lucky to find my Sam. He understands me better (annoyingly) than I understand myself. He is kind and compassionate, he knows my limits, he says he hates surprises but secretly he loves them, like me, and he knows exactly my sense of humour. I giggle the most with him and our silly antics. We are both dreamers and always think of thrilling plans. He is so much more than a husband: he is my soulmate, and someone I don't like being without.

I know we are a great team and I know we support each other though bad times and of course if anything should happen to anyone you love you would step in to help or support! However, it is hard for me not to feel I have put him through some terrible things with my heart, which makes me so sad to think about. Occasionally

I wonder, *What if he was with a clear-chested* Baywatch *babe?* But he reassures me that I'm for him and he is for me. In no way are we perfect. We bicker like all couples, and since Covid we now call each other Mr and Mrs Grouch.

It is so hard finding someone you trust as much as family. We are all different and how we give, expect and show love is all very diverse. There is a fantastic book by Gary Chapman called *The Five Love Languages*. As someone who is bad at expressing my feelings, it has taught me a thing or two about both myself and Sam.

When I think about Sam and my relationship, I obviously think about how much we love each other but two other huge areas of our relationship are respect and fun. In different ways we have both been through tough times in our lives; it may not have brought us together or attracted us to one another but there is affinity there that I have never had with anyone else. Whatever the core values of your marriage are, it's still worth investing in them even when sh*t has hit the fan! These core values should stand in your relationship whatever you are going through and should help you weather any storm. Try and make fun one of your core values, as without fun your energy levels will be so depleted and you will be all business and just plain ratty.

I proposed to Sam with a red Haribo ring in 2016 (a leap year), and he got very cross with me for popping the question. He then reproposed a short while after. Which felt like a long while after to me!

231

I feel like the luckiest person. I have fantastic friends and family, I have my health (which is hard – I exercise, I am now careful with alcohol and mindful of immunity and stress) and I have found a partner in crime and life who I can't wait to spend the rest of my life with. I am grateful and feel like one lucky duck that Sam chose me and puts up with me!

Due to the trials I have been through, my attitude is that life is unpredictable and very few things are within our control, but surrounding yourself with fantastic people that you love and that you feel love you can make it just that much easier and more manageable. My family taught me who I can be and to try to always see the positive. I recommend being grateful for all you have, from the big to the small, as so much can change at a flick of a switch.

My experiences have taught me that suffering is universal and that we are all more similar than we would like to admit. They have given me a good attitude, and it has taught me to always be kind to all I meet, to ask questions and to listen to the answers. We have all experienced pain, grief and joy. We all seek out acceptance and a life worth living.

'The more you are motivated by love, the more fearless and free your actions will be.'
Dalai Lama

Chapter 14
Cure

When I sat down to write the final chapters of the book, I had to take a little break. I found writing the earlier chapters so physically, mentally and emotionally draining and hard to do. I thought that 'Cure' would be a short chapter – there is no cure. And then I thought long and hard. I beat the odds! I survived 12,337 days (and counting) longer than people thought I would!

Yes, at times I feel like a patchwork quilt or a bashed-up teddy which needs fixing with a new button for an eye every so often. Every patch or additional amendment (operation) its emotionally expensive and painful, but there are wonderful moments and beautiful places along the way. All the old patches (scars) are a reminder of these things and they will stay with me for ever. They tell a story.

Life expectancy

'In the end, it's not the years in your life that counts, it's the life in your years.'
Stieglitz, E. J. Advert in 1947 for *The Second forty years.*

Nobody knows when they're going to die, and even the healthiest of us can suddenly drop dead. Life expectancy is always something I have preferred to ignore. I have however, recently started taking much better care of myself. We never knew how long I would live for. We just kept going.

There was an article written by the British Heart Foundation that says my generation of heart patients are the guinea pigs, and doctors will have to wait and see what happens next with us. We are the first of our kind. If you're an expert, don't let me know and don't place bets. For me, ignorance is bliss. My family and I are doing pretty well nowadays.

Since I surpassed the age of twenty-one, I have assumed I will get to a ripe old age. I don't expect anything less now. One of my sisters thinks I will outlive them all. I also never expected to leave my family and I always felt the doctors knew what they were doing to keep me around. As women live longer than men, Gem and I have made a plan to go to the same old peoples home. I already have a pacemaker fitted and a real love for *Murder, She Wrote*, so I think I'll fit in well.

Tip

Hug more. Hugging releases oxytocin which some refer to the 'hugging drug' or 'cuddle hormone'. It lowers stress, reduces inflammation, improves wound healing, lowers heart rate and stress and, I believe, makes you happy. I am a touchy-feely person and I always have been; from the moment I learned to hug, I was hooked – I love it. I think it is because it is reassuring. If all your senses are blurred or don't function as they should, you know touch will work. I love them (just not straight after an op). Be careful around me – I may force you into one. ☺ It's my drug of choice!

My Cure

The cure was love. Mum's chocolate cake, playing post office with my sisters, sleeping with Inky in her basket, dressing Puff the cat up and forcing him into prams, singing *Lion King* tunes in Africa, breakfast for dinner, my sisters' amazing poems, my dad's scrambled eggs, sailing as a family, farm chores with my family, and so much more. Not everything was fun, but everything was together.

My motto now is *Live, enjoy life with my family and don't worry: what will be, will be.* I try and do this so I enjoy everything in the time I have. I speak about luck a lot, because I feel so lucky.

It was the right place, right time, right care and right love that got me to where I am now.

'It is part of the cure to want to be cured.'
Lucius Annaeus Seneca

Chapter 15
Future

'The future belongs to those who believe in the beauty of their dreams.'
Unknown

Who knows what the future holds? I don't feel limited; my imagination is pretty powerful about the future. Because of my journey I am determined to do more to help others. I am here because of so many people. They say it takes a village to raise a child, but for me it took a city! All sorts of people, of all sorts of walks of life![40] One dream I have is to get people healthier (mentally and physically), encourage healthier mentality, being more active and just plain moving more.

'The future depends on what you do today.'
Mahatma Gandhi

---

[40] I watched a video of Arnold Schwarzenegger speaking at an American university. He spoke about how he didn't make it on his own, and why he was not a self-made man. He succeeded thanks to a lot of help from a lot of people. He made the point that the students were also there due to a lot of people and help and that now is the time to help others. It's true.

Covid

The pandemic affected all of us in so many ways and taught us a lot about each other and ourselves. I wish individuals with Covid turned green or there was some really obvious feature, but no, it is silent and invisible. Quite scary, really.

Due to my heart, I was in the vulnerable category, so Sam and I self-isolated from March 2020 until around March 2021, with two al fresco pub trips in August 2020. We were very careful (and responsible) as we didn't want to be an added burden to the already stretched NHS. We were home-birds during the first lockdown in the UK and believed the virus was all around us, so we just stayed in.

Sam bought the exercise bike, which we loved. We were determined to make the most out of our situation and what was available to us. We wanted to see if we could cycle around the world on it; we spent hours each in the saddle during this time. Annoyingly, the electronic dial was not equipped for the distances we were going and kept resetting to 0. As the crow flies, we got from London to central Africa, and then it got too frustrating to keep a note. My knees now are a bit noisier walking upstairs than they ever were before, but I am still glad I was able to move as much as I did in our London flat with no garden.

You may get an understanding of my mental state, when I tell you that my hands are completely scarred by antibacterial hand gel. Which is a small price to pay for feeling safe. It's a reminder that I have limitations, being in a vulnerable category during a pandemic. In the second lockdown we realised we had gone a bit mad and started going for walks outside. Luckily, Sam and I were both able to get jabbed and boosted early. There would have been no point one of us being jabbed and not both of us with me in the house. I catch everything!

Covid has definitely changed us as a couple and our sense of humour is worse than ever, but it was lovely having my husband to myself one-on-one for so long. We chatted and made plans for the future. I have a new appreciation for small things being present for your friends.

> *'The greatest gift you can give another is the purity of your attention.'*
> Richard Moss

I was conflicted by wanting to volunteer, especially as I had the time and capacity. But realistically, I was too vulnerable to be on the front line. I felt again grateful for scientists and their life saving technology. I am a PRO-vaxxer!

Making Life

I'm an optimist, through and through. However, I never thought I would live long enough to think about having babies or looking after babies. I was always told I could not have children. On my first date with Sam, I said, 'If you are with me there will be no biological children.' I think he thought we should see how that night went before making huge life decisions, but this didn't put him off.

Even if I didn't have any barriers for having children I wouldn't go into it lightly. It's a big decision. Sam and I thought and spoke at length about it all. With modern medicine, so many new doors have opened for so many people. As a child I was told once I couldn't have children, and this was my belief. When I was then told as an adult that there was a glimpse of hope, it was very exciting. But changing my mindset was difficult. We spoke with our magic cardiologist from Southampton who was all too eager to make our dreams a reality, but also made it very clear that there were huge risks.

Having put my family and husband through so much, I didn't think it was fair to put myself in danger and once again ask for the NHS's help (I appreciate I sound unusually protective of the NHS), and my family's for the sake of our fulfilment. But I understand others may make a different choice. I feel even the healthiest women struggle during pregnancy, so I thought putting that much strain on my heart would be foolish. I must also mention that I had never been the type of woman who had always dreamed of carrying my own child: it was never a specific aspiration of mine. So we took the hard decision, but the right decision for us, that we would investigate other options. And so begun our journey to have a child, which continues today.

My biggest fear was that I would pass on what I have to someone else. I know this is an extreme statement, but I want my particular condition to stop with me. Not just for the NHS but to prevent human suffering, and above all I don't want anyone I love (or anyone at all) to have to go through the tube- extraction procedure. Experts said I am more likely to pass on my flat feet than my heart problem, but an insole is easier to fit than a pacemaker.

I have chuckled at the thought of having a C-section – due to the scars I already have on my body, my front would end up with a very strange winking face! The pacemaker being the wink, the central scar a nose and the C-section as a weird smile!

Sam and I have never felt we needed children to complete our relationship, knowing if this was it ,it was fantastic. We know if it is meant to be, it is meant to be. A while back, I started a list of names I liked the sound of, which may have been foolish. I will need to own a lot of animals to make my name aspirations come true. Sam likes a few of them, and he is up for owning 'Cleo the cat' one day.

As much as I am an optimist, my fertility journey made me realise that I am tired of making serious and sensible decisions related to heart problems. However, I know that weariness is short lived and heart problems are for ever, and it is important to make the right decision and not the emotional decision. Our fertility journey started a long time ago (with so much research) but we couldn't really *do* anything until the end of the pandemic. It felt like there were two years in which Sam and I couldn't do what we wanted, when we wanted t,o and then we had a new season of fertility obstacles to overcome and decisions to make, which are tough and tiring.

Just about everything to do with fertility is like blowing out a candle and trying to catch the smoke. It is a wearing and gruelling process: all the unknowns are very difficult and whichever path you take; at every corner something can go wrong. It's very painful and emotionally exhausting. A fertility journey is a different weariness from my operations, as I have chosen this path– but the end goal of achieving something wonderful and the drive needed to get there are the same. A fertility journey is not a life-saving necessity like a heart operation, but it is living life to the fullest.

If everyone had to go through the same thought process to have children, overpopulation wouldn't be a problem. As of now, we are still waiting on several moving parts to see what the next steps are.

It can be bad, but I am resolved to be positive. I try and remember that if I mope around all day, I will be unfulfilled and miserable. I know I must express myself and there will be bad days, but I want to make sure the good ones are great. I try and remind myself to open my eyes and see the countless wonderful things in the world. Nevertheless, due to how hard 'making life' has been it has given me a new compassion for those going through terrible times. Going through my heart journey and being considered terminal and critical has given me an absolute empathy.

Death

'Those we love never truly leave us. There are things that death cannot touch.'
Jack Thorne

I have no plans to die soon and in fact I am gunning for 112, but I should include a word on death here. The only certain thing is death, but I plan on having a wonderful life before then! I feel we should all strive to do so. I try not to be sad or angry – it is what it is. I make the best of it; it is as simple as that. Elbert Hubbard said, 'Do not take life too seriously. You will never get out of it alive.' I have never taken life too seriously – I didn't have the time or the energy – I just wanted to live.

When I was in my late teens, I wrote my will and final service partly because I didn't want anyone else to have a task like that and partly because Mum had said how important it is to make sure it is as you would want it for yourself. When I do go, I plan on making it a fun service, as uplifting as possible and not sad and depressing. Mum's best friend, Mimi, died a decade after she visited me in hospital. Her funeral dress code was 'colourful'. She never wore drab colours. She was the most colourful woman I've ever known. I loved how bright her funeral was. I am borrowing her dress code for mine.

Planning your funeral and buying life insurance are a bit like bringing an umbrella out on a cloudy day. If you don't bring it, it will rain, if you do it won't. For some reason life insurance companies don't want to insure me, but the search goes on for one that will.

As my final act on this earth, I am hoping they forget to take my pacemaker out before I am cremated and that I go out with a bang. No one will be injured in the explosion and it will be a fun final hoorah.

There are a few appealing things about death: apparently bodies look younger, calmer and truly at peace – and they say that 21 grams disappears at death, which is thought to be the person's soul. What I don't like about death is the idea of not seeing that person for the foreseeable future. I also don't understand giving flowers – I hated receiving them when I was growing up. They give off a smell of death when they start to turn, and you watch them slowly die, day by day! I can't bear it.

At home we never spoke about death or heaven, but we kids had learned what death was through owning hamsters. They only live for two to three years and if you were like our family and got Harriet instead of Harry, they do the opposite of death and make a lot of life – at a frightening speed!

Perhaps this is why I have never feared dying and I was never scared of the idea of heaven, it seemed like a fluffy haven filled with old friends. I also knew from a young age that earth wasn't always a great place to be, so there had to be somewhere great all the time. I always assumed heaven would be like the strange oasis dreamland I made up as a kid. I imagined that it was like Noah's Ark or the Garden of Eden: mystical, where anything could happen, and you could go on fun adventure quests, and there were no limitations like ill-health; it was sunny and warm, and yes, God's voice is probably Morgan Freeman's. It would smell of hyacinths or lily of the valley and be filled with the people you have loved over the years – and those who loved you, including your old pets.

This is a product of a Church of England upbringing, lots of TV, children's books, a very optimistic nature and creative imagination – but as an adult, I still believe there is something good waiting. Perhaps not glitter waterfalls, but one can hope.

For those looking for help with bereavement, GOSH has a bereavement support service and there are many excellent charities like Winston's Wish and Child Bereavement UK.

'Grief is the price we pay for love.'
Queen Elizabeth II

Before death

'I'm in that awkward stage between Birth and Death'
Mark T. Greene

Death is motivating, having a limiting time frame to work within is motivating and before I die, I want to try and make myself, my family and Sam proud. I want to help others. I want to be a force for good. I feel I survived for a reason; I'm not totally sure what that reason was, but I'm going to try and find out!

A while ago someone challenged me on the topic of what I would like to read in my obituary and it has made me think more about my use of time, I am now more conscious of how I spend it and I am more mindful of getting my top-priority projects complete. I have thought hard about what I want my life to mean and what I want to show for it. I don't want to waste my life opportunity or any opportunity.

My parents were and are amazing at collecting for charity, and when I was a lot younger, we always did something for our school, where we lived or charities which meant something to us. There are so many which have worked tirelessly, to provide something amazing and special to all that encounter them, and I wouldn't be here without them – GOSH and Starlight to name a just two. I wish to continue their work.

'Yesterday is gone. Tomorrow has not yet come. We have only today, let us begin.'
Mother Teresa

Like most humans, I want to achieve my goals, but my goals include keeping happy and healthy, doing my best to maintain strong relationships with those I love, and rekindling those that have faded. Bringing colour and joy to others' lives through my work, showing love and gratitude where I can, and giving back as best I can. All I want to do is leave the world a better place than I found it, if I can. It is hard to explain just how grateful I am for everything and everyone who has helped me, as well as those who will do in the future, and those who love me.

It has not been an easy road to get to this point. I never thought I would live past twenty-one, I never thought I would be a wife, I never thought I would have the option of becoming a mum one day. All these things have become possible for me because of amazing doctors, my family's support, and science. I feel infinitely lucky and grateful, and I am excited each day to live life to the full.

Above all, I never thought I would be blessed with such amazing family, friends and just … life! All these things have happened to me, but I hope that you and your life is as magic and as packed with as many if not more wonders. I recommend, keep saying yes to life like I did. I hope you will learn from our mistakes and take these lessons on board – maybe you have learned others along your own paths. Share your tales, send pictures.

At this moment I know many of you won't be able to see the wood through the trees, but just remember that there will be in the future a moment where you are on the beach with your family, on a walk or just sat together on the sofa watching TV. Visualise the future and visualise being together at home: this will keep you going. It kept me going! That and Mum's chocolate cake. ☺

It's also really important to remember that while things will not be plain sailing, there will be good times ahead, so do your best to live for the moment and enjoy the little things as much as you can.

'Enjoy the little things in life, for one day you'll look back and realise they were the big things.'

Kurt Vonnegut

Advice for life

Communicate with one another, look after one another and don't be scared to ask for help: you are not alone. The introduction to *Love Actually* said it well: 'love actually is all around' – so remember to take the time to look around! I love love! It's that simple.

I can't send enough good wishes to you as parents of little ones with heart conditions or those with heart problems, but you will be great. It is a marathon, not a sprint, so just take things as they come and do your best, and always remember that you are human.

'I've learned that people will forget what you said, people will forget what you did, but people will never forget how you made them feel.'

Maya Angelou

My ambition is to live happily and well and not dwell on what should or could have happened. I am not resentful of how I was born, as it wouldn't get me anywhere. I find joy in the small things and at the worst times. I am excited for the now and what tomorrow holds. I am sad and hold guilt that I brought this upon my family, but in theory I know this won't get me anywhere, and that it was out of my control; in practice that needs to sink deeper into my heart and reach my emotions and I do need to work on that sense of misplaced guilt. I truly hope you find your happiness and peace, whatever it may be. I find life hard, but as soon as I look at the good and start enjoying the bumps along the way, it really does become easier. I also know that the road I am on has potholes, but I have found it is best not to live in fear, just to be aware that there may be more to come and to just keep moving forward and adjust when necessary.

Acknowledgements

Growing up, Emma and Lizzy crashed into my scene in 1998, when we moved to the same village as them, almost opposite each other. They were like home to me! They were kind, fun, and they showed me how to roller-skate without getting worried. We had so much fun together: we made dens, bought bags of penny sweets, watched *EastEnders* for the first time, tried baked beans on toast for the first time – the list went on. They distracted me from my aches and pains, both physically and mentally.

Grace, a friend I met at my prep school; I don't know if she knew it, but it always felt as if she understood or knew the amount of energy I had and mirrored it with the activity we got up to. A film for quieter days and shopping or a walk for energetic days. Grace was so caring, thoughtful, always had the best food and films, and made me giggle non-stop.

Friends are the family you choose; I was blessed that the stork delivered me into a good family, but also that my friends were fantastic! What was amazing about Emma, Lizzy, Grace and Gem was that they never treated me differently. They saw me as more than just a girl with a heart problem, right from the start. They were extremely positive formative friendships. I don't think any of these fantastic girls will ever quite realise how incredible they were in every way, or how significant a part they played in making me who I am today, and my recuperation and I thank all four girls for this. You were the most wonderful friends and company I could have ever asked for.

Dr Cullen at UCL is a joyous Scottish man who always seemed happy to see me, which is always terribly flattering. He is totally lovely, a real natural with all things people, rapport-building and empathy related.

In 2018 I had an operation at Southampton General – I am a big fan of this hospital! The staff are so charming … maybe it's living by the sea. They are caring, friendly and I seem to really get on with everyone I encounter there, even in less-than-satisfactory circumstances, such as being in A & E in tachycardia (a very fast heart rate) Dr Smith is beautiful and wonderful. Dr Yue is so professional and my favourite doctor to try and make smile at Southampton; he is a marvel too! Dr Fitzsimmons looks like a supermodel and has such a presence and kindness of manner. I feel very lucky to be in the care of Dr Fitzsimmons and Dr Yue – long may it last. Furthermore, when I had a small blip in Cambodia, I travelled to Singapore to meet another doctor, Assistant Professor Pipin Kojodjojo (great name!) who showed true warmth and empathy and was lovely to meet during an emergency on foreign soil. I'd like to make a special mention of Dr Fiona Walker from UCLH too, who was with me from a very young age and was a joy to meet sporadically through the years: her compassion shone through always. And Nathalie Picaut, the GUCH clinical nurse specialist who supported our family in my youth so much and gave some much-needed relief to my parents at terrible times.

Thank you to my family, without whom I would not be who I am today. I will be forever grateful! I love you more than you will ever know and more than I could ever express. Thank you for giving me every opportunity to succeed, live and thrive. Thank you for being you.

Charlie, Nessie and Sammy, you are all great big sisters; I couldn't have asked for more. The moment you want to start that girl band, you let me know. I have always enjoyed looking for the Red Hearty Beast and giant squirrels with you and I hope we continue for ever.

To Mum and Dad, the best parents I could ask for. Sorry that this wasn't what you had planned, and thank you for not turning the stork around and sending it back where it had come from. Thank you for making life fun even at the hardest of times. And to all of my friends, thank you for all your love and belief in me. For those friends not mentioned, don't be hurt, it's actually a good thing! This means you met me when I was predominantly well. You know who you are, you know I love you.

To my dearest Sam, thank you for loving me, I'm sorry that loving me means life isn't always easy, but I am forever grateful you still do. I am so thankful I met you and you liked me and this continues. May our giggles never stop even when we are old. George Jung said, 'May the wind always be at (our) back and the sun upon (our) face(s). And may the wings of destiny carry (us) aloft to dance with the stars.' You are my best friend, my family, you are part of me.

'I need you (all) like a heart needs a beat.'
Unknown

Yes, I have written the word love ninety-one times, grateful twenty-one times and lucky (and luck) thirty-one times in this book – too many times, but I feel these things so strongly and I owe everything to love.

On a final note, my favourite memories are of when we are all around the kitchen table at dinner – a rare occurrence – and something happens to set one of us off. It can be anything. One off us starts shaking uncontrollably, another checks on the said person and then realises she is giggling so hard she can't talk, she then proceeds to speak in an ultrasonic pitch to try and explain what happened, their face going redder by the second. The giggles go around the whole table, slowly but surely. Then I turn to look at Dad who tries to look disapproving of what is going on, before he cracks too. This is my favourite thought when I think of our family. Laughter, simply laughter.

For love, family and friendship x

Dad, go to the start of the book please! ☺

Contact me

www.GerryShepherd.com
Instagram: Gerryshepherdwrites
Facebook Group:

Gerry and Her Pacemakers Community and Discussions
I have created a **Facebook group** for those that wish to swap advice, stories, and discuss topics further with others. Visit **Gerry and Her Pacemakers Community and Discussions** to join.

For those looking for a little fun…

I'm also the creator of Paced Fun, a series of books of Low-Energy Activities and Games for Kids with Congenital Heart Disease. Paced Activities and Games that you can do indoors with friends and family! Paced Fun books can be found on Amazon ☺

Charity Page

To find out more about charities that have touched our lives or give to any charities mentioned within the book please visit the links below: (In alphabetical order, no favourites here …)

British Heart Foundation
https://www.bhf.org.uk

Carmelite Sisters
https://carmelitesnottinghill.org.uk

Child Bereavement UK
https://www.childbereavementuk.org

GOSH – Great Ormond Street Hospital for Children
https://www.gosh.nhs.uk

Macmillan Cancer Support
https://www.macmillan.org.uk

Prostate Cancer UK
https://prostatecanceruk.org

Starlight
https://www.starlight.org.uk

Summerville Heart Foundation
https://sfhearts.org.uk

University Hospital Southampton NHS Foundation Trust
https://www.uhs.nhs.uk

Winston's Wish
https://www.winstonswish.org

References

ACLS. Date unknown. Conscious Sedation for Cardioversion.
https://acls.com/articles/conscious-sedation-for-
cardioversion/#:~:text=DCCV%20is%20a%20common%20proced
ure,mental%20trauma%20and%20potential%20PTSD
Sighted: 28th May 2024

Allen, C. Date unknown. Heart Matters. What is pulmonary
atresia? https://www.bhf.org.uk/informationsupport/heart-matters-
magazine/medical/ask-the-experts/pulmonary-atresia.
Sighted: 5 March 2022.

Blackmores.com 24 September 2018. 10 exercises to improve
your body and mind. https://www.blackmores.com.au/energy/10-
exercises-to-improve-your-body-and-mind
Sighted: 1 May 2024

Brouker, S. 3 October 2011. https://podcasts.ufhealth.org/poor-
bedside-manner-can-harm-patients'-health/.
Sighted: 15 February 2022.

E7 Health, 6 September 2016. Tips for a successful blood draw.
https://www.e7health.com/post/51/tips-for-a-successful-blood-
draw/.
Sighted: 10 October 2022.

Mayo Clinic, 21 January 2020. Positive thinking: Stop negative
self-talk to reduce stress. https://www.mayoclinic.org/healthy-

lifestyle/stress-management/in-depth/positive-thinking/art-20043950.
Sighted: 14 October 2012.

Nicholson, G and Nicholson M. Interview with my parents, 3 November 2020.

NHS. 2021. What is the opt out system in England?
https://www.organdonation.nhs.uk/helping-you-to-decide/about-organ-donation/faq/what-is-the-opt-out-system/.
Sighted: 25 October 2021.

Popovic, J. 3 September 2021. TV Statistics UK.
https://cybercrew.uk/blog/tv-statistics-uk/.
Sighted: 1 May 2024.

Paterson, S et al. 2003. Congenital heart disease statistics 2003.
British Heart Foundation Health Promotion Research Group
Department of Public Health, University of Oxford.
https://www.google.com/url?sa=t&rct=j&q=&esrc=s&source=we
b&cd=&ved=2ahUKEwiApJCFzq_2AhUHYcAKHcpSBL8QFno
ECCMQAQ&url=https%3A%2F%2Fwww.bhf.org.uk%2F~%2F
media%2Ffiles%2Fresearch%2Fheart-
statistics%2Fhs2003_cohd_statistics.pdf&usg=AOvVaw2bx_Rxr
RcQ2-o0J4z7D9JV.
Sighted: 5 March 2022.

Robinson, L. et al. July 2021. Laughter is the Best Medicine.
https://www.helpguide.org/articles/mental-health/laughter-is-the-
best-medicine.htm#.

Sighted: 1 May 2024.

Richards, E. 2021. What are your chances of winning the lottery? https://metro.co.uk/2021/04/09/what-are-your-chances-of-winning-the-lottery-2-14377628/. Sighted 17 January 2022.

Shepherd, M. 2022. Interview with my father-in-law.

Stieglitz, E. J. The Second forty years, advert in 1947. https://media.snopes.com/2017/02/Second-Forty-Years-ad.jpg Sighted: 27 March 2024.

Stroll, J. 2023. Average time per day spent watching broadcast TV in the United Kingdom from 2010 to 2022, by age (in minutes). https://www.statista.com/statistics/269918/daily-tv-viewing-time-in-the-uk-by-age/ . Sighted 1 May 2024.

Sudheer R et al. 2021. Pulmonary Atresia With Intact Ventricular Septum. https://pubmed.ncbi.nlm.nih.gov/31536272/ . Sighted: 5 March 2022.

Sugg, H. 2016. Changing Plate Size Could Be Key to Weight Loss. https://www.cookinglight.com/eating-smart/smart-choices/larger-plate-sizes-affect-portion-control. Sighted: 21 January 2022.

UK Government, 13 March 2017. Guidance. Health matters: obesity and the food environment. https://www.gov.uk/government/publications/health-matters-obesity-and-the-food-environment/health-matters-obesity-and-the-food-environment--2.

Sighted: 14 October 2021.

Printed in Great Britain
by Amazon

48133264R00152